MW01631105

BLACK CROSS RED STAR

The Air War Over the Eastern Front

VOLUME 2

In memory of

Voyennyy Tekhnik 1 Ranga Ivan Vasilyevich Antipov,

chief instrument engineer of 487 IAP – PVO and

grandfather of our good friend Vladislav Antipov, who has rendered invaluable assistance to the work on this book –

and to all airmen who gave their lives during the air war on the Eastern Front, 1941 – 1945.

BLACK CROSS RED STAR

The Air War Over the Eastern Front

VOLUME 2

Resurgence

January-June 1942

CHRISTER BERGSTRÖM • ANDREY MIKHAILOV

Pacifica Military History™

in association with

CLASSIC *PUBLICATIONS*

Printed in Italy

ISBN 0-935553-51-7

Design by Colin Woodman Design
Cover painting by Eugene V. Alexeyenko
Aircraft profiles by Claes Sundin, Jim Laurier and Tom Tullis
Maps by Claes Sundin and Andrey Mikhailov

The author can be contacted at either:
christer.bergstrom@blackcross-redstar.com or christer.bm@telia.com
The Black Cross/Red Star website is at www.blackcross-redstar.com

Library of Congress Cataloging-in-Publication Data

Bergström, Christer, 1958–
Black cross / red star : the air war over the Eastern Front / Christer Bergström, Andrey Mikhailov
p. cm.
Includes bibliographical references and index.
ISBN 0-935553-51-7
1. World War, 1939–1945–Aerial operations, German. 2. World War, 1939–1945–Aerial operations, Soviet.
3. World War, 1939–1945–Campaigns–Soviet Union. I. Mikhailev, Andrey. II. Title.

D787.B415 2000
940.54'217–dc21 037479

Contents

Foreword

Major a.D. Hansgeorg Bätcher
Luftwaffe Bomber Pilot

I salute the work by Christer Bergström and Andrey Mikhailov, which gives an objective description of the air war over Russia in 1942.

While serving with the Luftwaffe from the outbreak of World War II, in almost uninterrupted front-line duties throughout the war, I experienced the air war against the Soviet Union and have a particularly vivid memory of the air war over the Crimea in 1942, which I experienced as Staffelkapitän of 1. Staffel, Kampfgeschwader 100.

During those days we mainly operated from the Saki and Simferopol airdromes, and I carried out around two hundred sorties as bomber pilot over the Crimea. Our main targets were the ports of Sevastopol and Kerch, which were held by Soviet troops. We encountered strong resistance from powerful antiaircraft batteries and courageous Soviet fighter pilots, who did not hesitate to make nose-to-nose attacks on us.

We had a very good relationship with the civilian population. We lived together with the villagers and celebrated their holidays with them. When our unit was stationed in Saki, the flight crews were billeted in the village of Ivanovka. In 1994 I made a private trip to Yalta, and from there I paid a visit to Ivanovka. The older villagers, who still remembered 1942, gave me an overwhelmingly warm reception. They invited me and those who accompanied me (the interpreter and the guide) into the house where I once had been billeted. They served us their best food and spoke of the good memories they had of those days.

During the war, we soldiers were convinced that we had to wage this fight for our people and our Fatherland, and we were prepared to sacrifice our lives. On every sortie, no crew member knew if he would return safe.

Those of us who survived took part in the reconstruction of our destroyed country after the war. Unfortunately, these efforts in war and peace are no longer appreciated by some of our citizens.

I hope that this book will find a broad audience, and I am sure that it will contribute to dismantling the remaining hostility between our peoples.

Hansgeorg Bätcher
Major a.D.
Bomber pilot with KG 27, KGr 100/KG 100, KG 4,
Kommodore KG(J) 54

Foreword

Guards Polkovnik Aleksandr Aleksandrovich Pavlichenko

VVS Bomber and Ground-attack Pilot

We, the former front-line soldiers, often look back at those days of the war that were so hard to all of us. Why? Because the war had something to tell all of us. It taught each one of us of his own value. Even when a man was tormented by the hell of shame, he had pangs of conscience when he could be forgiven for some mistake. To us, the war was a reference mark to which we adhere to even present time.

The war rallied all of us, but each man had his own personal experience, his own first taste of combat, his own fear, his own first setbacks and successes. But there was hardly any happiness in this. I can't remember a single combat sortie when I was not subjected to fire from the ground. Attacks by enemy fighters were nothing rare, particularly early in the war when the relation of forces were not in our favor.

On every operation there were mutual losses. Both sides had their heroes, their patriots. It couldn't be otherwise. It was necessary to cultivate a belief in victory. Undoubtedly, the people on both sides suffered hard.

I served in aviation for more than thirty-two years. For eight years, between 1933 and 1942, I served in civil aviation, during which time I accumulated more than five thousand flight hours. After that, I served twenty-four years with the VVS—advancing from ordinary pilot to command a Diviziya, from Leytenant to Polkovnik.

Aviation is my profession and my pride. After all, the following words were not said for nothing:

Not in vain the people regard as the pride of the nation,
Those who were, who are, who will be in the aviation!

Having made it through two wars—the war with Finland and the Great Patriotic War of 1941-1945—I am able to look back on 138 combat sorties with the Su-2, the Il-2, and the Il-10. I was shot down three times and injured three times. But due to some kind of miracle, I survived. All of us who managed to stay alive are indebted to our fallen comrades. We shall never forget them. We shall not allow them to be forgotten!

At the outbreak of the war, I served with 210 BBAP. During the course of the war, 220 men of this regiment were killed in combat; 85 of them were pilots. 108 GShAP, with which I flew from December 1943 until May 1945, lost 117 men in combat; fifty-eight of them were pilots. It is clear that there was no such thing as an invulnerable aircraft, even if the Il-2 was considered a "Flying Tank."

The authors of this book have made an effort to review, to reconstruct, and to compare the outcome of air operations during the war. This is a most difficult task, if one has an objective, truthful, and documentary approach. After all, not every bullet or every bomb hit the intended target. The pilot's battlefield was the sky. How difficult is it to find out what happened to an aircrew that was blown up in midair by a direct hit of an antiaircraft shell or shot in pieces by fighters over enemy-held territory? For instance, between June 1941 and April 1942, 210 BBAP, outfitted with Su-2s, carried out 3,474 combat sorties and dropped sixteen thousand bombs. Theoretically, this was sufficient to wipe out four divisions of ground troops. But the real efficiency did not exceed 10 to 12 percent.

Nevertheless, the authors, having made this interesting approach, have arrived at staggering results. The reader will be convinced of this.

I wish that I could tell all authors that deal with the history of these events: Don't try, don't you dare try, to speak in our place. Don't you dare to depict us as downtrodden, benighted, deceived, or credulous. Our life was full-blooded and honest. There was everything in it. We are the only ones who can tell you what was falsehood and what was real life. After all, there are several among us that still are alive, although we are passing away. God forbid that the lively, sacred, warm light of memory shall fade.

It is no coincidence that there is a slogan at the entrance of the museum of 108 GShAP in Lyubertsy that reads: "*To uphold the purity of the past and the present means to believe in the future.*"

Aleksandr Aleksandrovich Pavlichenko
Guards Polkovnik (Ret.)
Bomber pilot with 210 BBAP, Ground-attack pilot with 108 GShAP
Honorary citizen of the cities of Rava-Russkaya, Konotop, and Lyubertsy

Glossary

and Guide to Abbreviations

AAA: antiaircraft artillery.
AB: *(Aviatsionnaya Brigada)* Soviet aviation brigade; usually composed of a few regiments and/or independent squadrons.
AD: *(Aviatsionnaya Diviziya)* Soviet aviation division.
ADD: *(Aviatsiya Dal'nego Deystviya)* Soviet Long-range Aviation; an independent branch of aviation, directly subordinate to Stavka VGK. Formed on March 5, 1942.
Adler: "Eagle" (the name of KG 30).
AE: *(Aviatsionnaya Eskadrilya)* Soviet aviation squadron.
Aerial victory: A confirmed shot-down enemy aircraft.
Alfarez: Spanish military rank, equivalent to USAAF second lieutenant.
Airacobra: U.S.-designed single-engine Bell P-39 single-seat fighter.
AM: Refers to Aleksandr Mikulin, Soviet designer of aviation engines.
AM-35A: Soviet high-altitude twelve-cylinder liquid-cooled Mikulin engine.
AM-38: Soviet low-altitude twelve-cylinder liquid-cooled Mikulin engine.
ANT: Refers to Andrey Nikolayevich Tupolev, Soviet aircraft designer.
AP: *(Aviatsionnyy Polk)* Soviet aviation regiment.
Aufklärung: Reconnaissance (German).
Aufklärungsgruppe: German reconnaissance aviation group.
AufklObdL: *(Aufklärungsgruppe Oberbefehlshaber der Luftwaffe)* German reconnaissance aviation group of the commander of the Luftwaffe.
Ar: (Arado) German aircraft designer.
Ar: (Arkhangel'ski) Soviet aircraft designer.
Ar-2: Soviet dive-bomber version of the SB twin-engine bomber.
Ar 95: German single-engine Arado three-place reconnaissance biplane.
Aviabrigada *or* **Aviatsionnaya Brigada**: Soviet aviation brigade.
Aviadiviziya *or* **Aviatsionnaya Diviziya**: Soviet aviation division.
Aviaeskadrilya *or* **Aviatsionnaya Eskadrilya**: Soviet aviation squadron.
Aviakorpus *or* **Aviatsionnyy Korpus**: Soviet aviation corps.
Aviapolk *or* **Aviatsionnyy Polk**: Soviet aviation regiment.
Aviatsiya Voyenno-Morskogo Flota: Soviet Navy Air Force, VVS-VMF.
Aviatsionnaya Shkola Pervonachal'nogo Obucheniya: Soviet primary flight training school.
Aviazveno Svyazi: Soviet liaison flight.
BA: *(Bombardirovochnaya Armiya)* Soviet bomber aviation army.
BAB *(Bombardirovochnaya Aviatsionnaya Brigada)* Soviet bomber aviation brigade.
BAD: *(Bombardirovochnaya Aviatsionnaya Diviziya)* Soviet bomber aviation division.
BAK: *(Bombardirovochnyy Aviatsionyy Korpus)* Soviet bomber aviation corps.
BAO: *(Batalyon Aerodromnogo Obsluzhivaniya)* Soviet airfield service battalion.
BAP: *(Bombardirovochnyy Aviatsionyy Polk)* Soviet bomber aviation regiment.
Barbarossa: Code name of the German attack on the Soviet Union in 1941.
BBAP: *(Blizhnebombardirovochnyy Aviatsionnyy Polk)* Soviet short-range bomber aviation regiment.
Bell: U.S. aircraft designer.
Beriyev: Soviet aircraft designer.
Bf: *(Bayerische Flugzeugwerke)* German aircraft designer; original designation of Messerschmitt 109 and 110.
Bf 108: German Messerschmitt single-engine liaison and training aircraft.
Bf 109: German Messerschmitt single-engine, single-seat fighter.
Bf 110: German Messerchmitt twin-engine, two-place heavy fighter and fighter-bomber.
Blitz: Lightning (the name of KG 3).
Blitzkrieg: "Lightning War."
BMW: *(Bayerische Motoren Werke)* German engine designer.
Boelcke: The name of KG 27 (adopted after World War I ace Oswald Boelcke).
Boston: British designation of U.S.-designed Douglas A-20 Havoc twin-engine light attack bomber.
BV: *(Blohm und Voss)* German aircraft designer.
BV 138: German Blohm und Voss three-engine, six-place reconnaissance flying boat.
Capitan Provicional: Spanish military rank, equivalent to captain.
Capitano Pilota: Italian Air Force rank, equivalent to captain.
Caproni: Italian aircraft designer.
Ca.311: Italian Caproni twin-engine reconnaissance-bomber.
Chayka: "Sea gull," Soviet Polikarpov single-engine, I-153 single-seat biplane fighter.
Che: Chetverikov, Soviet aircraft designer.
Che-2: Soviet Chetverikov twin-engine amphibian reconnaissance aircraft.
Chetverikov: Soviet aircraft designer.
ChF: *(Chernomorskiy Flot)* Soviet Black Sea Fleet.
Comandante: Spanish military rank, equivalent to lieutenant-colonel.
Curtiss: U.S. aircraft designer.
"Curtiss": An incorrect German identification of the Soviet Polikarpov single-engine I-153 single-seat biplane fighter.
DB: Daimler-Benz, German engine designer.
DB: *(Dal'niy Bombardirovshchik)* Soviet long-range bomber.
DB-3: Soviet Ilyushin twin-engine bomber.
DB-3F: Modified version of Soviet Ilyushin twin-engine bomber/torpedo bomber, redesignated Il-4 from March 26, 1942.
DBA: *(Dal'ne-Bombardirovochnaya Aviatsiya)* Soviet long-range bomber aviation; part of VVS; on March 5, 1942, reorganized into the independent ADD.
DBAP: *(Dal'nebombardirovochnyy Aviatsionnyy Polk)* Soviet long-range bomber aviation regiment.

DFS: *(Deutsche Forschungsinstitut für Segelflugzeuge)* Institute for Sailplane Research, German sailplane and glider designer.

DFS 230: German Gotha assault glider.

Direction: Supreme and centrally commanded Red Army operational zones on the Soviet-German front. This formation usually comprised several Red Army Fronts (i.e., army groups). The directions existed only for a brief period during the war. The Northwestern, Western, and Southwestern directions were formed on July 10, 1941, then disbanded in August and September 1941. New directions were formed briefly later in the war: the Southwestern Direction (December 24, 1941, through June 23, 1942); the Western Direction (February 1, 1942, through May 5, 1942); and the Northcaucasian Direction (April 26, 1942, through May 20, 1942).

Diviziya: Soviet aviation wing; usually composed of three to six regiments in 1942.

Do: Dornier, German aircraft designer.

Do 17: German Dornier twin-engine bomber and reconnaissance aircraft.

Do 24: German Dornier three-engine reconnaissance flying boat.

Do 215: German Dornier twin-engine, three-place bomber and reconnaissance aircraft.

Douglas: U.S. aircraft designer.

Edelweiss: The name of KG 51.

Ergänzungsgruppe: German replacement aviation group.

ErgGr: *(Ergänzungsgruppe)* German replacement aviation group.

Escadrila: Romanian squadron.

Eskadrilya: Soviet squadron.

Experten: German designation for fighter aces.

F: *(Fernaufklärung)* German long-distance (strategic) reconnaissance aviation.

FAB: *(Fugasnaya Aviatsionnaya Bomba)* Soviet high-explosive aviation bomb.

Falco: Italian Fiat single-engine CR.42 single-seat biplane fighter.

FARR: *(Fortele Aeriene Regale ale României)* Royal Romanian Air Force.

Fernaufklärungsgruppe: German long-distance (strategic) reconnaissance aviation group.

Fi: Fieseler, German aircraft designer.

Fiat: *(Fabrica Italiana Automobili Torino)* Italian aircraft and car designer.

Fiat BR.20: Italian Fiat twin-engine reconnaissance bomber.

Fi 156 Storch: German Fieseler single-engine liaison and reconnaissance aircraft.

Flak: *(Fliegerabwehrkanone)* German antiaircraft artillery.

Flieger: German airmen.

Fliegerdivision: German aviation division.

Fliegerführer: German "aviation command"; command of the aviation within a defined geographical area.

Fliegerkorps: German aviation corps.

Flotiliya: Soviet flotilla; a small regional fleet.

Flugzeugführerschule: German pilot training school.

Focke Wulf: German aircraft designer.

Freya: German early-warning radar equipment.

Front: Soviet equivalent of army group.

Fw: Focke Wulf, German aircraft designer.

Fw 189 Uhu: German Focke Wulf twin-engine, three-seat reconnaissance aircraft.

Fw 190: German Focke Wulf single-engine, single-seat fighter.

Fw 200: German Focke Wulf four-engine maritime reconnaissance bomber and transport aircraft.

G *or* **Gv**: *(Gvardeyskiy)* Soviet Guards; see below.

General der Jagdflieger: German fighter aviation General; the Inspector of Fighter Aviation.

General Wever: The name of KG 4 (adopted after the first chief of staff of the Luftwaffe, General Walther Wever).

German Cross in Gold: *(Deutsches Kreuz in Gold)* German military award, below the Knight´s Cross.

Geschwader: German aviation wing, composed of three or four *Gruppen*.

Geschwaderkommodore: German aviation wing commander.

GKO: *(Gosudarstvennyy Komitet Oborony)* Soviet State Committee for Defense.

Go 242: German Gotha airborne cargo glider.

Gorbatyy: "Hunchback," Soviet nickname for the Il-2 ground-attack aircraft.

Gosplan SSSR: *(Gosudarstvennaya Planovaya Komissiya USSR)* State Planning Committee of the USSR.

Greif: "Griffin," the name of KG 55.

Gruppe: German aviation group; usually three *Staffeln*, see below.

Gruppenkommandeur: German aviation group commander.

Gruppo: Italian aviation group.

Gruppo Autonomo Caccia Terrestre: An independent Italian fighter aviation group.

Grünherz: "Green Heart," the name of JG 54.

GST: *(Gidrosamolyot Transportnyy)* Transport hydroplane; Soviet license-built U.S.-designed Consolidated PBY-1 twin-engine maritime reconnaissance bomber hydroplane.

Guards: Honorary Soviet title to specially distinguished units.

GULAG: *(Glavnoye Upravleniye Lagerey)* Soviet Main Administration of Camps; NKVD department responsible for the maintenance of prisoners and prison camps.

Gv: See "Guards."

GVF: *(Grazhdanskiy Vozdushnyy Flot)* Soviet Civil Air Fleet; civilian aviation.

H: *(Heeresaufklärung)* German Army (tactical) reconnaissance aviation.

Hawker: British aircraft designer.

He: Heinkel, German aircraft designer.

He 46: German Heinkel single-engine, two-place reconnaissance aircraft.

He 59: German Heinkel twin-engine reconnaissance and torpedo bomber float biplane.

He 70: German Heinkel single-engine reconnaissance and liaison aircraft.

He 111: German Heinkel twin-engine, five-place bomber and torpedo aircraft.

He 113: Soviet misidentification of Bf 109 F and Bf 109 G fighters.

He 114: German Heinkel single-engine, two-place reconnaissance floatplane.

He 115: German Heinkel twin-engine, three-place torpedo bomber.

Heeresaufklärungsgruppe: German Army (tactical) reconnaissance aviation group.

Heinkel: German aircraft designer.

Henschel: German aircraft designer.

Hero of the Soviet Union: *(Geroy Sovyetskogo Soyuza)* The highest Soviet title of recognition for heroic feats.
Hindenburg: The name of KG 1 (adopted after the World War I German Army commander in chief and later president Paul von Hindenburg, who helped ensure Hitler's rise to power).
Holzauge: "Wooden Eye," wingman in German fighter pilots' slang.
Holzhammer: "Wooden Club," the name of KG 2.
Horst Wessel: The name of ZG 26 (adopted after a Nazi streetfighter "hero").
Hs: Henschel, German aircraft designer.
Hs 123: German Henschel single-engine, single-seat ground-attack biplane.
Hs 126: German Henschel single-engine, two-place army cooperation and tactical reconnaissance aircraft.
Hs 129: German Henschel twin-engine, single-seat ground-attack aircraft.
Hurricane: British Hawker single-engine, single-seat fighter.
I: *(Istrebitel')* Soviet designation for fighters.
I-15: Soviet Polikarpov single-engine, single-seat, fixed-gear biplane fighter.
I-15bis: Soviet Polikarpov single-engine, single-seat, fixed-gear biplane fighter.
I-16: Soviet Polikapov single-engine, single-seat fighter.
I-18: An incorrect German name for the MiG-1 and MiG-3. In reality, the MiG-1 prototype was I-200, while the serial MiG-3 had no other designation.
I-26: Alternate designation for Soviet Yakovlev Yak-1 single-engine, single-seat fighter.
I-61: An incorrect German name for MiG-1 and MiG-3.
I-152: Alternate designation for Polikarpov I-15bis.
I-153: Soviet Polikarpov single-engine, single-seat fighter biplane.
I-301: An incorrect German designation for the Soviet single-engine LaGG-3.
IA: *(Istrebitel'naya Armiya)* Soviet fighter aviation army.
IA PVO: *(Istrebitel'naya Aviatsiya PVO)* Soviet fighter aviation of the PVO, a part of PVO established in January 1942. Previously, fighter units allocated for PVO duties were part of the VVS and were subordinated to PVO only operationally.
IAB: *(Istrebitel'naya Aviatsionnaya Brigada)* Soviet fighter aviation brigade.
IAD: *(Istrebitel'naya Aviatsionnaya Diviziya)* Soviet fighter aviation division.
IAK: *(Istrebitel'nyy Aviatsionnyy Korpus)* Soviet fighter aviation corps.
IAP: *(Istrebitel'nyy Aviatsionyy Polk)* Soviet fighter aviation regiment.
I.A.R.: *(Industria Aeronautică Română)* Romanian Aeronautical Industry, Romanian aircraft designer.
I.A.R. 39: Romanian single-engine, three-place light bomber, liaison, and reconnaissance biplane.
Il: Ilyushin, Soviet aircraft designer.
Il-2: Soviet Ilyushin single-engine, single-seat (in 1941-42) ground-attack aircraft. Also referred to as *Shturmovik*, the Soviet term for ground-attack airplane.
Il-4: Designation of Soviet Ilyushin twin-engine, DB-3F bomber and torpedo aircraft from March 26, 1942.
Ilyusha: Soviet nickname for the Il-2 ground-attack aircraft.
Immelmann: The name of StG 2 (adopted after World War I ace Max Immelmann).
Ishak: "Jackass," nickname of Soviet Polikarpov I-16 single-engine, single-seat fighter.
J: *(Jagd)* German fighter.
Jagdflieger: German fighter pilots.
Jagdgeschwader: German fighter aviation wing.
Jagdstaffel: German fighter aviation squadron.
Jagdwaffe: German fighter aviation arm.
JG: *(Jagdgeschwader)* German fighter aviation wing.
Ju: Junkers, German aircraft designer.
Ju 52: German Junkers three-engine transport aircraft.
Ju 86: German Junkers twin-engine, four-place bomber and reconnaissance aircraft.
Ju 87: German Junkers single-engine, two-place dive-bomber.
Ju 88: German Junkers twin-engine, four-place bomber/dive-bomber and reconnaissance aircraft.
Ju 90: German Junkers four-engine civilian airliner; also used as military transport aircraft.
Junkers: German aircraft designer.
Junkers Jumo: German aircraft engine.
KA: *(Krasnaya Armiya)* Red Army.
Kaczmarek: German fighter pilots' slang for wingman.
Kampfflieger: German "combat aviators"—bomber aviators.
Kampfgeschwader: "Combat Wing"—German bomber aviation wing.
Kapitan 1-go (Pervogo) Ranga: Captain (i.e. a ship commander) of the 1st Rank, a Soviet naval rank equivalent of army Polkovnik.
Kapitan 2-go (Vtorogo) Ranga Captain (i.e. ship commander) of the 2d Rank, a Soviet naval rank equivalent of army Podpolkovnik.
Kapitan 3-go (Tretyego) Ranga: Captain (i.e. ship commander) of the 3d Rank, a Soviet naval rank equivalent of army Mayor.
Kapitan-Leytenant: Soviet naval rank equivalent of army Kapitan.
Katyusha: "Little Katya," Soviet rocket-missile; unofficial name of Soviet rocket-projectile systems and occasionally of the rocket-projectiles themselves.
KBF: *(Krasnoznamyonnyy Baltiyskiy Flot)* Soviet Red Banner Baltic Fleet.
Kette: "Chain, " a German tactical air formation of three aircraft.
KG: *(Kampfgeschwader)* German bomber wing.
KGr: *(Kampgfruppe)* German bomber group.
KGrzbV: *(Kampfgruppe zu besonderen Verwendung)* German special-purpose (transport) bomber group.
Kittyhawk: Version of the U.S.-designed Curtiss P-40 single-engine, single-seat fighter.
Klimov: Soviet designer of aviation engines.
Knight's Cross: One of the highest German military awards.
Kommandeur: See *Gruppenkommandeur*.
Kommodore: See *Geschwaderkommodore*.
Komsomol: *(Kommunisticheskiy soyuz molodyozhi)* Soviet Communist Youth League.
Közelfelderitö-század: Hungarian tactical reconnaissance squadron.
Kriegsmarine: German Navy.
KüFlGr: *(Küstenfliegergruppe)* German coastal aviation patrol group.
KV: *(Kliment Voroshilov)* Soviet heavy tank.

La: Lavochkin, Soviet aircraft designer.

La-5: Soviet Lavochkin single-engine, single-seat fighter.

LaGG Lavochkin-Gorbunov-Gudkov, Soviet aircraft designers.

LaGG-3: Soviet Lavochkin-Gorbunov-Gudkov single-engine, single-seat fighter.

Legion Condor: Condor Legion, the name of KG 53.

LeLv: *(Lentolaivue)* Finnish aviation squadron.

LeR: *(Lentoregiment)* Finnish aviation regiment.

LG: *(Lehrgeschwader)* German aviation training wing.

Lotfernrohr Lotfe 2 d: German mechanical-optical bombsight.

Lotfernrohr Lotfe C 7: German mechanical-optical bombsight.

Lotfernrohr Lotfe 7 H: German gyroscopical bombsight.

Löwengeschwader "Lion Wing, " the name of KG 26.

Lufbery circle A tight circle in which an aircraft formation flies in trail behind the leader to form a closed circle. Originally conceived by the American World War I ace Raoul Lufbery as a defensive maneuver. See *Oboronitel'nyy krug*.

Luftflotte: German air fleet.

Luftwaffe: German Air Force.

Luftwaffenkommando: German "air force command," an aviation command within a defined geographical area.

M: *(Motor)* Soviet engine.

M-82: Soviet two-row fourteen-cylinder air-cooled Shvetsov radial engine.

M-105: Soviet twelve-cylinder liquid-cooled Klimov engine.

Macchi: Italian aircraft designer.

MAGON GVF: *(Moskovskaya Aviatsionnaya Gruppa Osobogo Naznacheniya GVF)* Soviet Moscow Aviation Group of Special Purpose of GVF. Formed in July of 1941 from units that were withdrawn from the Moscow Directorate of the GVF.

Maggiore Pilota: Italian Air Force rank equivalent to major.

Magyar Királyi Honvéd Légierö: Royal Hungarian Air Force.

"Martin bomber": An incorrect German identification for the Soviet twin-engine SB bomber.

Mauser: German arms designer.

MBR: *(Morskoy Blizhniy Razvedchik)* Soviet short-range naval reconnaissance aircraft.

MBR-2: Soviet Beriyev single-engine reconnaissance hydroplane.

Mc.200 Saetta: Italian Macchi single-engine, single-seat fighter.

Me: Messerschmitt, German aircraft designer.

Me 210: German Messerschmitt twin-engine, two-place heavy fighter.

MG: *(Maschinengewehr)* German machine gun.

MG 17: German Rheinmetall 7.92mm aviation machine gun.

MG 81: German Mauser 7.92mm flexible aviation machine gun.

MG FF: German Oerlikon 20mm aviation automatic cannon.

MG 151: German Mauser 15mm automatic cannon.

MG 151/20: German Mauser 20mm automatic cannon.

MiG: Mikoyan-Gurevich, Soviet aircraft designers.

MiG-3: Soviet Mikoyan-Gurevich single-engine, single-seat fighter.

Military Council: *(Voyennyy Sovet)* The Soviet collective institution of military and political leadership where major questions of military activities were mainly discussed in principle The topics for discussion included operational planning; the creation and buildup of military forces; the supervision of training; and supplying the troops.

MK: *(Maschinenkanone)* German automatic cannon.

MP-1: Unarmed passenger/transport version of Soviet Beriyev MBR-2 single-engine hydroplane.

MTAP: *(Minno-Torpednyy Aviatsionyy Polk)* Soviet mine-torpedo aviation regiment.

Nahkampfführer: German close-support air command within a defined area.

NBAP: *(Nochnoy Bombardirovochnyy Aviatsionnyy Polk)* Soviet night bomber aviation regiment.

Neman: Soviet aircraft designer.

NJG: *(Nachtjagdgeschwader)* German night-fighter wing.

NKPB: *(Nochnoy Kollimatornyy Pritsel Bombardirovshchika)* Soviet bombsight for nocturnal bombing.

NKPB-3: Soviet bombsight for nocturnal bombing.

NKPB-4: Soviet bombsight for nocturnal bombing.

NKPB-7: Soviet bombsight for nocturnal bombing.

NKVD: *(Narodnyy Kommissariat Vnutrennikh Del)* Soviet People's Commissariat for Internal Affairs.

O. A.: *(Osservazione Aerea)* Aerial Italian reconnaissance.

OAG: *(Osobaya Aviatsionnaya Gruppa)* Soviet special aviation group.

Oboronitel'nyy krug: Soviet defensive air maneuver in which the aircraft formation flies single-file behind the leader, forming a closed circle. See Lufbery circle.

Oerlikon: German arms designer.

OIAE: *(Otdel'naya Istrebitel'naya Aviatsionnaya Eskadrilya)* Soviet independent fighter aviation squadron.

OKH: *(Oberkommando des Heeres)* German Army High Command.

OKL: *(Oberkommando der Luftwaffe)* German Air Force High Command.

OKW: *(Oberkommando der Wehrmacht)* German Armed Forces High Command.

OMRAP: *(Otdel'nyy Morskoy Razvetyvatel'nyy Aviatsionnyy Polk)* Soviet independent naval reconnaissance aviation regiment.

OPB: *(Opticheskiy Pritsel Bombardirovshchika)* Soviet optical bombsight.

OPB-1: Soviet bombsight for daylight bombing.

OPB-2M: Soviet bombsight for daylight bombing.

ORAE: *(Otdel'naya Razvedyvatel'naya Aviatsionnaya Eskadrilya)* Soviet independent reconnaissance aviation squadron.

OSAE: *(Otdel'naya Sanitarnaya Aviatsionnaya Eskadrilya)* Soviet independent medical aviation squadron.

OSAG GVF: *(Osobaya Severnaya Aviatsionnaya Gruppa GVF)* Soviet Special Northern Aviation Group of GVF. Formed in July 1941 based on the Leningrad Directorate of the GVF.

OSNAZ: *(Osoboye Naznachenie)* Any Soviet special-purpose unit. Same as a task force.

Osoaviakhim: *(Obshchestvo Sodeystviya Oborone, Aviatsionnomu i Khimicheskomu Stroitel'stvu)* Soviet Society for the Support of Defense and of Aviation and Chemical Construction.

OUTRAP: *(Otdel'nyy Uchebno-Trenirovochnyy Aviatsionnyy Polk)* Soviet independent training aviation regiment.

P-39: U.S.-designed Bell Airacobra single-engine, single-seat fighter.

P-40: U.S.-designed Curtiss Warhawk/Tomahawk/Kittyhawk single-engine, single-seat fighter.

PAK: *(Pritsel Aviatsionnyy Kollimatornyy)* Soviet aviation reflector gun sight.

PAK-1: Soviet reflector gun sight.

Panzer: German tank.

Para: "Pair," a Soviet tactical air formation composed of two aircraft.

PBAP: *(Pikiruyushchiy Bombardirovochnyy Aviatsionnyy Polk)* Soviet dive-bomber aviation regiment.

PBP: *(Pritsel dlya Bombometaniyas Pikirovaniya)* Soviet dive-bombing bombsight. Combined reflector gun sight/calculating bombsight for dive-bombing.

PBP-1: Soviet combined reflector gun sight/calculating bombsight for dive-bombing.

PC: *(Panzerbombe, cylindrisch)* German armor-piercing bomb.

Pe: Petlaykov, Soviet aircraft designer.

Pe-2: Soviet Petlaykov twin-engine dive-bomber.

Pe-3: Soviet Petlaykov long-range fighter-interceptor version of the Pe-2 dive-bomber.

Pe-8: Soviet designation of Petlaykov four-engine heavy bomber from March 1942.

Pegmatit: Soviet variant of RUS-2 early-warning radar that could be broken down into components small enough for soldiers to carry.

Petlyakov: Soviet aircraft designer.

Pik As: "Ace of Spades," the name of JG 53.

Polikarpov: Soviet aircraft designer.

Polk: Soviet regiment.

PQ: Code name for U.S. and British Soviet-bound Arctic shipping convoys.

PS: *(Passazhirskiy Samolyot)* Soviet passenger aircraft.

PS-84: Soviet license-built U.S.-designed Douglas DC-3 commercial airliner. Like the American C-47 military variant, the PS-84 could function as a military transport and cargo plane

PVO: *(Protivo-Vozdushnaya Oborona)* Soviet Air Defense; Troops of the Home Air Defense.

QP: Code name for U.S. and British Arctic shipping convoys returning home.

R: *(Razvedchik)* Soviet reconnaissance.

R-5: Soviet Polikarpov single-engine light bomber and reconnaissance biplane.

RAG: *(Reservnaya Aviatsionnaya Gruppa)* Soviet reserve aviation group (of the *Stavka VGK*).

RAP: *(Razvedyvatel'nyy Aviatsionnyy Polk)* Soviet reconnaissance aviation regiment.

Rata: "Rat," German and Spanish nickname for Soviet single-engine Polikarpov I-16 single-seat fighter.

Re 2000: Italian Reggiane single-seat, single-engine fighter.

Redut: Soviet truck-borne variant of RUS-2 early-warning radar.

Reggiane: Italian aircraft designer.

Regia Aeronautica: Royal Italian Air Force.

Reich: "Empire" or "Realm"; the Third Reich, Hitler's designation for Nazi Germany.

Repülöcsoport: Hungarian aviation groupment.

Revi: *(Reflexvisier)* German reflector gun sight/bombsight.

Rheinmetall: German arms designer.

Rotte: German tactical air formation composed of two aircraft.

Rottenflieger: German wingman.

Rottenführer: German *Rotte* leader.

RS: *(Reaktivnyy Snaryad)* Soviet airborne rocket projectile.

R/T: radio-telephone.

RUS: *(Radioulavlivatel' Samolyotov)* Soviet early-warning radar equipment.

RUS-2: Soviet mobile early-warning radar.

RVGK: *(Rezerv Verkhovnogo Glavnongo Komandovaniya)* Soviet Reserve of the Supreme High Command.

R-Z or **R-zet**: Soviet Polikarpov single-engine light bomber-reconnaissance biplane. The successor to the R-5.

S: *(Schlacht)* German ground-attack.

SAD: *(Smeshannaya Aviatsionnaya Diviziya)* Soviet composite aviation division.

Saetta: Italian Macchi Mc.200 single-engine, single-seat fighter.

SAGr: *(Seeaufklärungsgruppe)* German maritime reconnaissance aviation group.

SAP: *(Smeshannyy Aviatsionnyy Polk)* Soviet composite aviation regiment.

Savoia-Marchetti: Italian aircraft designer.

SB: *(Skorostnoy Bombardirovshchik)* Soviet high-speed bomber; and a particular Soviet Tupolev twin-engine bomber.

SBAP: *(Skorostnoy Bombardirovohchnyy Aviatsionnyy Polk)* Soviet high-speed bomber aviation regiment.

SC: *(Splitterbombe, cylindrisch)* German cylindrical splinter (shrapnel) bomb.

SchG: *(Schlachtgeschwader)* German ground-attack aviation wing.

Schlachtflieger: German ground-attack airman.

Schlachtgeschwader: "Assault Wing," German ground-attack aviation wing.

Schwarm: "Swarm" or "Flight," German tactical air formation composed of four aircraft.

Schwarmführer: German *Schwarm* leader.

SD: *(Splitterbombe Dickwand)* German hard-covered splinter (shrapnel) bomb.

SF: *(Severnyy Flot)* Soviet Northern Fleet.

ShAD: *(Shturmovaya Aviatsionnaya Diviziya)* Soviet ground-attack aviation division.

ShAP: *(Shturmovoy Aviatsionnyy Polk)* Soviet ground-attack aviation regiment.

ShKAS: *(Shpital'nyy-Komaritskiy Aviatsionnyy Skorostrelnyy)* Soviet 7.62mm rapid-firing aviation machine-gun designed by Shpital'nyy and Komaritskiy.

Shkola Voyennykh Pilotov: Soviet military flight training school.

Shturmovik: Soviet term for ground-attack aircraft. Usually refers to the Il-2.

ShVAK: *(Shpital'nyy-Vladimirov Aviatsionnaya Krupnokalibernaya)* Soviet large-calibre 20mm aviation cannon designed by Shpital'nyy and Vladimirov.

Shvetsov: Soviet aviation engine designer.

SKG: *(Schnellkampfgeschwader)* German high-speed bomber wing.

SOR: *(Sevastopol'skiy Oboronitel'nyy Rayon)* Soviet Sevastopol Defensive District.

Squadriglia: Italian squadron.

SS-Obergruppenführer German SS rank equivalent to Generalleutnant.

St: See Stuka.

Stab: German staff.

Staffel: German aviation squadron usually composed of twelve aircraft.

Staffelführer: German acting aviation squadron commander.

Staffelkapitän: German aviation squadron commander.
Stavka VGK: The Soviet Supreme High Command.
StG: *(Sturzkampfgeschwader)* German dive-bombing wing.
Storch: German Fieseler Fi 156 single-engine liaison-reconnaissance aircraft.
Stuka: *(Sturzkampfflugzeug)* German dive-bomber; usually refers to Junkers Ju 87.
Stukageschwader: German dive-bomber aviation wing.
Su: Sukhoy, Soviet aircraft designer.
Su-2: Soviet Sukhoy single-engine, two-place light bomber.
T-34: Soviet medium tank.
TAD: *(Transportnaya Aviatsionnaya Diviziya)* Soviet transport aviation division.
TAP: *(Transportnyy Aviatsionnyy Polk)* Soviet transport aviation regiment.
Taran: Soviet air-to-air- ramming.
TB: *(Tyazhyolyy Bombardirovshchik)* Soviet heavy bomber.
TB-3: Soviet Tupolev four-engine heavy bomber.
TB-7: Designation of Soviet Petlaykov Pe-8 four-engine heavy bomber prior to March 1942.
TBAP: *(Tyazhyolyy Bombardirovochnyy Aviatsionnyy Polk)* Soviet heavy bomber aviation regiment.
Teniente: Spanish military rank equivalent to lieutenant
Tomahawk: British designation (adopted by the Soviets) of the U.S.-designed Curtiss P-40B and P-40C single-engine, single-seat fighter.
Totenkopf: "Death's Head," the name of KG 54.
Transportstaffel: German transport aviation squadron.
Tu: Tupolev, Soviet aircraft designer.
Tupolev: Soviet aircraft designer.
U: *(Uchebnyy)* Soviet basic flight trainer.
U-2: Soviet Polikarpov single-engine, two-place training/light bomber/multirole biplane.
UAG: *(Udarnaya Aviatsionnaya Gruppa)* Soviet strike aviation group, a groupment of aviation regiments.
UT: *(Uchebno-Trenirovochnyy)* Soviet advanced flight trainer.
UT-1: Soviet Yakovlev single-engine, single-seat aerobatics training aircraft.
UTI: *(Uchebno-Trenirovochnyy Istrebitel')* Soviet advanced fighter trainer.
UTI-4: Two-place training version of the Polikarpov I-16 fighter.
VA: *(Vozdyshnaya Armiya)* Soviet air army.
Victory: *see* "aerial victory."
Vitse-Admiral: Soviet vice admiral, naval rank corresponding to army General-Leytenant.
VMF SSSR: *(Voyenno-Morskoy Flot SSSR)* Naval Forces of the USSR.
VNOS: *(Vozdushnoye Nablyudenie, Opoveshchenie i Svyaz')* Soviet aerial observation, information, and communication.
VO: *(Voyennyy Okrug)* Soviet military district.
Voyennoye Aviatsionnoye Uchilishche: Soviet secondary military flight training school.
VVS: *(Voyenno-Vozdushnye Sily)* Soviet Military Air Force.
Wehrmacht: The German Armed Force.
Wehrmachtführungsstab: German General Staff of the Armed Forces.
Westa: *(Wetterkundungsstaffel)* German weather-reconnaissance aviation squadron.
Wetterkundungsstaffel: German weather-reconnaissance aviation squadron.
Wiking: "Viking," the name of KG 100.
WNr: *(Werknummer)* German aircraft construction number.
Yak: Yakovlev, Soviet aircraft designer.
Yak-1: Soviet Yakovlev single-engine, single-seat fighter.
Yak-7: Soviet Yakovlev single-engine, single-seat fighter.
Yakovlev: Soviet aircraft designer.
Yer: Yermolayev, Soviet aircraft designer.
Yer-2: Soviet Yermolayev twin-engine long-range bomber.
Yermolayev: Soviet aircraft designer.
Z: *(Zerstörer)* German heavy fighter
ZAB: *(Zazhigatel'naya Aviatsionnaya Bomba)* Soviet incendiary aviation bomb.
Zerstörer: "Destroyer," German heavy fighter.
Zerstörerstaffel: German heavy fighter aviation squadron.
Zerstörergeschwader: German heavy fighter aviation wing
ZG: *(Zerstörergeschwader)* German heavy fighter aviation wing.
Zveno: Soviet tactical air formation composed of three or four aircraft.

Soviet Alternative Aircraft Designations

ANT-6: TB-3.
ANT-42: TB-7.
B-3: Douglas A-20 light attack bomber (deriving from the British designation Boston Mk.III; applied to other A-20 models as well).
"Curtiss": An incorrect German identification for the I-153 biplane fighter.
"Douglas": Alternative Soviet designation for PS-84.
I-18: An incorrect German name for MiG-1 and MiG-3. In reality, the MiG-1 prototype was I-200, while the serial MiG-3 had no other designation.
I-26: Yak-1.
I-61: An incorrect German designation for the MiG-3.
I-152: I-15bis.
I-301: An incorrect German name for the LaGG-3; in reality, I-301 was the designation of LaGG-1, the non-serial prototype of LaGG-3.
Il-4: Designation of DB-3F from March 26, 1942.
"Martin": An incorrect German identification for the SB bomber.
Pe-8: Designation of TB-7 from March 1942.
SB: ANT-40 (incorrectly described in German sources as SB-2 or SB-2bis/SB-3).
SB-RK: Dive-bomber version of SB. The most common designation is the Ar-2.
TB-3: ANT-6.
TB-7: ANT-42.

Note: Soviet airmen frequently misidentified Bf 109 F and Bf 109 G fighters as "He 113s." In reality, the Heinkel He 113 single-engine fighter was not mass-produced and never saw first-line service with the Luftwaffe. Soviet pilots also misidentified Bf 109F fighters as "Me 115" on some occasions in late 1941 and early 1942.

Central and Eastern Europe 1942

The Northern and Central Combat Zones of the Eastern Front, December 1941 through Spring 1942

Key to locations south of Lake Ladoga		
1 = Schlüsselburg	4 = Lavrovo	7 = Lyuban
2 = Tosno	5 = Kobona	8 = Finev Lug
3 = Mga	6 = Voybokalo	9 = Myasnoy Bor

The Southern Combat Zone of the Eastern Front, January 1942

Far Northern Combat Zone of the Eastern Front

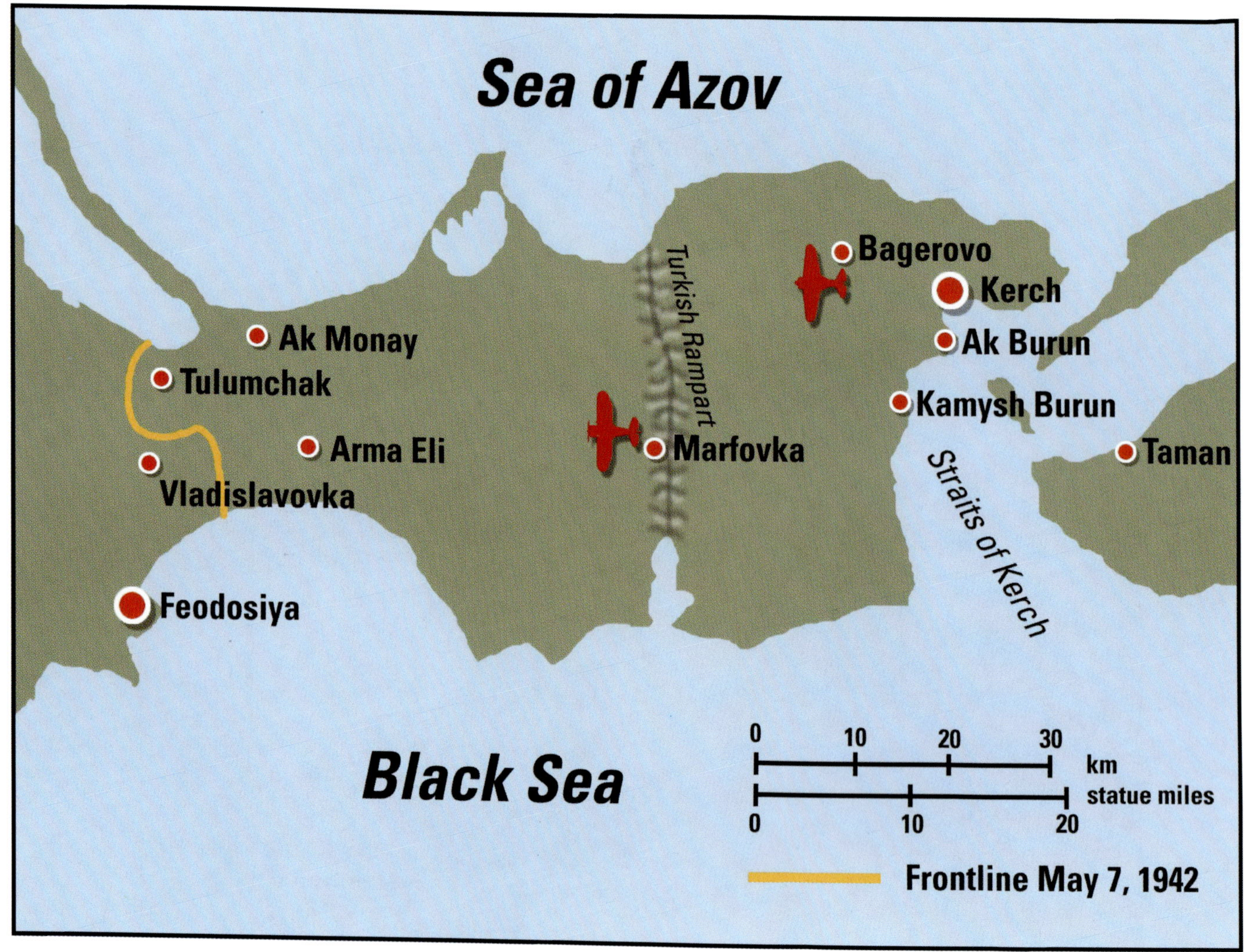

Kerch Peninsula, eastern Crimea

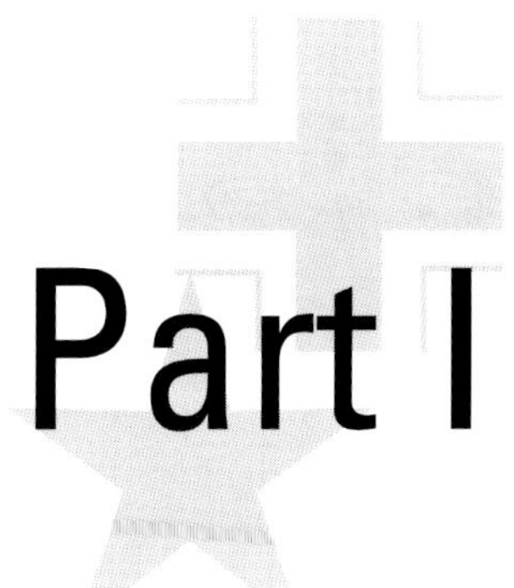

Part I

The Legacy of Barbarossa

Two Messerschmitt Bf 110 Zerstörer ("Destroyers") of I./SKG 210—recommissioned as I./ZG 1 in January 1942—in the air over the Eastern Front.

Chapter 1 

Two Crippled Armies

Operation Barbarossa, Adolf Hitler's attack on the Soviet Union on June 22, 1941, initiated the largest and deadliest military campaign in the history of mankind. The German war machine, the most modern of its kind – experienced and refined from service in the Spanish Civil War and twenty-two months of war against ten European nations – was able to deal a horrendous blow against a Red Army that had been severely crippled by Secretary-General Josef Stalin's purges in the late thirties. The German trump card was Reichsmarschall Hermann Göring's Luftwaffe. On the first day of the war alone, as many as two thousand Soviet aircraft may have been destroyed in the border areas, including more than three hundred in aerial combat.

A Luftwaffe He 111 bomber in flight over the Eastern Front. Although it inflicted immense losses upon its Soviet adversary, the Luftwaffe was unable to gain absolute air supremacy on the Eastern Front. (Photo: Bundesarchiv.)

But the German invaders were unprepared to meet such determined opponents as the soldiers and airmen of the Red Army. Despite enormous losses, the Soviets kept offering a frantic resistance that in the long run wore down Hitler's armed forces. Even though the cream of the Red Army in Europe was virtually annihilated three times in a space of four months in 1941 – at Minsk in July, at Kiev in September, and at Vyazma in October – new reserves brought in from the Asian regions of the USSR and new recruits were always able to fill in the gaps.

By December 6, 1941, two thirds of the Luftwaffe force that had been set against the USSR had been put out of commission. At that moment, a series of Soviet counterattacks along large tracts of the front turned the Wehrmacht's victory march into a retreat.

A common misconception of the Soviet winter offensive is that of numerically superior Soviet forces striking a German Army that was paralyzed by Arctic temperatures. In reality, the Red Army had exhausted its last reserves by that time, and the Soviet forces that opened the counterattack at the gates of Moscow were numerically inferior to the Germans in all types of combat arms except aviation. In the sector where the German Army Group Center was operating, there were 1.1 million Soviet troops facing 1.7 million Germans; 7,652 Soviet artillery pieces versus 13,500 German; and 774 Soviet tanks as compared to 1,170 German.[1] There was indeed a cold spell in late November and early December 1941, bringing temperatures down to minus 20- to minus 30-degrees Celsius – and occasionally below minus 40 degrees. But from December 8 on, a low pressure system in the Moscow area brought mild air.

Temperatures had risen to between zero and minus – five degrees Celsius when Generalfeldmarschall Fedor von Bock, commanding Army Group Center, reported to the Wehrmacht High Command on December 9 that his army group could no longer withstand the attack.[2] Three days later, when von Bock made another desperate telephone call to the OKH to report the situation as critical, rainshowers thawed the snow.

What saved Moscow was exhaustion and strung-out supply lines on the German side in combination with a last-ditch effort by the Soviet troops. By concentrating the bulk of what remained of the Red Army and providing the best equipment for the defense of the capital, the Soviets were able to deal the Wehrmacht its first large defeat. Army Group Center almost collapsed. Its soldiers fell back, often in disorder, bewildered and demoralized.

Adolf Hitler was absolutely furious, and before the turn of the year, five senior commanders had resigned or been sacked – Generalfeldmarschall Walter von Brauchitsch, the chief of the German Army High Command (OKH); Generalfeldmarschall Fedor von Bock, commanding Army Group Center; Generalfeldmarschall Gerd von Rundstedt, commanding Army Group South; Generaloberst Heinz Guderian, commanding the Second Panzer Army; and Generaloberst Erich Hoepner, commanding the Fourth Panzer Army. The Führer ordered Generalfeldmarschall Günter von Kluge, the new commander of Army Group Center, to offer a "fanatical resistance," and issued his famous Halt Order, which forbade any retreat.

The German withdrawal however should not obscure the fact that the Red Army still was deeply marked by defeat. The losses it sustained during the summer and fall of 1941 had been replaced only to a small degree, and even though many factories had been evacuated from the Ukraine and the Donets Basin, the Soviet war industry as a whole still was in disarray. The Soviet main point of concentration was confined to a two-hundred-mile sector with Moscow at its center.

To the north of this combat zone, the surviving Soviet soldiers and airmen had fought for months, suffering losses, and were receiving all but the scrap from the reserves. The city of Leningrad had been surrounded by German and Finnish forces since early September 1941, and with the seizure of Tikhvin – a railroad junction located one hundred miles southeast of Leningrad – on November 10, 1941, the Germans managed to block the main rail line on which supplies to Leningrad were brought via Lake Ladoga. Leningrad was already subject to a deepening famine, and within a short time more than one thousand inhabitants would succumb to starvation each day.

Prior to the successful counterattack at Moscow, the Soviet Northwestern and Leningrad Fronts and the air forces were on the verge of collapse. Battle fatigue was spreading throughout their ranks.

On December 5, 1941, 13 IAP of the Soviet Red Banner Baltic Fleet Air Force's 61 AB reported Starshiy Leytenant Petr Kulakov missing during a flight in the Lake Ladoga-Leningrad area.[3] In fact, Kulakov flew directly to a German airfield and handed himself over to the enemy.

Kulakov's story is quite revealing of the harsh lot of the Soviet airmen serving in the northern combat zone since the opening of the German invasion. He had claimed one Finnish SB shot down; but on July 24, 1941, what Kulakov thought was a "Bf 110," which he attacked and shot down, turned out to be one of the new Soviet Pe-2s piloted by 57 BAP/VVS-KBF's Leytenant Chechetin. The pilot and the navigator survived, but the radio operator was killed. For this Kulakov was sentenced to eight years forced labor, the sentence suspended to the end of the war.

Having flown fifty combat missions against Luftflotte 1 over the Baltics and Leningrad since June 1941, Kulakov had experienced directly the sufferings and hardships of the VVS aviators encountering the superiority of the Bf 109. He was shot down twice but managed to bail out safely. This narrow escape, and the

Interrogation of a downed Soviet pilot at JG 54's air base at Relbitsy in the winter of 1941-42. (Photo: Trautloft.)

A Junkers Ju 87 B taxies out for another dive-bombing mission on the Eastern Front. The Stuka was the symbol of the German Blitzkrieg. It usually dived against the intended target at an angle of about 70 degrees, which enabled the pilot to place the bombs with high precision. Thanks to the dive brakes, the descent could be carried out at a fixed speed. When the pilot levelled out from the steep dive, he experienced three to five Gs of pressure, and during this phase of the attack the Stuka crew was most vulnerable to enemy fighter attacks. (Photo: Roba/Mombeek.)

forced labor that awaited him, quickly brought down Kulakov's fighting spirit.

VVS-KBF ace Leytenant Vasiliy Golubev and his wingman, Leytenant Dmitriy Knyazev, had flown with Starshiy Leytenant Kulakov of 13 OIAE/VVS-KBF on a fateful sortie on August 13, 1941. As they were bounced by JG 54 Bf 109s, Golubev saw that Kulakov, who was leading the I-16 formation, just left the scene and abandoned his subordinates. In the ensuing combat, both Golubev and Knyazev were shot down.

A few days later, Kulakov was shot down for the third time. This time he was injured and ended up in the same naval hospital in Leningrad where Golubev was being treated. Golubev later told historian Carl-Fredrik Geust that he was so upset to find out that Kulakov had escaped from the combat on August 13 that he assaulted Kulakov physically.[4] It was during this stay at the hospital that Kulakov decided to defect.

Starshiy Leytenant Kulakov actually stayed with JG 54 for several months. According to former airmen of JG 54, he eventually volunteered for the anti-Soviet air unit, composed of Soviet airmen in German captivity, which the Germans set up late in the war. According to the same source, Kulakov was later shot to death by a partisan.[5]

Perhaps Kulakov's defection alone is no strong indication of combat fatigue, but other factors support the supposition that fatigue alone was not the issue. His unfortunate relationship with Golubev and other men of VVS-KBF following his escape from the melee in August 1941 and the punishment awaiting him for his unfortunate destruction of a Pe-2 were no less important. It is interesting to note how the circumstances surrounding Kulakov's defection were described in a report issued by the chief of the supreme political directorate of the Soviet Navy, Armeyskiy Komissar Vtorogo Ranga Ivan Rogov, on March 19, 1942:

> On one of the airfields of 61 AB/KBF, the deputy commander of an Eskadrilya, Starshiy Leytenant Kulakov, took off together with his wife in an I-16 in broad daylight in December and flew over to the enemy. This occurred due to the fact that there was an insufficient organization of the service of the airfield; elementary orders and military discipline was absent, and the men who were present when Kulakov took off showed no vigilance. It is incredible that the technicians who prepared the aircraft for the flight, the duty officers, and the flight officers all were unable to see that a woman was entering a combat aircraft. And yet, no one issued any warning and no one undertook any measures to prevent Kulakov's escape.[6]

As the Kulakov incident was taking place, exhausted and inadequately equipped soldiers on both sides were fighting over the town of Tikhvin. Historian Werner Haupt describes the state of the German Eighteenth Army at this forward position: "Supply came to a standstill. There were no first aid dressings, no ammunition, and no rations that could make it through the snow drifts."[7]

The troops of General Armii Kirill Meretskov's Fourth Soviet Independent Army were inadequately trained and poorly equipped, but they nevertheless managed to seize Tikhvin on December 9, 1941. The importance of this liberation to the beleaguered city of Leningrad cannot be underestated. On the same day as Tikhvin was liberated, only nine or ten days of bread stocks were available in the city. The restoration of the Tikhvin – Volkhov – Voybokalo railroad line alone saved Leningrad from collapse. But Meretskov's force was too weak to achieve any major breakthrough and thus halted at the Volkhov River, forty miles farther to the west. Leningrad would remain surrounded, with the supply line across the frozen surface of Lake Ladoga its only lifeline.

In the southern combat zone of the Eastern Front, the Soviet Southern Front was in no better state. Only through a skillfully organized flank attack was it able to oust the Germans from Rostov at the end of November 1941, but following this, the planned Soviet offensive, faced with determined German resistance, bogged down. German Army Group South made a tactical retreat to the area of Taganrog and the Mius River, forty miles to the west of Rostov, effectively supported by bombers of KG 27 and KG 51, the dive-bombers of StG 77, and the newly arrived ground-attack aircraft of Stab and I./ZG 1.

On December 1, 1941, only 185 operational aircraft remained available to VVS-Southern Front.[8] In addition, the bulk of these aircraft were obsolescent models – as was the case with VVS-Southwestern Front on its northern flank – so the Bf 109 fighters of Luftflotte 4 were in almost complete control of the air in the southern combat zone – an ironic situation, since at the start of the war the Soviet air forces in the Ukraine had been equipped with a greater number of modern aircraft than in any other sector. But by December 1941 these aircraft had been rooted out in severe air battles, and with the Soviet emphasis placed on the Moscow sector, the units in the south received almost exclusively, obsolete Polikarpov fighters to compete with the Bf 109s for air superiority. Starshiy Leytenant Aleksandr Pavlichenko, of 210 BBAP on the Southern Front in late 1941, recalls: "The fighter pilots were frustrated. They waited and hoped: 'Perhaps tomorrow we will receive modern aircraft?'"[9]

The preparations for a new Soviet offensive in the Mius-Taganrog region were detected by German air reconnaissance, and on December 7, StG 77 delivered heavy strikes against these Soviet troop concentrations. On this day alone, StG 77 claimed seventy trucks destroyed. Next day the Stukas returned in force, reporting the destruction of several vehicles, eight tanks, and one artillery battery.

With their attack columns broken up following these concentrated dive-bombings, the Soviets attempted to compensate for weakness on the ground by launching their air force in an all-out effort against the Mius front line. "We carried out many sorties and attacked railway stations or military trains," recalls Kapitan Aleksandr Pokryshkin of VVS-Southern Front's 55 IAP. "The hardest thing was to get the novice pilots to maintain their position in combat formation. As soon as the Messerschmitts appeared the novice pilots would close up tighter and trouble the formation leader. Instead of concentrating on the target, one had to watch out not to collide with one of the new pilots."[10]

December 9 saw intense air activity over the Mius front, resulting in frightening Soviet losses. The Germans claimed twenty-two Soviet aircraft shot down[11] – including two I-15 biplanes, one I-16, and one DB-3 by Hauptmann Kurt Ubben of III./JG 77, his personal victories numbers fifty-eight to sixty-two; three I-15s by Leutnant Emil Omert of the same unit (victories thirty-six to thirty-eight); and an I-16 – his sixtieth – by the Gruppenkommandeur of I.(J)/LG 2, Hauptmann Herbert Ihlefeld.[12]

During the month of December 1941, the fighter units of Luftflotte 4 claimed 135 victories for a single operational loss in combat against the air forces of Southwestern and Southern fronts. The most successful unit was III./JG 52, which scored ninety kills without loss.

Also taking part in the battle on the southern combat zone were the Italian Mc.200 Saetta fighters of 22 Gruppo Autonomo Caccia Terreste. On December 25 the Italians claimed five victories in the air over the Mius sector. Two days later the pilots of 369 Squadriglia came home with reports of nine aerial kills, including six I-16s. They suffered no losses.

VVS-Southern Front filed forty-four aircraft lost on operations against thirty-eight victories from December 1 through December 22.[13]

The principal threat to the Luftwaffe in the area during this period was ground fire. The Soviet antiaircraft artillery

Leutnant Hermann Graf is carried triumphantly on the shoulders of pilots and groundcrew of 9./JG 52 after achieving another victory in the winter of 1941-1942.

On December 8, 1941, Hermann Graf and his wingman, Unteroffizier Alfred Grislawski, bounced a formation of R-Z light bombers and I-16 fighters that were attacking the SS Brigade Leibstandarte Adolf Hitler on the Mius front. In a matter of minutes, Graf claimed two R-Zs and one I-16 for his thirty-fifth to thirty-seventh victories, while Grislawski claimed one each of the Soviet aircraft types for his tenth and eleventh victories. The impact of this fighter onslaught was so great that SS-Obergruppenführer Josef "Sepp" Dietrich, the commander of SS Leibstandarte, paid a visit to the German fighter base at Taganrog that same evening to congratulate the two Bf 109 pilots. (Photo: Grislawski.)

enjoyed a healthy respect among the German fliers. A hard blow was dealt against 2./StG 77 on December 26 when five Ju 87s were shot down or severely damaged by AAA during raids against Soviet troop concentrations at Stalino. All the airmen managed to return to base unhurt, even though two crews went down in Soviet-held territory. Hauptmann Helmut Bruck, Gruppenkommandeur of I./StG 77, landed his Ju 87 twice on the steppe and picked up these downed airmen before Soviet troops arrived.

Even if the Soviet troops in the northern and southern combat zones lacked the strength to defeat their enemies, they still triumphed in the sense that they forced the Wehrmacht onto the defensive all along the front. Nowhere was the Wehrmacht able to mount even a relief offensive – except for the Crimea. And that was the second place where the Germans were dealt a substantial military blow towards the end of 1941.

On December 8, 1941, Hitler ordered the commander of the German Eleventh Army, Generaloberst Erich von Manstein, to launch a renewed offensive against the heavily fortified harbor city of Sevastopol in the western Crimea. In preparation for this offensive, the Luftwaffe initiated an intense bombardment against artillery positions, ships in the port, and both of Sevastopol's airfields. Von Manstein's offensive commenced on December 17.

The Soviets countered by landing General-Leytenant Vladimir L'vov's Fifty-first Army in von Manstein's rear on December 26 – on the Kerch Peninsula, the easternmost part of the Crimea. Although stormy weather was a major obstacle to the Soviet landings, the adverse weather conditions also prevented German bombers and Stukas from interfering effectively against the assault. Three days later, five thousand soldiers of General-Mayor Aleksey Pervushin's Forty-fourth Army were landed at Feodosiya on the Crimean southern coast, sixty miles farther to the west. Under improving weather conditions, the German airmen were dispatched against this larger threat, sinking two transport ships and damaging two others on December 30 and December 31. Nevertheless, by December 31, 22,919 Soviet soldiers had been landed in the Feodosiya bridgehead.

In total, 42,000 Soviet troops, 198 cannon, 256 mortars, 43 tanks, and 1,579 tons of supplies were landed at Feodosiya and Kerch during the last days of December, forcing Generaloberst von Manstein to discontinue the offensive against Sevastopol and turn to the defensive.

Regardless of their small numbers and inferior equipment, the Soviet air forces were very active in this area. Operating from inside the besieged fortress of Sevastopol, the airmen of VVS-ChF, the Soviet Black Sea Fleet Air Force, continuously raided German supply columns and even the German Eleventh Army headquarters at Sarabuz. From December 28 onward, the I-153s of 347 IAP and the I-16s of 268 IAP were in constant action, providing the Fifty-first Army at Kerch with close-support attacks. Due to adverse weather conditions and a low serviceability rate, the German fighters in this area – III./JG 77 – managed to shoot down only eight Soviet aircraft between December 25, 1941, and January 1, 1942. The Soviets admitted thirty-nine aircraft lost.

At the turn of the year, the immense German victories on the Eastern Front in 1941 had turned into a severe crisis. The powerful Luftwaffe, which had spread fear over the entire European continent for more than two years, had been reduced largely to an appendix to the army. Heavy losses, both due to combat and the adverse conditions in the East, had cut the number of operational Luftwaffe aircraft on the Eastern Front in half. This further reduced the freedom of action of the Luftwaffe commanders.

The main doctrine of the Luftwaffe still was the Blitzkrieg – "Lightning War" – doctrine of tactical support. Germany went to war with the concept of achieving a swift and decisive victory as its only option. But the Blitzkrieg air war doctrine did not mean the sole use of the air force as flying artillery. This task was assigned to close-support aircraft such as the Ju 87 Stuka, the Hs 123, and the Bf 110 fighter-bomber. According to Blitzkrieg doctrine, the task of the medium bombers – considered to be the backbone of the Luftwaffe – was to disrupt communications in the area behind the enemy's front and take out headquarters, airfields, ports, bridges, and the like. This method was one of the main elements to the German successes in Blitzkrieg warfare against countries such as Poland in 1939 and France in 1940 – and against the Soviet Union during the opening phase of Operation Barbarossa. Nevertheless, the powerful Soviet counteroffensive at the gates of Moscow in December 1941 and the subsequent heavy losses in artillery equipment increased the need for using even Luftwaffe medium bombers as flying artillery. In light of the surprisingly low availability of Luftwaffe close-support aircraft, it is obvious that Hitler had gone to war with a far-from-complete rearmament.

The resurgence of the military capacity of the Soviet Union toward the end of 1941 is remarkable. Not only had the cream of the Red Army been annihilated during the summer and fall of 1941, the territories lost by the Soviets included a very large part of the country's natural resources: Mines with 63 percent of the coal production,

68 percent of the iron mines, and an agricultural area where 38 percent of the Soviet grain had been produced were occupied by the Germans. Meanwhile, Germany, the most modern industrial nation of the world, controlled the entire western European continent with all its industries, labor force, and natural resources – the bulk of which could be concentrated to the war efforts against the USSR.

At the beginning of 1942, the Eastern Front was Germany's only major battle arena. Across the English Channel, Great Britain held out, but her potential for threatening Germany's war effort still remained very weak. A force numbering about five hundred RAF strategic bombers carried out regular, but – in early 1942 – largely ineffective nocturnal bombings of German cities. In daylight the threat from the RAF was so low that only two Jagdgeschwader were needed to keep the western European air space under German control. The United States had entered into the war against Germany and Italy only on December 11, 1941, and it would be a long time before the Americans would be able to provide Germany any real opposition in Europe.

Apart from the Eastern Front, the only combat zone that involved German ground troops at that time was the North African coastline of Libya and Egypt. Here, a handful of divisions on each side – equivalent to the forces that fought over a single city on the Eastern Front – were occupied in a relatively small-scale war of attrition.

For all that it was so heavily concentrated on the Eastern Front, the Wehrmacht was not able to hold the crippled Red Army at bay.

Chapter 2

The Luftwaffe in Early 1942

At the end of 1941, Germany's war industry found itself in a severe crisis, an ironic situation since the needs of the German economy had been one of Hitler's principal reasons for invading the USSR.[14] Germany had indeed seized some of the most important industrial areas and mine regions of the USSR but had largely failed to benefit from the conquest since the bulk of the industrial base in these regions had been dismantled and evacuated east by the Soviets. Moreover, the German occupation authorities and businessmen who took charge of the mines shortsightedly devoted most of their time to looting rather than to business. The German authorities also largely failed to take advantage of the tens of millions of potential laborers in the occupied areas. In a critical report, the German Armament Inspector for the Ukraine asked: "If we shoot all the Jews, let the prisoners of war die, subject large parts of the population of major cities to famine, and let parts of the population in the countryside succumb to starvation – then one must ask: Who is going to uphold production here?"[15]

In Germany itself, massive conscription created a severe labor shortage that converged with shortages in key raw materials.

The chief of supply and procurement of the Luftwaffe, Ernst Udet, was unable to cope with the mounting disorder in aircraft production planning. Udet was a famous World War I fighter ace, and it was only his personal fondness for Udet that made the commander in chief of the Luftwaffe, Reichsmarschall Hermann Göring, place him in this high position. But Udet lacked the required competence for the mission, and the disarray of aircraft production drove Udet to commit suicide in November 1941.

Output of close-support aircraft was in a particularly troublesome situation. The Bf 110, Willy Messerschmitt's twin-engine design that had been originally intended as a long-range heavy fighter, then reduced to the role of fighter-bomber, suffered a complete production breakdown. The monthly output of Bf 110s fell from 123 in February 1941 to only 1 in December 1941 – and not

Two Messerschmitt Bf 110 Zerstörer ("Destroyer") of I./SKG 210—recommissioned as I./ZG 1 in January 1942—in the air over the Eastern Front. After displaying its shortcomings in air-to-air combat, the twin-engine Bf 110, which was originally designed as a heavy fighter, was converted to the fighter-bomber role during the Battle of Britain and by SKG 210 during Operation Barbarossa. Heavy losses in combination with the need to convert the aircraft to yet another role—that of night-fighter against increasing RAF night raids against German cities—next compelled the OKL to withdraw most of the remaining Zerstörer from action on the Eastern Front in the fall of 1941. Three months later, during the Soviet winter offensive the new night-fighters were reconverted to the fighter-bomber role and rushed back to the Moscow front. The redesignation of I. and II./NJG 4 to ZG 26 and the subsequent shift back to the Eastern Front considerably weakened the German night-fighter force in Western Europe.
(Photo: Kriegstagebuch I./SKG 210 via Bobek.)

even 1 in January 1942 – at a time when the Bf 110 units were being rushed back to the Eastern Front to help stem the tide of the Red Army's Winter counteroffensive! The disaster resulted from Messerschmitt's miscarriage of producing an aircraft type that was intended to be the successor of the Bf 110, the Me 210. The Me 210 proved to be a construction failure, but it was not withdrawn before serial production had begun. Only slowly was the Bf 110 production crisis resolved, and forty-two Bf 110s were delivered in March 1942. The Ju 87 Stuka – the very symbol of the Blitzkrieg – had been obsolete for modern aerial warfare by the outbreak of the war. During the Battle of Britain, increasing losses of Ju 87s to RAF fighters compelled the Luftwaffe commanders to pull back all remaining aircraft of this type from combat service.

Although the Stukageschwader experienced a revival during the first months of Operation Barbarossa, in the summer of 1941, the appearance of new and faster Soviet fighter planes made it obvious that a successor was needed. Production of the Ju 87 also was planned to be phased out. The output of Ju 87s decreased and almost terminated toward the end of 1941. But since no adequate replacement types were available, the needs deriving from the critical situation on the Eastern Front compelled the Germans to reinstate the Ju 87 into production from January 1942. A new version, the Ju 87 D, better armored, better equipped and with stronger defensive armament, entered service in early 1942, replacing the old Ju 87 B. But the dominant weakness of the Ju 87 – its slow speed – was not overcome. Nevertheless, it should be stressed that most airmen of the Stukageschwader, who generally were characterized by their high combat spirit, received the new Ju 87 D with great enthusiasm. Friedrich Lang, who flew as an Oberleutnant with I./St.G. 2 in 1942, said: "This aircraft was easy to handle. Its armament and bomb load was increased within one year from one 500-kg bomb and one fixed and one flexible machine-gun to one 1,800-kg bomb, two fixed 7.92mm machine guns and a fixed twin 7.92mm machine gun." The output of Ju 87s increased from 476 in 1941 to 960 in 1942.

With the creation of the first Schlachtgeschwader – ground-attack wing – in 1942, the Luftwaffe considerably improved the structure of its ground-attack force. But the technical equipment did not follow the improvements in organizational structure. At the beginning of 1942, the only operational aircraft type expressly designed as a ground-attack plane remained the old Hs 123 biplane. In January 1942, one Staffel – 10.(S)/LG 2 (later to be reformed into 8./SchG 1) – was the only unit operating this aircraft type on the Eastern Front. The bulk of the aircraft composition of SchG 1 was Bf 109 Es with liquid-cooled aircraft engines and thus extremely vulnerable to ground fire.

A new aircraft type entirely designed for the ground-attack role was being completed in early 1942 – the heavily armored twin-engine Hs 129. But the Hs 129 proved to be a disappointment as it entered service in May 1942. The French-designed Gnôme-Rhône 14M engine had a dangerous tendency to seize without warning during operations on the Eastern Front. Two other major deficits of this aircraft type were relatively slow speed and the lack of any rear firing armament, which contributed to making the Hs 129 somewhat vulnerable to enemy fighters. Moreover, these aircraft had rather poor visibility to the sides and rear, which made it difficult to spot attacking enemy fighters in time to evade them.

Another weakness of the Luftwaffe on the Eastern Front was the virtual absence of a night-fighter force, even though most of the Soviet medium bomber raids had been shifted to the hours of darkness from the fall of 1941.

Taken as a whole, the Luftwaffe fielded some of the best combat aircraft in the world in early 1942. The greatest success of the German aircraft industry in 1941 had been the new Focke-Wulf Fw 190 fighter. Equipped with a powerful air-cooled radial engine, the Fw 190 was faster than the Bf 109 F – and better armed. Nevertheless, the Bf 109 would remain the only German fighter active on the Eastern Front during most of 1942.

From a technical point of view, the fighter planes were the trump card of the Luftwaffe during the remainder of the war. Together with the Soviet Yak-1 and the British Spitfire Mk V, the Bf 109 F "Friedrich" remained the best fighter plane in European skies in early 1942. The Bf 109 F-2, equipped with a 1,175-horsepower DB 601 N engine, could reach a maximum speed of around 370 miles per hour. The Bf 109 F-4, which slowly started succeeding the Bf 109 F-2 in mid-1941, had a more powerful engine – the 1,350-horsepower DB 601 E – which gave it a maximum speed of 390 miles per hour. The F-4 also came equipped with a nose-mounted MG 151 15mm cannon rebored to 20mm.

In the bomber units, the old Do 17 horizontal medium bomber disappeared from service with the Kampfgruppen on the Eastern Front as III./KG 3 was reequipped on Ju 88s in December 1941 and 15.(Kroat)/KG 53 left first-line service. From then on, Do 17s only served as long-range reconnaissance aircraft. The Do 17's replacement, the Ju 88, was the best German combat airplane on the Eastern Front in 1942. It was a fortunate combination – a fast medium bomber that could dive-bomb with sufficient accuracy. The aircraft was supposed to dive at an angle of about 50 degrees, but Ju 88 crews state that they frequently dived at 60 to 70 degrees. The Ju 88 was aimed at the target with the Revi bombsight, which could be swung in elevation to account for a headwind. The bombs were released automatically during the pullout, after a set time interval. Thus, the Ju 88 could be used with considerable effect against pinpoint targets such as bridges, ships, and even moving tanks, and its high speed often allowed it to escape fighter interception.

The twin-engine He 111 was the backbone of the Luftwaffe's horizontal bomber fleet. In late 1941 the modified He 111 H-6 – supplied with improved armor protection – was introduced. He 111 production increased from 950 in 1941 to 1,337 in 1942. In 1942 the aircraft was used in versatile roles as horizontal bomber, torpedo plane, minelayer, and transport. Hansgeorg Bätcher, who was an Oberleutnant and Staffelkapitän 1./KG 100 in early 1942, describes the He 111 as an outstanding aircraft in 1942 – "excellent handling characteristics, a bit slow, but with a great ability to withstand damage." It was very popular among the flight crews.

One of the most significant roles played by a single German aircraft type on the Eastern Front in 1942, was that of the three-engine Ju 52. The Ju 52 had made its first flight on October 13, 1930, and for the next fifteen years, the chassis was never changed – a measure of the farsightedness of its designer, Ernst Zindel. This old and slow transport plane served by the hundreds in all combat zones, providing surrounded German troop contingents with vital supplies, bringing up ammunition and fuel to advancing Panzer spearheads or forward airstrips, evacuating wounded, and so forth.

The Focke Wulf Fw 189, which succeeded the Hs 126 as the German Army's main tactical reconnaissance aircraft in 1942, was a constant headache to the Soviets. It was well protected against fighter interception; armament of the principal version, the Fw 189 A-2, consisted of twin MG 81 Z machine guns in the dorsal turret, a twin MG 81 Z in the rear of the nacelle, and two fixed forward-firing MG 17s in the wing roots. In addition, the Fw 189 had excellent maneuverability, and the view from the glass cockpit allowed the crew to detect fighter interception from almost any angle. Nevertheless, the Soviet fighter pilots hunted the Fw 189, which they called *Rama* ("Frame"), with a particular eagerness. (Photo: Roba/Mombeek.)

Among all Luftwaffe units on the Eastern Front, the heaviest losses during Operation Barbarossa had been suffered by the Heeresfliegerverbände – the Nah-, Panzer- and Fernaufklärungsstaffeln subordinate to the German Army. Chiefly outfitted with the old Hs 126, these tactical reconnaissance units registered 259 aircraft as totally destroyed and 231 damaged until the end of 1941 – compared to the 366 that had been at hand at the onset of Operation Barbarossa. It is hardly surprising that the tactical reconnaissance units underwent the largest reorganization among all German aviation units during 1942. Due to frequent coordination difficulties between the Luftwaffe and the army's tactical reconnaissance aviation, the army aviation units were disbanded and the Heeresaufklärungs units were placed under Luftwaffe control in February 1942. Moreover, the gradual replacement of the Hs 126 with the new twin-engine Fw 189 resulted in a radical improvement of the technical standing of the Heeresaufklärungs units in 1942.

The Henschel Hs 126 was the backbone of the German Army's tactical reconnaissance arm. It provided an invaluable contribution to German military achievements during the Blitzkrieg, but it was approaching obsolescence and suffered heavily at the hands of modern fighter aircraft. Heeresaufklärungsgruppe 13 alone lost at least eighty-seven Hs 126s destroyed or severely damaged on the Eastern Front between June and December 1941. In 1941, this aircraft type was removed from production to be succeeded by the twin-engine Fw 189, which provided the crew with a far better chance of survival in the face of fighter interception. (Photo: Roba/Mombeek.)

Fw 189 A-1, 3.(H)/14, Eastern Front 1942

Chapter 3

The VVS in Early 1942

At the beginning of 1942, the structure of the VVS still was based on the irrational division between the front air forces, the army air forces, and the long-range bomber aviation (DBA). This division of command and responsibility seriously hampered the efficiency of Soviet aerial operations. At the same time, the Soviet aircraft industry was heading for a remarkable revival from immense difficulties. In the fall of 1941, almost the entire industry in the western parts of the USSR had been evacuated to the east. Production resumed under utterly primitive conditions, often beneath the open sky. Under these circumstances, the monthly output of Soviet aircraft fell from 2,329 in September 1941 to 627 in November of that year. But through frantic efforts and concentrating production resources, output figures rose sharply. By January 1942 monthly production surpassed one thousand aircraft.

Another Ilyushin Il-2 Shturmovik is manufactured. The winter of 1941-1942 was the most difficult time of the war for the Soviet aircraft industry. The loss of large industrial regions in the western part of the USSR and the evacuation of several aviation plants led to a decline in aircraft production from 2,329 aircraft in September 1941 to only 627 in November 1941. Nevertheless, all difficulties were overcome, and by the first quarter of 1942, 3,740 aircraft were produced—compared to 3,177 aircraft in the fourth quarter of 1941. In the second quarter of 1942, 6,004 aircraft of all types were produced. The story of Aircraft Production Plant No. 18—the main Il-2 factory—is the most telling. The evacuation of this plant from Voronezh to Kuybyshev (the location of Aircraft Production Plant No. 295) was initiated in early November 1941. Only one month later—on December 10, 1941—the first Il-2 was assembled in Kuybyshev from parts that had been produced in Voronezh and evacuated with the new factory. On December 29, 1941, a trainload with the first twenty-nine Il-2s produced in Kuybyshev left for Moscow, and by the end of January 1942, the daily output of Aircraft Production Plant No. 18 reached seven aircraft. (Photo: Author's collection.)

Production of a new single-engine ground-attack plane, the Il-2 Shturmovik, received top priorities. Considered the triumph of Soviet aviation technology, the Il-2 with its heavy armor shield earned the nickname "Cement Bomber" from German fighter pilots. Another important advantage of this aircraft was its strong landing gear, enabling operation from almost any makeshift airfield.

But the putative "invulnerability" of the Il-2 should not be exaggerated. The aircraft's weak spot was the unprotected radiator in its belly. In combination with the absence of dive brakes that forced the Il-2 to make shallow dives at no more than 30 degrees, it would have seemed natural for the Il-2 pilots to remain "on the deck" during the entire combat sortie. But the most common operational flight altitude of the "Ilyusha," as the Soviets called it, was between 800 and 6,000 feet. Aleksandr Yefimov, who served as a Leytenant and Il-2 pilot with 198 ShAP in 1942, explains:

> Low-level attacks did not allow the pilots to take advantage of the full striking capacities of the Shturmovik. During low-level attacks we had to use delayed-action bombs in order to evade damage to our own aircraft. Furthermore, the accuracy of the bombing was significantly hampered by the tendency of the delayed-action

bombs to bounce back into the air before exploding. And the Il-2s faced the danger of being hit by these ricocheting bombs. And we could not make full use of our cannon and machine guns during low-level attacks, since it was impossible to hit targets in trenches, ramparts, and behind folds in the landscape.

Furthermore, we also experienced problems related to finding the target during flights at tree-top level. Our Shturmoviks had to fly along some reference line (like a road or a river) in order to find the target area. On occasion, fighters or dive-bombers that flew at a higher altitude were used to guide the Shturmoviks. With this, the moment of surprise was lost.[16]

A Curtiss P-40 Tomahawk fighter in Soviet service. The airplane seen here might be the Tomahawk IIA, serial number AH976, which belonged to 126 IAP/6 IAK PVO and which was damaged in an accident on October 28, 1941. According to Soviet sources, a total of 247 Tomahawks were received – 230 in 1941 and 17 in 1942. In 1942 the Tomahawks were phased out in favor of the improved P-40 Kittyhawk. (Photo: Viktor Kulikov photo collection.)

But the principal reason why Il-2s generally carried out their attacks from medium-high flight altitude was that most Il-2 losses were from antiaircraft fire. By approaching at medium-high altitude and not a low level, the pilots could locate their target more rapidly, which enabled them to carry out quick strikes without exposing themselves to AAA for protracted periods. Withal, the Il-2 was a formidable ground-attack plane, perhaps the best of its kind during World War II, and gained a healthy respect from the German ground troops.

The VVS fighter units operated with a versatile aircraft mix in 1942. The slow and obsolescent Polikarpov fighters – I-15bis, I-153 Chayka, and I-16 Ishak – were successively phased out, but whereas only few fighter aviation regiments still were outfitted with the I-15bis and I-153 biplanes in 1942, the I-16 monoplane would stay in operational service in relatively large numbers throughout 1942. With its excellent maneuverability, the I-16 could be a quite tough opponent even against faster Bf 109s.

The modern MiG-3 had been designed as a high-altitude fighter, based on the belief that the upcoming air war would be fought at high altitudes. But on the Eastern Front, the air war mainly took place at low or medium altitudes in response to both sides concentrating on close-support missions near the front lines. Moreover, the MiG-3 was equipped with the high-altitude AM-35A engine, and the first Il-2s used the low-altitude version of the same engine – both of which were manufactured on the same production line. So in late 1941 the MiG-3 was removed from production for the sake of producing more engines for more Il-2s. Existing MiG-3s remained in service in large numbers during the first months of 1942.

Instead of MiG-3s, large numbers of LaGG-3s and Yak-1s were assigned to the fighter units. Out of 9,918 Soviet fighters produced in 1942, nearly two-thirds would be Yakovlev fighters.

The Yak-1, the first in this series, was comparable to the Bf 109 F in all respects – at least at low and medium flight altitudes. The first Yak-7s built for combat were converted two-seat Yak-7UTI training fighters; they entered service in the fall of 1941, but the evacuation of the production plants delayed large-scale serial production until early spring 1942. Although easier to handle than the Yak-1, the Yak-7 was heavier and slightly slower. The Yak-7 and Yak-7a variants were armed with one 20mm cannon and two 7.62mm machine guns, but the Yak-7B, which was introduced in April 1942, was armed with one 20mm cannon and two 12.7mm machine guns.

The LaGG-3 – which reached its peak of production in 1942, with 2,771 manufactured – was never able to compete with the Bf 109, but it was successively improved throughout 1942.

Lend-Lease fighters that the British and the Americans delivered to the USSR starting in late 1941 – Hawker Hurricanes and Curtiss P-40 Tomahawks –

generally performed poorly compared to the Bf 109. Soviet fighter pilots found the British Hurricane to be outdated and cumbersome. Furthermore, the standard Soviet aviation fuel in 1941 – 42 was the B-70 formulation, with an octane rating between only 70 and 75. Since the Hurricane's Rolls-Royce Merlin engine was designed for a considerably higher octane rating the Soviet fuel wore them down rapidly, decreasing its performance and frequently causing flight accidents. Bf 109s shot down scores of American Tomahawks flown by British and Commonwealth pilots in North African skies in 1941 and throughout 1942. Nevertheless, this airplane was superior to both the Hurricane and the I-16, and it at least fared no worse on the Eastern Front than in North Africa. Inexperienced Soviet pilots generally disliked the Tomahawk, but veterans like Podpolkovnik Boris Safonov, Kapitan Petr Pokryshev, and Kapitan Petr Pilyutov could use its advantages – maneuverability and reliable radio equipment – to compensate for its liabilities – low speed and poor climbing performance – with adequate tactics. Although he was not especially enthusiastic about the Tomahawk, 154 IAP ace Kapitan Petr Pokryshev had this to say about it: "Horizontal maneuver – good, fire power – as one can wish, radio equipment – we never had anything like it before." The reliable radio equipment installed in all American or British aircraft was the dominant advantage of all Lend-Lease aircraft that reached service with the VVS.

The Soviet bomber force – considered the backbone of the VVS before the war, just as the bomber force had been considered in the Luftwaffe – was in a dismal state at the end of 1941. The modern, all-metal Pe-2 bomber still was not built in any large numbers due to the Stavka's decision to concentrate on the production of Il-2 ground-attack planes and to the shortage of aluminum coinciding with the evacuation of the industries from the western territories of the USSR. Just 125 Pe-2s were manufactured in January 1942, and only later in the year was output of this aircraft type able to reach any significant figures.

The Soviet SB and DB-3 twin-engine medium bombers had suffered heavy losses in the face of German fighters and AAA during daylight operations in the summer of 1941. In August 1941 the five Korpusa of DBA were disbanded, and only seven weakened Divizii remained. The commands of the various fronts used these forces – together with the SBs of the front air forces – for tasks for which the DBA was not intended, such as low-level close-support missions. Only by shifting the bulk of medium and heavy bomber sorties to nighttime in the fall of 1941 would the DBA be saved from a complete annihilation. While the SB had given ample proof of its obsolescence and was successively disappearing from first-line service, the improved version of the DB-3, the DB-3F (re-designated Il-4 in March 1942), would remain the backbone of the Soviet long-range air force throughout the war. During night operations, the difference between the early DB-3 and the DB-3F was decisive. While the engines of the DB-3A and DB-3B had exhaust stacks both above and beneath the engines – and thus could be detected from both above and below – the engines of the DB-3F only had exhaust stacks beneath. Most DB-3F engines also were equipped with special flare dampers, although this equipment reduced the power of the engines.

A formation of Ilyushin DB-3F torpedo planes. Redesignated Il-4 in March 1942, this aircraft type would remain the standard Soviet long-range bomber and torpedo bomber throughout the war. From the fall of 1941 it was mainly deployed on night-bombing missions.

Due to difficulties arising from the evacuation and reorganization of the aircraft industry by that time, the higher prioritization on other aircraft types resulted in a relatively low industrial output of these bombers in 1942. Through 1942 a total of 858 DB-3Fs/Il-4s were manufactured at four aircraft plants – No. 126 in Komsomol'sk-na-Amure, No. 81 in Moscow, No. 23 in Fili, and No. 39 in Irkutsk. (Photo: Rybin.)

An Ilyushin DB-3 2M-87b bomber. The early DB-3 models were starting to be replaced by the more highly developed DB-3F, before the war. The heavy losses in 1941 resulted in the near disappearance of early DB-3 models from the first-line combat units. (Photo: Creek.)

In the front air forces and the army air forces, most bomber and ground-attack operations were carried out by Il-2s, Pe-2s, and Su-2s in daylight, and by a mixed composition of SBs and vastly obsolete R-5, R-Z, and U-2 biplanes at night. The biplanes, in fact, played a remarkable role during most of the war. From late 1941 on, the Soviets converted large numbers of U-2 trainers into light bombers and brought them to first-line service for nuisance missions at night. During the crisis of the VVS in late 1941 and early 1942, the U-2s were responsible for a large share of total VVS activities. They operated under the most primitive conditions and rarely succeeded in dealing any true material losses to the Germans, but they had a psychological effect that should not be underestimated, depriving German soldiers and airmen of their badly needed sleep at night. The U-2 was so successful that it not only remained in service with the VVS until the end of the war, but the Luftwaffe copied its combat methodology later on.

The risk of hitting friendly troops frequently kept the Soviet night bombers well away from the front lines. Thus, their main targets were army bases, airfields, depots, railway junctions, and so forth – mostly between five and thirty miles behind the German front line. Some raids were also conducted against targets deep in the German rear area.

From the end of 1941, the Soviets also paid increasing attention to aerial reconnaissance. The number of aerial reconnaissance regiments – RAPs and ORAEs – was increased, and these were equipped largely with Pe-2s or Pe-3s. Some of the most experienced bomber aviation regiments were transformed into reconnaissance units.

Chapter 4 

Equipment and Methods

A common conception of the Eastern Front in World War II is that of a rather primitive or crude type of warfare, and this is to a certain extent true regarding technology. Some of the most refined technical developments of the early 1940s never were used or were only used on a limited scale, and the use of radar was scarce throughout the war. Most air surveillance was carried out by visual sightings from observation posts at the front. In early 1942 the Soviets had RUS-2 early warning radar stations installed at a few specially protected targets, such as Moscow and Leningrad. RUS-2, which was set up in fixed installations, mounted on trucks (called Redut), or in deployed in a portable version (called Pegmatit), had a range of between sixty and ninety miles.

On the Eastern Front the Germans only made use of radar in northern Norway and for brief periods at Leningrad. The German Freya early warning radar, operating on a 2.4-meter wavelength, had a range of eighty to a hundred miles. Because of the higher priority given to the defense of the Fatherland against RAF night bomber raids, there were no dedicated German night fighter units on the Eastern Front in early 1942.

Unlike fighters and ground-attack aircraft, all multi-engine Soviet bombers were equipped with radio transmitters and receivers. This photo shows an RSB-bis, the standard radio equipment in Soviet bombers in 1941-1943, in a DB-3F. (Photo: Kurayev via Antipov.)

In the field of navigation, bombsights and gun sights, the situation was better, and both sides had quite similar equipment. While fighters and ground-attack aircraft navigated visually, the German bomber crews were provided with a radio navigation beacon however of a more simplified nature than in western Europe. Hansgeorg Bätcher of I./KG 100 describes the situation: "We were provided with only one radio beacon for navigation, not the three-axis beacon that was common in the Western Theater of Operations."[17] On the Soviet side, the night bombers of the DBA navigated through an increasingly well-organized network of radio homing beacons from late 1941. On occasion, Soviet partisans even marked the target with flares or by lighting fires.

With the introduction of the German gyroscopic reflector bombsight Lotfernrohr Lotfe 7 H, which automatically calculated drift during high-altitude horizontal bombing, the German medium bombers achieved a considerably increased bombing accuracy in 1942. Soviet bombers were outfitted with similar bombsights – OPB-1M or OPB-2M for daylight bombing, and NKPB-3, NKPB-4, or NKPB-7 for nocturnal bombing. But such Soviet aircraft like the U-2 light night bomber, a converted biplane trainer,had no bombsight. The U-2 pilot simply aimed by counting the seconds after the target had disappeared below the forward edge of the lower wing. It was virtually the same with the Il-2 and German fighter-bombers such as the Bf 109.

For air combat, the German Reflexvisier Revi 12 reflector gun sight had a roughly equal counterpart in the Soviet standard PBP-1a gun sight.

Communication by radio transmitter (R/T) was the main difference between the Luftwaffe and the VVS regarding technical equipment. All German aircraft had modern and reliable radio transmitters and receivers, which naturally was an enormous advantage in aerial combat. The Soviets were only slowly taking steps in that direction. Most fighters and ground-attack aircraft produced by the Soviets in 1942 were outfitted with radio receivers, but only a small proportion was also equipped with transmitters. This however did not apply to the multi-place aircraft – DB-3s, Pe-2s, TB-3s, TB-7s, SBs, and even the obsolete R-5s and R-Zs – which were all outfitted with both radio receivers and transmitters. On the other hand, the Luftwaffe for some inexplicable reason never installed radio communication *between* fighter pilots and the aircraft they were supposed to escort. This particular disadvantage did not appear on the Soviet side, once radio transmitters and receivers were at hand.

The absence of radio transmitters in most Soviet aircraft was an important reason for the generally vast advantage the German fighters held in air combat. But there were several other causes for this well-documented advantage. Both the doctrine and the mentality of the German fighter pilots were concentrated on achieving personal victories, promoting a "hunting mentality" and combat tactics against which their opponents of 1942 – both in the VVS and the RAF – often stood little chance.

Because the VVS lacked adequate ground-attack aircraft – the Il-2 Shturmovik – until the summer of 1942, heavy demands for ground-attack missions were placed on the Soviet fighter aviation regiments, and the Soviet fighter pilots frequently were caught in a vulnerable position by the Bf 109s. The technique favored by the Jagdflieger was a high-side gunnery run against lower flying enemy formations. In this maneuver the German fighter pilots took advantage of the speed built up in a dive combined with the superior climb performance of the Bf 109 to place themselves above the Soviets for a new attack.

Not even when they were used in the pure fighter role could the Soviet fighter pilots employ the same pursuit methods as their German counterparts. Whereas the Jagdflieger were free to choose if they would accept combat, the Red Falcons frequently were instructed to remain covering a particular object during the entire sortie. Fixing fighters to a point defense may have provided the Red Army ground troops with a morale boost (German ground troops frequently asked themselves: "*Wo bleibt die Luftwaffe?*" – Where is the Luftwaffe?), but it forced the Soviet fighter pilots to accept any aerial engagement, whether the conditions were favorable or not, and the Soviet pilots had only limited possibilities of pursuing the enemy. Added to this was the obvious fact that the Soviet aircraft – with the exception of the Yak-1 – were inferior or vastly inferior in most aspects to the Bf 109.

A Messerschmitt Bf 109 F during a landing approach following a free-hunt sortie on the Eastern Front. Unlike most other air forces, the Luftwaffe had only a single standard fighter plane during the early years of the war, the Bf 109. In early 1942, all German Jagdgeschwader on the Eastern Front had been operating nothing but Bf 109s for several years. This permitted the veterans to fully exploit the type's advantages. In early 1942, no enemy fighter plane could out-dive or out-climb the Bf 109, and this made it perfect for German hit-and-run tactics against enemy aircraft formations. The Bf 109 F was considerably faster than the old Soviet Polikarpov I-15bis, I-153, and I-16 fighters. And it was superior in all respects to the MiG-3, the LaGG-3, and Lend-Lease P-40s and Hurricanes. Only in the Yak-1 did the Bf 109 meet its equal on the Eastern Front in early 1942. In 1941 and 1942, the Jagdgeschwader shot down an average of about twelve Soviet aircraft for every Bf 109 lost in combat. (Photo: Trautloft.)

The principal reason for the inequality in pure dogfighting, however, was the increasing gap of pilot training standards between the Luftwaffe and the VVS. From late 1941 it was not uncommon that young Soviet airmen arrived from the flight training schools with no more than thirty or forty flight hours in training aircraft and eight to ten flight hours on combat planes. This was a result of the immense losses in 1941; the Soviets were left with no other option but to reduce the curricula of the flight training schools.

That no more than 1,666 German fighter pilots left pilot training schools in 1942 clearly indicates the Luftwaffe had not yet started reducing the training curricula. Furthermore, almost three years of war had developed a core of veterans within the Luftwaffe units – men who were absolute masters in aerial combat, virtual flying war machines. These "Experten" were the main force of the Luftwaffe. Although few in numbers, they were one of the most important German assets in the air war on the Eastern Front.

On top of this, the new Soviet aircraft that arrived at front-line aviation units in early 1942 were plagued by defects from hasty production under primitive conditions in the evacuated factories. According to a report issued by 230 ShAD in June 1942, production deficiencies reduced the maximum speed of some Il-2s by 25 to 30 miles per hour. This forced pilots to hold the engines at maximum power during combat flights, which rapidly wore down the engines.[18]

The Soviets also had to operate under another disadvantage. Their air combat tactics still relied on the obsolete tactical thinking that had characterized the VVS operations in 1941 – and would do so well into mid-1942. In contrast to the German belief in subordinate initiative, the entire Red Army was handicapped by an archaic and authoritarian attitude. This was felt at all levels, often frustrating efforts to improve methods and material. Sometimes, a display of independent judgment could be hazardous to an individual soldier's or airman's health. Soviet fighter ace Kapitan Aleksandr Pokryshkin spent much of the winter of 1941 – 42 teaching novice pilots of his regiment, 55 IAP, the hard-earned conclusions that he and other veteran pilots had drawn from the air combats in 1941. His lectures were not always according to the book, and word of this soon spread. One day General-Mayor Aleksandr Osipenko, the commander of 20 SAD, to which 55 IAP was assigned, entered the lecture hall in the midst of a discourse by Pokryshkin. Pokryshkin was drawing two different methods for ground attack: the old one – from the Soviet prewar tactics book – and the new one, which was more effective according to his front-line experiences. Suddenly Osipenko rose and interrupted Pokryshkin. He gave the "new thinker" a sharp reprimand and ordered him to teach exclusively according to the old dogma. Pokryshkin and Kapitan Pavel Kryukov, who led the 55 IAP Eskadrilya that had been formed for the training of novice pilots, were warned against tutoring their own tactics.[19]

In this way, Soviet airmen entered first-line service with tactical thinking that reduced their efficiency and made them easy prey for German fighters.

On another occasion this same winter, Aleksandr Pokryshkin was one of many highly awarded Soviet pilots invited to a special meeting with the chief engineer of 20 SAD. In a lecture lasting several hours, the engineer tried to explain to the pilots that all Soviet aircraft types, such as the MiG-3, the I-16, and even the I-153 biplane, were superior to the Bf 109. "I could not see the reason for this lecture," Pokryshkin commented in his memoirs. "After all, his audience was made up of experienced airmen who had met the Messerschmitts and Junkers on several occasions, and who knew how good these aircraft were."[20] At the end of the meeting, Pokryshkin could not stand it any more and decided to raise his voice. He asked permission to speak. The hall became death-silent, but undauntedly Pokryshkin spoke out. He agreed that MiG-3 had certain advantages, but that it was too heavy and that the Bf 109 was more maneuverable at lower altitudes and also more heavily armed. He expressed the urgent need for new and better aircraft. The reaction from the senior commander to Pokryshkin's rebellious candor mirrors the general command attitude in Josef Stalin's society. "My words found no response," Pokryshkin wrote. "Instead, I found myself charged with accusations of an 'unpatriotic attitude.' I decided to keep such appraisals to myself in the future. I returned to my regiment in a dismal state of mood. Only when I started flying combat missions again was I able to get rid of this uneasy feeling."[21]

It was hardly surprising that the VVS would remain handicapped well into 1942 by the rigid and divided structure with which it had been so disastrously hobbled in 1941. Individual ground army commanders jealously guarded their air forces, rigidly tying them to the army's sector even if there were greater

The first LaGG-3s were something of a disappointment to Soviet fighter pilots. The type proved to be considerably slower and less maneuverable than the Bf 109 F, so several measures were taken to improve its performance. The first of these was carried out with the eighth production series in Fall 1941, from which the two 7.62mm ShKAS machine guns were removed. This reduced weight and thus improved flight performance. In return, the armament was limited to only one 20mm ShVAK or 23mm VYa cannon and one 12.7mm UB machine gun. Compared to the Yak-1, the lighter LaGG-3 remained difficult to handle and still had inferior performance, but it had the stronger structure and thus the higher ability to withstand battle damage. (Photo: Seidl.)

needs in other areas. The division between front air forces, the PVO, the army air forces, the DBA, and the navy air force caused severe coordination problems.

Meanwhile, the Luftwaffe was able to outweigh its declining numerical strength on the Eastern Front with its flexible structure, which allowed Fliegerkorps or Luftflotten commanders to concentrate aircraft in particularly endangered sectors. This flexibility was increased from the end of 1941, with the independent Fliegerkorps, Fliegerführer, and Fliegerdivisionen assuming the operational role of the larger Luftflotten. Frequently, Gruppen were shifted from one front-line sector to another, creating power points against which the more rigid VVS had no chance of competing. For instance, II./StG 1 operated in the central combat zone in early 1942, then took part in the opening of the German summer offensive in the southern combat zone, and returned to the central combat zone to help counter the Soviet offensives later that summer. After a short while it was back in the southern combat zone, operating over Stalingrad. III./KG 1 saw action all over the front line during 1942, from Leningrad in the north to Stalingrad in the south.

Designed as a high-altitude interceptor with a maximum speed of 400 mph at 24,000 feet flight altitude, the Soviet MiG-3 fighter proved to be inferior to the Bf 109 F during air combat on the Eastern Front, where most air fighting took place at relatively low altitudes. A major disadvantage of the MiG-3 was that it was rather difficult to handle. Relatively few Soviet pilots had the skills needed to exploit the MiG-3's advantages. (Photo: Via Rosipal.)

Various figures on the total aircraft strength on the Eastern Front in January 1942 have been given in different sources. Historian Heinz A. F. Schmidt gives the figure of 3,688 Soviet aircraft in first-line service,[22] and historian Percy E. Schramm gives the figure of 1,500 German first-line aircraft in service on the Eastern Front in January 1942.[23] In addition, approximately 200 aircraft from Germany's allies – including 110 Finnish – were opposed to the Soviet Union.

Part II

The Soviet Winter Offensive

American Lend-Lease Curtiss P-40 Tomahawks of 126 IAP taking off for a combat mission on the Moscow Front during the winter of 1941-1942. 126 IAP was the first unit to be equipped with P-40 fighters. The two best pilots of the regiment during that period were Kapitan Vladimir Kamenshchikov and Starshiy Leytenant Stepan Ridnyy, each of whom achieved eight individual and shared victories during the first month of the war, and on August 9, 1941, both were named Hero of the Soviet Union.

Stepan Ridnyy was killed on February 17, 1942, with a final tally of nine individual and twenty-one collective victories. By August 1942, when he was transferred to 788 IAP, Vladimir Kamenshchikov had amassed eighteen individual and fifteen shared victories. During the Battle of Stalingrad Kamenshchikov added another sixteen individual and shared victories to his score, thus positioning himself among the top VVS aces of that time. In February 1943, Mayor Kamenshchikov was appointed commander of 38 GIAP, but he was killed in action on May 22, 1943. (Photo: Viktor Kulikov collection.)

Chapter 5

Flying Artillery on the Central Combat Zone

One area in which the Soviets held a significant advantage over their German adversaries was in the ability to cope with the extreme cold that reigned on the Eastern Front in early 1942. This advantage alone led to decisive results in January of that year.

By early 1942, German Army Group Center was in complete disarray. The strongholds at Kalinin on the northern flank and Kaluga in the south had been abandoned, and the troops were falling back, often in panic. Self-assured Soviet ground troops advanced mainly by infiltration, avoiding German strongpoints and passing over snow-covered fields and through deep forests instead of along roads. Cavalry, ski troops, and partisans haunted the German rear area. The Germans avoided a complete breakdown in the central combat in December 1941 only by bringing in substantial Luftwaffe reinforcements.

Since the transfer of Luftflotte 2 to the Mediterranean area late in 1941, General Wolfram Freiherr von Richthofen's Fliegerkorps VIII was in control of Luftwaffe operations in the Moscow combat zone. Von Richthofen had received numerous reinforcements in December 1941, and had approximately two-thirds of all Luftwaffe aircraft in service on the Eastern Front at his disposal. At the turn of the year, Fliegerkorps VIII could muster the following bomber, close-support, and fighter units:

Fighter units: Stab, II., III. and IV./JG 51 (Bf 109 Fs);
I. and II./JG 52 (Bf 109 Fs).
Zerstörer units: II./ZG 1 (Bf 110s); I. and II./ZG 26 (Bf 110s).
Dive-bomber units: II./StG 1 (Ju 87s); III./StG 2 (Ju 87s).
Ground-attack units: II.(S)/LG 2 (Bf 109 Es); 10.(S)/LG 2 (Hs 123s). (On January 13 these two units were reformed into the new SchG 1.

The bomber units assigned to Fliegerkorps VIII were brought together under a special command umbrella, Gefechtsverband Bormann, led by the Geschwaderkommodore of KG 54, Oberst Ernst Bormann. Early in January 1942, Gefechtsverband Bormann could muster the following units: Stab, I. and II./KG 3 (Ju 88s); Stab and II./KG 4 (He 111s); III./KG 26 (Ju 88s); II./KG 30 (Ju 88s); Stab, II. and III./KG 53 (He 111s); 15.(Kroat)/KG 53 (Do 17s); II. and III./KG 76 (Ju 88s); and II./KG 100 (He 111s).

In addition, more than a hundred Ju 52 transport planes under the command of Oberst Fritz Morzik had been brought in to provide forward positions of Army Group Center with airlifted supplies.

While the transport planes helped to improve the supply situation, bombers, Stukas, Zerstörer and fighter-bombers were in relentless action over the battlefield, dealing heavy blows to the advancing Soviet troops. But after the new year, this activity stopped abruptly. "Suddenly there were only small groups of enemy aircraft in the air," recalls Soviet fighter pilot Arkadiy Kovachevich, who served as a Starshiy Leytenant with 27 IAP of 6 IAK/Moscow PVO during this time. "This puzzled us, for our air reconnaissance had reported large concentrations of German planes at Klin and other German airfields."[1]

The reason for the paucity of German aircraft was the dramatic change in the weather. Temperatures in the central combat zone fell sharply after Christmas 1941, and on January 4, 1942, they plummeted to minus – 42-degrees Celsius. It was at this point that "General Winter" made his real entrance into the war. Unlike the Soviets, the Germans had virtually no means to cope with the Arctic cold on the primitive front-line airfields. "Eighty percent of the aircraft park of the Luftwaffe was paralyzed at temperatures below minus – 20 degrees Celsius," states historian Heinz Kiehl.[2] "Due to the

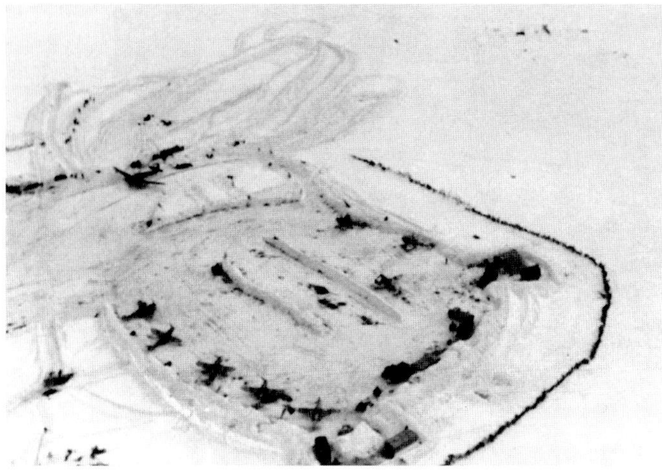

A Bf 109 F Staffel in the parking area of a front-line Eastern Front airfield in the winter of 1941-1942. Standing on the runway is a Focke Wulf Fw 58 Weihe liaison aircraft.

During flights over German-held territory in early January 1942, Soviet airmen were stunned to see large numbers of Luftwaffe planes on the airfields – and very few airborne. Soviet fighter pilot Starshiy Leytenant Arkadiy Kovachevich recalls how the Soviets attempted in vain to thaw out the engines of the German aircraft that were seized at Klin Airdrome with heating lamps. Despite all efforts, the fuel remained too thick. (Photo: Trautloft.)

sudden cold spell, hardly any aircraft could be made serviceable, since there was no heating equipment available," reads a report from JG 52: "II./JG 52 lost its entire technical equipment, including a large part of its aircraft park at Klin."[3]

According to a report issued by the Air Defense of the Soviet Western Front, German air activity over the Western Front sector in January 1942 dropped to one-third of the activity of the previous month.[4]

"Only when we seized the airfield at Klin did we understand the reason to for this German passivity in the air," said Arkadiy Kovachevich: "Several German aircraft were captured there, all of them intact, but with their engines frozen. The desperate Germans had even attempted to thaw out the engine of a Messerschmitt 109 by wheeling the nose of the plane into a house!"[5]

Luftwaffe Oberst Hermann Plocher wrote: "Aircraft engines which had been stopped overnight in the extreme cold were difficult, if not impossible, to start. Warming ovens and all sorts of expedients were devised in an effort to solve this problem. Planes designated for standby-alert were often placed with their noses in 'alert boxes,' heated shacks which kept the engines warm enough to start on short notice."[6]

With their front crumbling, the few German aircraft that could be sent into the air were mainly committed to close-support missions whether they were fighters or medium bombers. While this mirrored the Soviet doctrine for the use of air power, it came about through the acute lack of artillery on the German side. Thus, most of the combat missions were restricted to areas near the front, and the overall air strategy was reduced to a series of improvisations, deriving from the daily changing needs for air support on the ground. Even the Jagdflieger, who had been trained to seek victories in aerial combat, had to set aside their ambitions and carry out hazardous low-level strafing attacks or fighter-bomber raids against the advancing Soviet troops.

The VVS dominated the skies in January 1942. The troops of Army Group Center had suffered from repeated Soviet air attacks since the opening of Operation Barbarossa, but what they had to endure in January 1942 was worse than anything previously experienced in this conflict.

Sitting in front of his MiG-3, Starshiy Leytenant Arkadiy Kovachevich and another pilot of 27 IAP study the flight route of an upcoming combat mission on the Moscow Front in January 1942. Kovachevich served from the beginning of the war in June 1941 until the fall of 1944, and in late 1941 his score stood at four individual and three shared victories. In the fall of 1942, he was posted to the "ace regiment" 9 GIAP. By that time his score had reached nine individual and six shared victories. In December 1942 and January 1943 he attained four more victories and was appointed Hero of the Soviet Union. In the summer of 1944 he assumed command of 9 GIAP. Kovachevich was credited with a total of twenty-six personal and six shared victories. (Photo: Kovachevich.)

Pe-3, Kapitan Aleksey Ostayev, commander of 208 SBAP, Chkalovskaya, Soviet Union, winter 1941-1942
Ostayev was killed in action on July 1, 1942.

On January 1, 1942, the Soviet Western Zone could muster about one thousand serviceable aircraft, divided between the air forces of the Kalinin and Western fronts, VVS-Moscow Military District, 6 IAK/PVO, the independent aviation groups under General-Leytenant Ivan Petrov and General-Mayor Yevgeniy Nikolayenko, and the DBA.[7]

The VVS had developed several ingenious methods and devices to keep its aircraft operational in spite of extremely low temperatures. Powerful heating lamps were commonly used to prevent engine liquid from freezing. In addition, the Soviets had the advantage of operating several of their aviation units from well-equipped air bases constructed prior to the war – in stark contrast with Luftwaffe units that often were stationed at makeshift airstrips.

Thus, the Soviet numerical superiority in the air in the central combat zone at the onset of the winter offensive became even more accentuated in January 1942. Frequently using two crews for every aircraft to maintain the largest possible air activity, the frontal aviation, the independent aviation groups, the aviation units of Moscow Military District, and even the air-defense units of 6 IAK/PVO operated predominantly in close-support, but they also ranged against German supply lines and airfields in the vicinity of the front. Since there still were only a few Il-2s and Pe-2s at hand, most of the daylight missions were carried out by fighters in the role of fighter-bombers. At night, U-2s, R-5s and R-Zs took over against the same targets.

Relentless air strikes meant that transporting goods destined for front-line troops which had been unloaded at Vyazma was a virtual death ride. With most of the vehicles rendered useless due to the cold – only 15 percent of the 100,000 Luftwaffe vehicles on the Eastern Front remained in working condition in January 1942[8] – these columns were mainly horse drawn, and the plowed roads leading to the frontlines soon became littered with frozen horse carcasses and overturned wagons.

Air combat was relatively rare, but when it occurred, the Luftwaffe fliers were up against tougher opposition than ever before on the Eastern Front. On January 3, thirteen German aircraft were claimed destroyed in the air or on the ground

208 SBAP's Kapitan Aleksey Ostayev in the air in his Pe-3 over the German lines on the central combat zone in early 1942. Originally equipped with SB bombers, 208 SBAP was dealt heavy losses during the initial weeks of the German invasion in June 1941. After it had lost fifty-five aircraft and thirty-eight crews, it was withdrawn from first-line service in late July 1941. It was then reformed and served as the basis for three new regiments. One of those regiments, which retained the designation 208 SBAP, was posted to 6 IAK-PVO at Moscow with its twenty Pe-3s on October 15, 1941. During the next three months, the regiment conducted 683 combat sorties and claimed the destruction of 34 tanks, 212 lorries, 6 trains, and 33 enemy aircraft, while at the same time losing ten Pe-3s, twelve pilots, and nine navigators. For its participation in the defense of Moscow the regiment received an official message of thanks from the commander of the Western Front, General Armii Georgiy Zhukov. On January 19, 1942, 208 SBAP once again was withdrawn from the front – this time to transition to Il-2s. During this break, it was redesignated 208 ShAP.

Kapitan Ostayev, one of 208 ShAP's Eskadrilya commanders, was a veteran from the Winter War against Finland and had been appointed Hero of the Soviet Union in March 1940. He was killed in action on July 1, 1942. (Photo: Petrov.)

Known as "alert boxes," heated shacks like this were erected by Luftwaffe groundcrew on the Eastern Front in early 1942 to prevent engine liquid from freezing. Shown here is a JG 51 Bf 109 F in January 1942. (Photo: Trautloft.)

Outfitted with skis, these Soviet Polikarpov U-2 trainer biplanes converted to the light-bomber role were able to operate from makeshift airfields covered with deep snow. During a nocturnal mission on February 21, 1942, the U-2 piloted by Mayor Sergey Melnik, commanding 708 NBAP/VVS-Kalinin Front, was shot down, and for more than a week the injured Melnik hid in a snow cave in German-held territory. A woman from a collective farm rescued him, and she managed to amputate both of his frostbitten feet by herself. Mayor Melnik was kept hidden until Soviet troops liberated the area – in March 1943! After receiving medical treatment, he returned to active service and continued to fly combat missions in U-2s. (Photo: Grubich.)

by the Soviets, three of them by 157 IAP's Leytenant Petr Shemendyuk. During an escort mission for Il-2s, Shemendyuk bagged two. A little later he had an encounter with the Bf 109s of I./JG 52. He claimed one shot down but was also hit and force-landed in friendly territory.

On January 4 Kapitan Nikolay Dunayev was leading six MiGs of 16 IAP, 6 IAK/PVO homeward after successfully strafing a German column in the Medyn area, eighty miles southwest of Moscow. One of the Soviet pilots, Leytenant Ivan Shumilov, felt a terrible fatigue. This sortie had been his third low-level attack that day. Recently, the Germans had strengthened their mobile antiaircraft artillery considerably, turning each low-level air attack into a real venture with death. The twenty-two-year-old pilot also had not recovered completely from a terrifying event five days earlier. On December 30, 1941, a Bf 109 had shot his fighter down in flames. Shumilov had been too low to bail out, and as the flames licked his face and hands, he bellied into the deep snow. Reflecting the soaring combat spirit of the Soviet airmen in the Western Zone during these days, Shumilov was soon back in action again.

Five days later, while flying as the last man in the formation, he spotted another column of enemy vehicles on the ground. Since he had no possibility of communicating with his comrades – only the leading aircraft was equipped with a radio-transmitter, and the remainder were outfitted with receivers only – Shumilov decided to attack alone. He made two gunnery runs, which used up all of his ammunition.

By this time, Kapitan Dunayev's main group was twenty-five miles to the east. As Shumilov started climbing in an easterly direction, he suddenly noticed tracer bullets passing on his right. He looked behind him, and the blood froze in his veins: Seven Bf 109s came diving against him.

Shumilov immediately throttled back. The MiG-3 appeared to stand still in the air, threatening to stall – a hazardous maneuver. Three Bf 109s flashed past Shumilov and then broke in separate directions, probably to avoid gunfire from the MiG-3. Of

Luftwaffe personnel inspect the remains of a downed Soviet fighter on a cold winter morning in early 1942. This airplane is an early LaGG-3, from one of the first seven production series. It was manufactured in 1941. (Photo: Creek.)

course, the German pilots could not know that the Soviet fighter had no bullets to send against them. Unarmed, outnumbered seven to one, and with a terrible speed disadvantage, Shumilov realized that there was only one thing to do. When a fourth Bf 109 came dashing beneath his MiG, the Soviet pilot increased speed and pushed the stick forward. The next moment, the propeller of his fighter struck the Messerschmitt's cockpit. The impact was terrible. In a fraction of a second, the rotating propeller blades of the MiG-3 shattered the glass canopy of the Bf 109 and shredded the German pilot to the waist. Then, as both airplanes shivered and shook, the MiG's propeller and reductor were violently torn away and the Soviet plane caught fire. Shumilov jettisoned his canopy and attempted to bail out, but the air current squeezed him against the fuselage of the descending aircraft. He felt he was falling helplessly to his death together with his doomed machine. For the second time in less than a week, burning fuel scorched his face and body.

Shumilov didn't know how long his body remained with the airplane, but suddenly freezing air told him that he had come free. His parachute deployed, and only seconds later he hit the ground at high speed.[9] He was picked up by Soviet ground troops, who had seen both the MiG and the Messerschmitt crash close to each other about five hundred yards from the small hamlet of Shemyakino.

Illustrating the high combat spirits of Soviet airmen in the central combat zone in early 1942, Leytenant Pavel Peskov smiles confidently in front of his LaGG-3 fighter.

5 GIAP, with which Peskov served, was one of the first VVS Guards units, an honorary title awarded for above-average achievements in combat. Originally designated 129 IAP, it was recommissioned as 5 GIAP in December 1941 in recognition of the sixty-two enemy aircraft it destroyed in the air along with twenty on the ground during a ten-week-period. In January 1942, several of the most skilled Soviet fighter aces were counted within its ranks: Mayor Vasiliy Zaytsev, who scored twelve victories in only sixteen aerial combats by January 1942; Mayor Nikolay Gorodnichev with eleven victories by January 1942; Mayor Grigoriy Onufriyenko, whose score stood at ten at the beginning of 1942; Batalyonnyy Komissar Anatoliy Sokolov, with eight victories by December 1941; and Kapitan Ivan Meshcheryakov, victor in seven aerial combats by the time of his death in February 1942.

Pavel Peskov's personal score stood at seven kills in January 1942, and he would achieve another thirteen victories by the end of the war. (Photo: Seidl.)

Provided with such excellent air support, three armies of General Armii Georgi Zhukov's Western Front, spearheaded by General-Mayor Pavel Belov's 1st Guards Cavalry Corps, was able to split the connection between the German Fourth Army and Second Panzer Army south of Kaluga. At Sukhinichi, fifty miles southwest of Kaluga, four thousand German soldiers of the 216th Infantry Division arrived from France only to be enveloped by the Soviet Tenth Army. "Very strong enemy air activity, repeated bombings and low-level attacks by fighters," was reported from the Germans in Sukhinichi on January 6.[10]

On the northern flank of Army Group Center, the VVS initiated an offensive against enemy airbases in order to open the way for an upcoming ground offensive. Between January 4 and January 7, VVS-Kalinin Front's 569 ShAP, 5 GIAP, and 193 IAP, and the independent aviation group under command of General-Leytenant Ivan Petrov, claimed the destruction of nine Ju 52s on the ground in the Rzhev and Velikiye Luki areas. A tenth German airplane was shot down in the air – reportedly a "Do 217," possibly Narednik (Technical Sergeant) Zdenko Kopetzki's Do 17 of 15.(Kroat)/KG 53, which was reported missing on January 7. On January 8, KG 76 suffered a severe setback, registering six Ju 88s brought down by ground fire in the same area.[11]

During this period, the DBA concentrated on night raids against the railway line leading from Smolensk to Vyazma. Despite heavy AAA opposition, the bomber crews caused some severe disruption of German supply transports. The operation that was carried out against the railway junction at Vyazma by forty-eight bombers – flying separately or in small groups – on the night of January 4 – 5 was particularly successful, as is confirmed by German Army reports.

Adolf Hitler, who had assumed overall command of the German Army in December 1941, had daily outbursts of fury in which he accused the army commanders of treason. Convinced that most of his generals were nothing but defeatists, he dismissed the commander of the Fourth Panzer Army, Generaloberst Erich Hoepner, on January 8, and had him expelled from the ranks of the Wehrmacht. The same day, he issued a statement wherein he pointed out the morale strength of the Soviet troops and demanded that it was "the duty [of all German soldiers] under all circumstances not to prove to be inferior in this regard."[12]

A particular cause of Hitler's concern was Belov's cavalry corps, which advanced rapidly toward the northwest from the Sukhinichi sector, threatening to sever the so-called "Rollbahn," the highway from Warsaw to Moscow that constituted the life artery of Army Group Center. The Führer ordered the surrounded 216th Infantry Division to hold Sukhinichi "under all circumstances" to act as a breakwater against the Soviet offensive tide in this area. An airlift operation by the Ju 52 transport of KGrzbV 172 – was organized, and Hitler personally instructed the twin-engine bombers of Fliegerkorps VIII to concentrate on low-level attacks in support of the Sukhinichi garrison.

Although there were repeated occasions when navigation problems over the snow-covered landscape and the constantly shifting front lines led to erroneous Luftwaffe bombings of German troops, these raids enabled the troops at Sukhinichi to hold out. But the concentration of Fliegerkorps VIII to the Sukhinichi area in the south left the northern flank of Army Group Center with virtually no air support. And here, General-Polkovnik Ivan Konev's Kalinin Front opened a major offensive on January 8 against the German Ninth Army east of Rzhev. Farther to the north, the Soviet Northwestern Front launched a massive attack on January 9 in the Ostashkov area on the border between Army groups Center and North, 200 miles northwest of Moscow. Dispatching the bulk of its air force to support the offensive, Northwestern Front immediately succeeded in tearing a large gap in the German front line.

A sudden low-pressure system that brought rising temperatures and heavy snowfalls complicated the situation. These adverse weather conditions, however, did not prevent the Soviet airmen from maintaining constant pressure on the Germans. Even in blizzard and fog, the fighter-bombers, Shturmoviks, and Pe-2s dived out of the low clouds and wrought havoc on German troop columns. On January 11 the VVS-Kalinin Front claimed to have destroyed fifteen trucks and two artillery pieces during operations against the retreating German Ninth Army.[13] Two days later, the forwardmost troops of the Kalinin Front reached Sychyovka between Vyazma and Rzhev, forty miles north of the Rollbahn. With the attack forces of the Western Front that had penetrated the German lines behind the surrounded Sukhinichi steadily continuing toward the Rollbahn from the south, a gigantic pincer movement developed, threatening to envelop the bulk of Army Group Center.

At this stage, it was evident even to Hitler that the battle for Moscow had been irrevocably lost, and that only a withdrawal from the forwardmost positions could save Army Group Center. On January 15 Army Group Center was finally allowed to pull back to a defense position along the line Rzhev – Gzhatsk – Yukhnov, some ninety miles to the west of Moscow.

The Soviets countered the German retreat by conducting a large-scale airborne troop landing behind the German lines. This was initiated on January 18 and January 19, when twenty-one PS-84s – license-built American DC-3s – of MAGON GVF carried out forty-eight sorties – thirty-four of them were successful – and dropped 642 paratroopers from the 201st Airborne Brigade of 5th Airborne Corps behind German lines in the Ugra area south of Vyazma. The operation continued for five days, and a total of 1,642 troops were landed at the cost to MAGON GVF of six PS-84s, of which three were lost in operational accidents.

According to a widespread German version of the event, a large portion of these Soviet troops were dropped without parachutes. "Under interrogation, numerous Soviet prisoners testified that they had been flown to the target areas, where they were simply pushed or thrown without parachutes from the planes", wrote Oberst Hermann Plocher.[14] In reality, the Soviets – who had pioneered the airborne doctrine (the German paratroopers, the "Green Devils," were formed on the basis of the Red Army model, and the British, Americans, and others followed duly) – had no reason to take such primitive and brutal measures. The German story possibly originates from the fact that the parachuting was supplemented by troops of the 250th Independent Rifle Regiment who were unloaded from transport planes landing on an improvised airstrip near Plesnyovo in German-held territory. It is also conceivable that captured soldiers of the 250th Independent Rifle Regiment invented this story in order to obscure the location of this airfield.

The German crisis reached its climax. Weary and despairing troops – the Wehrmacht definitely had failed to win the competition of moral strength that Hitler had demanded – embarked upon a dreary retreat, mostly on foot. Feldwebel Peter Stahl, a Ju 88 pilot in KG 30, described the sight that met Luftwaffe airmen who flew above the battlefield on January 17:

> We are offered a sorrowful view: long columns of our own soldiers strenuously stumbling back. Everywhere one can see abandoned vehicles,

> some half-covered with snow, and others just recently abandoned.
>
> As we fly past the columns and small groups of soldiers at low altitude, it is evident that they are half unconscious out of fatigue. They pay no attention to us. We pass by burning villages. The enemy won't be able to use them as living quarters when he pursues our troops.
>
> The entire horizon is filled with columns of black smoke. It is a merciless war.[15]

The Luftwaffe units that were supposed to support the troops were in no better state. Although the problems deriving from the Arctic temperatures were slowly overcome through an increased use of "alert boxes" and other heating measures, mounting losses wore down several Luftwaffe units. Losses through air combat remained very limited – VVS-Western Front only claimed six German single-engine fighters, three Hs 126s, and two "miscellaneous aircraft types" shot down from January 1 through January 20[16] – but ground fire and, most of all, the primitive conditions on the front-line airstrips, rapidly depleted the strength of several Luftwaffe units. After thirteen of their bombers had been destroyed or damaged during the first three weeks of January, III./KG 53 and the Do 17-equipped 15.(Kroat)/KG 53 had to be withdrawn from first-line service.

At the same time, Hauptmann Erich Woitke's II./JG 52 was left with six unserviceable Bf 109s. This unit became subject to the harsh makeshift methods that General Walter Model, the new commander of the Ninth Army, undertook in order to save the situation in the endangered Rzhev sector. What followed when the highly trained men of II./JG 52 were sent to the trenches – in minus – 45-degrees Celsius – is symptomatic of the demoralized state on the German side during these days. Oberleutnant Johannes Steinhoff, the Staffelkapitän of 4./JG 52, described the events on January 20: "At night, Woitik [sic] received a telephone call warning him of a Russian breakthrough and instructing him to man the defensive positions. But he was so drunk that he didn't pay any notice. The outcome of this was a disaster. The Russians killed several pilots and members of the ground crew during this ice-cold night. The injured adjutant [Oberleutnant Carl Willi Hartmann, an ace with eighteen victories to his credit] was abandoned during the retreat. Later we found him dead. Woitik was court-martialled. The verdict was demotion and conditional sentence."[17]

On January 21 General-Polkovnik Andrey Yeremenko's Fourth Assault Army of the Northwestern Front seized the large German supply depot at Toropets, seventy miles southwest of Ostashkov, and severed the rail line between Rzhev and the western interior. At this point, the gap between Army Group North and Army Group Center caused by the Northwestern Front's offensive had increased to eighty miles. There was no cohesive German front in this vast area. Although the German Ninth Army still held a salient at Rzhev, on the northern flank of Army Group Center, there was little hope that this army could do much to improve the situation. The Ninth Army was in fact threatened with being surrounded through a pincer movement by the Soviet Kalinin and Western fronts. The Thirty-ninth Army and 11th Cavalry Corps of the former front made deep penetrations toward Vyazma from the north, while Western Front's Thirty-third Army and 1st Guards Cavalry Corps advanced toward Vyazma from the southeast.

Only by pulling together his last reserves – arming support units and grounded Luftwaffe men (such as those of II./JG 52) – was the energetic new commander of the German Ninth Army, General Model, able to save the situation. On January 21 Model initiated a counterstroke at Sychyovka, south of Rzhev.

This proved to be the beginning of the end of the German disasters during the winter of 1941 – 42. The Luftwaffe was slowly starting to resurge. More and more "alert boxes" came into use, and various other improvised methods – such as lighting fires beneath the aircraft engines on the ground – helped to gradually defeat "General Winter." With this, and the method of continuously pulling out worn-down aviation units and replacing them with fully equipped units that had been rested in Germany, Fliegerkorps VIII managed to increase its presence in the air.

During the latter half of January, II./KG 54 and I./KG 77 arrived to replace the badly mauled III./KG 53 and 15.(Kroat)/KG 53. Together with the Stukas of Hauptmann Gustav Pressler's III./StG 2, the two new Kampfgruppen were immediately dispatched to save the Ninth Army from envelopment. The Soviet fighter pilots tried their utmost to interfere, and on January 21, Kapitans Ivan Meshcheryakov and Vasiliy Yefremov of the crack 5 GIAP each claimed one Ju 87 – whereas III./StG 2 registered one Ju 87 damaged due to fighter combat. Meanwhile, 180 IAP's Leytenant Sergey Dolgushin bagged a Bf 109 for his fifth victory – possibly the plane piloted by I./JG 52's Leutnant Ernst Gelich, who was killed in action in the Rzhev area. Next day, 5 GIAP claimed two Ju 87s while Sergey Dolgushin and Leytenant Sergey Makarov of 180 IAP each bagged a Ju 87 and a Bf 109 in the vicinity of Rzhev. III./StG 2 registered two Ju 87s lost with both crews perishing on January 22.[18] A few days later, both Dolgushin and Makarov were recommended to be appointed as Heroes of the Soviet Union – for seven individual plus four shared victories, and ten individual plus thirteen shared victories respectively.

Yet, by this time, the Luftwaffe exercised an increasing pressure all along the front line. On January 22 and January 23, the commanders of the Soviet Western Front complained about intense Luftwaffe bombing and strafing of their troops in the Medyn area, southeast of Vyazma. At Sukhinichi in the south, Zerstörer and bombers of Fliegerkorps VIII carried out "rolling attacks" in support of another German counterattack, which succeeded in establishing contact with the surrounded troops of the 216th Infantry Division on January 24.

But the VVS continued to pay back. During the air combats in this area on January 24, the commander of II./JG 51, Oberleutnant Hartmann Grasser, was shot down shortly after achieving his forty-fifth victory. Grasser force landed in enemy territory but was able to reach the German lines, notwithstanding an injured eye. Striking against the air transport fleet at Smolensk that flew in supplies to the Sukhinichi garrison on January 25, the DBA succeeded in destroying six Ju 52s on the ground, and a seventh was shot down.[19] Also on that day, 5 GIAP lost Batalyonnyy Komissar Anatoliy Sokolov, an ace with eight victories, during an intercept mission against German bombers.

On January 27, the Soviets renewed the airdrop operation at Vyazma. Thirty-nine PS-84s from MAGON GVF and twenty-five four-engine TB-3s were concentrated to fly General-Mayor Aleksey Levashov's 4th Airborne Corps behind the German lines. However, the operation, which commenced on January 27, was ill fated from the outset. The 648 paratroopers that were dropped on the first day landed more than ten miles from the intended drop zone and became scattered over a fifteen-mile-wide area. The same day, a Bf 110-reconnaissance plane discovered the departure airbase at Grabtsevo – and shot down a LaGG-3 over the airdrome before returning home with the valuable information. A few hours later, Major Wilhelm Spies's I./ZG 26 and Major Waldemar Krüger's II./KG 3 mounted all available aircraft against the airfield. Twelve TB-3s, one Pe-3, and the entire fuel store were destroyed, and the runway was severely damaged. The only German aircraft lost during this mission was the Bf 110 piloted by Major Spies. A veteran from the Spanish Civil War and credited with twenty aerial victories, Knight's Cross holder Spies was one of the top Zerstörer aces.

During the following days, the airborne troop landing continued in the face of repeated Luftwaffe attacks, while VVS-Western Front directed strong fighter forces to the area. These operations saw the loss of four German fighters on January 29.[20] A total of 2,497 Soviet paratroopers were dropped by February 2.

Without doubt, the VVS proved to be a most serious opponent to the Germans in the central combat zone during January 1942. During that month, the frontal aviation of VVS-Western Front carried out 4,175 combat sorties, while only 666 Luftwaffe sorties were registered in the same area. The frontal aviation of VVS-Western Front claimed twenty German aircraft shot down, and in raids against ground targets, 1,920 vehicles, 64 tanks, 117 railway wagons, and one railway engine were reported as destroyed.[21] In addition, the antiaircraft artillery of the Western Front was credited with shooting down thirty-four enemy aircraft.[22] For these successes, VVS-Western Front registered seventy-four aircraft lost on combat flights – including twenty-four fighters or fighter-bombers, thirteen medium bombers or dive-bombers, seven Il-2s, and thirty biplanes (U-2s, R-5s or R-Zs).[23]Meanwhile, the fighters and antiaircraft artillery of the Moscow PVO were credited with the shooting down of forty-three enemy aircraft.[24]

Largely due to the Moscow PVO, any deep intrusion by the Luftwaffe into the Moscow area was made increasingly hazardous. This particularly was the case with long-range reconnaissance missions, which usually were carried out singly. Two Fernaufklärungsstaffeln of Fliegerkorps VIII, 4.(F)/11 and 4.(F)/14, registered eleven Ju 88s missing in action during January 1942.[25]

By now, fatigue was spreading on both sides. On January 30, Unteroffizier Walter Tödt of I./JG 52 wrote in his diary: "The anniversary of the *Machtergreifung* [Hitler's seizure of power in 1933]. There are no patriotic feelings. What remains is only a stubborn will to do one's duty!" Having lost a total of nineteen Bf 109s and twelve pilots since mid-November 1941 – against seventy aerial victories – this Jagdgruppe was pulled out of first-line service and transferred to Germany ten days later.[26] In JG 51, it was felt that 7. Staffel was suffering from such low combat spirits that Oberstleutnant Friedrich Beckh, the Geschwaderkommodore, decided to have it disbanded. Its pilots were divided between 8. and 9. Staffeln.[27]

On the Soviet side, a report on the operations of VVS-Western Front in January 1942 noted: "Insufficient organization of the air defense of our troops and an incomplete use of available air defense means, together with the impossibility of the few fighters available of fulfilling all requests from the armies, resulted in significant losses to our troops."[28]

The rapid advance also had negative effects on the Red Army. Not only were supply lines strung out, but the VVS fighters and ground-attack planes were deprived of one of the initial Soviet advantages – well-equipped air bases. As the frontal aviation regiments were moved forward to airstrips deserted by the Luftwaffe, the Soviets encountered many of the problems that previously had beset only their counterpart.

A Bf 110 Zerstörer formation on patrol over the Eastern Front. The radio operator of a Bf 110 took this shot during a combat mission. The concentration of four 7.9mm MG 17 machine guns and two 20mm MG FF cannon, all fixed for fire forward from the nose of the Bf 110 turned the aircraft into a formidable weapon during strafing missions. (Photo: Roba/Mombeek.)

To the south of the Rollbahn, the Soviet advance had reached its peak when General-Mayor Belov's 1st Guards Cavalry Corps and the Thirty-third Army reached the suburbs of Vyazma in late January and early February. The cavalry force also managed to connect with the 8th Airborne Brigade of General-Mayor Levashov's 4th Airborne Corps in this area. A few days later, the support provided by the Luftwaffe played a significant role in the German counterattack that managed to surround Belov's cavalry troops and parts of the Thirty-third Army. This compelled the Stavka to discontinue its airborne troop landing in this sector.

With the immediate threat against the Rollbahn from the south thus removed, Fliegerkorps VIII could shift its focus to the Kalinin Front's broad advance to the south on the northern flank, and its aircraft fell upon large concentrations of Soviet soldiers on wide snow-covered fields that offered little protection against air attacks.

Gefreiter Siegfried Wittmer, radio operator in a Ju 88 of 6./KG 54, describes one of these missions on February 2:

Croatian Air Force personnel in front of a Do 17 Z of 15.(Kroat)/KG 53 in the winter of 1941-1942. Shortly after Ante Pavelic's Croatian Ustasha government was installed in April 1941, a Croatian air unit was formed to participate in Hitler's war against the Soviet Union. In late 1941, a Croatian Do 17-equipped unit arrived on the Eastern Front to form 15./KG 53. This staffel suffered heavy losses and was withdrawn from first-line service at the end of January 1942. It returned to the Eastern Front later that year, but in October 1942 it was finally shifted back to Croatia to help combat Marshall Tito's Communist partisans. The crest below the aircraft's cockpit is Ustasha's red and white insignia.

"We dropped our fragmentation bombs from low level. The Soviet soldiers lay flat on their backs and opened fire against us with rifles, submachine guns, and machine guns. Suddenly our left engine was on fire. [My pilot] Leutnant [Johannes] Griessler managed to pull up above a small forest. I jettisoned the canopy. We were down to only 120 feet. After another half mile we bellied in on the snow-covered ground. I destroyed the radio equipment. The aircraft burned up. Armed with a submachine gun we started to walk."[29] After four days of walking, the exhausted bomber crew managed to reach the German lines.

Heavily armed Bf 110s of the newborn Zerstörergeschwader dealt the Soviet ground troops particularly bloody losses. Oberleutnant Johannes Kiel of I./ZG 26 wrote: "There were Soviet troops on all roads, and they were unable to take cover, because these roads were nothing but narrow tracks that had been created by snowplows, huge mountain walls of snow rose on both sides of them. Congested like sheep herds, tightly squeezed between vehicles and other equipment, entire battalions often were caught without any chance of survival from our air attacks. There was no escape from these ravines of death; flying at low level, we mowed them down on road after road, and saw the snow becoming stained red by all the blood."

The declining number of Soviet fighters available at the front did their utmost to defend their first-line troops, and the strafing Bf 110 Zerstörer earned a particular hatred among the Soviet fighter pilots. On February 3, Bf 110s of II./ZG 1 were spreading terror among a Kalinin Front supply column at Toropets when five MiG-3s bounced them. Two Bf 110s were lost. The Gruppenkommandeur, Hauptmann Rolf Kaldrack, was killed in a taran. With this, the Zerstörer arm had lost two of its most outstanding pilots in a week's time. "Schlitzohr" Kaldrack had been awarded the Knight's Cross for eleven victories after the Battle of Britain. He had headed II./SKG 210 with great success during Operation Barbarossa and at the time of his death was credited with twenty-one aerial victories. Six days later, Kaldrack was posthumously awarded the Oak Leaves, the first Zerstörer pilot so honored.

Two years of Blitzkrieg had made the German soldiers dependent on air support. Deprived of this weapon during the extreme cold spell in early January, they lost their foothold. Now that the Luftwaffe appeared above their heads once more, dealing increasingly severe blows against the Soviets, the troops of the German Ninth Army turned to counterattack again. On February 5 they managed to isolate the Kalinin Front's Twenty-ninth Army, which had driven a deep southern-pointed wedge southwest of Rzhev. Farther to the west, German troop reinforcements brought in from France forced the Soviet Third and Fourth Assault armies to discontinue their advance.

The Rzhev area, where the German Ninth Army held a deep salient from the south to the north – with strong Soviet forces on both sides – developed into the principal point of both sides' efforts. Oberstleutnant Friedrich Beckh, the commander of JG 51, concentrated two of his Jagdgruppen in this sector, and following a series of fierce

A VVS-Kalinin Front Pe-2 – apparently from Kapitan Nikolay Laukhin's 128 BBAP – warms up its engines at a forward airstrip before another mission in the Rzhev area. One of the most successful pilots of this regiment was Leytenant Nikolay Musinskiy, who by April 1942 had carried out 103 combat sorties and claimed two enemy aircraft in aerial combats.The modern Pe-2 bomber proved to be one of the German fighter pilots' deadliest adversaries in the air over the Eastern Front. On February 10, 1942, 7./JG 51's Staffelkapitän, Oberleutnant Helmut Lohoff, intercepted a VVS-Kalinin Front Pe-2 in the Rzhev sector. Lohoff made a stern attack against a Pe-2, which dived to the deck. Lohoff was able to down the Pe-2 – filed as his seventeenth victory – but the Soviet pilot had forced him to reduce too much speed. Thus Lohoff's Bf 109 stalled and belly-landed in the deep snow close to a Soviet advance road where Oberleutnant Lohoff was immediately captured. (Photo: Red Army Museum, Moscow.)

air combats, local German air superiority was secured. On February 8, 5 GIAP's Kapitan Ivan Meshcheryakov, credited with seven aerial victories, failed to return from a combat mission in the Rzhev area.[30] Two days later, 180 IAP's Leytenant Sergey Makarov was shot down when he and his wingman were bounced by Bf 109s. He was appointed Hero of the Soviet Union posthumously on May 5, 1942.

But even if the Luftwaffe was regaining its strength in the central combat zone, its air operations still were faced with determined opposition. On February 10 Fliegerkorps VIII registered five bombers and four Bf 109s lost to hostile activity, while the Soviets filed only eight of their own aircraft lost on the entire Eastern Front. Counted among the Luftwaffe casualties that day was Feldwebel Gerhard Wille, a thirteen-victory ace in 8./JG 51. Twenty-one-year-old Wille was last seen entering combat with three Il-2s and a DB-3 over the Rzhev sector.

The relentless low-level missions against Soviet troops resulted in significant losses to both sides. On February 11 seven more planes from Fliegerkorps VIII were shot down. On February 13 Ju 88s from II./KG 54 annihilated an entire ski column, knocked out one tank, and set three trucks on fire during a single mission. Next day, two crews of the same Gruppe – including the Gruppenkommandeur, Hauptmann Heinz Gehrke – were lost to ground fire during a mission against troops intended to relieve the surrounded Soviets southwest of Rzhev.

From mid-February, the role played by the air forces on both sides increased dramatically. The Soviet commanders once again turned to their airborne troops. They went in for severing the Warsaw – Moscow highway – which runs parallell to and south of the Rollbahn – and joining forces with the Soviet Fiftieth Army, which operated in the area south and southwest of Yukhnov. The intention was to encircle and annihilate the German troops in the Yukhnov area, and to break the German defense positions to the south of Vyazma. This in turn could have created favorable conditions for encircling the entire German Ninth Army. For this purpose, General-Mayor Levashov's 4th Airborne Corps staged the third large-scale airborne operation behind the German lines at Vyazma on February 17.

The bombers of 1 DBAD, 2 DBAD, 26 DBAD, 42 DBAD, and 133 DBAD were concentrated for the task of isolating the German battlefield by staging intense raids against lines of communications in the area. Other aviation units targeted the Luftwaffe on the ground. VVS-Kalinin Front carried out large-scale attacks against Dugino Airdrome, twenty miles north of Vyazma, on February 18 and February 20.[31] But the increasing presence of German fighters forced the Soviets to launch most of their bombing operations in the hours of darkness, and these missions were characterized by poor organization and a lack of coordination between the DBA and the front and army aviation units. This, in combination with inadequate equipment for night bombing and intense German antiaircraft fire, rendered most bombing missions ineffective. The repeated Soviet air raids against the Orsha Airdrome on February 21 and February 22 only succeeded in putting three Ju 88s of KG 3 and KG 77 out of commission. Nevertheless, the participating aircrews filed hollow unsubtantiated success reports – Polkovnik Yevgeniy Loginov's 1 DBAD alone claimed to have destroyed forty-two German aircraft on the ground at Orsha, Smolensk, and Vitebsk between January 23 and February 22.[32]

Meanwhile, Fliegerkorps VIII was successfully brought into action against the Soviet attack forces on the ground. Soviet fighters did what they could in this situation – and scored their largest successes against the Bf 110 Zerstörer. Oberleutnant Johannes Kiel of I./ZG 26 recalls a sortie during one of these days: "The Bolsheviks had no idea from where death appeared. As though struck by lightning, an entire company lay flat in the snow; none of these soldiers would ever rise again. We continued our deadly flight. Two horse columns became our next targets, and we tore the horse bodies apart with machine-gun fire. Suddenly there was a cry in the R/T: 'Enemy fighters to the right!' There were only two planes, but they attacked us from above. Before we were able to turn around, they had positioned themselves on the tail of our rear aircraft. In the next moment we could see how it started emitting smoke. By that time, I had pulled myself together and was able to evade the second fighter attack. As the two birds of prey attempted to disengage, I took a short cut and overtook one of them. I got the climbing fighter right in front of my nose guns, and my bullets ripped large parts away from its fuselage and wings. Gone and out! Instead of pursuing the other fighter, I decided to see what had happened to my comrades that had been hit. I saw their aircraft just as it belly-landed in a cloud of spraying snow."

During this period 4./ZG 26 took a heavy beating. On February 18 the Staffelkapitän, Oberleutnant Eduard Tratt, was injured by ground fire, and over the following days three of the Staffel's crews were lost in action. The Zerstörer nevertheless dealt crippling losses to the 4th Airborne Corps on the ground and in the air.

On one of the last transport flights to the Vyazma area, on February 23, a TB-3 of 3 TBAP that was carrying General-Mayor Aleksey Levashov and the entire staff of

Pe-2, VVS-Kalinin Front (probably 128 BBAP), Soviet Union, Winter-Spring 1942

the 4th Airborne Corps to the landing area came under attack by a Bf 110. A 20mm round hit Levashov. The pilot of the transport plane, Mayor Aleksandr Mosolov, made a rapid forced landing, but Levashov's life could not be saved. Next day, the airborne assault ended. By then, 7,373 soldiers had been flown into the landing area in 612 aircraft sorties, 443 of which completed the mission successfully.

Five of II./ZG 1's Bf 110s were shot down during the last five days of February. It seems as though 120 IAP was responsible for quite a large part of the losses suffered by this Zerstörergruppe. On February 28 an Eskadrilya of 120 IAP led by Kapitan Viktor Tomilin intercepted three Bf 110s of II./ZG 1 over the battlefield between Medyn and Vyazma. Tomilin managed to shoot down the leading aircraft while the other two escaped. Later that day another flight of 120 IAP MiG-3s led by Leytenant Sergey Rubtsov attacked a formation of German bombers, possibly He 111s of II./KG 53, escorted by the same Zerstörergruppe. The Soviet fighters attacked head-on and claimed two bombers and a Bf 110 shot down without loss. II./KG 53 filed one He 111 shot down, while both Zerstörer claimed by 120 IAP on this day can be verified with German loss files. On March 1 Leytenant Rubtsov and another pilot of 120 IAP claimed two more II./ZG 1 Bf 110s, both of which can be verified in German loss lists. One week later 120 IAP was established as the twelfth VVS Guards aviation regiment.

Overcoming fierce resistance, the Soviet 4th Airborne Corps managed to accomplish its task. By February 28, its soldiers had advanced thirteen miles to the south and southeast and reached the line on which they intended to join forces with the Soviet Fiftieth Army. But under the pressure of incessant Luftwaffe attacks, the Fiftieth Army failed to penetrate the German defenses and thereby establish direct contact with the airborne corps. The 4th Airborne Corps had to switch to the defense, but it continue to fight in the German rear area for a prolonged period. The German situation in this sector was saved in large part by efforts of the Luftwaffe.

By the end of February, the Soviet winter offensive had been strategically halted all across its lines of advance. The significance of the Soviet victory at the gates of Moscow should not be underestimated. Indeed, the German Army had been dealt its first large defeat in World War II. The entire Army Group Center had been thrown to the brink of collapse just after victory had seemed to be within its reach, and it was pushed back between forty and two hundred miles. The Wehrmacht had sustained 175,000 casualties during the first two months of 1942 – most of them in Army Group Center – and only barely managed to save the situation – at the cost of immense suffering. On the other hand, the Soviets failed to achieve any major strategic goal, apart from saving Moscow. Their aim of surrounding and annihilating Army Group Center had not been accomplished.

As one of the most successful MiG-3 regiments during the battle for Moscow 120 IAP was adopted as the 12 GIAP on March 7, 1942. This photo was probably taken on March 8, 1942, when 12 GIAP's fighters were lined up for a visit by the commander of VVS Moscow Military District, General-Mayor Nikolay Sbytov, who congratulated the regiment for its ascension to Guards status. On March 10, 1942, Leytenant Sergey Rubtsov – an ace with eight individual and shared victories – was quoted in *Pravda:* "We vow to live up to the honorable rank of Guardsmen. We assure our government and the leader of the Red Army, Comrade Stalin, that we will multiply our energy to annihilate the enemy." On March 27, 1942, the Guards banner was officially handed over to 12 GIAP. Next day, Starshiy Leytenants Rubtsov and Churmantayev claimed two German bombers shot down in the Mozhaysk area. (Photo: RART.)

Some statistics for February 1942 are quite indicative of the increased Luftwaffe activity that played a major role in the overall situation. In the sector of the Soviet Kalinin Front alone during February 1942, according to VVS documents, the Luftwaffe carried out 2,866 combat sorties (2,781 in daytime) and VVS-Kalinin Front carried out 6,667 combat sorties (3,939 in daytime) – resulting in 67 air combats involving 344 aircraft from both sides.[33] Eighty-two German aircraft were claimed shot down by VVS-Kalinin Front.

It was also clear that Fliegerkorps VIII, once it had overcome the difficulties deriving from the cold spell in early January, was regaining the German initiative in the air. This was above all due to the fighters of JG 51 – in particular II. and IV. Gruppen, which abandoned its fighter-bomber

MiG-3, 12 GIAP/6 IAK/Moscow Corps District of the PVO, Soviet Union, March 1942

Note that the original outer wing panels have been exchanged for outer wing panels without slots from an earlier MiG-3 variant. These outer wing panels are still in their original green camouflage. It is apparent that an engine exchange has recently taken place. Note also that the propeller blades are partly red.

missions and started challenging the VVS formations in air combat again in February. Claiming ninety victories against only four Bf 109s shot down, II./JG 51 was the most successful Jagdgruppe of Fliegerkorps VIII during the defensive battle of January and February 1942. At the end of February 1942, three pilots of II./JG 51 had acheived scores of forty victories apiece – Leutnant Hans Strelow, Oberfeldwebel Wilhelm Mink, and Oberfeldwebel Otto Tange. In IV./JG 51, Leutnant Bernd Gallowitsch and Feldwebel Franz-Josef Beerenbrock were top-scorers of the period.

Serzhant Olzan Tapkhanayev, gunner in a 128 BBAP Pe-2 on the Kalinin Front in early 1942. The new twin-engine Soviet Pe-2 bomber, which appeared in relatively large numbers for the first time during the Soviet offensive in the winter of 1941-1942, was a most unpleasant surprise to German fighter pilots. Fast, able to withstand relatively heavy punishment, and armed with two 12.7mm UB and three 7.62mm ShKAS machine guns, it was by far the best Soviet bomber in 1942 against fighter interception. But the designer of this formidable aircraft, Vladimir Petlaykov, would not live to see the peak of its success; he was killed in a flight accident with a Pe-2 on January 12, 1942. (Photo: Viktor Kulikov collection.)

In review, the Red Army's ability to turn the tide at the gates of Moscow in the winter of 1941 – 42 was an extraordinary achievement. The main reasons given in most accounts are the unusually low temperatures – for which the Wehrmacht was not prepared – combined with over-extended German supply lines and, not least, the Soviet determination to fight back. A further key factor to the German setback was the lack of support from the Luftwaffe in January 1942, another effect of the extreme cold. During the Blitzkrieg in the early years of the war, the German ground troops grew increasingly spoiled by continuous air support. By the summer of 1941 the Germans on several occasions had shown a tendency to keep their heads down as soon as there was no air support immediately available. Without a doubt, the weak opposition from the air was an important factor to the Soviet successes on the central combat zone in January 1942. This further underlines the role played by the Luftwaffe in the entire German concept of warfare.

In February 1942 the radically increased presence of the Luftwaffe above the Soviet lines and rear areas was a factor of equal importance with the over-extended Soviet supply lines and German reinforcements in halting the Soviet offensive efforts. Fliegerkorps VIII in fact increased its air activity in February by more than seven times compared to the previous month. The growing emphasis Soviet air commanders placed on air-base raids from mid-February onward serves as a confirmation of the deadly threat from the air against the Red Army. Nevertheless, the campaign against the Soviet winter offensive undoubtedly was one of the most difficult battles fought so far by the Luftwaffe. Of this, a member of the ground crew of II./JG 52 wrote: "Toward the end of February we were withdrawn from the front and relocated to Königsberg, where we received new equipment. We had entered combat with 142 men, and now we returned with only 37 remaining! The rest were all dead, injured, or in the hospital with frostbite!"[34]

As was the case with the Soviet ground troops, the combat spirit among the airmen of the VVS soared in the winter of 1941 – 42. It was only due to inadequate training of a large part of its airmen that the VVS failed to play the same decisive role as the Luftwaffe. Still, the Soviet Air Force was able to deal repeated – and in several cases, rather heavy – losses to the retreating German troops and their supply lines during the winter offensive. In launching several large airborne operations behind the German lines, the Soviet fliers surpassed anything the Luftwaffe was able to attain in this field.

 Chapter 6 

Fire Brigade in the Northern Sector

In the northern combat zone, between Lake Ladoga and the area around Lake Ilmen, the Red Army mainly focused on raising the German blockade of Leningrad, which had been going on since September 1941. The Soviet offensive immediately to the south of Lake Ladoga in early December 1941 had pushed the Germans out of the advanced position at Tikhvin, thus relieving Leningrad of its most acute supply difficulties. Although the means available to the Soviets were too limited to permit any major breakthrough, this outcome also thwarted the hopes of Germany's Finnish ally for a united German-Finnish military operation along the eastern shores of Lake Ladoga. Moreover, the Soviet Seventh Independent Army had halted the Finnish Army along the Svir River, which connects Lake Ladoga and Lake Onega, between 50 and 150 miles inside Soviet territory from the 1939 border.

For all that, the Soviet offensive could not prevent the besieged Leningrad from becoming the scene of a terrible famine. Nevertheless, a combination of scarce Luftwaffe resources and the powerful air defense of Leningrad – above all the antiaircraft artillery – saved the city from air raids during the first three months of 1942. But apart from this, the Soviet air forces in the northern combat zone were not able to achieve many successes in early 1942.

Since the cream of VVS had been concentrated in the Moscow battle zone, only weak and crippled Soviet air forces remained in the northern combat zone following the costly air battles in 1941. On January 12, 1942, VVS-Leningrad Front reported the strength of 139 serviceable aircraft, and the air force of the new Volkhov Front had 211 serviceable aircraft. More than half of the latter were obsolete biplane night bombers – U-2s, R-5s, and R-Zs. The Air Force of the Red Banner Baltic Fleet, VVS-KBF, which operated over the Gulf of Finland and Lake Ladoga, could only muster ninety-one serviceable airplanes. In the area immediately to the south of Lake Ilmen, the situation was even worse – seventy-nine aircraft were all that remained of VVS-Northwestern Front on December 22, 1941.[35] By that time, VVS-

An R-Z crew studies a map prior to a nocturnal mission over the German rear area during the winter of 1941-1942. The old single-engine R-5 and R-Z reconnaissance biplanes and the U-2 biplane trainers that were converted to the night-bomber role played an important part in VVS operations in the northern combat zone throughout the first half of 1942.

On December 17, 1941, when the Volkhov Front was created, VVS-Volkhov Front could muster only 118 combat aircraft. During the following months, the reinforcements allocated to this air force were mainly the single-engine biplane night bombers. In early January 1942, six new LBAPs outfitted with these biplanes were assigned to VVS-Volkhov Front, and four more LBAPs arrived before the end of the month. This is a striking illustration of the weakened state of the Soviet Air Forces following the disastrous losses in 1941.

The R-Z was the last serial-produced Soviet reconnaissance biplane and successor to the R-5. Developed in 1935, the R-Z was equipped with an M-34 engine (840-horsepower at sea level, 750-horsepower at 10,000 feet), which provided a maximum speed of nearly 200 miles per hour at 11,700 feet—compared to the R-5's 140 miles per hour speed at that altitude. The R-Z was armed with a fixed 7.62mm PV-1 machine gun in the nose and a turreted rear-firing 7.62mm ShKAS. It could carry a bombload of 880 pounds. (Photo: Grubich.)

In late 1941, Major Hannes Trautloft, the Geschwaderkommodore of JG 54 Grünherz, arranged for his unit to be billeted in the old Czar palace at Krasnogvardeysk. Erected in 1766, the palace was turned into a museum following the October Revolution. The palace garden, with its artistic pavilions, statues, and monuments served as an exemplary recreation facility for the Grünherz fighter pilots between combat missions. The small town south of Leningrad named Krasnogvardeysk—originally named Gatchina, and in 1923//-1929 called Trotsk after Leon Trotsky—occupied a central role in the annals of JG 54. The surviving veterans of this Jagdgeschwader still recall the days when they were billeted in the last Czar's luxury rooms. Shortly after its liberation in January 1944, the town regained its original name. Today the central archive of VMF is housed in Gatchina. (Photo: Trautloft.)

Northwestern Front had not received a single airplane replacement for more than two months! Thus, Soviet aviation was incomparably weaker in this sector than in the central combat zone. Furthermore, the VVS forces that were based in the Leningrad – Lake Ladoga area had to fight both the Luftwaffe and portions of the Finnish Air Force. One advantage on the Soviet side, however, was that Leningrad PVO was provided with a chain of ten RUS-2 early warning radar stations, with a range of between sixty and ninety miles.

As the Soviet offensive from Tikhvin was halted at the Volkhov River, connecting Lakes Ladoga and Ilmen, Generaloberst Alfred Keller instructed his Luftflotte 1 to intensify armed reconnaissance over the so-called "Ice Road," the supply "life line" across the frozen surface of Lake Ladoga to Leningrad. Luftflotte 1 had been responsible for air cover for Army Group North since the opening of the invasion of the USSR. This air fleet was composed of only a single air corps, Fliegerkorps I, which mustered 115 aircraft on January 15, 1942 – 44 Bf 109 fighters, 32 Ju 88 and He 111 bombers, 26 transport and liaison aircraft, 8 Ju 87 dive-bombers, and 5 Ju 88 reconnaissance planes. On the credit side, the units of Luftflotte 1 operated from well-equipped airdromes in or close to the former Baltic countries, which were in turn tied directly to the Luftwaffe's infrastructure in Germany. Thus, Fliegerkorps I was not hampered by the cold as was Fliegerkorps VIII farther to the south. In combination with a comparatively lower qualitative standard of the Soviet aviation units in this sector, this gave the air war in the northern combat zone in the winter of 1941 – 42 a completely different character than that in the central combat zone.

The primary responsibilities of Soviet aviation in the northern combat zone were divided between air defense of Leningrad, air cover for the transport route to Leningrad across Lake Ladoga, and close support for the front troops. In late 1941, 123 IAP of 7 IAK/PVO, along with the Red Banner Baltic Fleet's 11 IAP, 13 IAP, and 12 OIAE had been allocated to the defense of the Ice Road. These forces were reinforced by VVS-Leningrad Front's 39 IAD and 7 IAK/PVO's 158 IAP on New Year's Day. On January 2, VVS-KBF formed a special aviation task force for operations in the southern Ladoga region; it consisted of sixty-four aircraft of the naval 5 IAP, 13 IAP, 57 ShAP, 71 IAP, 42 ORAE, and 13 OIAE.

Since the new year opened with clear skies (and minus – 25-degree-Celsius weather), intense air battles evolved over Lake Ladoga evolved during the first days in January – in which the Bf 109s of JG 54 Grünherz would prove their vast superiority. JG 54, the only Jagdgeschwader in the Leningrad area, had some of the most highly motivated German airmen on the Eastern Front during that difficult winter of 1941 – 42. Credit for JG 54's morale must be given to the Geschwader-kommodore, Major Hannes Trautloft, who took great personal care of his men. The large and well-equipped bases at Siverskaya and Krasnogvardeysk also contributed to keeping spirits high among the Grünherz men. At the latter base, the men were billeted in the Czar's former residence.

The atmosphere among these highly trained German fighter pilots form a sharp contrast to what the Soviet defector Starshiy Leytenant Petr Kulakov of 13 IAP/VVS-KBF said about the Soviet airmen in the same area during his interrogation: "The mood among the old fliers is very negative. In any case, there are very few old pilots remaining. Most pilots are very young novices who have arrived at the front directly from the schools. Some of them flew their first sorties only in 1941. The attitude among the younger pilots is quite different. They are fanatical and naïve, very narrow, and incapable of realizing the seriousness of the situation. The pilots evade combat with the Messerschmitts. The word 'Messerschmitt' is even prohibited among us."[36]

Winter-camouflaged Curtiss P-40 Tomahawks warming their engines. The American-designed Tomahawk disappointed the Soviet pilots who received it. "I had expected more from the American planes, but our Yak-1s proved to be considerably better," wrote one of the pilots in 158 IAP, Leytenant Mikhail Satalkin, in his diary. The main advantage of the P-40 was its reliable R/T equipment, a device that most Soviet fighter planes still lacked in 1942. As had been noted by the British in North Africa during the previous year, the Tomahawk was hopelessly inferior to the Bf 109 F. Nevertheless, a skilled pilot could overcome its inferior speed and climbing performance by utilizing its excellent maneuverability. Kapitan Petr Pilyutov, a 154 IAP ace, stated that the Tomahawk "is able to twist around its own tail. With this plane one can turn in on any Messerschmitt." A German fighter ace once described a turning combat with P-40s as "tantamount to suicide." (Photo: Viktor Kulikov photo collection.)

Throughout January 1, the Bf 109s of JG 54 conducted constant strafing missions and fighter sweeps over the Ice Road, claiming six railway engines and fourteen motor trucks destroyed. During a mission by four Bf 109s of 7./JG 54 in this area, Unteroffizier Gerhard Raimann suddenly caught sight of a lone four-engine TB-3, painted all over in black, that came lumbering in above the frozen surface of Lake Ladoga at low altitude. "Four-engine transport plane below! I attack!" Raimann excitedly cried in the R/T.[37] The huge TB-3 attempted to make it across the lake with twenty passengers, but it didn't stand a chance without a fighter escort. "A few seconds later I could see the four-engine transport plane fall in flames and crash onto the ice on Lake Ladoga," Major Trautloft later wrote in his diary. "The word *Abschuss* crackles in my headphones, and that was the end of the game."[38] Sixteen of the passengers were killed and the other four were rescued with severe injuries.[39] In addition, the chief of staff of VVS-KBF, Polkovnik D. I. Surkov, was killed when a Grünherz pilot shot down the UTI-4 in in which he was traveling over Lake Ladoga. And that was not the only serious loss the Soviet air forces sustained in this area on New Year's Day.

Mayor Vladimir Matveyev, the commander of 158 IAP, was something of the equivalent on the Soviet side in this region to Major Hannes Trautloft: one of the most popular and respected VVS unit commanders at that time. Early on January 1, 1942, he took off at the head of four Tomahawk fighters to patrol above the Ice Road. In the vicinity of Zelenets Island, Matveyev spotted two Bf 109s that were strafing a truck convoy on the ice. He pressed the transmit button of his R/T and called out: "Enemy ahead. Attack!"

A pilot of Oberleutnant Hans-Ekkehard Bob's 9./JG 54 calmly climbs out of the cockpit of his Bf 109 F after a successful combat sortie. The veterans of this Staffel had every reason to remain tranquil, considering the weak opposition they encountered in the air during this period. They opened the new year by claiming four victories – two by Unteroffizier Rudolf Damoser, and one each by Oberfeldwebel Friedrich Rupp and Feldwebel Alfred Kromer. But the 9./JG 54 log has the following entry for January 1, 1942: "Our novice pilots give us less pleasure. Unteroffizier Höger crashed his aircraft during landing, and it is a miracle that he managed to survive." Novice pilots were a constant source of headaches for the veterans even though they stood a far better chance of surviving than VVS novices. (Photo: Trautloft.)

Leytenant Gennadiy Tsokolayev in the cockpit of his I-16 Mark 24 in early 1942. His aircraft displays the Guards emblem; 13 IAP/VVS-KBF, with which Tsokolayev served, was adopted as 4 GIAP/VVS-KBF on January 18, 1942. Tsokolayev, who was among the most experienced pilots in that unit, completed his pilot training in 1938 and saw action against Finland during the Winter War in 1939//-1940. Through April 1942, Tsokolayev amassed a total of six individual and eleven shared victories, and on June 14, 1942, he was appointed Hero of the Soviet Union. Gennadiy Tskoloayev survived the war but was killed in a traffic accident on July 13, 1976. (Photo: Petrov.)

Just as the four P-40 Tomahawks put their noses down, a second Rotte of Bf 109s bounced them from the rear and above, headed for the lead Soviet fighter. Leytenant Vasiliy Kharitonov got on the tail of these two Bf 109s and reportedly shot one of them down. As he turned to attack the next enemy fighter, Kharitonov found even more Bf 109s appearing on the scene. He also saw his commander pursue a Bf 109 while a second enemy fighter approached Matveyev's Tomahawk from below. Tracer bullets hit the Tomahawk right in the belly. The fighter fell into a spin and sent Mayor Matveyev plunging to his death. Oberleutnant Hans-Ekkehard Bob's 9./JG 54 returned from the first mission carried out that morning with four victory claims,[40] possibly including Matveyev.

13 IAP/VVS-KBF also took a heavy beating by JG 54 over Lake Ladoga that day. (The date is somewhat unclear; an official Soviet source places the date at January 4;[41] but for various reasons the actual date seems to be January 1.) Five I-16s from 13 IAP/VVS-KBF, divided into two groups, were on patrol over the western part of Lake Ladoga when the commissar of 1 AE, Starshiy Politruk Seven Dmitriyevskiy, spotted a formation of German bombers. Dmitriyevskiy, leading two other I-16s, had just turned in against the bombers when six Bf 109s appeared on the scene. After a stiff turning combat, Serzhant Dmitriyev's Ishak was set burning and the pilot bailed out. Next, a Bf 109 got on Dmitriyevskiy's tail while he was still pursuing the bombers. One or two 15mm shells exploded in the engine of his I-16, which immediately burst into flames. The small Ishak turned over, went into a steep dive, and crashed into the ice close to the coast, killing Starshiy Politruk Dmitriyevskiy. Shortly afterward, Serzhant Aleksandr Baydrakov's I-16 was badly hit and this pilot had to disengage.

Then the three-plane Zveniya led by Leytenant Gennadiy Tsokolayev, of 13 IAP/VVS-KBF's 2 AE, and Kapitan Aleksandr Agureyev, deputy commander of the

Polikarpov I-16 Mark 24, Starshiy Leytenant Gennadiy Tsokolayev, 4 GIAP/VVS-KBF, Leningrad, Soviet Union, early 1942
Tsokolayev was accredited with 20 aerial victories. Note the freshly painted Guards emblem beneath the windscreen. 13 IAP/VVS-KBF was redesignated 4 GIAP/VVS-KBF on January 18, 1942.

same regiment's 3d Eskadrilya, were scrambled. Shortly after takeoff, as they had reached 6,000 feet and still were climbing, a Bf 109 Staffel bounced them. The three I-16s led by Kapitan Agureyev, flying top cover, received the brunt of the attack. Both Serzhant Zaboykin's and Agureyev's I-16s were severely damaged and disengaged, with the latter limping back toward the base escorted by the third fighter of the Zveno. Having thus neutralized the Soviet top cover, the Bf 109s went straight after Gennadiy Tsokolayev's flight. These three Soviets soon found themselves involved in a desperate struggle for survival. While Leytenant Tsokolayev, one of the most skillful fighter pilots in VVS-KBF, managed to evade all attacks by using everything his aircraft had to give, Serzhant Nikolay Shchegolyov was wounded.

Only when the other 13 IAP/VVS-KBF I-16s that remained airborne intervened did the German fighter pilots disengage. But Kapitan Agureyev's crippled I-16 couldn't be saved. Unable to complete the landing approach, the aircraft clipped the top of a tree, was thrown into a dense fir grove, and caught fire. Agureyev managed to get out of the aircraft only seconds before the fuel tanks blew up.

By that time, three more formations, each comprised of nine Ju 88s escorted by Bf 109s, appeared on a heading toward the Kobona area and the Ice Road. The 13 IAP/VVS-KBF pilots went after them, and in the ensuing clash another two I-16s were damaged. In total, the combat this day cost 13 IAP/VVS-KBF one pilot killed and five wounded, with three aircraft destroyed and seven damaged.

With 13 IAP/VVS-KBF more or less neutralized, Yak-1s, LaGG-3s, and P-40 Tomahawks from 5 IAP/VVS-KBF and 39 IAD were sent into the air as further reinforcements. During a twenty-five-minute dogfight, three of these fighters were shot down.

In total, JG 54 reported thirteen Soviet aircraft shot down on the first day of 1942. Its own losses are uncertain. In his diary, Major Trautloft reported that there had been no losses, but the Luftwaffe's files indicate that JG 54 lost two Bf 109s this day, one shot down above Lake Ladoga and one in a take-off accident.

The Soviet airmen fared no better on January 2. The debacle started in the morning, when KG 1 and KG 4 mounted concentrated raids against the western stretch of the Ice Road and the loading port of Osinovets. Meanwhile, six Bf 109s from 7./JG 54 spotted a group of VVS-KBF "I-18s" above Novaya Ladoga Airdrome – probably LaGG-3s of 5 IAP/VVS-KBF. Oberfeldwebel Karl-Heinz Kempf made a high-side attack and claimed two of the Soviet fighters shot down. Later, during the same mission, the German formation became entangled with I-16s (apparently from VVS-Volkhov Front), resulting in Oberfeldwebel Kempf's claim for two, and his wingman, Unteroffizier Hans Halfmann, claimed one.

At the same time, the Soviets sent five Pe-2s, escorted by eight I-16s, against the airfield at Siverskaya. There they succeeded in taking out six Bf 109s, four Ju 88s, and twenty trucks. One soldier was killed and ten were injured. Oberfeldwebel Kempf and the other pilots of 7./JG 54 arrived over the airfield just after the Soviets had unloaded their bombs. Kempf blew one of the Pe-2s out of the sky with his last rounds of ammunition. Thus, he had achieved at least five kills in a single sortie,[42] bringing his total victory score to forty-one. Two days later, Kempf was awarded with the Knight's Cross.

In early 1942 the Wehrmacht had suffered its worst defeat since the outbreak of the war, but it was still able to mount an imposing striking force. In this situation, Josef Stalin intervened in a fateful manner. Soviet General Armii Georgiy Zhukov, Moscow's savior, proposed concentrating the Red Army's offensive on the central zone. Here, the ratio of forces was most favorable to the Soviets. But Stalin, the dictator who had panicked six months earlier, now was absolutely euphoric. He rejoiced at stopping the Wehrmacht at the gates of Moscow and openly spoke of "victory in 1942." On January 5, 1942, Stalin declared his position to the Stavka VGK: "Now the moment has come to launch a general offensive along the entire front!"

Zhukov protested, arguing that the Red Army was still too weak to undertake such a large-scale operation against a determined enemy. Nikolay Voznesenskiy, the head of Gosplan SSSR, the State Planing Committee, supported Zhukov's view. Voznesenskiy explained that it was impossible to deliver the material to support a general offensive along the entire front line from the Black Sea to Leningrad. But it was Stalin's view that counted – and only his. Within the general climate of fear that permeated all echelons of Soviet society, there was little place for criticism. Stalin's obedient sycophants rushed to the dictator's support and characteristically lashed out against the critics. Georgiy Malenkov, the secretary of the Communist Party Central Committee, and Lavrentiy Beriya, the Peoples Commissar of Internal Affairs, dismissed Voznesensky scornfully and accused him of "being unable to see anything but obstacles."

Stalin referred to a discussion that he had had with Marshal Sovetskogo Soyuza Semyon Timoshenko, the commander of the Southwestern Front. "I have spoken to Timoshenko," Stalin said in his normal calm manner, "and he is for active operations in the southwestern direction as well." Timoshenko had asserted that the time had come to "make mincemeat of the Germans."

"Anyone else who wants to speak on this matter?" Stalin asked, and, as no one raised his voice, he concluded: "With this, I regard the matter as settled."

Two days later, all Front commanders had already received instructions to launch a general offensive. Thus was the Soviet winter offensive doomed. After the meeting, the Chief of the General Staff, Marshal Sovetskogo Soyuza Boris Shaposhnikov, told Zhukov that Stalin had made up his mind beforehand. It should be underlined that the vastly exaggerated Soviet appraisals of the Wehrmacht's losses apparently played a sinister role in Stalin's fateful decision.

A 1 GMTAP/VVS-KBF DB-3F prepares to take off. 1 GMTAP was one of the most famous and highly decorated regiments of the Soviet military aviation. Thirty-three of its aviators became Heroes of the Soviet Union – the highest total for any aviation regiment – and ten other 1 GMTAP aviators became Heroes of the Soviet Union after being transferred to other units. But the price for these successes was high. On the eve of the war, 1 MTAP was completely outfitted with DB-3T torpedo bombers. Until the end of 1941 the regiment flew 1,520 combat sorties and lost 77 aircraft. As a result, the number of DB-3Ts on hand dropped dramatically, and 1 MTAP's principal aircraft became the DB-3F, as shown on this photo. On January 18, 1942, the unit was adopted as a Guards unit, becoming 1 GMTAP.

Another record that was established by 1 GMTAP is that two of its war-time pilots became two of the most longest serving C-in-Cs of VVS-VMF (from 1955 AVMF – the Aviation of the VMF – Yevgeniy Preobrazhenskiy, who served from February 1950 to May 1962, and Ivan Borzov, who succeeded him and remained at this post until July 1974). (Photo: Viktor Kulikov collection.)

On January 7 the Soviets opened their major offensive in the northern combat zone with simultaneous attacks by the Volkhov Front against the German lines at the Volkhov River and by the Northwestern Front to the south of Lake Ilmen. The air forces of the Leningrad and Volkhov fronts were tasked to interdict the German supply route along the Volkhov River, and to delay and destroy German troop columns. With mainly single-engine trainers converted to the role of night bombers available, this task was impossible to accomplish. Equipped with bombsights of World War I standards, the U-2, R-5, and R-Z biplane bombers that operated during the hours of darkness were unable to do more than create nuisance to the German troops. Meanwhile, daylight operations conducted by VVS-Leningrad Front achieved very little in the face of JG 54's spirited defense. On the first day of the offensive, three VVS-Leningrad Front bombers escorted by five Tomahawks of 158 IAP attempted to reach and attack Siverskaya Airdrome. They were intercepted by Bf 109s from I./JG 54, whose pilots shot down two – credited to Hauptmann Franz Eckerle and his wingman – and forced those remaining to disengage.[43]

Generaloberst Keller decided to concentrate his forces against the Volkhov Front, and on January 8, the Ju 88s and He 111s of KG 1 and KG 4 were brought in against the congestion of Second Assault Army troops who advanced across the ice of the Volkhov River near Chudovo. "The bombers created a total chaos among the columns, which brought a considerable relief to our infantry," wrote Major Trautloft in his diary.[44] Provided with the dominant task of covering their troops and lines of communication with air cover, the VVS-Volkhov Front and VVS-Leningrad Front fighters rose in full strength – only to be butchered by Trautloft's fighters. JG 54 reported fourteen victories against only one loss. The pilot of the downed Bf 109, Feldwebel Wilhelm Quak, managed to evade capture for two days but was finally seized in a completely exhausted condition and brought to the airbase at Novaya Ladoga, where he was introduced to Soviet fighter pilots.

After only two days, the Soviet Second Assault Army had lost about three thousand men, and the entire venture had to be discontinued. The German Eighteenth Army managed to hold its positions both at the Volkhov River and around Leningrad.

But to the south of Lake Ilmen, the situation was different. While ground-attack planes and fighters of VVS-Northwestern Front strafed the positions of the

German Sixteenth Army, the seventeen Bf 109s of I./JG 51 had to be evacuated from Staraya Russa to Dno in advance of the rapidly advancing Soviet troops. On January 10 thick fog at Siverskaya and Dno grounded the Bf 109s, while the bombers that carried out low-level attacks against the advancing Soviet troops were met with intense small-arms fire from the ground. Three bombers were downed, and the new Gruppenkommandeur of I./KG 4, Major Heinz Alewyn, had to bail out of his burning He 111. The Germans were unable to prevent Staraya Russa from being surrounded, and on January 13, VVS-Northwestern Front mounted heavy raids against the town. The wooden houses burned like torches, and only the brick and concrete buildings withstood the firestorm.[45]

Meanwhile, the southern wing of the Northwestern Front operated in cooperation with the Kalinin Front, farther to the south, to strike against the seam between German Army groups North and Center at Ostashkov, ninety miles southeast of Lake Ilmen. Prevailing fog and snowfalls continued to hamper Luftwaffe operations. On January 13, I./JG 51's Feldwebel Egon Grosse, an ace with twenty-eight victories, was severely injured when bad weather forced his airplane down near Staraya Russa. He later died from his injuries.

Having received considerable reinforcements, the Soviet Second Assault Army took advantage of the situation in order to reopen its offensive on January 13 at the Volkhov River between Chudovo and Novgorod. Marching straight against the German fortifications in fog and raging blizzards, the Second Assault Army tore a six-mile wide gap in the German front lines at Myasnoy Bor. Its cavalry forces advanced thirty miles in five days and reached Finev Lug, thus severing the rail connection between Novgorod and the German troops south of Leningrad.

Raging with fury, Hitler fired the commander of Army Group North, Generalfeldmarschall Wilhelm Ritter von Leeb, and replaced him with Generaloberst Georg von Küchler. On the Soviet side, on January 18, commander in chief of the Soviet Fleet, Admiral Nikolay Kuznetsov, appointed four aviation regiments as the first Guards aviation regiments – three of them from VVS-KBF: Podpolkovnik Yevgenniy Preobrazhenskiy's 1 MTAP/VVS-KBF (which had carried out the difficult Berlin raids in 1941) became 1 GMTAP/VVS-KBF; the Northern Fleet's 72 SAP became 2 GSAP/VVS-SF; 5 IAP/VVS-KBF became 3 GIAP/VVS-KBF; and 13 IAP/VVS-KBF became 4 GIAP/VVS-KBF.

The same day, January 18, Northwestern Front outflanked the German II Corps and the bulk of X Corps – ninety-five thousand men – at Demyansk, a forward post and communication center fifty miles southeast of Lake Ilmen, and advanced westward on both flanks of this garrison. A few days later, fifty-five hundred German soldiers were isolated at Kholm on the Lovat River, fifty miles farther to the southwest.

Hitler ordered the encircled forces to stay put rather than attempt a breakout. Demyansk was even officially declared a "fortress" – Festung Demyansk. By holding these two strategic communication centers, the Germans thwarted all Soviet possibilities of expanding their advance much farther to the west.

An air supply operation to the besieged garrisons commenced in an atmosphere of urgency. Only seventy-five operational Ju 52s were available for this task, so Generaloberst Keller decided to allocate the He 111s of I./KG 4 to fly in supplies and reinforcements to Demyansk and Kholm in towed DFS 230 and Go 242 gliders.

The first forty Ju 52s landed on the narrow airstrip at Demyansk on January 20. During the following days, sixty to one hundred Ju 52 sorties made it to Demyansk. Major Trautloft dispatched 9./JG 54, commanded by the able

Transport flights by Ju 52s were vital for the ability of the German garrison at Demyansk to hold out during the first months of 1942. Designed in 1930, the Ju 52 had made its operational debut with the Bolivian Air Force during the Chaco War of 1932-1935. Ten years later it still was an excellent transport plane, and it was the predominant Luftwaffe transport throughout the war. A total of 4,845 Ju 52/3m were manufactured by October 1944 – including aircraft produced in France and Hungary. (Photo: Wagner/Stein via Rosipal.)

DB-3F, 1 GMTAP/8 BAB/VVS-KBF, Soviet Union, early 1942

Oberleutnant Hans-Ekkehard Bob, to reinforce the fighters of I./JG 51 already operating in this area.

By this time, the limited forces of VVS-Northwestern Front were concentrated to support the operations on the southern flank – where the gap that had been torn between German Army groups North and Center had been widened to eighty miles – so there was only limited counteraction on behalf of the Soviet airmen against the first supply flights to Demyansk and Kholm.

On January 19 a cold front cleared the skies. "A clear blue sky and minus – 29 degrees Celsius. We can start flying again!" an enthusiastic Major Trautloft wrote in his diary. Hauptmann Bruno Dilley's I./StG 2 Immelmann arrived at Dno Airdrome after a long period of rest in Germany with the first of the modified Ju 87 D version to reach the Eastern Front. Other famous Stuka pilots in I./StG 2 included the Staffelkapitäne of 1. and 3. Staffeln, Knight's Cross holders Oberleutnant Friedrich Lang and Oberleutnant Alwin Boerst. The latter had carried out more than three hundred dive bombings, and Lang would celebrate his five hundredth combat sortie in February 1942. Later on, both were among the four Stuka pilots who were awarded the Swords to the Knight's Cross with Oak Leaves.

As the skies now cleared, Dilley's highly motivated Stuka fliers were brought into relentless action, dealing heavy blows against the Soviets wherever their new Ju 87s appeared. Historian Georg Brütting describes how they put an armored train out of action:

> I./StG 2 attacked an armored train on the railway Staraya Russa-Bologoye to the east of the encirclement area at Demyansk. The well-aimed artillery fire from this armored train created a difficult situation for the German troops in this sector. The dive-bombing took place in clear winter weather, commencing from an altitude of

A Ju 87 D is loaded with bombs for a dive-bombing mission. I./StG 2, which introduced the Ju 87 D on the Eastern Front, was commanded by one of the Luftwaffe's most formidable Stuka veterans, Hauptmann Bruno Dilley. On September 1, 1939, three days after his twenty-sixth birthday, Dilley carried out the first hostile action in World War II by dropping bombs over Polish targets at 0435 hours, ahead of the scheduled attack on Poland. By the time he arrived at the Eastern Front in mid-January 1942, Dilley had flown over Poland, Norway, France, England, the Balkans, Malta, and North Africa. He survived 650 combat sorties and ended the war as a Major in command of a Stuka/Schlachtfliegerschule.(Photo: Roba/Mombeek.)

> 9,000 feet. The aircraft dived against the wind toward the front line. After releasing their bombs from a very low flight altitude, the pilots flew out of the target area almost on the deck, and thus managed to evade the antiaircraft artillery. The bombs were dropped with accuracy. Six of the long, white-painted rail wagons fell across the railway.
>
> After the landing at Dno, the command post of I./StG 2 received a radio message from the ground troops reporting that the armored train still maintained its unpleasant activity. The Stukagruppe hurriedly prepared another raid against the same target. This time the Russians had called in fighters to protect the remainder of the armored train. As an additional protective measure, the commander of the armored train had dispersed the wagons. One of the wagons had been moved 200 yards closer to the front line. The accurately dropped bombs completed the destruction and the army command sent its gratitude for the completely successful work.[46]

During this period, Hauptmann Dilley's unit was rushed to and fro between the sectors to the north and to the south of Lake Ilmen like a fire brigade. Since the bulk of VVS-Northwestern Front was concentrated to the southern flank at Toropets, fighter opposition was only light in the Staraya Russa – Demyansk area. But during operations against the deep penetration of the Soviet Second Assault Army north of Lake Ilmen, the war diary of I./StG 2 noted increased opposition from Soviet fighters. This is hardly surprising, since VVS-Volkhov Front was receiving considerable reinforcements – however, mostly U-2 and R-5 biplanes – and reached a strength of 313 aircraft by the end of January. The air force of Second Assault Army increased from three to eight aviation regiments, and seven new aviation regiments were allocated to the Fifty-ninth Army. Nevertheless, the Bf 109s of JG 54 managed to save I./StG 2 from losses to Soviet fighters throughout the months of January and February. During the periods when I./StG 2 operated south of Lake Ilmen, JG 54 relentlessly strafed the troops of Second Assault Army. The Kampfgruppen and Stukagruppen meanwhile were tasked to attack railroad lines and airfields east of the Volkhov River. These air operations did not entirely halt the Soviet troops, but the pace of the Soviet advance was considerably reduced.

The Soviet fighter pilots did whatever they could to relieve their hard-pressed ground troops but largely failed in this task. Although the Ju 88s and He 111s of KG 1 and KG 4 operated predominantly in daylight, the rate of combat losses in these Kampfgeschwader was only 1.2 percent during January 1942, and most of these losses appear to have been the result of ground fire.

Engagements with the Bf 109s of JG 54 still were all but encouraging to the Soviet fighter pilots. On January 20, six P-40 Tomahawks of 154 IAP, led by the ace Kapitan Petr Pokryshev, clashed violently with the Bf 109s of JG 54 near Leningrad. Pokryshev was a veteran from the Winter War, in which he had achieved two victories, although he was also shot down twice. As they patrolled the sky in the area of Pogostye, Pokryshev's Tomahawks were bounced by six Bf 109s that came out from the sun and behind the Soviet formation.

Flying at the rear of the Soviet formation was another distinguished ace, Leytenant Andrey Chirkov, who had scored the first victory of VVS-Leningrad Military District on the second day of the war. Chirkov turned head-on against a Messerschmitt. Both Chirkov and the Grünherz pilot opened fire. In the last moment the Bf 109 attempted to avoid a collision, but it was too late. As the two airmen broke off, the Tomahawk's wing struck the Bf 109, and Chirkov's plane was thrown into a spin. The pilot had no alternative but to bail out, even though he was over German territory. While Chirkov rode to the ground in his parachute, the Bf 109 limped away and finally made a belly-landing in the deep snow. Chirkov found himself alone in the wilderness behind enemy lines. He had lost his flying helmet and gloves during the descent. That day, Major Hannes Trautloft noted the temperature in his diary – minus – 29-degrees Celsius. After a two-day walk through the thinly held German lines, the frostbitten and exhausted Andrey Chirkov managed to reach Soviet lines.

On January 23 – a day with clear skies and a temperature of minus – 49-degrees Celcius[47] – Oberleutnant Max-Hellmuth Ostermann, one of the deadliest Grünherz aces, brought home his fifty-fourth and fifty-fifth victories. Next day, he chalked up number fifty-six. On January 25 Ostermann spotted an MP-1 – the civilian version of the single-engine MBR-2 hydroplane – escorted by two VVS-KBF I-153s on an air transport mission from Priyutino to Novaya Ladoga. The MP-1 had no chance at all. Four crewmen and five passengers in the airplane were killed[48] as Ostermann triumphantly scored another victory. Three days later, Ostermann brought home his sixtieth victory.

Regardless of heavy snowfall and low cloud ceiling, Hauptmann Franz Eckerle, the Gruppenkommandeur of I./JG 54, managed to achieve his fifty-first victory against a Soviet fighter on January 31. That day,

Leytenant Mikhail Satalkin of the Tomahawk-equipped 158 IAP, wrote in his diary:

> Today I lost three comrades: Leytenant Golovach, who had taken off on a reconnaissance mission, was forced to return due to engine malfunction. But he wasn't able to reach the airfield and crashed into a dense forest. The engine was separated from the fuselage. His dead body was recovered from the completely burnt-out wreck.
>
> Leytenant [Vasiliy] Kharitonov had to make a forced landing, but his aircraft stood on its nose. He was sent to the hospital. In the evening [Starshiy Leytenant Ilya] Shishkan crashed in his aircraft and suffered a jaw fracture. He was also hospitalized.

During the month of January 1942, Luftflotte 1 carried out a total of 3,185 combat sorties. KG 1 and I./KG 4 carried out 913 bomber sorties in the Volkhov area and 473 in the Demyansk area; the pilots of JG 54 contributed with 1,152 sorties – 736 alone over the Volkhov sector – resulting in ninety-nine victory claims.[49] The Soviet airmen's chances of survival during this difficult period can be read by the statistics of VVS-Northwestern Front: Of seventy-nine aircraft at hand in late December 1941, thirty-two were shot down in January 1942.[50]

Each day resulted in new bitter losses to the Soviet fighter units, and combat spirits among many of the survivors plunged. Starshiy Leytenant Ivan Chulkov, an ace in the Soviet 41 IAP with nine personal and two shared victories, was reported missing during a sortie over the Volkhov battlegrounds on February 2, possibly the victim of II./JG 54's Feldwebel Herbert Broennle, who scored the only victory reported by JG 54 that day. The repeated loss of experienced pilots was particularly hard in this situation, where VVS replacements were made up of only half-trained fliers.

Some weak attempts by the Soviet air forces to neutralize JG 54 on the ground backfired. Alerted by a Freya early-warning radar installation that recently had been brought in, I./JG 54 knocked down three of six Pe-2s that attempted to raid Siverskaya Airdrome in daylight on February 3. Two days later, the Grünherz fighters warded off an unusually strong Soviet fighter interception against He 111s of KG 1. Seven Soviet fighters were claimed shot down in this melee, and the German bombers escaped unscathed. Among the downed Soviet airmen was 3 GIAP/VVS-KBF ace Starshiy Leytenant Georgiy Kostylev, who survived with injuries. On February 7 another Soviet ace was killed when 740 IAP's Politruk Aleksey Godovikov rammed a German Ju 88 reconnaissance aircraft in the Tikhvin area – his fifth victory.

Soviet replacement pilots were inadequately trained and proved to be unable to fulfill their tasks as wingmen. In 4 GIAP/VVS-KBF, Serzhant Viktor Golubev (not to be confused with Leytenant Vasiliy Golubev) was shot down and had to bail out of his burning Ishak. Leytenant Dmitriy Sotsenko and Serzhants Vladimir Bakirov and Semyon Gorgul – all from the same unit – were also wounded, while Leytenant Mikhail Alekseyev survived unscathed when he was shot down.

Poor air support was the dominant weakness of the Soviet offensive across the Volkhov River. In daylight, the Germans made effective interference by Soviet aircraft impossible. Instead, VVS-Volkhov Front carried out an impressive number of sorties against German lines of communication and airfields during the hours of darkness, but since mainly obsolete U-2s, R-5s, and R-Zs were used, the effect was almost negligible. Only when adverse weather conditions over the German airfields between February 10 and February 12 prevented fighter interception was the VVS able to deliver effective daylight strikes against railroad stations, supply trains, and lines of communication without significant loss. Leytenant Vasiliy Golubev of 4 GIAP/VVS-KBF recalls that the Soviet fighter pilots were in bad need of a morale boost at this time.

The sad remnants of a downed Soviet MiG-3 fighter. (Photo: Balss.)

Hauptmann Franz Eckerle, the I./JG 54 Gruppenkommandeur, was one of the Luftwaffe's most popular unit commanders. He also was a most talented fighter pilot, and following his thirtieth victory he was awarded with the Knight's Cross on September 18, 1941 (as seen in this photo). On February 7, 1942, Eckerle downed three Soviet aircraft – his victories numbered fifty-five through fifty-eight – and was thus recommended for the Oak Leaves to his Knight's Cross. But only one week later a VVS-KBF I-15bis put an end to this fighter ace's life. The Oak Leaves were awarded posthumously on March 12, 1942. (Photo: Trautloft.)

JG 54 was also dealt a disheartening loss on February 14. That day, Hauptmann Franz Eckerle, the successful commander of I./JG 54, charged a formation of eight I-16s and I-15bis near Turyshkino, seventeen miles southeast of Schlüsselburg on the southwestern shore of Lake Ladoga. Eckerle managed to shoot down one I-15bis – his fifty-ninth victory – but in the next moment, another I-15bis came up and hit Eckerle's Bf 109 with a hail of machine gun bullets. Eckerle's wingman, who was caught up in a difficult turning combat with the agile little Polikarpovs, managed only a glimpse as his commander's plane turned over on its back and went down steeply. A KBF report gives the following account of this combat: "At noon, four I-16s and four I-15bis carried out a reconnaissance mission in the area Voronovo-Mga-Tosno-Maluksa. Near the village of Turyshkino, the flight of four I-15bis of 3 AE, 71 IAP/KBF led by Mladshiy Leytenant Petrukhin was attacked by two Me-109s. After the second attack, one I-15bis went into a spin and hit the ground. The pilot was killed. As a result of the combat, one Me-109 was shot down and hit the ground near Lake Dolgoye at Lodva. The victory was shared between Mladshiy Leytenant Petrukhin, Mladshiy Leytenant Markov, and Serzhant Savosin"[51]

German front-line soldiers reported seeing the pilot of a Bf 109 bailing out over Soviet territory. According to accounts by Soviet soldiers who were captured in this area shortly thereafter, furious Soviet soldiers brought Eckerle into a forest, where they lynched him.[52] Major Trautloft noted that the loss of Eckerle shook the entire Gruppe. The most successful Grünherz ace, Hauptmann Hans Philipp, who had recently scored his seventy-seventh victory, took Eckerle's place at the head of I./JG 54.

During the next few days, the Soviet air forces stepped up their activities in an effort to relieve the Second Assault Army, which by now was suffering heavily from German flank attacks and bombardment from the air. On the night of February 15 – 16 and during the day on February 16, VVS-Volkhov Front dispatched all available aircraft against German motorized columns in the rear of the German Eighteenth Army at the Volkhov River. As a result, forty trucks with infantry and twenty horse-drawn ammunition carts were reportedly destroyed. But such incidents remained an exception, and the participating Soviet airmen suffered grievous losses. After intercepting one of these daylight raids, Hauptmann Hans Philipp was able to down three planes in twelve minutes.

On February 23 the Soviet air forces put on another burst of activity during daylight. While 2 GIAP of VVS-Volkhov Front conducted strafing attacks against the German troops that almost surrounded Second Assault Army's narrow penetration area, units of VVS-Leningrad

Luftwaffe losses in the northern combat zone were relatively light in early 1942, but on February 16, 1942, this 1./KG 53 He 111 was forced down in Soviet-held territory near Voroteyka after sustaining machine-gun hits. The entire crew was listed as missing. As this photo shows, the crashed He 111 was set on fire – possibly by the Soviets for propaganda purposes – a considerable time after it was shot down. (Photo: Viktor Kulikov collection.)

Front joined from the airfields on the southern shore of Lake Ladoga and in besieged Leningrad. The outcome brought about nothing more than new severe losses to the Soviet airmen. JG 54 reported eleven victories, including 158 IAP's Leytenant Mikhail Satalkin, who was listed as missing in air combat. German documents show that he was shot down by Hans Philipp. Satalkin was listed as Philipp's eighty-second victory. Two days later, a Rotte composed of Feldwebel Gerhard Lautenschläger and Feldwebel Rudolf Rademacher of I./JG 54 bounced seven P-40 Tomahawks and claimed five shot down, three by Rademacher.[53]

This gun-camera footage shows a Soviet fighter as it flies straight into the tracer shells from a JG 54 Bf 109. (Photo: Trautloft.)

By the third week of February, the Second Assault Army was finally halted. Within a short time, its triumphant march to relieve Leningrad had turned into a desperate fight to evade complete annihilation. The fifty-mile-deep penetration, similar to a long, narrow finger on the map, was a bold but disastrous maneuver. All efforts by Soviet airmen – VVS-Volkhov Front reportedly carried out 4,927 combat sorties during February 1942, of which 80 percent were close support of the ground troops – could not alter the situation. The majority of the Soviet air operations in this sector took place at night, and the relatively few missions that could be carried out in

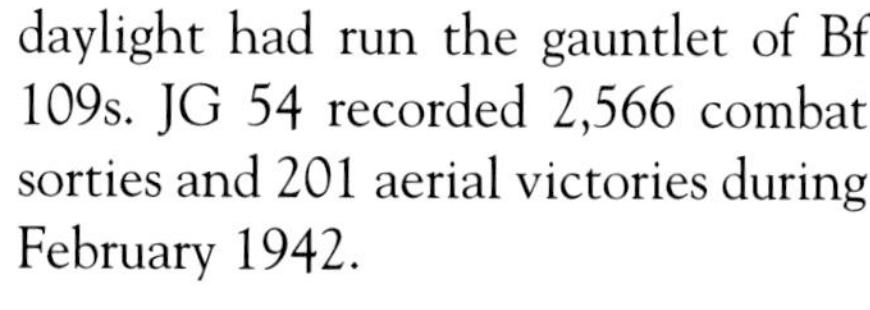
daylight had run the gauntlet of Bf 109s. JG 54 recorded 2,566 combat sorties and 201 aerial victories during February 1942.

It is clear that the Luftwaffe played a decisive role in the containment of the Soviet offensives in the northern combat zone in January and February 1942. Despite substantial numerical reinforcements, the VVS in this area remained vastly inferior to Fliegerkorps I. There was a severe shortage of day bombers, ground-attack aircraft, and – most important – fighters on the Soviet side. The rigid command structure of VVS-KA, which tied aviation units strictly to individual ground armies, also prevented the Soviets from countering the flexible German tactic of shifting the bulk of aviation units to the main point of concentration.

But even though the Soviet offensives in the northern combat zone were halted short of their strategic targets, they did succeed in one sense: They brought relief to besieged Leningrad. The extensive Soviet offensive operations forced Fliegerkorps I to turn its attention away from air operations against the Ice Road. This allowed the supply loads brought in to Leningrad to increase while thousands of civilians were evacuated across the ice on Lake Ladoga to freedom on the other shore.

Leytenant Mikhail Satalkin (far right) with a group of Soviet 158 IAP fighter pilots during the first difficult stage of the war with Germany. Satalkin experienced nothing but hardship during his service as a fighter pilot. He participated in the fighting over the far approaches to Leningrad in the summer of 1941, where he bailed out with severe injuries on August 4, 1941. Following medical treatment he returned to first-line service with the Tomahawk-equipped 158 IAP on December 2, 1941. His diary for the first two months of 1942 tells of a severe combat situation, his agony over the famine in Leningrad, and problems in relations between the pilots and the regimental commander. On February 23, 1942, Satalkin was shot down and killed, probably in combat with Hauptmann Hans Philipp, who had just succeeded the fallen Franz Eckerle as the I./JG 54 Gruppenkommandeur.

Second from the left in the photo is Starshiy Leytenant Aleksandr Bulayev, who is wearing the Order of the Red Banner and a medal on his chest. He scored fifteen individual and eight shared victories during the war against Germany. (Photo: Novikov.)

He 111 H-6 W.Nr. 4442,
Oberfeldwebel Willi Thoma (with Leutnant Heinrich Leske as observer, Feldwebel Erich Schmidt as radio operator, Obergefreiter Fridolin Szymanek as flight engineer, and Feldwebel Peter Jäger as gunner), 1./KG 53 Legion Condor, Riga, Latvia, February 16, 1942

This airplane was hit by Soviet ground fire and force-landed in Soviet-held territory near Voroteyke on February 16, 1942. The entire crew was listed as missing.

 **Chapter 7** 

Frustration in the South

During the first successful Soviet attack in the winter of 1941 – 42, German Army Group South was forced to evacuate Rostov, the gate to the Caucasus, and pulled back to the Mius River, ninety miles to the west. The retreat cost the commander in chief of the army group, Generalfeldmarschall Gerd von Rundstedt, his command; but his successor, Generalfeldmarschall Walter von Reichenau, was able to benefit from this timely retreat. While the front of Army Group Center collapsed, Army Group South was able to hold a line stretching from the northern coast of the Sea of Azov along the Mius and Donets rivers to an area east of Kursk, where it linked up with the right flank of Army Group Center.

During this period, the air war over the Ukraine was on a much smaller scale than that farther to the north. At the turn of the year, Generaloberst Alexander Löhr's Luftflotte 4 and its single air corps – Fliegerkorps IV – could deploy no more than 310 first-line aircraft to the eight-hundred-mile-wide front. The small air force of the Italian Expeditionary Corps, numbering approximately thirty Macchi MC.200 fighters of 22 Gruppo Autonomo

Krivoy Rog during the winter of 1941-1942. At least four Italian Caproni Ca.311s of 119th Squadriglia of 61st Gruppo O. A. are visible on the snowy airfield. Shortly afterward these aircraft were transferred to Stalino. There is also a Caproni Ca-133 transport plane, probably belonging to 22d Gruppo, which was left behind after the unit transferred to Zaporozhye. The small Italian Air Force detachment that participated in the war on the Eastern Front suffered grievously in the harsh winter conditions, and apart from a brief outburst of combat in early February 1942, carried out very few missions during the first months of 1942. (Photo: Collection D'Amico - Valentini.)

A Bf 109 F takes off from a snow-covered airfield on the Eastern Front in early 1942. (Photo: Trautloft.)

Caccia Terreste and a dozen SM.81 transport planes, was grounded during most of January due to an endemic lack of fuel.[54] According to German estimates, Luftflotte 4 was opposed by some 450 Soviet planes in January 1942. Soviet documents show that VVS-Southwestern Front mustered 236, and VVS-Southern Front 185 operational aircraft on December 1, 1941.

Stab, I., and III./KG 27, and the three Gruppen of KG 51, were the only bomber units remaining in Luftflotte 4 after the withdrawal of several units at the end of 1941 for rest and recuperation. The main task assigned to these Kampfgruppen was to strike against communication lines, particularly oil transports along rail lines in the Caucasus. The task of providing the ground troops with close support mainly fell on StG 77, Luftflotte 4's only Stukageschwader.

According to a report issued by the staff of VVS-Southwestern Front early in 1942, the bombers of Luftflotte 4 generally operated in formations of two to six planes, and occasionally singly or in formations of eight to fourteen planes. Only against railway stations did the Germans dispatch larger formations, divided among several flight altitudes. While the He 111s unloaded their bombs in horizontal flight, the Ju 88s often followed the example of the Ju 87 Stukas to carry out dive-bombings against pinpoint targets.

The dive-bombing generally opened with the Stuka formation circling over the target area, after which each airplane dived individually from 10,000 to 12,000 feet and unloaded one or two bombs apiece from an altitude of 1,000 to 1,200 feet. Each dive-bomber carried out three or four such attacks before returning to base.

Most German bomber missions were carried out without fighter escort. Fighter protection was provided mainly when the operations were carried out in support of a major ground battle or in regions with relatively strong Soviet fighter concentrations. When operating against such areas, or sectors with strong antiaircraft artillery coverage, the German bombers frequently conducted their raids in the twilight, at dusk or dawn. When they were intercepted by Soviet fighters, the German bombers used the tactic of dropping down to low to seek refuge in clouds.[55]

Conducting operations in several small groups was the most rational method, because of the limited number of bombers and Stukas covering such a vast area. Since no more than two Jagdgruppen – I.(J)/LG 2 (later redesignated I./JG 77), and III./JG 52 – were available in the Ukraine, fighter escorts could be provided only when they were vitally needed. In most cases, the Kampfgruppen and Stukagruppen had to rely on their defensive combat formations and the air gunners' skills to fend off hostile interception in the air.

The close cooperation of the highly skilled air gunners and the relatively low frequency of encounters with Soviet fighters kept the losses in German bombers and Stukas at a very low level. During the month of January 1942, KG 27 registered only three combat losses in the air, while KG 51 lost five, and StG 77 lost three planes.[56]

On the other side of the hill, the situation looked grim. Aleksandr Pavlichenko, who served as a Starshiy Leytenant and Su-2 pilot in VVS-Southern Front's 210 BBAP at this time, recalls: "On New Year's Eve 1942 the veterans of 210 BBAP sat together in the underground shelter at our air base. We counted our losses and found that only twelve crews had survived since June 22, 1941 – out of five Eskadrilii with a total of fifty crews!"

Most bomber units of the Soviet front aviation and the DBA had shifted mainly to night operations since the autumn of 1941. Since there were no German night fighters, losses were considerably reduced. During January 1942, VVS-Southern Front lost only three bombers – DB-3s of 21 DBAP and 81 DBAP – during night raids. In addition, VVS-Southern Front's 622 LBAP lost two R-5s,

Following the terrible bloodletting of the summer and fall of 1941, VVS fighter opposition was very limited, even against German single-plane reconnaissance flights. Based at Poltava, Hauptmann Walter Plotke's 2.(F)/22 conducted regular long-range reconnaissance missions throughout January and February 1942 while suffering but a single combat loss. This loss occurred on January 6, when Hauptmann Plotke's Ju 88 A-4 had to belly-land due to an engine fire. The entire crew was injured. The inspection of the airplane – as viewed in this photo led to the conclusion that it had to be scrapped. (Photo: Fregosi.)

and 654 NLBAP lost one U-2 during night operations in the same period.[57]

VVS daylight bombing operations generally were carried out by faster light bombers, primarily Su-2s, and fighter-bombers, mostly without fighter escort. These operations generally were confined to close support directly at the front.

Feldwebel Alfred Grislawski of 9./JG 52 recalls that during the first months of 1942 German airmen flew most missions without encountering any enemy aircraft. During January 1942 Grislawski´s logbook records eight combat sorties-–two fighter sweeps, three escort missions for StG 77, and three strafing missions – without spotting a single enemy aircraft in the air.

The Bf 109 aces, who had grown accustomed to achieving easy victories with only minimal peril to themselves, adopted all kinds of measures to draw their opponents into combat. Leutnant Hermann Graf of 9./JG 52 entered the following in his diary:

> One day we tried something which was rather uncommon. We made up a packet with chocolates and cigarettes, tied it to a small parachute, added an invitation to the Russians, and dropped it over the Russian fighter airfield south of Rostov. It read: "Comrades from the other side, we invite you to a dogfight over the Don delta south of Rostov tomorrow, Wednesday, at 1200 hours, altitude 4,000 meters. We guarantee that we will come with only eight machines, you can bring as many Soviet machines as you want! Horrido! In sincere friendship, your enemy."
>
> However we waited in vain.

With pilot training curricula radically cut to meet the needs created by combat losses, and given their inferior equipment, most Soviet airmen in this area who came across the Jagdflieger stood little chance of survival. But the low rate of aerial encounters during this period was the consequence of the limited number of aircraft available to both sides, rather than a Soviet reluctance to take to the air.

On Wednesday, January 7, Leutnant Hermann Graf came across a formation of I-16 fighters and sent two plunging to the ground. Next day Feldwebel Leopold Steinbatz, a very aggressive pilot of 9./JG 52, managed to surprise two Soviet fighters and a bomber in the air over the Soviet rear area on the Mius front. Steinbatz described this event in a letter to his wife:

> Today was my lucky day. Early this morning we took off on a free hunting mission and we actually spotted three Soviets. . . .
>
> I flew together with a young comrade who had never been in combat before as the three brothers appeared. Of course, I immediately attacked one of the fighters. With a short burst of fire I blew off his left wing and he went down vertically.
>
> Pulling up, I saw the second fighter below. He was watching his descending comrade. I dived again and attacked him. I hit his radiator and he made a forced landing. We shot the aircraft on fire.
>
> Now the turn had come for the third aircraft, the bomber. My wingman had been attacking him but wasn't able to bring him down. As I approached him, he fired like mad. I came in very close, and then I shot him in flames with a few rounds. Burning, he crashed into a village. The crew had no chance to bail out, since they had been flying at an altitude of no more than 450 feet.

With these kills, "Poldi" Steinbatz had achieved his fortieth to forty-second victories, for which he was awarded the Knight's Cross. That same day, his Staffelführer, Hermann Graf, caught and shot down another Soviet aircraft, his forty-fifth victory.

Only for a brief period during the latter half of January 1942 did the air war in the southern combat zone flare up. This increased activity was in connection with a Soviet attempt to achieve a major breakthrough.

Su-2, Mladshiy Leytenant Grigoriy Sivkov with Mladshiy Leytenant Petr Zemlyakov as gunner/bombardier, 3 Eskadrilya/210 BBAP/VVS-Southern Front, Budyonovka, Soviet Union, December 28, 1941

Sivkov carried out his first combat sortie with this airplane on December 28, 1941. Sivkov was twice appointed Hero of the Soviet Union – on February 2, 1944 and August 18, 1945.

On January 16 Unteroffizier Horst Schlick of I./JG 77 noted in his diary:

> For weeks we hadn't seen anything of the enemy in the air... Joking before take-off, I said that today there will be some fighting where I am. And suddenly – at first we see them as small dots, like a swarm of bees – we find ourselves in the midst of sixty Russians – I-153s, I-16s, and Yaks. Looking back at my compatriots – we flew in the strength of a Schwarm – I noticed that they were 1,000 meters above the Russians. I applied full throttle and climbed as fast as I could. [Oberleutnant Erwin] Clausen attacked a Rata. I can still see this aircraft falling out of the formation with Clausen on its tail, at a distance of 100 meters. A short burst from Clausen's guns ignites the Russian bird. He rolls over his left wing and hits the ground, burning, next to a main road. This was Clausen's twentieth and the Gruppe's three hundredth victory. Having almost run out of fuel, Clausen and I land in Taganrog."[58]

Among the Soviet airmen that were shot down by I./JG 77 this day was 210 BBAP's Starshiy Leytenant Aleksandr Pavlichenko, who recounts: "This happened on January 16, 1942, in the region of Makeyevka in the Donbass. We were returning from a reconnaissance mission. We were flying at an altitude of 4,500 feet, already above our own territory, as Me 109 fighters jumped us and shot our aircraft in flames. We bailed out and went down in our own territory eight miles from the front line. The aircraft spun down and exploded on impact three or four miles from the place where we took ground."

This engagement preceded the combined Soviet offensive, which opened on January 18 at the Donets River in the Izyum area, seventy miles southeast of Kharkov. The Soviet offensive caught Army Group South in the midst of a command crisis. General-feldmarschall Walter von Reichenau, the commander in chief of the army group, had suffered a heart attack on January 12, and was killed when the transport plane that attempted to bring him to medical treatment in Germany crashed. His successor, Generalfeldmarschall Fedor von Bock, the former commander of Army Group Center, who had been fired by Hitler in December 1941, took over just as the Soviet Southwestern and Southern fronts launched their hitherto most powerful offensive.

The operation was initiated with a totally unexpected outburst of Soviet raids on German air bases. On January 18, three of 4 ShAP's Il-2s made a swift attack against Mariupol Airdrome on the northern coast of the Sea of Azov and managed to put three I./JG 77 Bf 109s out of commission,[59] although two of the precious Il-2s failed to return from this mission.[60] On the ground, General-Leytenant Dmitriy Ryabyshev's Fifty-seventh Army achieved a deep breakthrough during the initial phase. Within a few days, however, these Soviet troops were faced with massive German air attacks. On January 22 the Luftwaffe was reported to have destroyed more than 230 vehicles and 9 artillery pieces. Nevertheless, in spite of repeated Luftwaffe attacks, the Soviets managed to seize the main supply store of the German Seventeenth Army at Barvenkovo, thirty miles southwest of Izyum, on January 23. To the north of the Fifty-seventh Army, the Soviet Sixth Army raced across the frozen steppe and reached Lozovaya, farther to the west, on January 25. Thus, the Soviets had driven a fifty-mile deep wedge into the German lines and severed the strategically vital rail line from Kharkov to southeastern Ukraine.

Starshiy Leytenant Aleksandr Pavlichenko served as an Su-2 light-bomber pilot with VVS-Southern Front's 210 BBAP during the early stage of the war. Pavlichenko, who was a civilian airline pilot, was posted to the Su-2-equipped 210 BBAP on January 9, 1941, and participated in early operations against invading German and Romanian forces with this unit in the summer of 1941. In October 1941 he was assigned to command 3 AE/210 BBAP. Pavlichenko, who recalled the first three months of 1942 as a most difficult time, was shot down on three occasions. (Photo: Pavlichenko.)

The air forces of the Southern and Southwestern fronts made a maximum effort to deliver decisive strikes against the retreating German troop columns, supply lines, and airfields. Starshiy Leytenant Pavlichenko recounts: "We carried out intensive air operations. Each crew never flew less than three sorties per day, sometimes even four or five sorties a day. We suffered losses on almost every mission, mostly through enemy fighters. The Messerschmitt pilots showed a very high self-confidence. Early in 1942 I lost several close friends, all of them experienced men and good people."

Il-2, Kapitan Nikolay Zub, Eskadrilya-commander in 4 ShAP/VVS-Ninth Army/VVS-Southern Front, Novo-Aleksandrovka, Soviet Union, early 1942

The text on the fuselage of the Il-2 is a typical patriotic slogan which frequently was painted on Soviet combat aircraft, and reads, in translation "Death to the Fascist Occupiers!"

The Soviet inferiority in the air proved to be the decisive factor. On January 26 Pavlichenko was once again within a hairsbreadth of being killed by the Bf 109 pilots of I./JG 77: "We were out on a bombing mission with seven Su-2s in the Slavyansk area. Suddenly we were bounced by a group of enemy fighters. They raked my plane with cannon and machine-gun fire during the initial attack. Something burning pierced my right arm above the elbow. I felt that I couldn't use my right arm, so I grabbed the stick with my left hand. I felt a heavy pain; it was as if my right arm was burning. Warm blood trickled down on my waist." Despite his bullet wound, Pavlichenko managed to bring the aircraft back to base for a safe landing.

As VVS losses mounted, even R-5s and R-Zs were dispatched in daylight close-support sorties. On February 3 and February 4, I./JG 77's Oberleutnant Friedrich Geisshardt and Oberleutnant Erwin Clausen spotted and shot down three R-5s or R-Zs of 622 LBAP and 672 LBAP. Between February 1 and February 9, these two LBAPs sacrificed nine R-5s and R-Zs.[61]

After several weeks without any flight activity, the Italian fighter pilots of 22 Gruppo Autonomo Caccia Terreste resumed operations in defense of Izyum. On February 4 and February 5, the Italian pilots reported fifteen Soviet aircraft destroyed on the ground and five more in the air as a result of low-level attacks against the VVS-Southern Front airdrome at Krasnyy Liman, southeast of Izyum. These claims are largely exaggerations, since VVS-Southern Front lost no more than eight aircraft during enemy air-base raids between October 1941 and March 1942.[62]

Largely through the prolonged exertion of the airmen of Fliegerkorps IV, the Soviet offensive was finally halted, although it left a deep wedge in the German front line. On most days during this operation, the airmen had been forced to fly under terrible weather conditions – low clouds and heavy snowfall. The battle came to a stalemate in February. By that time, combat fatigue among the German airmen was a major concern to the commander of Fliegerkorps IV. Many of these fliers had been in constant action since the summer of 1941, and in December 1941 the medical personnel of KG 51 noted frequent cases of nervous exhaustion among flight crews.

During February 1942 blizzards and icy winds that swept over the airfields on the Ukrainian steppe grounded most of the air activity. Forced to inactivity, shivering with cold, and with their stomachs rumbling with hunger, the German airmen cursed inadequate supplies and had much time to ponder their situation. Here they were, hundreds of miles from home, deep inside a devastated and hostile country, with no outlook for any immediate end of the war. First they had been promised victory in 1940, then in 1941. Now the Wehrmacht had become bogged down in a strenuous defensive situation that not one of them could have anticipated when they spearheaded Hitler's invasion of the USSR. The following lines from the diary of Leutnant Hermann Graf of 9./JG 52 during this winter are significant: "Yesterday we received the last food rations of our Gruppe. Then followed a hungry day." Leutnant Graf heard Feldwebel Leopold Steinbatz exclaim: "Oh, Hermann [Göring], what has become of your heroes! Nowadays we run around like nothing but a bunch of hobos." No wonder the mood dropped below zero on the German side.

Lacking any other targets of opportunity, Hauptmann Hubertus von Bonin, the commander of III./JG 52, ordered four Bf 109s to strafe a Soviet antiaircraft position on Friday, February 13. "It wasn't that I was an out-and-out-coward, but I always had a great fear of this type of missions," wrote Leutnant Adolf Dickfeld, who was one of the three pilots selected to accompany von Bonin.[63] The attack was carried out at low level. Von Bonin, his wingman, and Dickfeld managed to return to base despite AAA hits on all three Bf 109s, but Leutnant Heinrich Freitag went missing. Dickfeld recalls that "the CO called him, but no answer."[64] Four days later, the Soviet newspaper *Pravda* ran a long article asserting that Leutnant Freitag had deserted to the Soviets. According to *Pravda*, he had landed his fully intact Bf 109 at a Soviet air base. The following statement appeared in the article:

> Russia, 15.II.42. – I, the son of Sebastian Freitag's family from Reising, have gone over to the Russian side in order to struggle against the rapacious robbers from Germany.
>
> The immediate reason for my desertion was the derisions of my commanders over me – intimidations and arrests. I have witnessed the horrible scenes in Kharkov, where innocent Russians were hanged from the balconies. From what I have heard I understand that they are executing all the Jews. Germany is carrying out a murderous war against Russia and halts at nothing, using derision and torture of prisoners. There is no doubt that the Russians will achieve victory. One only has to get acquainted with the Russian people—everywhere you are met with an exceptional cohesion and confidence in victory. I have met with Russian airmen, and we

> understand each other perfectly. During one of our discussions we talked about the inevitable fall of Hitler.
>
> *Freitag, Heinrich.*[65]

On February 22, I-16s from 88 IAP buzzed III./JG 52's base at Kharkov. Together with a few bombs that hit a hangar, thousands of white leaflets fluttered from the Ishaks. According to the war diary of 88 IAP, 28,300 leaflets were air-dropped that day.[66] Disregarding orders not to read any enemy propaganda, the men of III./JG 52 picked them up and were stunned to find a text similar to the one quoted above, ending with an exhortation to follow Leutnant Freitag's example. Adolf Dickfeld wrote: "Freitag's case remained a topic of discussion for some time, because we weren't sure whether he had been forced to land and branded a deserter, or if he had really gone over to the other side."[67]

Heinrich Freitag returned to Germany after his Soviet captivity on December 4, 1949.[68]

Another case of this kind of desertion from Luftwaffe ranks reportedly took place shortly afterward, when Leutnant Herbert Baumgartner of 2./KG 27 flew his He 111 to the Soviet airfield at Leninsk. As in Leutnant Freitag's case, leaflets were air-dropped over KG 27's base at Kirovograd a few days later. The text, allegedly written by Baumgartner, urged "the pilots Leutnant Krenz and Lessmaier, Oberleutnants Wagner, Lohmann and Klein" to join him.

Two Soviet bomber crewmen have a smoke while waiting for the ground crew to ready their DB-3F for another combat mission. Since they were fighting in their own territory to defend the Motherland, the Soviet soldiers and airmen generally endured hardships better than most Germans. Vasiliy Kurayev, who was a Starshina in early 1942 and served as a radio operator with the DB-3F-equipped 8 BAP in the southern combat zone, states: "Yes, that was a hard time, but our task was clear. We knew that our Motherland depended on us, and we could endure anything." (Photo: Kurayev via Antipov.)

Even if such cases remained isolated, it is obvious that the stamina of the Soviet airmen was stronger. Starshiy Leytenant Aleksandr Pavlichenko describes the situation at his base in the third week of February: "There had been very heavy battles, and all that remained of the two regiments that were based on our airfield was sixteen Su-2s in 210 BBAP and twelve I-16s in 289 IAP. But we nevertheless continued to carry out our orders."[69]

On February 23 – Red Army Day – six I-16 pilots of Podpolkovnik Ivan Taranenko's 289 IAP were briefed to escort nine Su-2s of Pavlichenko's 3 Eskadrilya/210 BBAP against German troops in the Barvenkovo-Slavyansk area south of Izyum. The two groups took off in clear weather at 0930 hours. After they crossed the front lines, the Soviet aircraft ran into twelve Bf 109s from I./JG 77. Pavlichenko recalls:

> Our fighters started maneuvering sharply and the combat started. My formation pulled tighter together and our aft gunners opened fire. It was clear that our fighters were unable to hold the Bf 109s at bay, so the I-16s went into a defensive circle. By this means, each plane covers the one that flies in front of it. We carried on without fighter support, but the enemy fighters paid no attention to us.
>
> We flew to the target area and released our bombs from an altitude of 3,300 feet. Following this we regrouped and turned back for home. The sight we met really stunned us: There was a huge "roundabout" in the air. We soon noticed that it was our fighters. Until now they had been flying in circles. They were surrounded by eighteen to twenty Me 109s at different altitudes. The German pilots obviously attempted to exhaust our fighters, then aimed at forcing them down one by one. I thought that our fighters soon would be running out of fuel, since we had had the time to reach the target and return. I ordered my pilots to follow me and then passed below the I-16s' circle. This apparently confused the German fighter

> pilots. They hardly could have expected our nine Su-2s to join into the center of the air combat. In the wake of the German confusion, the I-16 pilots guessed my thoughts and rapidly started diving beneath us. Having passed below our formation, they placed themselves in front of us. Covered by our aft gunners, the I-16s rocked their wings, signaling us to follow them, and started diving. We decreased speed in order not to overtake the fighters and went down to 300 feet. The stunned Germans didn't pursue us, and we soon managed to reach friendly territory, and our airfield.
>
> We allowed the I-16s to land first. The engines of two fighters stopped while they were landing. As we climbed out of our aircraft, the fighter pilots came up to us and thanked us for saving them.

Statistics speak for themselves: In 88 IAP, only eight I-16s remained serviceable at the end of February 1942. As a consequence, one of the three Eskadril'i was disbanded. The situation was even worse in VVS-Southern Front's 4 ShAP, which was left with three Il-2s, of which only one was serviceable at the end of February.[70]

During the two first months of 1942, I./JG 77 pilots operating against VVS-Southern Front claimed seventy-four victories against only two combat losses in the air. According to Soviet loss files, VVS-Southern Front counted sixty-one aircraft downed in combat during the same period.[71] To these losses should be added those suffered by VVS-Sourhwestern Front. III./JG 52, which operated against VVS-Southwestern Front from the Kharkov airdrome, recorded approximately forty victories against three combat losses from the end of December 1941 to the end of February 1942. Total combat losses sustained by the Luftwaffe in Ukrainian airspace during the period January through February 1942 amounts to thirty-five aircraft.

Given their weak numbers in the air it is little wonder that the Soviets failed to achieve any major alteration of the strategic situation in the Ukraine during the winter of 1941 – 42.

 Chapter 8 

Winter Battles in the Crimea

In the Crimean skies the Luftwaffe airmen faced a considerably stronger resistance than they faced over the mainland. The effectiveness of the opposition was due in part to the skillful airmen assigned to General-Mayor Nikolay Ostraykov's VVS-ChF – most notably the Yak-1-equipped 5 Eskadrilya of 32 IAP/VVS-ChF, which operated from within the besieged city of Sevastopol. By the turn of the year, the most successful pilots of this Eskadrilya were Starshiy Leytenant Konstantin Alekseyev with seven personal victories by January 1, 1942, and Starshiy Leytenants Mikhail Avdeyev and Boris Babayev, and Leytenant Nikolay Shilkin, each with six kills. (This Eskadrilya was later folded into 8 IAP/VVS-ChF, where a famous veteran of the Battle of Odessa, Kapitan Konstantin Denisov, guaranteed high combat spirits for the new members of the unit.) Through the end of January 1942, 8 IAP/VVS-ChF was credited with eighty-eight victories in 930 aerial engagements since the outbreak of the war.

In early 1942 the Soviet air forces in the area were in constant action, night and day, against German supply bases, airfields, and troop positions in the Crimea. The Bf 109 pilots of Major Kurt Ubben's III./JG 77, based at Sarabuz, were the Soviets' main rivals in the struggle for air superiority. Apart from Ubben, who had surpassed his sixty-victory mark in December 1941, this unit included aces such as Leutnant Emil Omert with thirty-eight victories and Oberleutnant Wolf-Dietrich Huy with thirty at the start of 1942.

At the turn of the year as well, the initiative in the Crimea had slipped from the hands of Generaloberst Erich von Manstein's Eleventh Army. The surprise landings of Soviet troops to the army's rear at Kerch and Feodosiya in the eastern Crimea had forced Manstein to cancel the assault against Sevastopol in December 1941. On January 5, 1942 the situation was further complicated when a battalion of Soviet naval infantry landed at Yevpatoria, a port on the western side of the Crimean Peninsula. Here the civilian population also rose en masse against the occupation forces.

The Luftwaffe was tasked to save this situation. The commander in chief of the Luftwaffe, Reichsmarschall Hermann Göring, personally intervened to improve the circumstances in the Crimea. He called General Robert Ritter von Greim, the commander of Fliegerkorps V (based in Belgium), to Göring's residence at Karinhall and ordered von Greim to depart for the Crimea, where he was to form a new tactical operations staff, Sonderstab Krim, to make air support in the Crimea more effective.

From the onset of the Soviet amphibious landings, parts of StG 77, KG 27, and KG 51 were concentrated against the seaborne supply route to the Soviet beachheads. On January 5 the Soviet transport ships *Nogin* and *Zyryanin* were sunk and two others were damaged in air attacks off Feodosiya. Meanwhile, III./JG 77 claimed three SBs shot down that same day, and Soviet fighters brought down one Bf 109 of III./JG 77 and an He 111 from III./KG 27.[72]

Air raids and, in particular, heavy storms prevented the Soviets from reinforcing and supplying the troops ashore at Yevpatoria. Subjected to ceaseless dive-bombing attacks by II. and III./StG 77, resistance in this sector succumbed after a few days. The victorious Germans took a bloody revenge on the population, which had risen against them. On January 12, "1,300 partisans were executed," was laconically noted in the diary of the German High Command.[73]

By that time, General von Greim was preparing air support for the counterattack aimed at ousting the troops of the Soviet Crimean Front from the Kerch Peninsula in eastern Crimea. Despite inadequate supplies of fuel, ammunition, and spare parts, Sonderstab Krim made skillful use of its forces. The medium bomber units – III./KG 27 (He 111s) and III./KG 51 (Ju 88s) – were instructed to concentrate on targets at sea and the Soviet

Black Sea ports; the Ju 88s of 4.(F)/122 were dispatched on reconnaissance sorties to find suitable targets for these bombers; II. and III./StG 77 would provide close support for the attacking ground troops; and III./JG 77 would provide fighter cover for all these missions.

The German offensive opened on January 15 with Stuka raids against Soviet strongholds, artillery batteries, assembly areas, and troop concentrations. Soviet bombers were immediately called in to reduce the German pressure from the air by attacking Sonderstab Krim's airfields. In a daylight raid on January 15, 12 DBAP hit III./JG 77's base at Sarabuz and managed to put two Bf 109s out of commission. Leytenant Nikolay Krotkov, the pilot of one of the bombers that was shot down during this raid, reportedly crashed his doomed plane into a hangar at Sarabuz.[74]

Since most Soviet fighters in this area were based at distant airfields on the Taman Peninsula in the northwestern Caucasus, the Luftwaffe encountered only light fighter opposition above the battle arena on the Kerch Peninsula, leading Oberst Hermann Plocher, von Greim's chief of staff, to surmise that "Soviet flyers rarely accepted aerial combat and usually fled to protective fire of their own antiaircraft guns."[75] The Soviets had a completely different view:

Knight's Cross holder Oberleutnant Wolf-Dietrich Huy served as the 7./JG 77 Staffelkapitän in the Crimea in early 1942. During that time he competed with his Gruppenkommandeur, Hauptmann Kurt Ubben, and Leutnant Emil Omert for the position as III./JG 77's top scorer. Huy's personal victory tally stood at thirty-five on January 23, and his eagerness almost cost him his life that day when his Bf 109 was hit by a burst of fire from the well-known Soviet naval ace Starshiy Leytenant Mikhail Avdeyev. Following this staggering experience, Huy grew more cautious. Posted to North Africa in late summer of 1942, Huy was shot down by an RAF Spitfire and ended up in British captivity. Altogether, Wolf-Dietrich Huy was credited with a total of forty aerial victories on more than five hundred combat sorties. (Photo: Huy via Salomonson.)

> Enemy aviation operated with impunity, since our fighters, operating from inadequate and distant airfields on the Taman Peninsula, rarely appeared for 10 – 15 minutes. When our fighters arrived, the enemy was leaving; he bided his time until the departure of our planes, then he fiercely attacked Feodosiya again. It was a great mistake that the transport of sufficient antiaircraft artillery was not planned in the first supply trains.[76]

Although initially successful, the German offensive would be short-lived. On January 18, the same day the Wehrmacht recaptured Feodosiya, the Soviet offensive against Army Group South in the Izyum sector compelled Generaloberst Alexander Löhr, commanding Luftflotte 4, to shift the two Kampfgruppen and one Stukagruppe from Sonderstab Krim to the Kharkov area. Generaloberst von Manstein saw no other option but to cancel his attack against the Kerch Peninsula. Counting the aborted assault against Sevastopol in December 1941, this was von Manstein's second cancellation of a major attack in less than two months.

After several days of unfavorable weather conditions – including snowstorms – that prevented most flight activity, VVS-ChF on January 23 launched all available aircraft in the beleaguered Sevastopol base against the German Eleventh Army's supply bases. Some of the best pilots in 8 IAP/VVS-ChF were instructed to escort 40 BAP/VVS-ChF Pe-2s against Simferopol, forty miles northeast of Sevastopol. Meanwhile, Oberleutnant Wolf-Dietrich Huy led his 7./JG 77 on a fighter patrol. With thirty-five victories to his credit at that time, Huy was among the top scorers in JG 77. He had already been awarded the Knight's Cross, and within two months he would receive the Oak Leaves as well.

Huy's Bf 109s intercepted the Soviet formations in the target area. While the Pe-2s managed to get through, the fighters of both sides clashed violently. As the Soviet fighters formed a Lufbery circle *(Oboronitel'nyy krug)*, Oberleutnant Huy dove straight into their formation and clung to the tail of Starshiy Leytenant Konstantin Alekseyev's plane. But Huy was unfortunate to have placed himself in front of Starshiy Leytenant Mikhail Avdeyev, whose excellent marksmanship was well known throughout VVS-ChF. Avdeyev fired a long burst. "Everything happened very quickly," recalls Huy. "Before I had time to place myself in a firing position, another Russian took a shot at me and hit my engine, which stopped abruptly and then started to emit smoke."[77] Relieved from this threat, Alekseyev turned against another Bf 109 and reportedly shot it down after a short duel. The two Bf 109s that Avdeyev and Alekseyev claimed they shot down actually force-landed, and both pilots survived. Huy's 7./JG 77 was compelled to disengage without having achieved success.

Despite having only limited forces at hand, Generaloberst Löhr decided to launch one of his best bomber units against the flow of Soviet reinforcements to the forces that had landed on the Kerch Peninsula. On January 29, I./KG 100 Wiking was instructed to transfer from Kirovograd in the Ukraine to Saki in the Crimea to raid Soviet shipping in the Black Sea. But a supply shortage had left I./KG 100 in miserable condition. There were no more than eight serviceable He 111s at hand. On January 29 one He 111 was lost on a mission over the Straits of Kerch. Furthermore, the aircrew were trained for minelaying and had no experience in antishipping attacks. Had it not been for the twenty-eight-year-old Staffelkapitän of 1./KG 100, Oberleutnant Hansgeorg Bätcher, the allocation of this Kampfgruppe to the Crimea would have passed without any particular notice.

During one of his first days in Saki, the commander of I./KG 100 received a wire from Generaloberst Löhr: Air reconnaissance had spotted a seventy-five-hundred-ton Soviet tanker that was supplying the entire Soviet army at Kerch with fuel. Löhr demanded that this ship be destroyed, and he specially asked the commander of I./KG 100 to pick Oberleutnant Bätcher's crew for this task. As Bätcher recalls:

> Löhr had particularly mentioned which crew he wanted to fulfil this task, which was most uncommon. I gathered my crew quite undramatically and told them: "Tonight, boys, we're going to put this tanker underwater." We took off late at night and soon were closing in on Kerch. I decided to make one pass at high altitude to see if it was possible to make a high-altitude bombing run, and the Russians immediately opened a fierce fire. There was an enormous amount of Flak in the port. "It can't be done in this way," I told my crew, "We have to do it in another way." I flew out over the sea, went down to low altitude, almost skimming the waves, and turned around against Kerch again. Approaching the target area, I throttled back so the Russians wouldn't detect us from the sound of the engines, and, gliding in over the port, I caught sight of the tanker in front of me. I leaned toward my observer and said, "I'll release the bombs myself," since I figured I could make the best assessment in this situation. Flying straight toward the tanker, I gave full throttle and dropped the bombs. With roaring engines, my Heinkel passed above the tanker and out of the port area. My SC 500 bomb hit accurately, exploding amidships. And we managed to escape at high speed, before the Russians even managed to fire a single shot against us.

On Sunday January 24, 1942, III./JG 77's Leutnant Emil Omert wrote the following lines in his diary: "Low-level attacks against Russian field positions. Air combat with an I-15 and an R-5 during a fighter sweep. I shot down the I-15 and was credited with a probable victory against the R-5." Omert, who had celebrated his twenty-fourth birthday in Sarabuz nine days earlier, achieved his fortieth victory in this action and he was thus awarded the Knight's Cross. The photo was taken immediately after he landed following this successful sortie. Emil Omert achieved a total of seventy aerial victories before he was shot down and killed in combat with American heavy bombers over Romania on April 24, 1944. (Photo: Roba/Mombeek.)

The date for this incident has not been exactly established. The corresponding pages in Bätcher's flight book are missing, but according to German historians Ulf Balke and Georg Brütting, this mission took place on February 6.[78] Nevertheless, there is no mention of any bomb damage on any large vessel in this area in Soviet records for this date. It is possible that the tanker hit by Oberleutnant Bätcher was the *Emba*, which was severely damaged on January 29 by a German bomber at Kamysh-Burun, the port seven miles to the south of Kerch.

The airmen of I./KG 100 soon found their new mission to be most hazardous because a large antiaircraft artillery force had been brought into the area. "Those of us who were young did not pay much attention to this during those days," recalls Oberleutnant Bätcher. "We thought, 'Okay, things can go wrong,

The frequency of Luftwaffe missions over the Black Sea in 1942 called for an extensive air-sea rescue organization. The Dornier 24s of Seenotstaffel 8 aided the confidence of German airmen during these missions. The Do 24 was originally designed on request by the Netherlands, which needed modern floatplanes in the East Indies. For air-sea rescue operations, six bunks were installed for rescued personnel and medical equipment was added. The three BMW-Bramo Fafnir 1,000-horsepower nine-cylinder radial engines allowed the Do 24 to achieve a top speed slightly above 200 miles per hour while affording it a range of 2,920 miles. Armament normally consisted of two MG 15 machine guns – one each in the front and rear turrets – and a 20mm cannon in the central turret. (Photo: Roba/Mombeek.)

but so what!' But to the older officers, those of around 35 – 40 years old, it was absolutely terrible. They had great difficulties in coping with those sorties."

Adverse weather conditions brought flight activity to a minimum during I./KG 100´s first weeks in the Crimea. Thick fog on February 1 kept III./StG 77 from completing an operation against Soviet artillery positions on the Kerch Peninsula. Meanwhile, a weather-reconnaissance Bf 110 of 3.(F)/11 was listed as missing over the Straits of Kerch, probably shot down by 249 IAP's Mayor Petr Kozachenko, veteran of the wars in China and against Finland.

The new VVS-Crimean Front – formed on January 28 – started to transfer some of its units across the Straits of Kerch to makeshift airfields on the Kerch Peninsula. It should be emphasized that the bulk of VVS-Crimean Front was made up of obsolete Polikarpov fighters and SB bombers. A strong concentration of fighters – mainly from VVS-ChF – also was made at the Taman Peninsula to ward off the raids by I./KG 100 against the supply line across the straits.

Hansgeorg Bätcher recalls that whenever Soviet fighters intercepted the fliers of I./KG 100, things were "very rough." Although they often manned obsolete planes, the Soviet fighter pilots gave proof of "a splendid bravery" according to Bätcher: "Generally, they attacked nose-to-nose, but because of the high closing speed in such attacks, they were rarely able to score more than a few hits. On occasion, they also attempted to ram us, but I never saw any case when they succeeded in this."[79]

Apart from the achievements of Oberleutnant Bätcher, I./KG 100 in fact scored only limited successes during the first weeks of its operations against Soviet shipping. The Soviets managed to bring almost a hundred thousand troops and hundreds of artillery pieces across the Straits of Kerch between January 20 and February 11. On the latter date Reichsmarschall Göring ordered the dissolution of Sonderstab Krim. Another assignment awaited General von Greim – the command of the Luftwaffe in the central combat zone. Instead, the Luftwaffe units operating over the Crimea were brought under command of Oberst Wolfgang von Wild's Fliegerführer Süd.

In the small hamlet of Ivanovka, near Saki, where the crews of I./KG 100 were accommodated, the German airmen who were grounded by bad weather had ample time to establish contact with the inhabitants. What the men of I./KG 100 were not aware of in 1942 was that

The assignment of I./KG 100 to Saki Airdrome in the Crimea alarmed the Soviets and provoked intense countermeasures. Between February 18 and March 1, 1942, 350 to 400 bombs were dropped on the base during twenty individual Soviet night raids. But due to powerful antiaircraft artillery fire, most bombs fell scattered. Only one airplane was totally destroyed on the ground and three others were regarded as irrepairable. (Photo: Bätcher.)

Undoubtedly the most famous German bomber pilot throughout the entire war on the Eastern Front was Hansgeorg Bätcher, who in early 1942 served as an Oberleutnant and Staffelkapitän of 1./KG 100 Wiking in the Crimea. In the words of aviation historian Georg Brütting, Bätcher "became an institution, not only within the Bomber Air Arm, but also among the soldiers in all combat zones." Bätcher had once applied for the Fighter Arm, but he had been rudely turned down by his commanding officer, who asked him in a sarcastic tone: "Bätcher, now you are a soldier; since when have the soldiers been free to choose?" Nevertheless, as a bomber pilot, Bätcher succeeded in achieving a reputation normally reserved for fighter pilots, the "darlings of the Third Reich". In almost uninterrupted front-line service from 1939 to 1945, Hansgeorg Bätcher personally undertook 658 bomber sorties – the highest number among all Luftwaffe pilots during the entire war. Among all bomber airmen during the war, only a few Soviet night-bomber pilots managed to complete a higher number of missions. (Photo: Bätcher.)

information about this new German bomber unit streamed from Crimean civilians to the Red Army's intelligence service. From February 18 on, VVS-ChF initiated a prolonged series of air raids against German airfields in the Crimea, most notably those at Saki and Sarabuz. Until the end of February, Saki Airdrome alone was subjected to twenty-one air raids, albeit without any significant damage being dealt to I./KG 100.

After the war a pilot of I./KG 100 who had been shot down and captured by the Soviets told Bätcher that his captors had shown him a detailed "KG 100 information booklet," complete with portraits and biographical dates of most airmen in the unit.

With improved weather conditions during the last days of February, both sides used various countermeasures against each other. On February 20, eight He 111s of III./KG 27 struck the railway station at Ak Monay, reporting "four direct hits on a freight train, hits on the railway tracks, and good results against motor vehicles and troop concentrations."[80] On the return flight four to six Soviet fighters intercepted the bomber formation, which lost two He 111s.[81] Meanwhile, Oberleutnant Bätcher took off from Saki Airdrome for an armed reconnaissance over the Black Sea. Spotting what he reported to be "a loaded 2,000-ton freighter," it took Bätcher only a few passes to destroy the unfortunate ship, probably the 1,900-ton steamer *Kommunist*, which disappeared en route from Novorossiysk to Sevastopol.

On the German side, the effective Soviet fighter interception against the eight He 111s of III./KG 27 compelled Fliegerführer Süd to concentrate on counter-air activities. On February 21 the Bf 109 pilots of Stab and III./JG 77 made fifty-three individual combat sorties in fourteen missions – free hunting, escort missions, scrambles, and a low-level attack against the airfield at Sem Kolodesey – but the results were meager: There were no losses on either side, according to the daily report from Fliegerführer Süd,[82] or at best a single I-153 claimed by Stabsfeldwebel Georg Seckel, according to JG 77 records.[83] Next day, Stab and III./JG 77 carried out a low-level attack against the airfield at Bagerovo and claimed five MiG-3s and one I-15bis destroyed on the ground. On February 23 I./KG 100 dispatched five He 111s against Sevastopol,[84] and during the following night, Bätcher once again attacked the tanker in Kerch that he had damaged a few weeks earlier, inflicting additional damage.[85]

Taken as a whole, Soviet winter operations in the Crimea were rather successful, with land, naval, and air units sharing the success equally. German accounts tend to rationalize the Wehrmacht's setbacks in the Crimea in terms of adverse weather conditions, inadequate resources, and supply shortages, but this does not take into account that the Soviets were beset by the same problems. Despite immense difficulties, the Red Army managed not only to cross the Straits of Kerch and hold the positions, but also to expand the landing area and bring in considerable reinforcements.

Soviet forces of the Crimean Front were now preparing for what the Stavka hoped would be the decisive battle for the Crimea. But the increased Luftwaffe activity directed against the Soviet air forces on the Kerch Peninsula and shipping in the Black Sea did not bode well for the Soviet's projected and hoped for outcome.

Part III

Stalemate

The Ju 87s of Stab and III./StG 1, and I./StG 2, played an important role in containing the deep Soviet penetration in the seam between German army groups North and Center in February 1942. One Stuka pilot, III./StG 1's Leutnant Erich Hanne, single-handedly destroyed sixteen tanks, twenty-six field pieces and antiaircraft guns, two armored trains and four supply trains, five bridges, and nine pillboxes during this period.

A particularly successful attack against the Bologoye rail junction in February 1942 was conducted by a combination of He 111s and I./StG 2 Stukas. The horizontal bombers carried out their bomb run at an altitude of 9,000 feet, and the dive-bombers followed from three thousand feet higher. Since the Soviet antiaircraft artillery concentrated on the He 111s, and continued firing on them as they left the target area, the Ju 87s were totally undetected as they struck the rail junction. As a result, the target was reportedly totally destroyed. (Photo: Roba/Mombeek.)

Chapter 9

The Demyansk and Kholm Airlift Operations

In February 1942 the Soviet winter offensive was contained all along the Eastern Front as a result of Josef Stalin's fateful decision to disperse his resources throughout the front-line areas.

One of the most dangerous Soviet breakthroughs – the eighty-mile-wide gap that had been torn in the seam between German Army groups North and Center by the Soviet Third and Fourth Assault armies of the Northwestern Front – was halted by a combination of German ground reinforcements from Western Europe and relentless Luftwaffe attacks. Fliegerkorps I and Fliegerkorps VIII both committed bomber units to the hilt against the roads and railways used to supply the two Soviet armies.

With the arrival of the Ju 88s of Stab and I./KG 3, the He 111s of II./KG 4 and II./KG 27, and the Stukas of Stab and III./StG 1 to Fliegerkorps I, the German strike capacity in the northern combat zone was considerably increased. The rapid advance by the Soviet Third and Fourth Assault armies had stretched their supply lines to one hundred miles, and air raids dealt the final blow to their ability to advance farther.

Most Luftwaffe bombing missions in the northern sector were concentrated against the railroad from Bologoye to Ostashkov, the main supply base of the two Soviet assault armies. During the course of these interdiction operations, German airmen claimed the destruction of nine locomotives and seventy-seven railroad cars. German fliers also interdicted traffic at seventeen locations, seriously damaging the rail lines at six points and heavily damaging the railroad depots and surrounding track installations.[1] Largely as a result of these air operations, the advance of the Soviet Third Assault Army was bogged down through lack of supplies after it had reached a point twenty-five miles west of the Lovat River, in the sector between Demyansk and Kholm, and at Velikiye Luki farther to the south. Shortly afterward, the Soviet Fourth Assault Army met the same fate forty-five miles east of Vitebsk – deep in the operational area of Army Group Center – where its vanguard elements ran into fresh German reinforcements that had been brought in from occupied France.

In the meantime, to the north of Lake Ilmen, the Soviet Second Assault Army was halted west of the Volkhov River. The principal concern of German Army Group North was then shifted to the encircled 95,000 soldiers of its Sixteenth Army´s II and X corps at Demyansk, fifty miles southeast of Lake Ilmen, and to the 5,500 soldiers who were surrounded in a very small area around Kholm, some fifty miles farther to the southwest. A huge air supply operation had been initiated on January 20, two days after the Demyansk garrison had been surrounded.

Hitler instructed Lufttransportführer Oberst Fritz Morzik, the commander of the air transport fleet that had been deployed to the central combat zone in December 1941, to provide the two strongholds with airborne supplies. Morzik's mission was to deliver 300 tons of supplies per day – plus troop reinforcement – to the Demyansk pocket alone. With aircraft and crews pulled from transport aviation units and blind-flight schools in all parts of German-controlled Europe to reinforce his fleet, Morzik was able to muster 220 transport aircraft in only a few weeks. At the height of the operation, approximately 500 transport planes participated – grouped into I./KG 4, KGrzbV Oels (later KGrzbV 500), KGrzbV Posen (later IV./KGzbV 1), KGrzbV 4, KGrzbV 5, KGrzbV 6, KGrzbV 7, KGrzbV 9, KGrzbV 105, KGrzbV 172, KGrzbV 600, KGrzbV 700, KGrzbV 800, KGrzbV 900, KGrzbV 999, and II./KGzbV 1 (later KGrzbV 500). Most of these units were equipped with standard three-engine Ju 52 transports, but there also were some old Ju 86s (in KGrzbV 7), and even a few civilian Ju 90 and Fw 200 airliners arrived to supplement

German reinforcements prepare to board a four-engine Ju 90 to be flown into the Demyansk pocket. The desperate situation at Demyansk compelled the Germans to commandeer a number of four-engine Ju 90 and Fw 200 civilian airliners from Lufthansa, the German national airline. (Photo: Roba/Mombeek.)

Morzik's forces. The bulk of the transport fleet was concentrated to Demyansk. Only KGrzbV 5 and I./KG 4, equipped with He 111s rigged for transport duties, were primarily tasked to fly in supplies to Kholm.

Demyansk and Kholm constituted two serious thorns in the side of the entire Soviet operation in this sector – both were located on the two main roads in the area immediately to the south of Lake Ilmen – but the Soviet commanders expected these two garissons to collapse within a matter of days, and initially did not bother to dispatch their weak fighter forces against the air transport operation.

In the Demyansk sector the Luftwaffe controlled the skies. The Bf 109s of Hauptmann Josef Fözö's I./JG 51, in charge of providing the air bridge to Demyansk and Kholm with fighter support, hardly saw any Soviet air activity during this period. Instead, Hauptmann Fözö instructed his pilots to carry out fighter-bomber missions against the Soviet lines. Between January 20 and February 16, Oberleutnant Hans-Ekkehard Bob – Staffelkapitän of 9./JG 54, which had been allocated to this sector to supplement I./JG 51 – conducted twenty-three sorties over Demyansk. Only on one occasion did he encounter any Soviet planes in the air – and the four MiG-3s that he came across that day, February 6, made a quick escape.[2] All efforts by forces of Soviet Northwestern Front to break through in the Demyansk – Staraya Russa sector were faced with intense German air attacks.

Typical of the soaring combat spirits on the German side, Hauptmann Bruno Dilley, the commander of I./StG 2 Immelmann, took off despite a low cloud ceiling to carry out a lone dive-bombing sortie northwest of Demyansk on February 12. Flying at low altitude over the Soviet lines, Dilley's Ju 87 became an easy target for Soviet ground fire. When his Stuka was seriously hit in the engine, Hauptmann Dilley had no option but to make a forced landing on a snow-covered field behind the Soviet lines. The Ju 87 overturned in the deep snow and Dilley was knocked out. The radio operator, Oberfeldwebel Ernst Kather, pulled Dilley from the wreckage, and after three days the pair managed to reach the German lines at Demyansk.

Only in mid-February did VVS-Northwestern Front begin paying full attention to the airborne supply operation to Demyansk and Kholm. To the Soviets, it was

A German Gotha Go 242 glider. Since the 75-yard landing strip at Kholm made landing extremely hazardous, supplies for the German garrison there were mainly parachuted or flown in by Go 242 and DFS 230 gliders towed by He 111s. The first operational use of the German DFS 230 assault glider had stunned the world when a handful of paratroopers landed on top of the Belgian fortress Eben Emael on May 10, 1940, and seized this strategic stronghold within a few hours. The larger Go 242 cargo glider, which could lift twenty-one fully-equipped soldiers or equivalent freight, entered service in August 1941. (Photo: Roba/Mombeek.)

Bf 109 F-4 W.Nr. 7221, Oberleutnant Heinrich Krafft, Staffelkapitän 3./JG 51 Mölders, Soltsy, Soviet Union, February 1942

I./JG 51's Bf 109 F "Yellow 7" during a patrol over the Demyansk area in February 1942. This particular Bf 109 was the personal airplane of Oberleutnant Heinrich Krafft, the 3./JG 51 Staffelkapitän. "Gaudi" Krafft was among the top JG 51 aces. Under his command, 3./JG 51 lost only two pilots during the first seven months of the war on the Eastern Front. In the same period, Krafft scored thirty-eight victories – added to the four that he had achieved prior to Operation Barbarossa. On March 18, 1942, he was awarded with the Knight's Cross following his forty-sixth victory. (Photo: Trautloft.)

vital to seize these two communication centers before the approaching spring thaws, which would prevent all transport operations outside the main roads.

III./JG 3, which replaced 9./JG 54 when it was redeployed to the area north of Lake Ilmen in mid-February, arrived just as VVS-Northwestern Front initiated its operation against the Demyansk air lift. On February 18, III./JG 3 registered "repeated engagements with strong Russian ground-attack and fighter units."[3]

The men of III./JG 3 returned to the Eastern Front following two months of well-deserved rest in Germany, and they were eager to reenter combat. By the time they arrived back in the USSR, their Geschwader carried the name-of-honor of the famous World War I ace Ernst Udet, who had committed suicide in November 1941. III./JG 3 also was fully equipped with the latest Bf 109 version, the Bf 109 F-4, which was faster than the Bf 109 F-2 and armed with the new 20mm nose-mounted cannon instead of the 15mm weapon available in the Bf 109 F-2.

After the intense fighting on February 18, the three top aces in 9. Staffel – Oberleutnant Viktor Bauer, Oberfeldwebel Eberhard von Boremski, and Oberfeldwebel Georg Schentke – brought home four victories, all against "MiG-3s" (probably misidentified for LaGG-3s).[4] Bauer tallied his fortieth kill with a double victory.

VVS-Northwestern Front could muster no more than 142 serviceable aircraft – including 32 fighters – by February 19, but a substantial reinforcement was underway. After only a few more days, the two Jagdgruppen discovered that they were no longer able to prevent Soviet fighters from maintaining standing patrols over the Demyansk pocket. The first two Ju 52s to arrive on February 20 were shot down. The lumbering Ju 52s, making the trip in ones or twos, were easy targets for the Soviet fighters, and losses increased day by day. Four Ju 52s were shot down on February 23, and six Ju 52s and one He 111 were shot down on February 25.[5]

On the latter date, seven Ju 52s of KGrzbV 9 landed at the small airstrip at Kholm. After only a few minutes, they were attacked by Soviet planes that put four of the

Makarovo Airdrome, February 3, 1942. Starshiy Leytenant Ivan Struzhkin, the deputy commander of a 514 PBAP Eskadrilya and his Pe-2 crew have just returned from a combat operation. Struzhkin was one of most experienced pilots of 514 PBAP/VVS-Northwestern Front. He participated in combat at Khalkhin-Gol during the Winter War, and by February 1942 had carried out 123 combat sorties against the Germans. He was shot down and his entire crew was killed on April 6, 1942 – possibly by 9./JG 3's Leutnant Rolf Diergardt, who scored his fifth victory against a Pe-2 that day. On July 21, 1942, Struzhkin was posthumously appointed Hero of the Soviet Union. (Photo: Igashov/United State Museum of Tatarstan GOM RT.)

transports out of commission. This was the first and only attempt by German aircraft to land at Kholm. It also marked a new phase in VVS-Northwestern Front's operation against the air transports. From February 26 on, Soviet bombers launched heavy air attacks against Demyansk, operating at dawn and dusk. III./JG 3 shot down three of the VVS-Northwestern Front U-2 raiders (claimed as "R-5s") on February 26, but this did not prevent the Soviet airmen from knocking out five Ju 88s and one Ju 52 on the ground the following night and day. The landing strip at Demyansk was soon littered with the burned-out hulks of transport planes.

On March 1 the German Sixteenth Army reported severe losses as a result of VVS air attacks.

Notwithstanding adverse weather conditions, Soviet bombers took off at dawn on March 3 to attack a large number of Ju 52s on the ground at Staraya Russa. Returning later that day, the Soviet bombers caught a Ju 52 formation of I./KGzbV 172 as it was returning from a supply mission. Total Soviet claims for the day were ten German transports destroyed. On March 4 they reported another eleven destroyed, and four more on March 5. Between February 22 and March 10, VVS-Northwestern Front and VVS-Kalinin Front claimed the destruction of sixty Ju 52s. Thirty-nine of these claims are verified in German loss lists.

Injured German soldiers are loaded onto a KGrzbV 600 Ju 52 at the Demyansk airdrome in February 1942. Operating from Korovye-Selo, KGrzbV 600 lost sixteen Ju 52s during its flights to Demyansk during February and March 1942. The airplane shown here is probably BR+AQ, which – piloted by Oberfeldwebel Gerhard Schulz – was shot down by Soviet fighters on February 28, 1942. (Photo: Roba/Mombeek.)

During these critical days, the German defenders at Demyansk and Kholm were able to hold out solely because of further intensified Luftwaffe raids against Soviet troops and supply lines. A particularly heavy burden was laid on I./KG 4, whose crews were committed to both supply missions to Kholm and close-support sorties. During the four days between March 6 and March 9, Fliegerkorps I aircraft completed 935 sorties and dropped 1,024 tons of bombs in this area.[6]

In mid-March, the focus of the battle shifted northward to the area between Lake Ilmen and Lake Ladoga. Here, the Soviet Second Assault Army still held a narrow, almost fifty-mile-deep, wedge into the German lines to the west of the Volkhov River. Although the Second Assault Army had been halted short of its goals – surrounding parts of the German Eighteenth Army and breaking the siege of Leningrad – the penetration constituted a Soviet success. This salient in the German Eighteenth Army's sector at Lyuban posed a serious threat to the supply routes to German troops south of Leningrad and on the northern sector of the front line along the Volkhov River. It also tied up considerable German resources, including both air and ground forces.

In this sector the VVS for the first time adopted the Luftwaffe's flexible tactic of concentrating large ad hoc forces to a certain area. Early in March the Stavka had assigned General-Leytenant Aleksandr Novikov the task of organizing a combined air force action in the area between Lakes Ilmen and Ladoga. Novikov was authorized to command units of the air forces of the Leningrad and Volkhov fronts, as well as parts of the long-range aviation. To further strengthen this force, eight aviation regiments from the Stavka reserve were attached to Novikov's ad hoc command.

With Novikov and the new commander of the long-range aviation, General-Mayor Aleksandr Golovanov, by his side, the Soviet Air Force dispatched two of its most formidable commanders to this sector. Their first mission was to organize massive air strikes against the German positions surrounding the Second Assault Army in the Lyuban wedge from March 10 through March 20.

On March 12 General-Mayor Ivan Fedyuninskiy's Soviet Fifty-fourth Army, launched an offensive from the southern shore of Lake Ladoga, with the intention of linking with the Second Assault Army and thus sealing off six German divisions in the Chudovo area of the Volkhov sector. To support this drive, Novikov grouped the eight aviation regiments from the Stavka reserve – 92 IAP, 160 IAP, 293 IAP, 484 IAP, 175 ShAP, 565 ShAP, 35 BBAP, 771 BBAP, and a group of twenty DB-3Fs – into a unified command under General-Mayor Sergey Rudenko. The Novaya Ladoga Aviation Groupment of VVS-KBF, including 4 GIAP/VVS-KBF, also participated in this operation.

On the first day of the offensive, Leytenant Vasiliy Golubev, recently appointed to command 3 Eskadrilya of 4 GIAP/VVS-KBF, was returning from an early combat mission in his I-16 Ishak when he spotted a Bf 109 Rotte flying at tree-top level close to his base. The 109s probably were waiting to pick off Soviet aircraft as they were landing. Several pilots and the whole ground staff watched the sky as Golubev shot down both Bf 109s, which crashed in the snow just outside the airfield. The German commander's aircraft was totally burned out, but on the rudder of the wingman's aircraft, the Soviets could count twenty-six victory marks. The pilot, probably Unteroffizier Hans Schwartzkopf of 1./JG 54, bled to death from his wounds as he tried to escape from the Soviets.

Major Hannes Trautloft (left) and his wingman, Oberleutnant Otto Kath, rest on a horse-drawn sleigh in front of the former's Bf 109 F at Relbitsy Airdrome in early March 1942, when the northern combat zone was still covered with snow. On the spring equinox of 1942, the thermometer in Relbitsy registered minus-25 degrees Celsius. In early March, Trautloft was severely disturbed by an acute toothache. This tough fighter pilot in fact feared dentists, but these problems did not interfere with his duties as Geschwaderkommodore. Trautloft and Kath both survived the war, the former with fifty-seven and the latter with six victories. (Photo: Trautloft.)

March 13 saw a number of fierce encounters between some of the most skilled aces of both sides in this area. JG 54's Major Hannes Trautloft describes a difficult encounter with what appears to have been the pilots of Vasiliy Golubev's Eskadrilya: "[Oberleutnant Otto] Kath and I engage six Ratas at an altitude of 6,000 feet above the penetration area at Pogostye. We whirl around for twenty minutes without being able to achieve any success. On the contrary, we have to fight hard to defend ourselves. The Russian squadron proves to be most skillful, vigilant, and aggressive. We are soaked with sweat as we land."[7]

Leytenant Vasiliy Golubev (left), the commander of 4 GIAP/VVS-KBF's 3 AE, and Starshiy Leytenant Petr Kozhanov, his political commissar, in early 1942. A number of unfortunate incidents in the winter of 1941-1942 culminated in a command reorganization, and the regiment's operations ran more smoothly from that point. Between March 12 and April 13, 1942, the regiment claimed fifty-four aerial victories against only two pilots lost. Although this is a considerable exaggeration of actual achievements – included in the Soviet claims are twenty-seven single-engine fighters, whereas only fifteen Bf 109s are known to have been destroyed or severely damaged in 4 GIAP/VVS-KBF's zone of operations during the same period – it is indicative of the soaring combat spirits among the naval pilots in this unit. Golubev and Kozhanov were among the top fighter aces in this famous regiment. Golubev survived the war with a total of sixteen personal and twenty-three shared kills to his credit. Kozhanov amassed thirteen victories on five hundred combat sorties by the time he was shot down and killed on May 5, 1943.
(Photo: 4 GIAP/VVS-VMF Museum.)

Five Ishaks of 3 Eskadrilya, 4 GIAP/VVS-KBF, took part in the combat over Pogostye, from which Starshiy Leytenant Petr Kozhanov returned with claims of two Bf 109s shot down. One Soviet pilot was killed when his damaged I-16 overturned during a forced landing.

An equally even and drawn-out combat was fought between four Bf 109s of 9./JG 54 and three P-40s of 154 IAP on the same day. In the heat of the combat, the Messerschmitt pilot Oberleutnant Wilhelm Schilling[8] and the Soviets[9] made one unsubstantiated claim apiece. (The Soviet victory was shared between aces Mayor Petr Pilyutov and Kapitan Andrey Chirkov.) A few minutes later, the same three Tomahawk pilots engaged a formation of five Ju 87s escorted by nine Bf 109s and reported the destruction of a Stuka – which also cannot be found in German loss records.

While experienced Soviet unit commanders managed to compensate for the disadvantages of aircraft inferior to the Bf 109, the German fighter pilots were able to score substantially against VVS pilots led by less able unit commanders.

Bf 109 F-4, Major Hannes Trautloft, Geschwaderkommodore, JG 54 Grünherz, Relbitsy, Soviet Union, early March 1942

One of the most successful tactics adopted by the Bf 109 aces was simply to patrol above the Soviet airdromes. Starshiy Leytenant Aleksandr Silantyev of the LaGG-3-equipped 160 IAP recalls March 1942 as a most difficult period:

> The Germans blocked our airfields... They flew in pairs, particularly near the fighter regiment's airdromes at Gremyachevo, Serebrennitsa, and Budogoshch... It's hard to talk about this today, but our commander took no counteractive measures to counter the blockade of our airfields... Our passivity encouraged the German pilots, and they became most impudent. . . . We paid a high price for poor command planning... On one of those days I witnessed the death of Kapitan Tikhomirov [41 IAP] over the airfield at Gremyachevo. He was returning to base after completing a mission and was out of ammunition when the hunters fell upon him. Tikhomirov was a very skillful and experienced pilot, but without any ammunition there wasn't much he could do against the Me 109 hunters.[10]

On March 13 Starshiy Leytenant Boris Zamyshlyayev, an ace in 185 IAP with seven individual and fifteen shared victories, was attacked by Bf 109s just as he was taking off from the airfield near Malaya Vishera, east of the Volkhov River. The Soviet pilot had no chance at all; he died in the flames of his burning MiG-3. II./JG 54's Hauptmann Dietrich Hrabak and Oberleutnant Joachim Wandel returned from that mission with three victory claims in all.

JG 54 claimed thirty-three kills against three losses on March 12, 13, and 14, while the veterans of 4 GIAP/VVS-KBF claimed fifteen victories against only one pilot lost.

From March 15, when the German Eighteenth Army blunted the Soviet counteroffensive from the north by launching an attack against the Lyuban wedge, the air war in this sector was further intensified. JG 54 claimed fifteen aerial victories without loss on March 15, and twenty-three against one loss the following day. Oberleutnant Wolfgang Späte of II. Gruppe was credited with three R-5 or R-Z biplanes transporting supplies to the Second Assault Army,[11] and a Yak-1 ended up as Major Hannes Trautloft´s thirtieth kill. Three days later, a Soviet plane shot down by Oberleutnant Max-Hellmuth Ostermann brought the total victory score for III./JG 54 to five hundred.[12] On March 19 the Gruppenkommandeur of III./JG 54, Knight's Cross holder Hauptmann Reinhard Seiler, added two victories to this total but was himself shot down. Seiler survived a forced landing and was soon back in action.[13]

Although the Grünherz fighters did not succeed in clearing the skies of Soviet aircraft, the bombers and Stukas of Fliegerkorps I were able to deliver significant assistance to the German ground operations. Between March 13 and March 19, a total of 1,561 Luftwaffe sorties were carried out and 1,616 tons of bombs were dropped in this small area. As a result of these air operations, the Eighteenth Army was able to close the bulge in the rear of Soviet Second Assault Army in what came to be known as the "Lyuban Pocket."

The Soviet situation in this area of operations grew increasingly desperate. Although half a million civilians were evacuated from the starving city of Leningrad across the Ice Road from January until the spring, the besieged city remained a virtual death camp. Thousands of people succumbed to famine every day. It is estimated that 300,000 people died from starvation alone in January and February 1942.[14] The total death toll for the siege of Leningrad, to the spring of 1942, is estimated at the horrendous figure of one million.

The troops of the Soviet Second Assault Army, who had made such a courageous attempt to relieve tormented Leningrad, were now caught in a death trap. An airlift operation began, but the means available were hopelessly inadequate. The only aircraft that could be used to fly supplies to the marshlands and deep forests west of the Volkhov River by this time were R-5s and U-2s, which landed on makeshift landing strips. The 460 tons of provisions brought in by biplane pilots in March was far from sufficient.

Poorly equipped Soviet airmen of fighter and ground-attack units fought desperately to alter the situation. On March 21 a force of LaGG-3s from 3 GIAP and Il-2s from 313 ShAP managed to catch the Stukas of 5./StG 2 by surprise as they were about to land after a combat sortie. Within a matter of minutes, six of the new Ju 87 Ds were destroyed or heavily damaged.[15] In general, however, the VVS fliers managed to inflict only limited losses on the Luftwaffe north of Lake Ilmen – which is evident even by the inflated victory claims made by the Soviets: From February 22 through March 21, VVS-Leningrad Front and VVS-KBF reported no more than seventy-two enemy aircraft shot down, including a number of Finnish planes.

The situation was different to the south of Lake Ilmen, where the main part of Fliegerkorps I was concentrated from March 21 in order to support the attempt of the German Sixteenth Army to establish a ground link with Demyansk. Contrary to the assessment in most Western accounts of the air war over Demyansk,

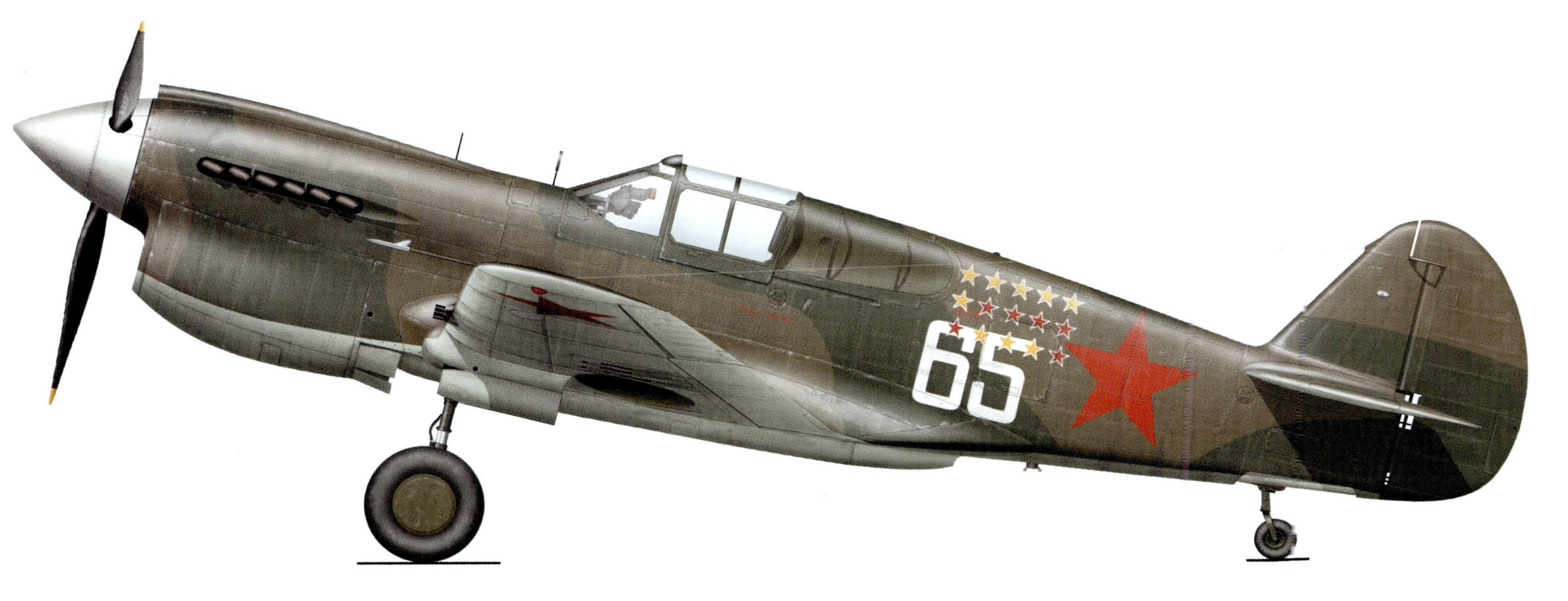

Curtiss P-40E Kittyhawk, Podpolkovnik Aleksandr Matveyev, commander of 154 IAP of General-Mayor Vasiliy Zhdanov's Aviation Group/VVS-Leningrad Front, Plekhanovo, Soviet Union, summer 1942

This P-40E was delivered by the British and thus carries standard RAF camouflage pattern. Matveyev led Mayor Petr Pilyutov and Kapitan Andrey Chirkov in combat against Oberleutnant Hans-Ekkehard Bob's 9./JG 54 at around 1000 hours on March 13, 1942.

Krasnogvardeysk, March 31, 1942. Hauptmann Hans Philipp returns from the sortie on which he claimed his ninety-ninth and one hundredth victories. When "Fips" Philipp left the Eastern Front for home leave in late 1941, he was JG 54's most successful fighter pilot. He returned to his unit in mid-January 1942 and experienced a new peak of successes. In February he was appointed Gruppenkommandeur of I. Gruppe, and on March 12 he became the first JG 54 pilot to be awarded the Swords to the Oak Leaves. Philipp achieved a total of 206 victories before he was killed in combat with American Thunderbolt fighters over Germany on October 8, 1943. (Photo: Trautloft.)

the Soviet fighter pilots there proved themselves to be highly motivated and skilled. Well aware of the terrible state of affairs in Leningrad, these pilots were determined to deal out the same suffering to the surrounded Germans at Demyansk and Kholm, and hunted the transport aircraft ferociously. Whereas historian Von Hardesty wrote about "the aenemic state of the Soviet fighter aviation in the winter of 1941 – 42,"[16] the following lines from Hannes Trautloft's diary entry for March 23, 1942, speak another language: "We have the impression that French pilots are flying with the Russians now. In the last days we have noticed a completely new tactic adopted by the enemy fighters [in the Demyansk sector]. They have stopped flying stubbornly close to each other. Instead, they guard each other mutually. Now and then one of these guys makes a roll, just as we have seen the French and the Tommies do. And the Russians have also grown more aggressive. One has to be damned alert!"

There were no French pilots in service with the Soviet Air Force at this stage of the war, but Trautloft's suspicion reflects the improved VVS tactics in the spring of 1942. If there is any substance in Trautloft's theory that non-Soviet pilots were in action with the VVS, it might have originated from the fact that three Spanish pilots served in the Demyansk area at that time. During the spring of 1942, three of the Spaniards who had been left behind in the USSR as the Spanish Civil War ended joined the Hurricane-equipped 964 IAP/PVO. Starshiy Leytenant Antonio Arias, appointed commander of that regiment's 2 Eskadrilya, had achieved at least fifteen aerial victories during the Spanish Civil War.

Twenty-three Ju 52s were shot down between March 17 and March 25.[17] On the latter date, only nine of the crews assigned to I./KG 4 in January remained alive. "Most crews carried out between 130 and 140 combat sorties during this period," according to one of the KG 4 pilots.[18]

While the bulk of the Soviet fighters were engaged in free hunting against the German transport planes, other tasks, such as providing bombers and ground-attack planes with escorts, were largely neglected. This inevitably resulted in an increase in losses among the latter. On March 26, for instance, only Starshiy Politruk S. D. Antipov returned from a three-plane formation that had been dispatched by 299 ShAP; the two other Il-2s were shot down by JG 54 Bf 109s. Nevertheless, the most experienced Il-2 fliers could strike back, which was demonstrated by Starshiy Serzhant Vasiliy Ryaboshapko of the same unit, who shot down two enemy aircraft – a Bf 110 on March 26 and another on March 28.[19]

III./JG 3 Udet was dealt a severe blow on March 28, when 7. Staffel engaged a formation of LaGG-3s southeast of Staraya Russa. The Udet pilots claimed five of their adversaries, but in doing so they lost two Bf 109s. Both pilots, who were reported as missing, were among the best of the Gruppe – Leutnant Eckhardt Hübner, credited with forty-seven victories, and Feldwebel Rudolf Berg, victor in seventeen engagements. In return, III./JG 3 claimed thirteen Soviet aircraft shot down that day. On March 31 Hauptmann Hans Philipp, commanding I./JG 54, brought home his ninety-ninth and one-hundredth victories, becoming the fourth pilot to reach the magical "100-mark".

By far the most intense air battle on the Eastern Front so far was being waged in the northern combat zone. The fact that Fliegerkorps I carried out more than 3,115 sorties on the Demyansk front in the last ten days of March 1942, dropping 3,316 tons of bombs, provides proof of the intensity of the air war in this sector.[20] Approximately half of the aircraft losses suffered by both sides on the entire Eastern Front in March 1942 occurred on the northern combat zone. Out of ninety-nine Luftwaffe aircraft lost on combat missions due to enemy activity or "unknown reasons" in the northern combat zone during March, fifty-four were Ju 52 transports.[21] Throughout the month the fighter units under command of Luftflotte 1 – III./JG 3, I./JG 51, and JG 54 – tallied 3,865 sorties and claimed 359 Soviet aircraft for the loss of 15 Bf 109s in combat.[22] These victories were divided as follows: 197 in the Volkhov-Leningrad area (155 fighters and 42 bombers) and 162 (128 fighters and 34 bombers) in the Demyansk-Kholm area. In operations in the latter sector, VVS-Northwestern Front recorded 110 aircraft (77 fighters and 33 bombers and Shturmoviks) lost in combat during March 1942.[23]

The bombers of Luftflotte 1 carried out 9,075 sorties in March 1942, during which 8,169 tons of bombs were dropped. Among the resultant totals for these missions was the destruction of 3,151 rail wagons. Luftflotte 1 recorded twelve bombers and eight Stukas lost,[24] but Generalquartiermeister der Luftwaffe files nineteen bombers and seven Stukas lost due to enemy action or "unknown reasons" in the northern combat zone in March 1942.[25] During the same period, VVS-Volkhov Front carried out 7,673 combat sorties, dropping 984 tons of bombs and claiming 99 German aircraft destroyed, approximately half of them on the ground.

Fighter pilot Aleksey Maresyev continued to fly combat missions with two artificial legs fifteen months after the unfortunate incident in April 1942 in which he spent nineteen days in the wilderness after being shot down. He scored his first victories while flying with the artificial legs during the air battles over Kursk in the summer of 1943. Maresyev ended the war with eleven kills. (Photo: Seidl.)

The month of April opened with intense Soviet air activity over the Demyansk battlefield. III./JG 3 chalked up fourteen victories on April 1 alone.[26] Two days later, Starshiy Serzhant Vasiliy Ryaboshapko, the Shturmovik ace of 299 ShAP, was killed when he collided with an Il-2 from 567 ShAP while returning from his twenty-seventh combat sortie.[27] Ryaboshapko was appointed Hero of the Soviet Union posthumously.

To bolster Soviet aerial assets, the Stavka organized six aviation regiments equipped with modern aircraft into the special aviation group 6 UAG, which was deployed to the Demyansk sector on March 30.[28] The airmen of 6 UAG immediately became involved in costly encounters with the pilots of JG 3 Udet, JG 51 Mölders, and JG 54 Grünherz. On April 4, nine Soviet aircraft were claimed by III./JG 3, including three MiG-3s by Leutnant Wilhelm Lemke and a LaGG-3 by Oberleutnant Viktor Bauer, his fiftieth kill.

Following one of the melees with III./JG 3 on April 4, Leytenant Aleksey Maresyev of 580 IAP had a remarkable experience. After downing two Ju 52s as they were taking off from a German airfield, Maresyev was jumped by ten Bf 109s. He tried to evade the attack, but his Yak-1 was hit by 20mm shells from a Bf 109 F 4 and went out of control. Maresyev's last memory was of a line of pine trees racing to meet him. When he came to, he found himself lying in deep snow. Both his legs were shattered.

Despite his injuries and the bitter cold, Maresyev survived in the wilderness for nineteen days. His only food consisted of a hedgehog that he was lucky to catch and a few frozen berries. Finally the half-dead airman was found by a detachment of Soviet partisans, who provided him with first aid, food, and warm clothing. The partisans radioed a message to their headquarters in Soviet-held territory, and Starshiy Leytenant Andrey Dekhtyarenko, Maresyev's Eskadrilya commander, soon arrived in a U-2 at an improvised landing strip in the forest to pick up his squadron-mate. The injured pilot was immediately flown to a military hospital in Moscow. There the doctors found that gangrene had set in, and they had to amputate both Maresyev's legs below the knee. For all that, Maresyev would return to front service the following year with two artificial legs and would take part as a fighter pilot in the battle of Kursk in 1943.

From the first week of April 1942 Lufttransportführer Oberst Morzik shifted tactics, abandoning single- and two-plane flights to the surrounded troops. The transports now started flying in large formations provided with heavy fighter cover, and this reduced losses considerably. Even though I. and III./JG 54 were assigned to the Leningrad sector and III./JG 3 was returned to Germany to reequip for the coming German summer offensive, Hauptmann Josef

Fözö's I./JG 51 and Hauptmann Dietrich Hrabak's II./JG 54 were quite sufficient to escort the transports. On April 5 one of Hrabak's best men, Oberleutnant Wolfgang Späte, brought down five Soviet fighters in two sorties – taking his victories to seventy-four.[29] Next day the Bf 109s escorted 360 Ju 52 sorties to and from Demyansk without a single loss. On the contrary, I./JG 51 and II./JG 54 claimed ten of the Soviet fighters that attempted to intercept the transports.

On April 8 Starshiy Leytenant Andrey Dekhtyarenko of 580 IAP reported the downing of four Ju 52s – and three Ju 52s were registered lost by KGrzbV 800 and 900 that day – the last success of its kind achieved by Soviet fighters against the Demyansk transports. At approximately this time, the VVS fighter pilots had to shift their attention to support of the ground troops of Northwestern Front, who were fighting hard against the German counteroffensive aimed at relieving Demyansk. Thus, during the remainder of April no more than five Ju 52s were lost to enemy action.

The German ground operation aimed at the relief of the Demyansk pocket made only very slow progress against tenacious Soviet resistance. Heavy thaws and resulting deep mud were a large obstacle to troop movements and caused the number of sorties carried out by Luftflotte 1 to drop by 40 percent between March and April.

It was only on April 20 that a small breach was opened into the "Demyansk fortress." The land corridor would remain very narrow and under constant Soviet artillery bombardment for a considerable period, so the large-scale airlift operations had to be continued for another month. In early May the Germans opened a land connection with the Kholm garrison.

Since several Luftflotte 1 units operated from better-equipped airdromes than those available to Luftwaffe units farther to the south, their operations were not terribly afflicted by the spring thaw. During the month of April Luftflotte 1 carried out a total of 5,859 sorties, air transport flights not included. III./JG 3, I./JG 51, and JG 54 claimed 261 Soviet aircraft shot down[30] against the loss of ten Bf 109s.[31] Throughout the spring of 1942 the German horizontal bombers and Stukas were committed primarily against Soviet lines of communication and troop concentrations, and they claimed the destruction of 2,764 rail wagons in April alone.

VVS-Northwestern Front registered 168 combat losses in April 1942.[32] VVS-Volkhov Front was nearly bled white during the fierce spring fighting; no more than approximately 160 serviceable Soviet combat aircraft – most of them U-2, R-5, and R-Z biplane night bombers – remained east of the Volkhov River. But the surviving Soviet airmen continued to put up a hard and increasingly skillful fight.

On April 20 Leytenant Ivan Likhobabin of VVS-Northwestern Front´s 402 IAP opened his victory account by claiming two Bf 109s near Staraya Russa, jointly with his regimental commander. Likhobabin would reach a score of five kills (including shared victories) before the end of the month.[33]

"From my own experience and numerous accounts by my pilots, I could note that the Russian fighter pilots had learned a great deal," wrote Major Trautloft in his diary on May 1. "Our aerial victories were achieved in increasingly hard combats. The Russians have become better fliers, more aggressive, and more alert."[34] That day, two Bf 109 pilots of 9./JG 54 were listed as missing following a combat with Soviet fighters near Leningrad.

Among the toughest opponents to Luftflotte 1 by this time was 485 IAP, which was led by the able Mayor Georgiy Zimin. Zimin, a bold innovator of new tactics, spurred his fighter pilots on and taught them to operate aggressively in the Schwarm-Rotte tactic adopted from the Germans. On May 7, the day after the men of 485 IAP had celebrated their commander´s thirtieth birthday, seven of these Hurricane pilots intercepted four German bombers and two Bf 109s in the Kirilovshchina-Domashi area near Demyansk. And they claimed one He 111 and two Ju 88s without loss.[35]

Soviet Hurricane pilots on alert. Mayor Georgiy Zimin, commander of the Hurricane-equipped 485 IAP in 1942, once characterized the Hurricane as follows: "It was an excellent aircraft for tourist flights above a picturesque country. But unfortunately we were forced to appraise it from another position." Notwithstanding this pronouncement in 1942, Zimin's 485 IAP became the most successful Hurricane unit – probably in all air forces. It was credited with sixteen victories against seven losses through April 1942, and fifty-four victories against seven losses through May 1942. (Photo: Seidl.)

A German ammunition train at Volosovo railroad station is strafed by VVS-KBF fighter-bombers. (Photo: 4 GIAP/VVS-VMF Museum.)

Three hours later, 485 IAP came across four Ju 88s and bagged one of them.[36]

Also on May 7 four Il-2 pilots of 299 ShAP reported a major success during an airstrike against Demyansk Airdrome – nine German planes destroyed on the ground, plus a Ju 52 (credited to Starshina Ivan Vovkogon) shot down in the air. Actually destroyed were two KGrzbV 500 Ju 52s. On May 8 Zimin's pilots claimed three Ju 88s and two Bf 109s shot down for the loss of one Hurricane.[37] During another encounter on May 8, 580 IAP's Starshiy Leytenant Andrey Dekhtyarenko claimed two He 111s and two Bf 109s while escorting Il-2s south of Lake Ilmen.

The Geschwaderkommodore of JG 54, Major Hannes Trautloft, and his wingman, Oberleutnant Otto Kath, had an encounter with what may have been Zimin´s Hurricanes on May 9. First the two German pilots attempted to intercept six Soviet bombers, but eight escort fighters drove the pair off. After a while, the Germans spotted another formation – three bombers and only one fighter – and attacked. Trautloft had just scored hits on one of the bombers, and was closing in to deal the coup de grace, when his earphones seemed to explode: "Break off! Break off! Turn left," Kath cried over the R/T.

A flight of Soviet fighters raced in from the right. Instead of turning left, Trautloft veered his Bf 109 to the opposite side. In the next moment, he flashed through the Soviet formation, then he pushed his stick forward and dove away – his speedometer showed 470 miles per hour – while Kath also disengaged from the red-starred fighters. Six Hurricane pilots of 485 IAP returned to base and filed a report of an engagement with three Bf 109s, of which one was claimed by Mladshiy Leytenant Bakharyov. Trautloft managed to pay them back some minutes later when he spotted a lone Pe-2 above Demyansk Airdrome and promptly shot it down – his fortieth victory.

To the north of Lake Ilmen, Oberleutnant Max-Hellmuth Ostermann, one of the most formidable aces in JG 54, was lucky to survive being shot down by a Soviet fighter on May 10, shortly after he had achieved his ninety-eighth victory. On May 11 five pilots of 4./JG 54 escorting an Hs 126 were intercepted by five 485 IAP Hurricanes. Although the Bf 109 F was vastly superior to the old Hurricane, it took a prolonged and stiff combat before Leutnant Hermann Leiste managed to shoot down Serzhant Gorodnichiy, who bailed out. Then the 4./JG 54 fliers chose to disengage rather than risk losing one of their own to these formidable opponents.

On May 12 Oberleutnant Ostermann scored his one-hundredth kill – but he was also shot down again, and this time injured by shrapnel from a shell. Next day JG 54 filed 8 victory claims – bringing its total to 2,222 since the beginning of the war – but 9. Staffel's Oberleutnant Hokan von Bülow and his wingman both went missing.

Upon his return from his May 9, 1942, combat flight, Major Hannes Trautloft celebrates his fortieth victory. His face still carries signs of the harsh air combat that he and Oberleutnant Otto Kath had had with what possibly were Hurricanes of Mayor Georgiy Zimin's 485 IAP. (Photo: Trautloft.)

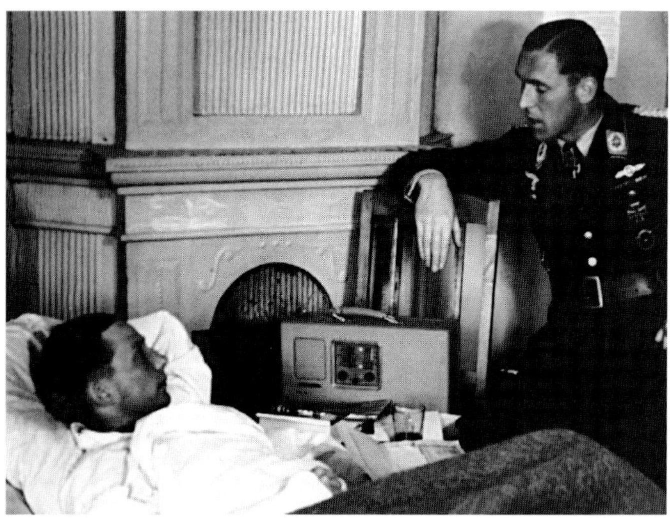

Oberleutnant Max-Hellmuth Ostermann is visited in hospital by his Geschwaderkommodore, Major Hannes Trautloft, in May 1942. On May 12, Ostermann was shot down for the second time in only three days, and this time he was injured. Only five days later, when he was awarded the Swords to his Oak Leaves, the ceremony took place in the hospital. After recovering from his injuries he was allowed a long home leave. In late summer 1942 Ostermann returned to first-line service and was shot down and killed in combat with a Soviet fighter shortly thereafter. (Photo: Trautloft.)

On May 16 Feldwebel Gerhard Lautenschläger, a 33-victory ace in 3./JG 54, was shot down and killed in combat with Curtiss P-40s. That his wingman, Leutnant Walter Nowotny, managed to destroy the P-40 on the tail of Lautenschläger's doomed Bf 109 could not outweigh the loss of such a formidable flier.

Around May 20 the bulk of the transport units were transferred to other areas, leaving three Gruppen to continue air supply operations to Demyansk until October 1942. By the end of May 1942 14,455 air transport sorties were carried out, 24,303 tons of weapons and supplies and 15,446 reinforcement soldiers were delivered and 22,093 injured flown out, which helped the surrounded German troops to hold out but only barely.

Historian Edgar Röhricht explains the grim realities of the Demyansk and Kholm airlift operations: "Even though 100 to 150 aircraft were committed, flying two or three daily missions, the supply situation deteriorated rapidly, leading to symptoms of malnutrition among the exhausted troops. The use of ammunition, particularly by the artillery units, had to be limited to a minimum, which resulted in increased losses. Even after the establishment of a land corridor, a large part of the supplies had to be flown in."[38]

A total of 265 transport aircraft were destroyed or severely damaged from all causes during the airlift operations to Demyansk and Kholm from February through May 1942, including 125 total losses due to enemy action or unknown reasons – 106 Ju 52s, 17 He 111s, and 2 Ju 86s. In addition, 387 airmen were lost.

VVS-Northwestern Front filed 408 aircraft losses, including 243 fighters, on operations from February through May 1942;[39] and the battle in the Demyansk sector between January 7 and May 20 cost Northwestern Front a staggering total of 245,511 casualties (the initial force was 105,700 troops).[40]

This photo illustrates the chaotic situation at Demyansk in early 1942. The upper aircraft, piloted by Unteroffizier Günther Vogel of KGrzbV 105, was damaged by Soviet fighters just as it was approaching to land at Demyansk, and it crashed into another Ju 52. Both aircraft were repaired and brought back into action. Unteroffizier Vogel's crew failed to return from a sortie to Stalingrad on December 7, 1942. (Photo: Roba/Mombeek.)

Ju 52/3m, Unteroffizier Günther Vogel, KGrzbV 105, Eastern Front, early 1942

Without doubt, the battles of Demyansk and Kholm were an important German success that possibly saved the entire situation for the Wehrmacht in this sector in 1942. It is beyond question that the Luftwaffe played the key role in this success. The airlift operation was one of the three most successful German air transport ventures during the entire war, together with the assaults against Norway in 1940 and Crete in 1941. It should nevertheless be pointed out that Oberst Morzik's forces enjoyed the advantage of large and well-equipped air bases in the Baltic countries that were linked directly to the Luftwaffe's infrastructure in Germany. This factor was not present during the next large-scale airborne operation – at Stalingrad – during the following winter.

It is also clear that the air force of the Soviet Northwestern Front had performed better than most accounts originating outside the former Eastern Bloc would indicate. The entire German air transport fleet was in fact heading for a complete breakdown due to the disastrous losses inflicted by Soviet airmen during the initial phase. Only through the combination of a reinforced German fighter presence in the area and radically altered tactics during the transport flights were the Germans able to maintain the air bridge.

The long-term consequences of the airlift to Demyansk and Kholm were quite serious, as historian Williamson Murray points out: "Unfortunately for the Luftwaffe, it had never possessed the resources to build a sizeable independent transport force; rather a significant percentage of transport aircraft served to transition future bomber pilots from single- to multi-engine aircraft. Thus, the only way to build up airlift capability for emergency situations like Demyansk or Stalingrad was to strip training establishments of instructors, pupils, and aircraft; in other words, to shut schools down. But the losses in training resources, particularly in instructor pilots, were not only irreplaceable but were enormous in their cumulative impact."[41]

In this way, the airlift operation to Demyansk must be regarded, after all, as a Pyrrhic accomplishment for the Luftwaffe.

Chapter 10

Target: Red Banner Baltic Fleet

In addition to its many responsibilities on and behind the battlefronts along the Volkhov River and in the Demyansk-Kholm area, Generaloberst Alfred Keller's Luftflotte 1 was committed against Soviet warships in the Gulf of Finland from the early spring of 1942 onward. The powerful Soviet Red Banner Baltic Fleet remained largely intact after the first year of war. An intense and relatively successful Stuka offensive had been made against these vessels in the port of the fortress island of Kronstadt in the Gulf of Finland in September 1941, but the damage dealt to the ships was not sufficient to take out their heavy guns, which continued to take a bloody toll among the German troops who besieged Leningrad. These potent warships also constituted a potential death threat to German ships crossing the Baltic Sea to Finland.

Because of this, and not the least due to political considerations, Keller was instructed to neutralize this threat before the ice that locked the Soviet ships into their base during the winter broke up. Since the Neva River in Leningrad, to which the KBF vessels had been transferred, was too shallow to actually sink any of the targeted ships, the vessels had to be bombed to pieces. The mission was given the code name Eisstoss – Ice Thrust.

After scrupulous preparations, including several photo-reconnaissance sorties, Keller dispatched his forces on the evening of April 4, 1942. More than one hundred aircraft from KG 1, KG 4, StG 2, and JG 54 joined together in a single concentration, the largest Luftwaffe formation to appear in the sky above Leningrad since the fall of 1941.

VVS-KBF scrambled its 3 GIAP, 4 GIAP, and 71 IAP, while Leningrad PVO dispatched 26 IAP against the raid. But the Soviet fighters were caught by the escorting Bf 109s at a lower altitude and suffered heavily without being able to deal the raiders any losses. During the drawn out air combat, JG 54 claimed twenty Soviet fighters shot down – including the two thousandth victory of the Grünherz-geschwader, scored by Oberfeldwebel Rudolf Klemm. Personnel losses on the Soviet side included 26 IAP ace Kapitan Vasiliy Matsiyevich and VVS-KBF veteran Leytenant Mikhail Maksimov, who was credited with three victories. Matsiyevich managed to bail out, but Maksimov was killed. The Soviet report of eighteen German planes shot down is totally unsupported, at least with respect to the Luftwaffe loss statistics,

A bombed-up Ju 87 D taxies out on the muddy runway at Krasnogvardeysk Airdrome in April 1942. By this time, both StG 1 and StG 2 had exchanged most of their Ju 87 Bs for Ju 87 Ds, which had been significantly redesigned with a more streamlined fuselage and cockpit area. The oil cooler was repositioned from the top of the engine to underneath, and instead of the large radiator beneath the nose, the D version's radiators were fitted to the inner sections of the wings. (Photo: Wagner/Stein via Rosipal.)

Vystav Airdrome on April 16, 1942. The Soviet jazz vocalist Klavdiya Shulzhenko (first row, center), is flanked by the commander of 4 GIAP/VVS-KBF, Podpolkovnik Boris Mikhailov (left), and V. F. Koralli, the director of Shulzhenko's jazz group. In the second row, from left, are Starshiy Leytenant Anatoliy Kuznetsov, Starshiy Leytenant Vasiliy Golubev, Batalyonnyy Komissar Stepan Khakhilev, Starshiy Leytenant Petr Kozhanov, and an unidentified pilot. This famous fighter unit did not participate in the air fighting over Leningrad in April 1942, but on the day this photo was taken, its pilots claimed three Ju 88s and a Bf 109 knocked down over Lake Ladoga. Hearing of this success, Klavdiya Shulzhenko's jazz group, which had played for 4 GIAP/VVS-KBF on the previous day, decided to pay an "extra visit" to the unit in order to congratulate these brave men. (Photo: 4 GIAP/VVS-VMF Museum via Dikov.)

according to which not a single German aircraft was lost over Leningrad on that date.[42]

But the raid in itself was a failure. The He 111 crews of KG 4 were unable to suppress the Soviet AAA batteries, and when the Ju 88s of KG 1 and Ju 87s of StG 2 came in to dive-bomb the ships, the intense antiaircraft barrage compelled many pilots to break off short of their targets. According to KBF reports, 58 of 132 German aircraft actually dropped their bombs over the mouth of the Neva River. Only one bomb hit the cruiser *Kirov*, but it went into the upper deck and passed through the side of the ship above the waterline without exploding. Near misses caused minor damage to the battleship *Oktyabrskaya Revolutsiya*, the cruiser *Maksim Gorki*, the destroyers *Svirepiy* and *Stoykiy*, and three submarines.[43]

An attempt by the He 111s of KG 4 to hit the ships the following night misfired completely.[44]

It stood clear to both sides that the operation had to be repeated, and Generaloberst Keller requisitioned the same kind of 1,000-kilogram armor-piercing bombs that had provided success against these same ships in 1941. While Luftflotte 1 was waiting for this delivery, the Soviets took action to suppress further attacks against the naval vessels by launching a series of raids against the Luftflotte 1 air bases. Krasnogvardeysk Airdrome, the main base of JG 54 – and the forward-most German airfield – was given the highest priority. From April 15 until the end of the month, it was subjected to incessant Soviet attacks by fighter-bombers and Shturmoviks in the daytime and bombers at night. Long-range artillery also was vectored against this target.

The action started on April 15, when twelve 26 IAP and 123 IAP MiG-3s, Yak-1s, and I-16s came buzzing with rattling machine-guns over the aircraft dispersal area at Krasnogvardeysk Airdrome. To Kapitan Vasiliy Matsiyevich, this attack was something of a personal revenge for having been shot down eleven days previously; he claimed two "Junkers" destroyed on the ground. In reality, only one Bf 109 sustained light damage during the raid. Two I./JG 54 fighters scrambled and engaged the Soviets in an uneven dogfight. 123 IAP's Kapitan Georgiy Zhidov shot down one of the Bf 109s (this can be verified with German loss records), but the Soviets lost the commanding officer of 26 IAP, Podpolkovnik Boris Romanov, when his MiG-3 was shot to pieces and exploded on the ground not far from Krasnogvardeysk. During the Soviet return flight, a lone Bf 109 pilot made a quick high-side attack and shot up one of the MiG-3s before he withdrew at high speed. The MiG-3 pilot, Leytenant Nikolay Shcherbina, belly-landed in friendly territory.

On April 18 twelve I-153s of 71 IAP/VVS-KBF were dispatched against Krasnogvardeysk,[45] where JG 54 pilots claimed three I-153s shot down.[46] The naval airmen struck the same airfield the very next day. "The Russians really are impudent," complained Major Hannes Trautloft, the Geschwaderkommodore of JG 54. "Between 0945 hours and 1046 hours, six I-153s escorted by six I-16s were airborne to strafe the German airfield at Krasnogvardeysk," the KBF report from this raid reads: "Twenty to twenty-five aircraft were found on the concrete parking grounds. Fifteen Ju 88s and Ju 87s were set on fire or destroyed. Two I-153s and one I-16 were shot down in air combat or by antiaircraft fire."[47] Starshiy Leytenant Aleksandr Shitov and Leytenant Yuriy Spitsyn of 71 IAP/VVS-KBF failed to return from this mission. Both were successful aces, Shitov having been credited with nine victories and Spitsyn with six. According to official Soviet sources, Spitsyn crashed his damaged I-153 into a group of parked German aircraft.[48] In reality, his I-153 was hit by German fire and crash-landed at Krasnogvardeysk, where Trautloft's men captured the Soviet pilot. (More than forty years later, Yuriy Spitsyn admitted that the self-sacrificing act that had destroyed two Ju 88s of 5.(F)/122 had been carried out by Shitov. Spitsyn's fate in captivity still remains clouded. After the

Polikarpov I-153, Starshiy Leytenant Aleksandr Baturin, deputy commander of 1 Eskadrilya/71 IAP/61 AB/VVS-KBF, Bychye Pole, Soviet Union, summer 1942

Two 71 IAP/VVS-KBF I-153s take off for a fighter-bomber mission. The near airplane is piloted by Starshiy Leytenant Aleksandr Baturin, who amassed a total of nine individual and an unknown number of shared victories through June 1942. Baturin was appointed Hero of the Soviet Union on October 23, 1942. He survived the war with the rank of a Mayor, credited with eighteen individual and twelve shared victories. (Photo: Petrov.)

war he reentered service with his old unit, but the stories he told his comrades – that he had piloted a Messerschmitt while in German captivity – soon reached the authorities' ears. A German pistol was reportedly found among his belongings, and Spitsyn was court-martialed and sentenced to prison.)

On April 24 Luftflotte 1 went after the large vessels of the Red Banner Baltic Fleet in Leningrad harbor for the second time, forty-four Ju 87s and eighteen Ju 88s escorted by twenty-eight Bf 109s of JG 54. This time, the code name given to the operation was quite ironic – "Götz von Berlichingen," which in German is understood to stand for the well-known phrase spoken by the principal character in Johann Wolfgang von Goethe's famous novel *Götz von Berlichingen*: "Kiss my ass."

Once again the fearsome Leningrad AAA frustrated the German effort. "The sky was filled with smoke clouds from exploding antiaircraft shells," Major Trautloft wrote.[49] The Soviet antiaircraft gunners claimed nine attackers, but most German pilots appeared to have broken off short of their target and thus evaded severe losses. Only one Ju 87 was shot down. The pilot went down with his airplane, but the radio operator managed to bail out.

Leytenant Yuriy Spitsyn (third from left) receives instructions from Batalyonnyy Komissar A. Pinyagin, the commissar of 71 IAP/VVS-KBF's 2 AE, at Kronstadt Airdrome in December 1941. The pilot to Pinyagin's left is Leytenant Pavel Pavlov, later appointed Hero of the Soviet Union. During the raid against Krasnogvardeysk on April 15, 1942, Spitsyn crash-landed his damaged I-153 on the German airfield and was subsequently interrogated by Major Hannes Trautloft. (Photo: 4 GIAP/VVS-VMF Museum via Dikov.)

"Where are the Russian airmen?" Major Trautloft thought as he watched the scores of Junkers planes that twisted around in the mottled sky, desperately fighting to evade the hundreds of antiaircraft shells. Trautloft's "colleagues" on the other side of the hill had scrambled their fighters too late, and only few of them managed to catch up with the Germans as they withdrew to the south. "Suddenly a red ball of fire drops from high altitude and flashes past me," Trautloft wrote: "A plane has been shot down! I get a glimpse of a red Soviet star on the tail fin. It goes straight down and crashes into the center of Leningrad." Then a LaGG-3, piloted by 11 GIAP's Starshina Shakh, got into firing position behind a Ju 87. Machine-gun bullets slammed into the cockpit of Leutnant Herbert Bauer's I./StG 2 Stuka, injuring the pilot, who was saved by the intervention of a Bf 109, and despite his injuries managed to bring his plane back to Krasnoye Selo Airdrome.

A recently downed Soviet fighter pilot is brought to interrogation in the spring of 1942. Soviet fliers who fell into the hands of JG 54 received good treatment, a sharp contrast with the ruthless treatment most Soviet POWs received in German captivity. (Photo: Trautloft.)

While the German airmen returned discontented, their adversaries were in a good mood as they landed at their airfields inside the besieged city. For the loss of only one of their own, fifteen German planes – of which no more than one can be squared with Luftwaffe loss records – were claimed by the enthusiastic Soviet pilots. What further spurred them on was that this German attack had been successfully repulsed. The cruiser *Kirov* (not *Maksim Gorki* as the Germans assumed) had sustained two direct bomb hits in the stern (killing seventy-eight men and injuring forty-six), and the battleship *Oktyabrskaya Revolutsiya* was slightly damaged by a near miss.[50]

Twenty-four hours later Generaloberst Keller dispatched forty Ju 87s against the same target. This time, not a single German plane managed to break through the antiaircraft barrage, and the raiders became entangled in a whirling dogfight with approximately thirty Soviet fighters outside the AAA zone. The Soviets claimed six and the Germans claimed four aerial victories. While no losses can be found in the files of the participating Luftwaffe units, all four claims made by JG 54 can be substantiated in Soviet sources. Hitler and Keller were furious and demanded an explanation as to why their airmen had failed to knock out any of the ships. "The Russian antiaircraft artillery is shooting damned well," Major Trautloft commented laconically.

The fourth operation against the Red Banner Baltic Fleet in Leningrad – on April 27 – confirmed that the mission was impossible. Only the training ship *Svir* was hit by a bomb – and destroyed. The German commanders had to accept the bitter fact that the air defense of Leningrad simply was too much for their airmen. A final raid against this target was carried out by only three Ju 87s on the last day of April.

Both air forces made meager performances during Operations Eisstoss/Götz von Berlichingen. Despite large claims, the Soviet fighters were unable to deal the attacking Luftflotte 1 formations any substantial losses. They managed to shoot down only three of the intruders – not the sixty-nine claimed in Soviet post-war accounts – during the April attacks against Leningrad.[51] The Soviet airmen also failed to inflict any significant damage on Krasnogvardeysk Airdrome despite repeated raids. Soviet accounts that the April 1942 strikes against this target forced the Germans to abandon the airfield are totally unfounded; the German personnel, who remained quite comfortably accommodated in the old Czar's residence nearby, were not that easily driven away.

The Luftwaffe's attempt to knock out the heavy vessels in Leningrad misfired completely. The main cause was the Leningrad AAA, which once again proved that it was one of the strongest concentrations of its kind in the war. The inaccurate German bombing and the comparatively low Luftwaffe loss rate during the missions against the KBF vessels in April 1942 indicate that a large portion of the German bomber crews simply broke off short of their target. Thus, taken as a whole, Operations Eisstoss/Götz von Berlichingen ended in a Soviet defensive victory.

What the Germans – and their Finnish allies – were not aware of was that the KBF never planned to deploy its heavy surface vessels in the Baltic Sea. Since the Gulf of Finland was heavily mined, and the shores were filled with German and Finnish coast artillery, the Soviets considered such a venture to be too risky. At the same time, the guns of the naval vessels were badly needed to support the defense of Leningrad, a place where the ships themselves were well protected, as shown. After the ice melted, the heavy vessels of KBF constantly changed their locations and shelled German troop positions almost daily in a radius of fifteen to thirty miles from Leningrad.

Following the failed attempt to sink the heavy vessels in Leningrad in the spring of 1942, no more large-scale

The Il-4 proved to be most suitable for torpedo and mining missions. During most of 1942, the crews of 1 GMTAP/VVS-KBF conducted mining and free-hunting torpedo sorties over the Baltic Sea and the Gulf of Finland. When 1 GMTAP's Starshiy Leytenant Vasiliy Balebin succeeded in destroying the first enemy escort ship through a direct torpedo hit during a lone free-hunting sortie, the enthusiastic C-in-C of the KBF, Vitse-Admiral Vladimir Tributs, "awarded" Starshiy Leytenant Balebin with a piglet. From then on, every torpedo pilot in VVS-KBF who managed to sink an enemy ship was presented with a piglet, which soon became known as "Balebin Piggys." (Photo: Authors' collection.)

attempts were made by the Luftwaffe to bomb the battleships and cruisers of the Soviet Red Banner Baltic Fleet. Instead, in May 1942, an extensive mine-laying operation was conducted in the Gulf of Finland. German and Finnish minelayers participated in this operation, as did Luftflotte 1. Under the code name Operation Froschlaich – Tadpole – the He 111s of Stab, I., and II. Gruppen of Oberst Hans Joachim Rath's KG 4 flew mine-laying sorties on eleven nights beginning May 27.

It is clear that Hitler exaggerated the threat from the heavy vessels of the KBF against the sea line of communication between Germany and Finland. During the entire war, the Soviets launched nothing but aircraft and submarines against these ships. On June 7, seven VVS-KBF Il-2s escorted by ten Yak-1s and six I-153s fell upon an Axis convoy near Hogland and claimed two patrol boats sunk.[52] The Il-4s of Podpolkovnik Yevgeniy Preobrazhenskiy's élite 1 GMTAP/VVS-KBF relentlessly carried out mine-laying and free-hunting sorties over the Baltic Sea and, even though 12,873 German and Finnish mines were laid in the Gulf of Finland during 1942,[53] several Soviet submarines made the passage into the Baltic Sea.

The largest support of the German shipping lanes to Finland was provided by the Swedish government, which allowed German transport ships bound for Finland to use Swedish territorial waters; it even allocated Swedish Navy vessels to escort these transports.[54] Nevertheless, the Soviets sunk forty-three vessels, including a number of Swedish vessels. For obvious reasons, the anti-shipping operations conducted by Soviet airmen over the Baltic Sea and the Gulf of Finland were far more effective than the Luftwaffe's effort to neutralize the Soviet warships at the AAA-lined quays of the Neva River in Leningrad.

Chapter 11

Springtime on the Moscow Front

It was clear in early March 1942 that the Soviet winter offensive in the central combat zone had been extended beyond its capacity. With the most acute situation at the front checked, Fliegerkorps VIII could shift emphasis from the role of flying artillery in the immediate front line to interdiction of the Red Army's supply lines.

The battle for air supremacy was considerably stiffened in early March, as the Soviet Air Force attempted to challenge the German threat from the air by instructing its airmen to start hunting the Luftwaffe both in the air and on the ground. This policy shift was not without success. On March 1, two Hs 123s and two Ju 87s of SchG 1 and StG 2 were destroyed at Dugino Airdrome, north of Vyazma.[55] As the Ju 88 crews of II./KG 54 raided Soviet supply lines in the Rzhev area on March 4 – claiming twenty-three trucks destroyed – they encountered fierce resistance from Soviet fighters and ground fire, and lost three Ju 88s, including the crew of the acting Gruppenkommandeur, Oberleutnant Günther Seubert. A fourth Ju 88 sustained heavy battle damage.[56]

The Germans also stepped up their air-base offensive in March – VVS-Kalinin Front reported that a total of 267 German aircraft completed fifty-six raids against its airfields in March 1942, compared to seventy-two aircraft dispatched on sixteen air-base raids in February – but it should be noted that the Soviets were more successful in their air-base raids. The increasing number of Il-2 Shturmoviks arriving in the western zone allowed the Soviets to undertake more air-base raids in the daytime, and this improved the effect considerably.

The sturdy Il-2 earned great respect from German ground troops. Generalleutnant Walter Schwabedissen noted that "the aggressiveness of the Soviet ground-attack pilots is favorably mentioned by most Luftwaffe and Army commanders reporting on the period 1942-43. They were impressed by the pilots' increasing operational toughness, their stubborn execution of assigned missions despite heavy losses, and their 'fighting heart and bold courage.'"

215 ShAP was one of the first units to be equipped with the new Il-2 in 1941. After reportedly destroying sixty-eight German aircraft (most of them on the ground), 183 tanks, 474 lorries, and 120 artillery pieces in under two months of combat action this unit was adopted as the 6th Guards Aviation Regiment, 6 GShAP, on December 6, 1941. (Photo: Viktor Kulikov photo collection.)

On March 5, six Il-2s of 6 GShAP were able to inflict more damage to Rzhev Airdrome than all the night raids in the previous month combined. Next day a large number of German aircraft – including the entire aircraft park of 2.(F)/11, twelve Do 17s and Fw 189s, and two aircraft of 3.(H)/21 – were destroyed at Vyazma Airdrome.

Nevertheless, the Soviet air-base raids failed to take the wind out of Fliegerkorps VIII. New thrusts by the Soviet Kalinin Front between

Ostashkov and Kalinin in the northern flank of Army Group Center on March 6 were beaten off by heavy German air attacks. While escorting a formation of Ju 87s, II./JG 51 fought off an interception attempt by twelve MiG-3s and I-16s and claimed four Soviets shot down against no losses of their own. That 728 IAP's Leytenant Andrey Borovykh and Starshina Aleksandr Novikov claimed to have shot down two Ju 88s from a flight of four in the same area on that day had no impact on the general situation.

To the south, in the vicinity of Vyazma, Stukas played a decisive role in clearing the Rollbahn – the main supply road to Army Group Center – of isolated elements of General-Mayor Pavel Belov's 1st Guards Cavalry Corps and the 8th Airborne Brigade.

After intercepting twelve Ju 87s from III./StG 2 escorted by fighters from IV./JG 51 southeast of Vyazma on March 7, six 168 IAP LaGG-3 pilots commanded by Leytenant Vasiliy Seryogin claimed seven Ju 87s shot down. (The official Luftwaffe loss statistics show only one Ju 87 lost.)

In January 1942, at the age of nineteen, Leutnant Hans Strelow was appointed Staffelkapitän of 5./JG 51 Mölders. Strelow was the most successful German fighter pilot during the defensive battles in the central combat zone of the Eastern Front during the winter of 1941-1942. A comparison between Soviet and German records indicates that approximately ten percent of all Soviet aircraft lost in aerial combat in the central combat zone between January and March 1942 were shot down by Strelow. In March 1942, he became the seventh pilot of Jagdgeschwader Mölders to be awarded the Oak Leaves – only six days after he received the Knight's Cross. (Photo: Author's collection.)

The intensified VVS activity against the Luftwaffe also led to increasing Soviet casualties. On March 9 VVS-Kalinin Front was dealt a severe loss when two 728 IAP Ishaks, piloted by Starshina Aleksandr Novikov and Starshiy Serzhant Igor Kustov, were bounced by a small group of Bf 109s. Only Kustov returned to base, injured and with his I-16 badly shot up. He reported that Novikov had saved him by drawing the attention of the Bf 109s to himself; in the ensuing combat, Novikov was shot down and killed. The twenty-year-old Novikov had begun his operational career in December 1941. He had demonstrated in his first sorties that he was a gifted fighter pilot and during his three-month front-line service, Novikov carried out ninety-three sorties and was credited with fifteen individual and shared victories.

The Luftwaffe's equivalent to Sasha Novikov in this combat zone was an even younger Leutnant from II./JG 51 named Hans Strelow, who enjoyed a comet-like career during the first months of 1942. Having achieved his first victory in June 1941, his total score had reached twenty-seven at the end of the year. On March 18, 1942, Strelow achieved the largest individual success by any fighter pilot during the Soviet winter offensive, claiming seven victories in one day – thereby raising his total victory tally to fifty-two. His combat report made on the same day he was awarded the Knight's Cross serves as testimony to his excellent marksmanship:

> Our mission was free hunting. I was first to spot the two Russian I-18 fighters. They flew at 600 feet flight altitude. We were down at 60 feet, which allowed us to make our attack unnoticed.
>
> The Russian wingman, positioned slightly behind and on the right-hand side of the leading aircraft, was singled out by [Feldwebel Wilhelm] Mink. As Mink set this I-18 ablaze, the second Russian realized what was going on and came turning round, attempting to get on Mink's tail. Apparently, he had not discovered me. I turned sharply to the right, and while still turning gave him three brief bursts with my cannon. Suddenly the Russian came veering against me. I pulled up steeply with the intention of making another attack from above. While still climbing, I saw the Russian fighter make a roll, and then it went down in spirals and hit the ground, exploding on impact. Mink's I-18 belly-landed on a field. We came down after it and destroyed it with our guns. Back at home we found that I had used no more than ten cannon rounds and forty-five bullets from each machine gun. This was my nicest victory ever: a fighter in a turning fight with only seven rounds!

Wilhelm Mink, who had downed the first MiG-3 in this combat, was awarded the Knight's Cross following his fortieth victory on March 19. But even if the Germans had regained their upper hand in air combat, they failed to destroy the Soviet airmens' determination to fight back.

Also on March 19, 441 IAP's Mladshiy Leytenant Yevgeniy Pichugin gave his life by ramming a Bf 110.[57] For this sacrifice, Pichugin was posthumously appointed a Hero of the Soviet Union.

Meanwhile, Gefechtsverband Bormann – the special command umbrella of bomber units assigned to Fliegerkorps VIII was shifted to operations mostly against the Soviet supply lines in the territory seized by the Soviets on the border between the Central and Northern army groups. Fliegerkorps VIII's War Diary noted: "Gef. Verb. Bormann carries out rolling attacks against movements on the railways and roads in the area Rzhev-Torzhok-Ostashkov-Toropets-Velizh-Belyy. Principal emphasis on disrupting the railway lines Torzhok – Soblago and Ostashkov – Toropets."

The Soviet fighter pilots made every effort to ward off these attacks. On March 21 five LaGG-3s of 5 GIAP, commanded by Mayor Vasiliy Zaytsev, engaged various Luftwaffe formations over the Kalinin battlefield and claimed five victories without loss. Next day three Yak-1s of 521 IAP made a daring attack against eighteen German bombers escorted by nine Bf 109s in the vicinity of Rzhev. According to the Soviet report, five Ju 88s were shot down against the loss of one Soviet fighter. It is possible that Major Arved Crüger, the Geschwaderkommodore of KG 77, who was lost in combat in the same area on that day, fell prey to these Yak pilots.

On Saturday, March 21, 1942, five 5 GIAP LaGG-3 pilots attacked various Luftwaffe formations and returned to base with five victory claims. One of these German planes, a Bf 110, fell before the guns of Starshiy Leytenant Ivan Laveykin. This twenty-year-old pilot served with 5 GIAP (formerly 129 IAP) from the beginning of the war and earned the respect of his comrades for his excellent marksmanship. In total, he was credited with twenty-four personal and fifteen shared victories, and ended the war as a Mayor. Ivan Laveykin passed away on December 2, 1986. This photo, taken in 1943, shows Laveykin wearing a Kapitan's shoulder straps. (Photo: Seidl.)

By this time the thaw started to affect operations on both sides. It had a particularly negative impact on fighter aircraft, whose narrow wheels and weak undercarriage were not constructed for the sleet on the runways of improvised Eastern Front airstrips. On mild days the fighters could take off only in the early morning, when the ground still was frozen. The rasputitsa – the deep, soft Russian mud – also created logistical problems which rapidly resulted in a scarcity in reserve parts and a subsequent drop in the number of serviceable aircraft. In II./JG 51, the few Bf 109s that remained operational were reserved for the most experienced pilots – and first and foremost, for the eager Leutnant Hans Strelow. Between March 19 and March 23, Strelow knocked down fourteen Soviet aircraft, and thus was responsible for a large part of the total VVS losses in the central combat zone during those five days. On March 24, when Strelow's victory tally stood at sixty-six, he received a message that he had been awarded the Oak Leaves – the youngest recipient of this award at the time.[58] Two days later, he celebrated his twentieth birthday at the start of a two-month home leave.

The rasputitsa contributed to dealing 1 GIAP/VVS-Kalinin Front a heavy blow on March 28. It was a warm spring day, and the quagmire-like forward airfield made any takeoff by the unit's Hurricanes unthinkable. But the Kampfgeschwader that operated from rear-area airdromes with concrete runways did not experience the same problems. One of these units dispatched ten Ju 88s against this Soviet fighter base, and thirteen 1 GIAP Hurricanes were put out of commission on the ground.[59]

On March 30, StG 2 reported a major success during a single attack against a large concentration of Soviet tanks, of which twenty-seven were knocked out. Only six Soviet fighters attempted to engage the Stukas, and five of these were claimed shot down by the escorting fighters of II./JG 51 – two each by Oberfeldwebel Alfred Rauch and Feldwebel Anton Hafner. Next day, on March 31, one of the most experienced pilots of 1 GIAP, Hero of the Soviet Union Starshiy Leytenant Vasiliy Migunov, was killed during an aerial combat with Ju 88s escorted by II./ZG 26 – reportedly as a result of engine failure.

During March 1942 the airmen of Fliegerkorps VIII claimed the destruction of 66 Soviet tanks, 106 artillery pieces, 123 railway engines, and more than 1,000 motor vehicles. In all 8,810 sorties were carried out (including 415 air-transport sorties and 264 night sorties), and 184 aerial victories were reported for the loss of 36 aircraft.[60] But the relationship between German victory claims and losses was by far not as favorable as in the northern and southern combat zones; Fliegerkorps VIII failed to achieve more than local air superiority. According to Soviet documents, VVS-Kalinin Front alone carried out 6,978 combat sorties (4,336 in daytime) in March 1942,[61] resulting in 203 air combats involving 590 Soviet and 933 German planes.[62] The cost for Fliegerkorps VIII's achievements during the defensive operations against the Soviet winter offensive between January and March 1942 was about two hundred combat aircraft – excluding transport, liaison, and reconnaissance planes – lost to enemy action. The hardest hit Geschwader was StG 2 Immelmann, which registered twenty-nine Ju 87s lost and ten severely damaged due to enemy action between January and March 1942.[63] Added to these losses were at least as many aircraft and airmen that succumbed to accidents.

According to Luftwaffe loss figures, 859 German aircraft were destroyed and a further 636 damaged to all causes on the Eastern Front between December 7, 1941, and April 8, 1942. The relationship between the Luftwaffe's victory claims and its own aircraft losses on the Eastern Front dropped from 8.4:1 during summer and fall of 1941 to 3.3:1 from December 1941 to March 1942, inclusive. In little more than nine months, through April 8, 1942, the war against the Soviet Union had cost the Luftwaffe 2,951 aircraft totally destroyed and 1,997 severely damaged.

The strength of both sides went into decline. By March 1942 total German tank losses on the Eastern Front had reached 3,486, and on March 30 no more than 140 German tanks were ready for action along the entire front line.[64] Both sides had fought to almost complete exhaustion, thus achieving a stalemate. On March 31 Generalfeldmarschall Günter von Kluge, the commander of Army Group Center, reported to Hitler that his troops were too fatigued to undertake the large-scale counterattack that had been planned. The badly mauled German Fourth Panzer Army had to be withdrawn from first-line service to rest and refit.

The situation was identical in the air forces. In March and the beginning of April, all ground-attack units of Fliegerkorps VIII – II./ZG 1, I. and II./ZG 26, and SchG 1 (formerly II. and 10.(S)/LG 2) – were pulled out of the

Inspection of a He 111 that made it back to base despite shot-up engines. The Soviet tactic of opening fire with even small arms against any enemy airplane that flew past was responsible for many of the Luftwaffe losses on the Eastern Front, particularly in the bomber units. (Photo: Balss.)

Oberleutnant Eduard Tratt, the 6./ZG 26 Staffelkapitän, lands his Bf 110 on a waterlogged airfield in front of an He 111, a Bf 110, and a Ju 52 in late March 1942. As a consequence of the serious situation on the Eastern Front, the new II./NJG 4 was reinstated as II./ZG 26 and quickly departed Germany for the Moscow combat zone. The reborn Zerstörer achieved large successes, but it also suffered heavily while repulsing the Soviet winter offensive. Eduard Tratt was injured by infantry fire at Rzhev on February 18, 1942, and on March 27, he was wounded by hostile fire a second time. A few days later, ZG 26 was again withdrawn from the Eastern Front. Later in the war, Tratt flew Me 410s against American heavy bombers over Germany and was killed in action on February 22, 1944. By that time he was the highest-scoring Zerstörer pilot, credited with thirty-eight aerial victories. (Photo: Trautloft.)

front to rest and recuperate. Simultaneously, the staff of Fliegerkorps VIII left the central combat zone in order to oversee operations in the Crimea. The remaining Luftwaffe units in the central combat zone were brought under the command of the new Luftwaffenkommando Ost, commanded by General der Flieger Robert Ritter von Greim. According to historian Percy E. Schramm, total strength in the Luftwaffe on the Eastern Front had declined to merely 650 combat aircraft by mid-March 1942.[65]

VVS records list 550 aircraft lost during the Rzhev-Vyazma offensive, from January 8 through April 20, 1942 – more than half the aircraft available to the Soviets in the central combat zone at the opening of the offensive. In consequence, VVS-Kalinin Front's 6 GShAP was left with only three serviceable Il-2s on April 3, 1942, while 128 PBAP could mount only six serviceable Pe-2s on that date. The three fighter aviation regiments in VVS-Third Assault Army could not muster more than twelve serviceable I-16s between them, and in VVS-Fourth Assault Army, the four fighter aviation regiments had no more than twelve operational LaGG-3s altogether.[66] JG 51 (given the name-of-honor 'Mölders' following the death of this famous air leader and fighter pilot) was responsible for the bulk of these Soviet losses; it claimed nearly five hundred victories against thirty-five Bf 109s shot down or badly damaged in combat during the period November 1941 – April 1942. On April 8, 1942, this Jagdgeschwader registered its three thousandth aerial victory.

Adding to the declining strength of the opposing forces, April brought increased spring thaws – which made large-scale operations impossible. The fighter planes had been able to take off only during the early hours of the day during the latter part of March, when the ground was still frozen, but the rasputitsa – with its notorious mud and slush created by the spring thaws – held them down for days at a time in April. JG 51 alone registered twenty-five landing or take-off accidents in April that resulted in severe damage to the aircraft involved.

According to Soviet documents, the number of aircraft taking part in aerial combat in the operational area of VVS-Kalinin Front dropped to 99 Soviet and 151 German through April 1942, and VVS-Kalinin Front lost 17 aircraft on operations during that month.[67]

Even if the Soviet winter offensive had bogged down – as a combined result of spring thaws and heavy losses – its aftershocks were enough to keep Army Group

Center fully occupied throughout the spring. The salients with fighting Soviet ground forces that remained after the deep Red Army penetrations became the principal concern of Generalfeldmarschall von Kluge. Each night, U-2s, R-5s, and R-Zs of the frontal aviation LBAPs and NBAPs landed on makeshift airstrips inside the salients and unloaded supplies. Other essential equipment airdropped by twin-engine PS-84s and four-engine TB-3s enabled the enveloped Red Army contingents to continue offensive operations that posed an ongoing threat to the Rollbahn. The most notable case was General-Mayor Pavel Belov's 1st Guards Cavalry Corps, which, together with elements from the 4th Airborne Corps, held a large area in the rear of the German Fourth Army southeast of Smolensk and south of Vyazma for three months. Since the Luftwaffe's entire night-fighter force was devoted to the defense of the Reich, the supply flights could be completed with only light losses.

Gefechtsverband Bormann's bombers contributed to the successive compression of these salients through random carpet bombing, but their main emphasis remained on operations against railway targets. Indeed, each bomber crew flew up to three such missions per day. The railroad stations and lines at Soblago, Goritzy, Gorbachevo, Gorov, Okhvat, Toropets, Dubno, and Yukhno were subjected to repeated aerial bombardment, which was increasingly troublesome to the Soviet commanders since the rasputitsa rendered most roads impassable.

A bellied-in Bf 109 F. Note that the upper propeller blade is intact, which indicates that the landing was carried out with a non-functioning engine. (Photo: Grislawski.)

Rarely encountering any fighter opposition during most of April and May, German bomber operations suffered only limited losses. KG 3 listed only seven Ju 88s shot down during May 1942, while II./KG 54 and I./KG 77 lost three Ju 88s apiece to enemy action.

The most serious fighter opposition was to be found at Soblago, on the rail line from Ostashkov to Toropets, where 630 IAP/PVO operated from a well-equipped airdrome. On May 3 Oberfeldwebel Johann Eibl of 2./KG 77 carried out a daring single-plane mission against this target. Eibl's Ju 88 was approaching Soblago at treetop level when two I-16s appeared. 630 IAP's Leytenant Nikolay Chebotaryov and Starshina Nikolay Dolenko immediately put the noses of their I-16s down from their position at 1,800 feet altitude and started diving against the German bomber. At a distance of 400 yards, one of the Soviet pilots launched RS-82 rocket projectiles. The rockets missed, and Oberfeldwebel Eibl made a 180-degree turn and increased speed while his radio operator, Unteroffizier Anton Hagel, opened fire with his two 7.92mm MG 81 machine guns. Then Eibl made a fatal mistake. He pulled up, intending to search for refuge in a low layer of clouds ahead. In that moment the second I-16 pilot launched his RS-82s, one of which exploded close to the bomber. Chebotaryov and Dolenko saw the Ju 88 lose altitude as thick black smoke

This German aerial reconnaissance photo shows a freight train burning in the wake of a bombing raid against a Soviet railroad station. Showcasing the destructive power of these attacks, 1./KG 77's Oberfeldwebel Horst Henning succeeded in destroying twenty-three trains, a feat that earned him the Knight's Cross on May 22. (Photo: Trautloft.)

Bf 110 E-2 W.Nr. 3794, Oberleutnant Eduard Tratt, Staffelkapitän 6./ZG 26 Horst Wessel, Dugino, Soviet Union, March 1942
Oberleutnant Tratt was injured by hostile fire in the Rzhev region while piloting this airplane on March 27, 1942.

poured out of both engines. Eibl nursed the crippled bomber down to a forced landing with retracted undercarriage on a field near the hamlet of Yamishche, ten miles northwest of Andreapol. The crew managed to abandon the aircraft and disappeared into a forest. Eibl's crew is still listed as missing.

On May 4, 1942, a young Serzhant of 5 GIAP scored his first victory against an He 111 – possibly of 1./KG 53 – in the same region. His name was Vitaliy Popkov, and he would end the war with a total of forty-one victories to his credit.

Mayor Vasiliy Zaytsev of 5 GIAP/VVS-Kalinin Front was one of the best-known Soviet fighter pilots in 1942. One of the maxims Zaytsev taught the novice pilots of his regiment was: "Never fear the enemy; he who fears the enemy will be shot down." On May 5, 1942, Zaytsev and five other 5 GIAP pilots were appointed Heroes of the Soviet Union. In this photo, taken in 1943, Zaytsev wears a Podpolkovnik's shoulder straps and carries two Red Banner Orders and the Lenin Order beneath the Golden Star indicating a Hero of a Soviet Union. On the right side of his chest he carries the Guards Unit Emblem. Zaytsev was credited with a total of thirty-four personal and nineteen shared victories during 427 combat sorties during World War II. He passed away on May 19, 1961, at the age of 50. (Photo: Viktor Kulikov collection.)

On May 5 a limited German counterattack in the Olenino-Rzhev sector, forty miles south of Ostashkov, drew the attention of the entire VVS-Kalinin Front. Operating from Budovo Airdrome near Torzhok, sixty miles north of Rzhev, 5 GIAP was dispatched on ground-attack missions in the area and engaged the Luftwaffe forces in stiff aerial combat. By the end of the day, the veterans of 5 GIAP had chalked up five kills. That same day five of the unit's pilots were honored as Heroes of the Soviet Union.

The Ju 88s of I./KG 77 were assigned to neutralize the Soviet fighters at Budovo Airdrome on May 12. A few 5 GIAP LaGG-3s managed to scramble before the bombs fell, but they were jumped by six JG 51 Bf 109s shortly after they left the ground. When Starshiy Politruk Vasiliy Bakhvalov, who had been appointed Hero of the Soviet Union during the Winter War against Finland in 1939/ – 1940, saw a Bf 109 Rotte pursue a badly shot-up LaGG-3, he turned in on the Messerschmitts. In the next moment a whole Schwarm came down on Bakhvalov. The air battle took place at very low altitude above the small village of Budovo. The lone LaGG-3 put up a magnificent fight, evading the every attacks by turning tightly just above the ground. More than once, the Soviet pilot managed to place himself in a firing position behind the Messerschmitts. One well-aimed burst left a Bf 109 trailing black smoke. Minutes later, the tracer bullets from Bakhvalov's guns disappeared into the fuselage of a second Messerschmitt. But finally the uneven fight came to an end.[68] Vasiliy Bakhvalov was buried in the central square of Budovo, close to where he was found dead. One Ju 88 of I./KG 77 failed to return from this mission.

As weather conditions improved, the air war intensified in late May. Between May 21 and May 23, a number of severe personnel losses were dealt to the Luftwaffe in the central combat zone. While dive-bombing the railroad station at Yukhno on May 21, the Ju 88 piloted by the Staffelkapitän of 5./KG 3, Knight's Cross holder Oberleutnant Ernst Petzold, sustained a direct hit by a 20mm antiaircraft shell in the cockpit that injured the pilot and the gunner. Bleeding from a deep wound, Petzold lost consciousness. But the fortuitous intervention of the observer, who took over the controls of the damaged plane and bandaged his injured airmen, enabled the crew to return to base. For this feat, General Ritter von Greim awarded the observer German Cross in Gold.

The 5./KG 54 crew of Unteroffizier Josef Andris, which went out against Soblago on the same day, did not have the same fortune; the aircraft was never seen again. Fifty-six years later, the remnants of the airplane and the bones of the crewmembers were found by a Soviet aircraft recovery group in cooperation with historian Vlad Antipov in marshlands located in a forest near Kalinin.

Leutnant Horst Deutschbein was appointed Staffelführer of 5./KG 54, but already on May 22 was listed as missing after another mission against Soblago. The log book of 630 IAP/PVO sheds some light on the fate of this crew: "While on patrol in his LaGG-3 at 2,000 meters altitude over Soblago railroad station, Leytenant [Georgiy] Gurov spotted three Ju 88s approaching for a bomb run. Then the lead airplane had dropped its bombs. After several gunnery runs, Gurov managed to set the lead Ju 88 on fire. Two crewmembers bailed out while two others remained in the cockpit. The airplane descended out of control and crashed 500 meters from the railroad station, exploding on impact. The crewmembers that had bailed out landed between two and three kilometers from the station. It turned out that the pilot of this aircraft was the commander of a bomber *Eskadra* that previously had been deployed at Peno. Both surviving crewmembers were captured."[69] Balancing this victory, 630 IAP's Leytenant Georgiy Sinelshchikov was killed in combat with four Bf 109s from JG 51.[70]

II./JG 51's famous ace, Leutnant Hans Strelow, also was lost on this May 22. Having recently returned to his unit from his long home leave following the award of the Oak Leaves on March 24, he took off on a free-hunting sortie in the area northeast of Orel. It was a well-known phenomenon that the initial period following home leave was particularly hazardous. Many pilots were lost on one of their first combat sorties shortly after a period of rest at home.

Strelow attacked a formation of Pe-2s, and shot down one of them. As he was pulling up from this attack, the rear gunner of the burning Pe-2 managed to hit the Bf 109's engine. Strelow had no option but to force-land in enemy-held territory. Fearing physical reprisals by Soviet soldiers, Strelow opted to take his own life before Soviet troops reached the Messerschmitt with sixty-seven victory bars painted on the rudder. Strelow's Bf 109 was the only loss in air combat registered by JG 51 in the central combat zone during May 1942.

Another hard loss was dealt II./KG 3 on May 22, when the Gruppenkommandeur, Major Waldemar Krüger, was shot down by AAA. The entire crew died in the crash near the Dechino railroad station on the line between Kaluga and Maloyaroslavets.

By this time, the German attempts to compress the Soviet salients in their rear area were gaining more and more momentum. Generaloberst Walter Model, the able commander of the Ninth German Army, often took to the air over the Soviet troops in an Fi 156 Storch to get a better overview of the situation. His Storch was subjected to light fire from the ground on numerous occasions, but this did not deter the bold Generaloberst. On May 23 he made one flight too many. Flying at 150 feet over the deep Soviet wedge between Belyy and Sychyovka, the slow Storch came under intense rifle fire from below. Both Model and his pilot, Feldwebel Wilhelm Haist, were injured, but the aircraft remained flying. With Model facing the prospect of bleeding to death, the injured pilot brought the Storch and its valuable cargo back over the German lines and landed as fast as he could. Model evaded death by a matter of a few minutes.[71]

A few days later the battle of the encircled Soviet forces died out. Most of the area was successfully retaken, but General-Mayor Belov was not beaten. In early June large parts of his 1st Guards Cavalry Corps and the 4th Airborne Corps managed to break out, overrunning the German 7th Infantry Division in the process, and finally reaching the Soviet front line.

A crash-landed Ju 88. Oberleutnant Peter Stahl, who flew Ju 88s in combat during most of the war, described this aircraft as "a diva." According to Stahl, "she was capable of carrying out surprising things by herself. She was particularly prankish during take off." (Photo: Roba/Mombeek.)

Due to the overall structure of the VVS, each commander of an individual army jealously guarded "his" air force. This frequently prevented armies locked in difficult situations from receiving necessary support from the air forces of neighboring armies, which might be less hard-pressed. The Stavka could provide the air forces of various fronts with additional resources, depending on the priority it gave to certain sectors, and indeed it did so. But the structure of the VVS did not allow for rapid redeployment of air force units to a sector where a sudden crisis developed – as could the more flexible Luftwaffe.

In March 1942 the commander in chief of VVS-KA, the Air Force of the Red Army, General-Polkovnik Pavel Zhigarev, analyzed the shortcomings of the VVS structure in a report to the Stavka. Zhigarev's opinion received a good reception, but he was relieved from his command (and sent to assume command of the Air Force of the Far Eastern Front) on April 10 for the VVS-KA's unsatisfactory showing during the winter offensive.

Stalin proposed that the commander of the new ADD, General-Mayor Aleksandr Golovanov, lead the reformation of VVS-KA; he wanted Golovanov to retain his post as head of ADD and at the same time command the entire VVS-KA. When Golovanov hesitated to take this double responsibility, Stalin turned to General-Leytenant Aleksandr Novikov, who had successfully commanded Soviet aviation in the northern combat zone during the difficult months of 1941. By concentrating aviation units from VVS-Leningrad Front, VVS-Volkhov Front, the ADD, and VVS-KBF over the Volkhov pocket under a single command in March 1942, Novikov had for the first time during the war demonstrated the efficiency of a coordinated and centralized use of aviation in the interest of two separate fronts.

Novikov's experience formed the benchmark upon which the military council of VVS-KA laid down the general outline for restructuring the Soviet Army Air Force. Appointed commander in chief of VVS-KA on April 11, 1942, Novikov introduced the Stavka to the final proposal for a new structure of the VVS: merging of the front air forces and the ground army air forces into air armies – Vozdushnye Armii (VA) – that provided a centralized command over all aviation units in operation over a certain army front.

The Stavka approved the plan, and on May 5, 1942, the first three air armies were formed: 1 VA, derived from VVS-Western Front and the aviation commands of its ground armies; 2 VA, derived from VVS-Bryansk Front and the aviation commands of its ground armies; and 3 VA, derived from VVS-Kalinin Front and the aviation commands of its ground armies.

During the next few weeks identical structural changes took place within the air forces deployed on the Southern Front (the new 4 VA), the Southwestern Front (the new 8 VA), the North Caucasus Front (the new 5 VA), and the Northwestern Front (the new 6 VA). Except for isolated special units the VAs were usually linked operationally to the ground forces, with each army front possessing its own operational VA.

Also of great importance was the progressive introduction of new tactics. Under Novikov´s influence, the VVS accepted the superiority of the German Schwarm (four-plane section) and Rotte (two-plane section) formations as the basic fighting elements and abolished the previous "Vic" or Kette three-plane-section of World War I heritage. That this had been demanded in vain by Soviet fighter pilots returning from the Spanish Civil War in the late thirties, and again by fighter pilots such as Starshiy Leytenant Aleksandr Pokryshkin during the fall of 1941, underlines the conservatism that had hobbled the Red Army for so long.

Paralleling the implementation of the structural changes, obsolete I-153s, I-16s, and SBs were gradually rooted out – by the Luftwaffe. From the summer of 1942, the only replacements sent to Soviet aviation units operating in daytime were more modern aircraft.

Their unsuccessful first winter offensive forced the Soviets to create a new air force structure with which they would eventually defeat the Luftwaffe. But in 1942 the most crucial factor, the men to fly the new airplanes and implement the new tactics, remained the Soviet Achilles heel. The thousands of experienced airmen lost during the costly air battles of the first months of the war were not as easily replaced as an airplane could be replaced, or changed as the structure of an organization could be changed. Moreover, increasing demands for replacement personnel shortened the time pilots spent in training courses; thus, from the spring of 1942 most new VVS airmen were inadequately trained. There were also severe "teething" problems for these VVS airmen with the introduction of new aircraft types, since the difficult combat situation forced the Soviets to send pilots into action in aircraft types with which they were not completely acquainted. The air war in the spring and summer of 1942 is defined by poorly trained Soviet airmen piloting new aircraft types (in which they might have only eight flight hours), encountering perfectly trained German fighter pilots with experience gained from hundreds of combat sorties in the same aircraft type.

Part IV

Resurgence of the Luftwaffe

An Ergänzungsgruppe/JG 77 Bf 109 E. Although III./JG 77 was the first unit to bring the new Bf 109 F-4 into action on the Eastern Front, both I./JG 77 and the reserve unit of this Jagdgeschwader, Ergänzungsgruppe/JG 77, still operated the old Bf 109 E model in the spring of 1942. In February 1942, a detachment from Erg/JG 77 was relocated to the Ukrainian front, where it conducted fighter-bomber missions against Soviet airfields and transport columns for several weeks. (Photo: Roba/Mombeek.)

Chapter 13

The Ukrainian Spring

The first spring thaws arrived in the Ukraine in early March and hampered or stalled most ground operations on the Mius-Kharkov front during the next two months. The main combat in the southern combat zone was focused around Slavyansk, south of the deep bulge at Izyum that the Soviets had achieved through their January offensive. Here, the German 257th Infantry Division managed to hold out, severing the road to Kharkov. The bulk of the air forces on both sides in the Ukraine were committed to close-support operations in this sector. While nothing more than a stalemate was achieved on the ground, the air war grew increasingly intense in March.

As the confrontation was shaping up, the aviation units of VVS-Southwestern Front and VVS-Southern Front finally began receiving larger numbers of modern aircraft. Yak-1 fighters were particularly welcome; with this superb aircraft the Soviets felt they could challenge the Bf 109 on equal terms. The two Fliegerkorps IV Jagdgruppen in the Ukraine – Hauptmann Hubertus von Bonin's III./JG 52 against VVS-Southwestern Front in the Kharkov area and Hauptmann Herbert Ihlefeld's I./JG 77 (supplemented by Ergänzungsstaffel/JG 77 and the Croatian 15./JG 52) against VVS-Southern Front in the Slavyansk area – soon learned that the "quiet days" of the past winter were done and gone.

Hubertus von Bonin was a veteran of the Spanish Civil War, in which he had achieved four aerial victories while serving with the Condor Legion. He commanded III./JG 52 between October 1941 and July 1943, during which time this unit developed into the most successful Jagdgruppe of the Luftwaffe. After that von Bonin succeeded Major Hannes Trautloft as the JG 54 Geschwaderkommodore. After achieving a total of 73 victories in World War II, von Bonin was killed in combat with Yak-9s on December 15, 1943. (Photo: Grislawski.)

On March 2 a Soviet fighter pilot achieved an important success with the downing of a Ju 87 south of Slavyansk. In this plane died one of the most successful Stuka pilots in the region, Oberleutnant Hermann Ruppert, a Knight's Cross recipient. Under Ruppert, 6./StG 77 had been a constant scourge to Soviet shipping in the Black Sea. Ruppert's fliers were credited with sinking five Soviet warships and four freighters and with damaging several other vessels.

On March 9 a flight of Yak-1 pilots of 296 IAP claimed a remarkable success. The day, a Monday, started "well" from the German point of view, with I./JG 77's Oberleutnant Erwin Clausen's return from a combat sortie with claims of five victories – four R-5s and one MiG-3, the latter recorded as his fortieth victory. A few hours later, six Bf 109s from 1./JG 77 were dispatched to escort II./StG 77. Flying at 6,000 feet, seven Yak-1s from 296 IAP spotted two German formations: six Ju 87s escorted by 1./JG 77, and a separate flight of twelve Bf 109 E fighter-bombers. A lone Ju 88 reconnaissance plane was also airborne in this area.

The Soviets decided to launch a head-on attack, firing RS-82 rocket projectiles as they came. This apparently caught the Germans by surprise. The leader of the Soviet formation, Kapitan Boris Yeryomin, recalled:

> We attacked the bombers and ripped their formation apart, and then I made a head-on

Bf 109 E-7, Ergänzungsgruppe/JG 77, Soviet Union, winter 1941-1942
Note the distinctive paint scheme of this airplane. It has been extensively resprayed over its original camouflage with RLM 70 and RLM 71.

> attack on the Messerschmitts. I managed to hit one of the fighters during my first pass. It fell to the ground like a flaming torch. Almost simultaneously, Leytenant [Aleksey] Salomatin set a second Messerschmitt burning – it went down not far from the first – and Leytenant [Aleksandr] Martynov shot down a third, while a fourth was set on fire by Serzhant [Dmitriy] Korol. During the fifteen-minute combat, our Eskadrilya destroyed one enemy bomber and four fighters. The engagement began at an altitude of 6,000 feet and finished at 150 feet. The remaining German planes disengaged.

A Yak-1 dives through the skies over the Eastern Front. This agile and speedy fighter boasted performance quite comparable to the Bf 109 F at altitudes below 15,000 feet, where most air fighting on the Eastern Front took place. (Photo: Authors' collection.)

The triumphant Yak-1s returned home without loss; only one Yak-1 had received a hit in the radiator, but the pilot, Leytenant Vasiliy Skotnoy, managed to nurse it back to a safe landing at the base. I./JG 77 made one victory claim – a "LaGG-1," which was registered as Oberleutnant Friedrich Geisshardt's forty-first victory. No losses were filed. It is interesting to find that I./JG 77 issued a report, according to which five Bf 109s force-landed due to lack of fuel on March 8. Later, the Soviet report increased the claims made by Yeryomin's pilots to five Bf 109s and two Ju 87s.

"This combat taught us much," Kapitan Yeryomin later wrote. "It convinced us that a fighter pilot's only sound tactic is to go on the offensive."[1] This statement should be taken in the context of the generally defensive doctrine that ruled the Soviet fighters at the time, where the rules of the day shackled air coverage to specific geographical areas and called on fighters to form defensive circles whenever German fighters attacked.

In a second action on March 9 at around 1730 hours, a flight of I./JG 77 Bf 109s bounced a formation of six I-16s led by 271 IAP's Starshiy Leytenant Sergey Luganskiy that were strafing German positions at Slavyansk. 88 IAP had been tasked to escort the ground-attacking Ishaks, but only had four planes serviceable following heavy losses during the past weeks.[2] 271 IAP's Batalyonnyy Komissar P. F. Novikov was shot down – possibly as Leutnant Günther Hannak's thirty-fourth victory. Pursued by a formation of Bf 109s, 88 IAP's Leytenant Boris Karasyov crashed into the ground as he attempted to escape at treetop level. Following a prolonged melee, the 88 IAP escort fighters managed to shepherd the five remaining 271 IAP Ishaks back to base.

271 IAP's Starshiy Leytenant Sergey Luganskiy was blamed for the loss of Batalyonnyy Komissar Novikov during an air action on March 9, 1942,. Luganskiy was seized by the NKVD counterespionage department and "tormented for a long time," according to Russian historian Nikolay Bodrikhin. Although he was rehabilitated, Luganskiy did not mention anything about this incident in his post-war memoirs. Following release from the clutches of the NKVD, he returned to first-line flying duty and eventually developed into one of the most famous Soviet fighter aces of the war, and he was twice appointed Hero of the Soviet Union. He ended the war with a total of thirty-seven personal and six shared victories on 390 combat sorties. Sergey Luganskiy passed away on January 16, 1977. (Photo: Seidl.)

Immediately after landing at the Barvenkovo airfield in the Izyum Bulge less than fifteen miles from where the combat occurred, one of the 88 IAP pilots, Leytenant Vasiliy Knyazev, took off again in order to search for the downed pilots. He found Batalyonnyy Komissar Novikov dead in the shattered remains of his I-16, but the wreckage of Karasyov's Ishak was empty. Karasyov was found alive but severely injured by Red Army soldiers the next day.

On March 14, 210 BBAP's Starshiy Leytenant Aleksandr Pavlichenko was shot down and severely injured by a Bf 109 near Krasnyy Luch in the Mius sector farther to the south. Pavlichenko recounts:

> The Messerschmitts attacked us from the left and from the right, and our Su-2 shook under the hits. "I'm hit! Hurry up and land," cried my radio operator. I looked back and saw how he bent down on his knees. While "Sasha" [the radio operator Starshiy Leytenant Aleksandr Pakhomov] lay groaning, more bullets shook the plane. The Germans concentrated on the wings, where they knew the fuel tanks were situated. I should have bailed out, but that would have meant sending "Sasha" to a certain death. I saw flames erupt from the right wing, and then we went into a spin. I remember glancing at the speedometer while we went down, and it showed 500 kilometers per hour [310 miles per hour]. I don't know how I managed to get out of the spin, but when I did I found that the enemy had disengaged. I was unable to recover the plane from the dive. My left wing hit the ground at an angle of 35 to 40 degrees. Then the right wing hit the ground. The aircraft overturned and our cockpit was flung 200 yards along the ground. We went down just next to an artillery column. They found "Sasha" hanging in his straps upside down in the cockpit, bleeding from a wound in his belly but still conscious and yelling: "Save my commander! Save my commander!" The artillerymen turned the aircraft over with a tractor, broke open the side of the cockpit, and pulled me out. I was unconscious. They put me on a horse-drawn carriage and drove me to hospital.

Starshiy Leytenant Aleksandr Pavlichenko with his radio operator, Starshiy Leytenant Aleksandr Pakhmonov. This photo was taken at Budenovka Airdrome in March 1942, only days before this crew was shot down by a I./JG 77 Bf 109. The injuries that Pavlichenko sustained on this mission occasionly left him totally paralyzed. Only due to an iron will was he able to recover and return to first-line service, where he flew Il-2s with 108 GShAP. His last combat sortie was carried out two days after the official end of the war, against German troops who continued to fight on in Prague. (Photo: Pavlichenko.)

> There it was found that my backbone was broken. My entire body was plastered, and I spent six months hospitalized. Only after two and a half months was I able to move the first parts of my lower body – my toes!

Pavlichenko's Su-2 ended up on the victory tally of either I./JG 77's Oberleutnant Werner Tismar or Günther Hannak – and it was one out of the seventy-four victories I./JG 77 and the Ergänzungsstaffel of JG 77 claimed during March 1942. Operating side by side with the Bf 109s of JG 77, the Italian MC.200 Saetta pilots of 22 Gruppo Autonomo C.T. also flew combat sorties over the Mius front whenever weather and supplies permitted, but taken as a whole, their contribution was limited. Between mid-January and the end of March 1942, the Italians claimed twenty-five aerial victories.[3] VVS-Southern Front recorded sixty-five aircraft lost on operations in March 1942.[4]

The end of a Soviet Su-2 light bomber. (Photo: Grislawski.)

Farther to the north, in the Kharkov area, III./JG 52 claimed 166 kills against 11 of its own aircraft shot down during February and March. The most successful Jagdstaffel in this Gruppe, 9./JG 52, brought down more than two hundred Soviet aircraft against only eight pilot casualties since the invasion of the Soviet Union.

Just returned from a seven-weeks home leave, 9./JG 52's Leutnant Hermann Graf engaged a formation of Soviet fighters on March 23, claiming two Yak-1s. But this success was subdued by the loss of the Staffelkapitän of 9./JG 52, twenty-seven-victory ace Oberleutnant Kurt Schade, who went down after sustaining hits from both an Il-2 and ground fire.[5] After the war, Schade described this fateful experience in the following laconic lines:

> I'm on fire! I bail out 30 kilometers behind the front!! And on the next day, I should have departed for home leave! My dreams are over!!!! I land in one-meter-deep snow. There are Russian soldiers in the nearby hamlet. And so I'm captured. Day and night there are interrogations, including beatings. "Special treatment" – not quite according to the Hague War Convention!! From April 1, 1942, I'm locked into the notorious GPU-prison Lyubyanka (not a particularly nice experience) in Moscow. Then Oranki POW camp, Yelabuga, Kazan (again fourteen days in jail), and Stalingrad...[6]

Appointed as Schade's successor, Leutnant Hermann Graf was in the air over the front line again four hours later. He brought down a Su-2 bomber, his fiftieth victory. On March 27, Graf filed his fifty-second victory. Next day, III./JG 52 reportedly knocked down ten Soviet planes without loss, and on March 30, I./JG 77 counted eleven kills – seven of them credited to Hauptmann Herbert Ihlefeld – over the Mius sector. That day III./JG 52 was less fortunate against VVS-Southwestern Front. Against only one claim – a Yak-1 brought down as Hermann Graf's fifty-eighth victory – three pilots were lost, two of them from 7th Staffel.

On the last day of March, Serzhant Pavel Lazyuka of 88 IAP managed to bring down two Bf 109s from I./JG 77. The I-16-equipped 88 IAP was mostly involved in strafing missions in the Slavyansk area during this period; during March 1942, it claimed 120 lorries and 11 German tanks destroyed for the loss of six I-16s.[7] As they strafed a German truck column on March 31, six 88 IAP I-16s were bounced by a Schwarm from 2./JG 77. Serzhant Lazyuka immediately turned head-on and launched four RS-82 rocket projectiles that exploded in the midst of the German formation, bringing down two and driving away the remainder. Both of Lazyuka´s claims can be verified in the Luftwaffe loss files, which is more than can be said of most Soviet claims made during this period.

During March 1942, VVS-Southern Front claimed eighty enemy aircraft destroyed,[8] but Fliegerkorps IV registered no more than twenty-nine aircraft lost on operations over the same period.[9] Even if the Luftwaffe loss files are not complete – and even with a few Italian aircraft added to the loss tally – VVS-Southern Front clearly made excessive overclaims in March.

Even though the Soviets claimed 1,074 Axis aircraft destroyed in March 1942, actual Luftwaffe combat losses on the Eastern Front that month were only about one-fifth of the Soviet claims. The German claims for March were also inflated – 1,040 Soviet aircraft shot down in aerial combat, 100 by AAA, and 251 destroyed on the ground – but closer to the truth than the Soviet success reports.

Kurt Schade completed his pilot training at Jagdfliegerschule Schleissheim in 1939 and was posted to JG 2 Richthofen the following year. In December 1940 he was transferred to III./JG 52, with which he achieved his first victory on June 26, 1941, against a 40 BAP/VVS-ChF SB during the interception of the Soviet air raid against Constanta. In November 1941 Schade assumed command of 9./JG 52, but he was shot down and captured by the Soviets three months later. On December 24, 1949, the Soviets put Schade into a refrigerated goods wagon for his trip home to Germany. (Photo: Schade via Salomonson.)

There are several reasons for the exaggerated Soviet success reports. First, the bulk of the Soviet claims were for aircraft destroyed on the ground. The number of enemy aircraft reportedly destroyed on the ground on the first day of the month alone – sixty-seven – was twice the number of German aircraft actually destroyed on the ground during the entire month. The exaggerated Soviet figures also are a reflection of the air combat situation. Lacking R/T equipment, Soviet fighter pilots frequently found themselves in confused combat with an unclear number of Bf 109s diving away after high-side gunnery passes, emitting thick exhaust smoke from their hard-pressed Daimler-Benz engines. In most cases there could be no radio calls to announce that a Soviet aircraft had been shot down, so

Yak-1, Kapitan Boris Yeryomin, commander 2 Eskadrilya/296 IAP/VVS-Sixth Army/VVS-Southwestern Front, Soviet Union, March 1942

The fortunes of war started turning against the Soviets once again in March 1942. By then, the radically shortened pilot training schemes – a measure that had to be undertaken in order for replacements to keep pace with combat losses – rendered the Soviet novice pilots virtually helpless against the Luftwaffe veterans. Despite this circumstance, combat morale appears to have remained at a high level in most aviation units, and it was further bolstered by the increasing overclaims that were made by VVS airmen during the period. This photo collage from *Leningrad Pravda* is illustrative of the description of the air war that was presented to the Soviet people.
(Leningrad Pravda via Dikov.)

a burning plane crashing into the ground may frequently have been interpreted by a Soviet pilot as being the Bf 109 he had shot at. There were cases of deliberately invented aerial victories – this phenomenon occurred on both sides – but most victories were claimed with some justification.

Nevertheless, questionable claims were made. It is interesting to note that I./JG 77 chalked up sixty-two victories against zero losses through April 1942. The Gruppenkommandeur, Hauptmann Herbert Ihlefeld (who scored his one hundredth kill on April 22), and his wingman, Oberleutnant Friedrich Geisshardt, made all but nineteen of these claims. This achievement is remarkable in light of the spring thaws that hampered Soviet aerial operations as well as the Soviet practice of conserving their forces in anticipation of an upcoming offensive – in the Kharkov area, in this case. The entire Ukrainian war zone was fairly quiescent during April, on the ground and in the air. A comparison with Soviet archival materials indicates that the I./JG 77 claims in April represent at least a two-fold exaggeration. In April 1942, VVS-Southern Front, against which I./JG 77 operated, noted only thirty-one aircraft lost on combat missions and seven non-combat losses.[10]

During this period, the Kampfgruppen of Fliegerkorps IV were dispatched on a number of strategic raids against industrial targets, including an ammunition factory at Tambov and an aircraft engine plant in Voronezh. On the night of April 22-23, fifty bombers carried out a three-hour long raid against the Krasnyy Oktyabr (Red October) tractor plant in Stalingrad, causing widespread damage. Meanwhile, German reconnaissance aircraft swept the Soviet rear area, detecting the build-up for the coming Red Army offensive to the north and south of Kharkov. On most occasions there was little or no Soviet fighter opposition. Total Luftwaffe combat losses in Ukrainian air space amount to five aircraft, at most, during all of April 1942.

VVS-Southern Front confined itself predominantly to small-scale night raids against German airfields and targets of opportunity. Poor navigational devices rendered those raids fairly ineffective.

On the night of April 24-25, 818 DBAP/3 UAG was able to destroy a Bf 109 at Mariupol Airdrome. This aircraft belonged to Croatian 15.(Kroat)/JG 52, which recently had arrived as a part of the build-up for the forthcoming Axis summer offensive. The personnel composition of 15.(Kroat)/JG 52 was quite disparate, and five of the squadron's twelve Bf 109 Es were seriously damaged in landing or take-off accidents during the first fortnight of its combat tour. Some Croatian pilots – such as the commander, Potpukovnik (lieutenant colonel) Franjo Dzal, or Narednik (technical sergeant) Veco Mikovic, who claimed three I-16s and two MiG-3s during March and April 1942[11] – were highly motivated to participate in Hitler's "Crusade against Communism." Others were influenced by Josip Broz Tito's resistance movement in Yugoslavia and secretly sympathized with the Soviets. On

Potpukovnik Franjo Dzal's Croatian 15./JG 52 is visited in the spring of 1942 by Hauptmann Herbert Ihlefeld, the I./JG 77 commander, who arrived in an early version He 70 used as a liaison plane. During March and April 1942, Dzal and his Croatian fighter pilots claimed twenty-four aerial victories, but during the same period, eleven of its Bf 109s were destroyed or severely damaged from all causes.

Herbert Ihlefeld passed away on August 8, 1995. (Photo: Roba/Mombeek.)

German fighter pilots inspect the remains of a downed Tupolev SB bomber. Note that the upper propeller blade of the starboard engine is intact, while all three blades of the port engine are curved to the side. This indicates that the starboard engine was not running during the forced landing. It also indicates that pilot was not killed in the air, as he was able to belly-land the airplane. Apparently the SB partially disintegrated during the landing or as a result of fire.

The twin-engine SB proved to be most vulnerable to hostile fire. Most of the SBs were shot down during extensive air combat in 1941, and in 1942 only a few survivors of the type remained in operational service. In 1942 the remainder were used mainly for nocturnal operations. (Photo: Trautloft.)

April 27 one of the Croatian pilots failed to return from a mission over Soviet-controlled territory. Satnik (captain) Berislav Supek belly-landed in Soviet territory. It is doubtful whether this actually was a desertion, although both the Soviets and Supek claimed so. A clear desertion however seems to have been the case with Natporucnik (first lieutenant) Nikola Vucina, who voluntarily flew his Bf 109 E to a VVS-Southern Front airfield on May 4. It is quite interesting to note that entries for May 1942 are missing from the 15./JG 52 log book.[12]

Starshiy Leytenant Aleksandr Pokryshkin of 16 GIAP was detailed to carry out reconnaissance flights with Vucina's Bf 109. In doing so he got a depressing insight into the low combat spirits of some of his fellow airmen. Flying the war booty close to the front-line, Pokryshkin spotted an airborne SB bomber. The sight of the Bf 109 was quite sufficient for the SB's pilot; without hesitating he put the nose of his bomber down and made an emergency landing in a field, heavily damaging his airplane. The scene was repeated during another sortie several days later: Approaching his airfield, Pokryshkin came across a U-2 whose pilot also panicked and made a forced landing, whereafter he ran all out to take cover. These incidents illustrate in a nutshell the prevailing weakness of the VVS in the Ukraine at this time, and it boded ill for the upcoming Soviet offensive in the area.

Chapter 14

Turn of the Tide at the Black Sea

On February 27, 1942, General-Leytenant Dmitriy Kozlov, the commander of the Soviet Crimean Front, initiated his long-planned breakthrough attempt from the Kerch Peninsula in eastern Crimea, but time had worked against him. The momentum of the past months, when the Soviets made a successful landing at Kerch and forced the Germans to abandon the assault on Sevastopol, was declining – in major part because the Luftwaffe units that had left the Crimea to blunt the Soviet counteroffensive in southeastern Ukraine in January had returned.

A formation of I-16 Ishaks. The Mark 24 I-16 viewed here was equipped with a 900-horsepower M-63 engine that produced a top speed of 296 miles per hour at 15,400 feet flight altitude. Although the new VVS-Crimean Front was rapidly built up to become one of the numerically strongest individual air forces of the VVS, most of its aircraft were obsolescent models such as this. (Photo: Authors' collection.)

Meanwhile, VVS-Crimean Front was beset by several disadvantages. There had been little time to prepare the airfields on the small Kerch Peninsula, and aircraft from four or five aviation regiments were crowded into each base. Furthermore, the bulk of the aircraft were obsolete variants.

Kozlov launched his attack on time, but thick fog curtailed air operations during the first two days. Despite desperate calls from the German ground troops, on February 27 Oberst Wolfgang von Wild, Fliegerführer Süd in the Crimea, could dispatch no more than three Luftwaffe aircraft on operations. The weak Luftwaffe close-air support promoted the Soviet venture, and the German ground troops were pushed back six miles on the northern flank.

The turning point came when the skies cleared on March 1. That day Oberst von Wild's units launched more than 120 sorties – 53 by fighters, 40 by dive-bombers, and nearly 30 by medium bombers. While conditions at the makeshift VVS-Crimean Front airstrips in the Kerch area still held most Soviet aircraft down, III./StG 77 was able to concentrate on armored units that had penetrated the German northern flank. The Stukagruppe claimed thirteen tanks and three motor vehicles destroyed without loss on the first day of March.[13]

General-Leytenant Kozlov was deprived of another of his trump cards, support from the guns of the Black Sea Fleet. The arrival of the torpedo bombers of Kampfgruppe II./KG 26 posed a serious threat to the ChF warships.

At the outbreak of the war, the Luftwaffe had lagged behind other air forces with respect to torpedo planes. In 1938 the Luftwaffe commander in chief, Hermann Göring, had ordered the "father of German torpedo aviation," Hauptmann Martin Harlinghausen, to "stop playing around with air torpedoes."[14] It was only after the successful British air-torpedo raid against the Italian naval base at Taranto on November 11, 1940, that Göring fully grasped the efficiency of torpedo aviation. Shortly afterward, two Kampffliegerstaffeln – 6./KG 26 and 1./KG 28 – were trained for air-torpedo missions and equipped with He 111 torpedo-plane variants.

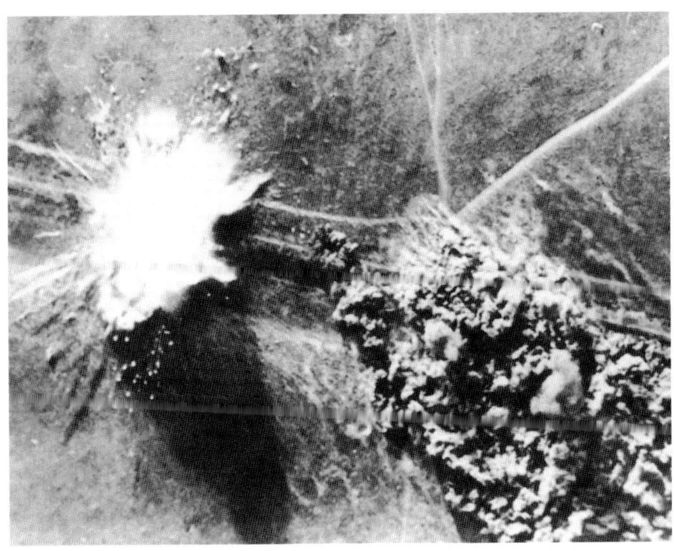

German bombs explode across a Soviet supply column. (Photo: Roba/Mombeek.)

The two Staffeln operated with considerable success over the Black Sea in the fall of 1941, sinking four Soviet freighters and damaging a tanker. It indeed was a great relief to Vitse-Admiral Filipp Oktyabrskiy, the commander of the Soviet Black Sea Fleet, when the torpedo units were withdrawn from the Eastern Front in November 1941.

Based on the successes achieved by 6./KG 26 and 1./KG 28, Harlinghausen – promoted to Oberstleutnant and appointed commander of the air-torpedo arm – set up the air-torpedo training school KSG 2 in Grossenbrode, Germany, and Grosseto, Italy. Hauptmann Werner Klümper, who had led an He 115 Staffel over the North Sea in 1940, was selected to command the school. 1./KG 28 was recommissioned as 4./KG 26, and within a short time, I. and II./KG 26 had been retrained as the Luftwaffe's first air-torpedo Kampfgruppen. The first Gruppe was dispatched to northern Norway to be used against the Allied northern supply convoys to the USSR, and II./KG 26 was directed to Fliegerführer Süd. The success was immediate.

The first victory was achieved on the night of March 1-2, when a II./KG 26 crew hit and severely damaged the 2,434-ton steamer *Fabritsius*. The ship was grounded at Cape Tuzla, where it later was destroyed in a storm.[15]

The return of the German torpedo planes greatly alarmed the commanders of the Soviet Black Sea Fleet. The news of the attack against *Fabritsius* compelled Vitse-Admiral Oktyabrskiy to limit the bombardment of enemy troops mainly to destroyers and flotilla leaders. Heavier vessels were held back unless guarded by powerful escort forces acting as an AAA deterrent.

General-Leytenant Kozlov's ground troops found themselves subjected to relentless air raids. On March 2 and March 3, III./ StG 77 inflicted considerable damage on Soviet truck and tank columns on the roads leading to the northern flank from Kerch. On March 3 Luftwaffe bombers hit and damaged the tanker *Kuybyshev* in the port of Kamysh-Burun south of Kerch, thus depriving the Crimean Front of much of its fuel. Finally, unexpected thaws alternating with blizzards mired the entire area to such an extent that Kozlov was forced to order the offensive terminated.

Discontented with the meager performances, Josef Stalin ordered VVS Crimean Front to be reinforced, and he sent one of his harshest senior political commissars, Armeyskiy Komissar Pervogo Ranga Lev Mekhlis, to the Crimea. Mekhlis, notorious for personally executing officers on the spot without trial, was a most unwelcome "guest" to the Soviets in this area. He immediately took a number of bureaucratic steps that weakened rather than bolstered the Soviet position. Disregarding the actual situation, he demanded that all attention be redirected to the offensive, and completely ignored defensive measures. While he kept the commanders of the aviation units occupied with preparing three detailed reports each day, he ordered an all-out effort by the airmen.

From the first week of March, VVS-Crimean Front and VVS-ChF initiated relentless attacks against German troop concentrations, artillery positions, and airfields. On March 8, VVS-ChF mounted its strongest air attack to date against Saki Airdrome, the home of II./KG 26 and I./KG 100 Wiking; the raiders dropped more than four

Sarabuz Airdrome, Crimea, in the spring of 1942. Two He 111 crewmen take a breather after another combat mission over the Black Sea. (Photo: Roba/Mombeek.)

hundred bombs. During a follow-up raid against the same target on March 9, five He 111s of I./KG 100 were severely damaged on the ground.

The increased Soviet activity was acutely felt, even at Nikolayev Airdrome, one hundred miles northwest of the Crimea. Posing as volunteer Hilfswillige – Soviet civilians assisting the Wehrmacht with fatigue-duty – partisans were able to put several Luftwaffe aircraft out of commission. On March 10 alone they completely destroyed three Ju 87s of StG 77, two Bf 109s of I./JG 77, and a Bf 110 of 4.(F)/122.

General-Mayor Nikolay Ostryakov, the commander of VVS-ChF, also participated in these operations. On March 11 he carried out a fighter patrol over Sevastopol in his personal Yak-1, which bore a tail fin painted navy blue. Ostryakov watched as two Il-2s of 18 ShAP attacked a German artillery position as it shelled a seaborne supply convoy arriving at Sevastopol. The German artillery was silenced as the gunners hastily took cover from the Shturmoviks' bombs, rockets, and machine guns. Nevertheless, heavy AAA fire met the two Soviet assault planes and both Il-2s were shot down. One of them made a belly-landing in no-man's land and Ostryakov saw its pilot climb to the ground. Without hesitation, the general pushed the stick forward, swooped down, and machine-gunned German soldiers who had left their position with the intention of capturing the Shturmovik pilot. Covered by devastating salvoes from the Yak-1, the Shturmovik pilot – Kapitan Mikhail Talalayev – managed to reach the Soviet lines and was soon back in action again.

Following Mekhlis's reckless demands, the Soviet Forty-fourth and Fifty-first armies reopened the ground offensive on the Kerch peninsula on Friday, March 13. By then, VVS-Crimean Front had been reinforced to a total of 581 combat-ready aircraft.

Both sides launched everything they could get into the air to support the ground battle, and large-scale aerial melees quickly evolved. "A stiff combat against a tenfold enemy superiority," III./JG 77's Leutnant Emil Omert reported on the first day of the new Soviet offensive.

Among several particularly skilled Soviet airmen who arrived to bolster VVS-Crimean Front was Mayor Mikhail Fedoseyev, one of the leading Soviet aces of the time. Fedoseyev, who was born in 1912 in Kazan as a worker's son, had participated in the Spanish Civil War as a fighter pilot. On August 4, 1938, he shot down his first enemy aircraft – a Bf 109 of the Condor Legion's J. 88 over Ebro. Until the fall of 1938, when the International Brigade was withdrawn from Spain, Fedoseyev carried out 160 combat sorties, took part in forty air combats, and was credited with seven victories. Awarded with the Lenin Order for these achievements, Fedoseyev was appointed commander of 6 OIAE (with the famous Kapitan Aleksandr Khalutin as his deputy), which later was reorganized into 88 IAP. In September 1939 he flew against the Poles over the western Ukraine, and at the outbreak of the war with Germany he commanded the newly commissioned 247 IAP, which was equipped with the best fighter aircraft the VVS could muster – the new Yak-1.

Under Fedoseyev´s command 247 IAP was credited with the destruction of forty-two enemy aircraft in the air. Fedoseyev took part in 169 combat sorties to February 1942, which yielded twenty-seven aerial combats and thirteen individual victories.

On March 16 Mayor Fedoseyev led the Yak-1s of his 247 IAP to intercept a formation of I./KG 100 He 111s as they flew against Kerch under escort by III./JG 77. In the ensuing combat, Fedoseyev claimed one Bf 109 shot down – his fourteenth individual victory – and an He 111 shared with three other pilots. Two other 247 IAP airmen claimed a second Bf 109. III./JG 77 registered two Bf 109s lost in aerial combat with a third suffering severe battle damage. On the opposing side, III./JG 77's Leutnant Emil Omert claimed a Yak-1 as his forty-fifth kill.

Next day, III./JG 77 airmen carrying out the Gruppe's final missions of its first combat tour on the Eastern Front could not prevent Soviet fighters from shooting down an He 111 of I./KG 100. On the

The end of an Il-2 Shturmovik. In February and March 1942, JG 77 claimed 150 victories in the Crimea, while VVS-Crimean Front alone filed 109 combat losses. (Photo: Grislawski.)

same day the 4,629-ton tanker *Kuybyshev* was hit and damaged in the port of Novorossiysk by III./KG 51 Ju 88s.

After twelve consecutive months of first-line service, Leutnant Omert and his comrades left the Crimea for rest and recuperation in Germany. In return, II./JG 77 arrived on station at Sarabuz Airdrome. Having exchanged their old Bf 109 Es for F-4s, these well-rested pilots were eager to pick up the fight after three months in Germany. Top scorers in this Gruppe were Oberleutnant Heinrich Setz (credited with forty-five victories by this time), Oberfeldwebel Rudolf Schmidt (thirty-three victories), Oberleutnant Anton Hackl (twenty-eight victories), and Gruppenkommandeur Hauptmann Anton Mader (twenty-seven victories).

Heinrich Setz joined II./JG 77 as a twenty-five-year-old Leutnant in July 1940 and scored his first victories against RAF aircraft over Norway's west coast. In July 1941 he was appointed Staffelkapitän of 4./JG 77, which he led until November 1942. Setz rose to fame during Operation Barbarossa, when he amassed forty-one kills in five months. With forty-five victories to his credit, Setz was awarded the Knight's Cross on December 31, 1941. In November 1942, he was placed in charge of I./JG 27 against the RAF, and on March 13, 1943, he was killed in action after shooting down three Spitfires in one combat – thereby running his total score to 138 victories achieved on only 274 combat missions. (Photo: Bundesarchiv.)

After a few quiescent days of ground fighting, German aerial reconnaissance noted signs that the Crimean Front was regrouping to intensify the offensive. The Luftwaffe reconnaissance units thus increased their activities over the Kerch Peninsula, and during a March 18 mission, Bf 110-equipped 3.(F)/11 lost its Staffelkapitän, Hauptmann Elmar Hornung with his crew – Oberfeldwebel Gerhard Lilienthal (pilot) and Unteroffizier Hans Stopf (radio operator). The German loss file records the cause as "unknown" and the entire crew was listed as missing.[16] On April 3, 1942, the *Krasnaya Zvezda*, the newspaper of the Red Army, reported:

> A Fascist aircraft appeared over the rifle detachment commanded by Leytenant Pich. The soldiers immediately opened an intense rifle and machine-gun fire, using incendiary and armor-piercing bullets. The fire hit the target and the plane descended steeply. The soldiers saw the plane crash in our territory. Mladshiy Leytenants Tupiyev and Baramidze and Krasnoarmeytsy Kekviashvili and Sirbiakvili rushed to the crash site and forced the Fascist airmen to surrender.
>
> The captured Fascists proved to be inveterate wolves. The commander of the crew carried three [sic] Iron Crosses. Oberfeldwebel Lilienthal and Unteroffizier Stopf admitted that they had flown over most European countries, dropping bombs over peaceful cities.[17]

Hans Stopf is reported to have died in Soviet captivity on September 11, 1942.[18] The fate of the two other crewmembers remains unclear to this day.

The Soviet onslaught opened again on March 19. From early that morning II./JG 77 was in constant action against large Soviet aviation formations. VVS-Crimean Front possessed an impressive number of aircraft – approximately 400 – but only 164 were "modern" types – 125 Yak-1, MiG-3, and LaGG-3 fighters; 21 Il-2s; and 18 Pe-2s.[19] Gruppenkommandeur Mader's airmen experienced a revival of air combat against obsolescent Soviet aircraft in 1941. They were thrilled by the impact of their new nose-mounted 20mm Mauser MG 151/20 cannon, with a velocity and rate of fire far superior to those of the old 20mm MG FF in the Bf 109 E. Before the day was over, Oberleutnant Heinrich Setz counted five victories and Oberfeldwebel Rudolf Schmidt and Feldwebel Ernst-Wilhelm Reinert each counted three. That evening Setz wrote in his diary:

> We have shot down 21 Russkiys. Personally, I brought home five, thereby reaching halfway to one hundred. At 0800 hours I take off on the day's first mission. As if by appointment, eight of the most modern Russian bombers arrive together with a considerable fighter escort. Within a matter of seconds, I had presented the infantry beneath to my 46th and 47th victories. Meanwhile, my wingman scored his 29th. The impact of the new cannon really impressed me. I remember the problems we had with some of these Russian aircraft previously, and now they are totally blown apart.[20]

attack. They now came in against the bombers from the rear in successive pairs. As soon as they noted that Terpugov was without his wingman, they immediately hurled themselves against him. Alone against three Messerschmitts, he was unable to cover the bombers on his flank. After the next Fascist attack, a DB-3F fell vertically, smoking heavily, and crashed into the ground. Shortly afterward it was followed by a second. Another four of our own fighters that had been scrambled from a forward airfield at Leninskoye appeared to assist us. But it was too late! Viktor Radkevich's victory cost us dearly"[24]

After the fight, "Toni" Hackl landed on the cratered airdrome at Sarabuz with mixed feelings. He had brought down three bombers – his twenty-ninth through thirty-first victories – and Oberfeldwebel Rudolf Schmidt had claimed a fourth, his thirty-ninth kill. But two of the Staffel's Bf 109s had been destroyed by the Soviet bombs and one of Hackl's most promising young pilots, Heinz Fröse, was missing.[25]

The 36 IAP aviators were even more angry. For several days afterwards they refused to speak to Radkevich.

All Soviet attempts to break through from the Kerch Peninsula were in vain. Met by a fresh panzer division and bolstered air attacks, the Crimean Front was effectively crippled. At the same time, Luftflotte 4 medium bombers subjected the Soviet supply shipping to relentless attacks, and the port of Kerch was reduced to rubble.

On April 2 a German reconnaissance plane spotted the large tanker *Kuybyshev* off Kerch. It had been repaired after the bomb damage it had suffered two weeks earlier and was now heading for Kamysh-Burun with 4,600 tons of badly needed fuel for the Crimean Front. A MiG-3 pilot from 7 IAP/VVS-ChF managed to shoot down the reconnaissance plane, but its radio message had already reached Fliegerführer Süd. An hour later Kapitan Vasiliy Chernopashchyenko of the same fighter unit reportedly brought down both bombers that were launched against the tanker – the second by a taran, which cost the Soviet pilot his life. But the tanker could not be saved. Hit by a torpedo in the stern, *Kuybyshev* violently caught fire and went down in the shallow waters of the Mariya Maddalina sand bank. There, the half-sunk tanker continued to burn for almost a week. This was such a terrible blow that the Crimean Front had to discontinue the entire offensive.

40 BAP/VVS-ChF debuted the new Pe-2 in service with the air force of the Soviet Black Sea Fleet in the summer of 1941, and these modern bombers achieved many successes in the Crimean battle zone. It was not uncommon for the twin endplate fin of this airplane to confuse VVS and Luftwaffe fighter pilots between Pe-2s and Bf 110s. (Photo: Viktor Kulikov collection.)

The transport capacity of the Soviet Black Sea Fleet had been reduced from 43,200 tons at the beginning of February 1942 to 27,400 tons at the end of March. Six transports had been lost and another six were under repair.[26] As small recompense, on April 2 VVS-ChF bombers hit and damaged the Romanian auxiliary cruiser *Dachia* and a torpedo boat.

In recognition of the courageous fighting in the air over the Crimea since the fall of 1941, the first two aviation regiments of VVS-ChF were adopted as Guards regiments on April 3. 2 MTAP was redesignated as 5 GMTAP/VVS-VMF and 8 IAP became 6 GIAP/VVS-VMF.

Every day from April 4 to April 8, the new Guards regiments and other VVS-ChF units raided the air bases at Saki and Sarabuz. 5./JG 77's Oberfeldwebel Rudolf Schmidt was shot down on April 6 as he intercepted a group of incoming 40 BAP/VVS-ChF Pe-2s between Yevpatoriya and Saki in western Crimea. The body of this formidable ace, victor of forty-two aerial combats, was never found.

The next Luftwaffe unit to intervene in the battle of the Crimea was KG 55, which bombed Tuapse on April 10, scoring hits on the destroyer *Sposobnyy* and the uncompleted cruiser *Frunze*. Intercepting Soviet fighters managed to bring down one of the He 111s. On April 17, II./KG 26 had another important success when two torpedo hits sank the 4,125-ton steamship *Svanetiya* between Sevastopol and Novorossiysk. Five hundred and thirty-five men were lost in this disaster.[27]

German air raids against the ports of Kerch, Novorossiysk, and Tuapse on April 19 were intercepted by scores of Soviet fighters. To the Bf 109 pilots of II./JG 77 a veritable "shooting party" developed. Thirteen victories were claimed – all but one by Oberleutnant Anton Hackl's 5. Staffel. Hackl personally contributed five kills to this total.[28] Moreover, the Ju 88s and He 111s were able to score hits on the tanker *I. Stalin* and three transport ships. Two days later, II./KG 51 sank a transport and damaged the mineship *Komintern* in the same area.

Against Soviet claims of seven Ju 88s shot down, only one Ju 88 was lost to fighter interception, according to German loss files.[29] Other Luftwaffe bombers were directed against Soviet air force ground installations, and VVS-ChF registered three MBR-2s and one GST damaged on a Sevastopol airfield.[30]

II./JG 77's Oberleutnant Heinrich Setz went after newly arrived VVS-Crimean Front Yak-1s: "Today I hunted the Yaks in their own aerie forty miles behind the front line," Setz noted in his diary. "First our bombers dropped their cargo, then I lie in wait. As I had expected, they came out. I darted toward one of these birds from an altitude of 12,000 feet."

In two such hit-and-run missions on April 21, Setz shot down three Yak-1s. The last one was his sixtieth victory.

An attempt by VVS-ChF to retaliate in like manner on April 24 backfired, and the Soviets lost six naval aircraft.[31] In return, however, II./JG 77's Feldwebel Franz Schulte, a twenty-five victory ace, was shot down and severely injured. Yet the hardest blow sustained by the Soviet Black Sea Fleet this day was dealt by III./StG 77. A concentrated dive-bomber attack completely devastated the ChF's 36th Aviation Repair Shop in Kruglaya Bay near Sevastopol. Among the forty-eight men killed were General-Mayor Nikolay Ostryakov and the deputy commander of VVS-VMF, General-Mayor F.G. Korobkov.

Ostryakov's death, especially, led to an outcry for revenge throughout the entire VVS-ChF. He had been very popular among all ranks and enjoyed a high and well-deserved respect. He had been one of the pioneers of Soviet parachuting and had developed mass parachuting in 1935 – for which he was awarded with the Order of the Red Star. Piloting an SB in the Spanish Civil War, Ostryakov had distinguished himself by breaking up an attack by the Italian Black Plumes Corps at Guadalajara and on another occasion scoring two bomb hits on the German battleship *Deutschland*.

A III./JG 52 Bf 109 F taxies out for another combat mission in Crimean skies in late April or early May 1942. (Photo: Grislawski.)

Hermann Graf (left) and Alfred Grislawski, inseparable friends in war and peace. During most of 1941 and in early 1942, Grislawski flew as the upcoming 9./JG 52 top ace's wingman. Graf's rise to fame started in the winter of 1941-1942, when he increased his personal victory tally from twenty to forty-five in slightly more than two months. Grislawski scored his first kill – an I-16 – on September 1, 1941. His period of real success opened in the Crimea in late April 1942, and during the next four weeks his tally rose from eighteen to forty-two. On July 1, 1942, Feldwebel Alfred Grislawski was awarded the Knight's Cross. By that time, Leutnant Hermann Graf had been awarded with the Knight's Cross with Oak Leaves and Swords. Both survived the war – Graf with 212 confirmed victories and Grislawski with 132. Graf, who spent five years in Soviet captivity, passed away on November 4, 1988. (Photo: Grislawski.)

Flying against Novorossiysk on April 28, thirty-three Ju 88 crews of I./KG 51 ran into vindictive MiG-3 fighter pilots of 7 IAP/VVS-ChF. As the pale-faced and exhausted German survivors returned to base afterwards, they described one of the fiercest Soviet fighter attacks they had ever encountered on the Eastern Front. Only close cooperation among the skilled German aerial gunners had prevented a complete rout. The MiG-3s brought down two Ju 88s and several returned with battle damage and injured crewmen. One of the missing Ju 88s was destroyed in an air-to-air ramming by Serzhant Leonid Sevryukov[32] – the second taran driven home by a 7 IAP/VVS-ChF pilot in less than a month. Soviet fighters and AAA claimed ten victories against only one loss, Serzhant Sevryukov's MiG-3.[33]

The increased Soviet air activity compelled Luftflotte 4's Generaloberst Löhr to dispatch another Jagdgruppe – III./JG 52 – to the Crimea. On April 29 this unit arrived at Zürichtal, twenty-five miles to the west of the front lines on the Kerch Peninsula. On April 30 Leutnant Hermann Graf, the Staffelkapitän of 9./JG 52, flew seven sorties over the Crimea, shooting down six Soviet planes. And his wingman, Feldwebel Alfred Grislawski, bagged two I-15bis in one engagement.[34]

III./JG 52 was an old acquaintance to the veterans of VVS-ChF. During the previous fall, this unit – and particularly Hermann Graf – had dealt the Black Sea fliers severe losses. As though the Soviets had been aware of who had arrived – which is far from impossible – Zürichtal Airdrome immediately became the focus of repeated raids by Soviet strafers.

Crimean partisans who kept surveillance on Zürichtal helped guide the Soviet fighters by radio. Hermann Graf noted in his diary how the men of III./JG 52 could hear the voice of a female partisan broadcasting news of takeoffs and landings at the base. "We called her 'Egg Lady,'" Graf wrote, "because we imagined that she was sitting somewhere with her radio-transmitter hidden in an egg basket, reporting our takeoffs and landings to her compatriots. Time after time, we had barely touched the ground, before the 'rivals' came buzzing at low level over the sea."

In due course Feldwebel Grislawski figured out a way to trap the Soviets. "Let's take off with the entire Staffel," he proposed to Graf. "Then we fly around, but without engaging any enemy aircraft, and return to the airfield with both ammunition and fuel available to deal the Ivans a nasty surprise."[35] Graf bought the idea.

"Once again we heard the 'Egg Lady' telling her stories about us," Graf wrote in his diary: "She definitely informed the Russians that we were about to land. In order to strengthen her in this belief, we made a wide turn, went down as if we were about to land, and then took off again. Having repeated this four times and still no sight of any Russian, I finally decided to land. I was just a few meters above the ground when I heard Grislawski cry that they were coming. Stick backwards, retract the landing gears, adjust the propeller pitch, and up we go!" Grislawski recalls that "We pursued the MiGs, Yaks, or LaGGs all the way back to Sevastopol, shooting them down one by one. Only one of the Russian pilots survived. He bailed out and his parachute got stuck in a pine tree in the mountains east of Sevastopol."

An I-16 downed by German fighters. The airplane in this photo is a Mark 5, one of the first I-16 serial variants. Due to the heavy losses of 1941, many VVS front-line units were re-equipped with such obsolescent aircraft drawn from flight training schools. While the bulk of the modern Soviet fighters were earmarked for the Moscow combat zone, the old I-16 became the most common VVS fighter in the southern combat zone. Out of thirty-three aircraft claimed shot down by 9./JG 52's Leutnant Hermann Graf between December 1, 1941, and April 29, 1942, at least seventeen were I-16s. (Photo: Wagner/Stein via Rosipal.)

In the early hours of May 2 Graf and Grislawski took off together with another famous ace of 9./JG 52, Feldwebel Leopold Steinbatz, to give the Soviets a taste of their own medicine – a low-level attack against a fighter base near Kerch. Two scrambling I-16s had just left the ground as the Messerschmitts came sweeping down. The VVS pilots didn't have a chance; they had to choose between engaging the Bf 109s with all odds against them, at a lower altitude, and considerably slower with their undercarriage down – or to start cranking the forty-four turns of the hoist ratchet it took to retract the landing gear into the wings.

One of the I-16s caught a full burst from Graf's cannon and machine guns and veered to the side, colliding with his wingman. Both aircraft crashed in a huge sheet of flame. These were Graf's seventieth and seventy-first victories.

At that moment other Ishaks came diving in against the three Germans, but they were obviously not aware of whom they had attacked. Three of these I-16s were shot down – two by Steinbatz and one by Graf. That day Hermann Graf surpassed his personal record by downing seven enemy aircraft.

May 3 saw a considerable increase in air activity by both sides. Heavy Luftwaffe raids were launched against Sevastopol, Bagerovo Airdrome on the Kerch Peninsula, and the port of Anapa in the northwestern Caucasus. VVS-ChF carried out 262 sorties, striking German troops at Sevastopol and the airfields at Saki, Sarabuz, and Yevpatoria.

During one of these missions, Oberleutnant Heinrich Setz and his 4./JG 77 had a tough encounter with 9 IAP/VVS-ChF. Early in the morning, Setz led a group of Bf 109s in a swift hit-and-run attack against a formation of about thirty I-153 biplanes over the Kerch front. Setz and Feldwebel Ernst-Wilhelm Reinert managed to destroy two I-153s, and then Setz decided to lead his fighters further behind the enemy front, searching for more "easy victims."

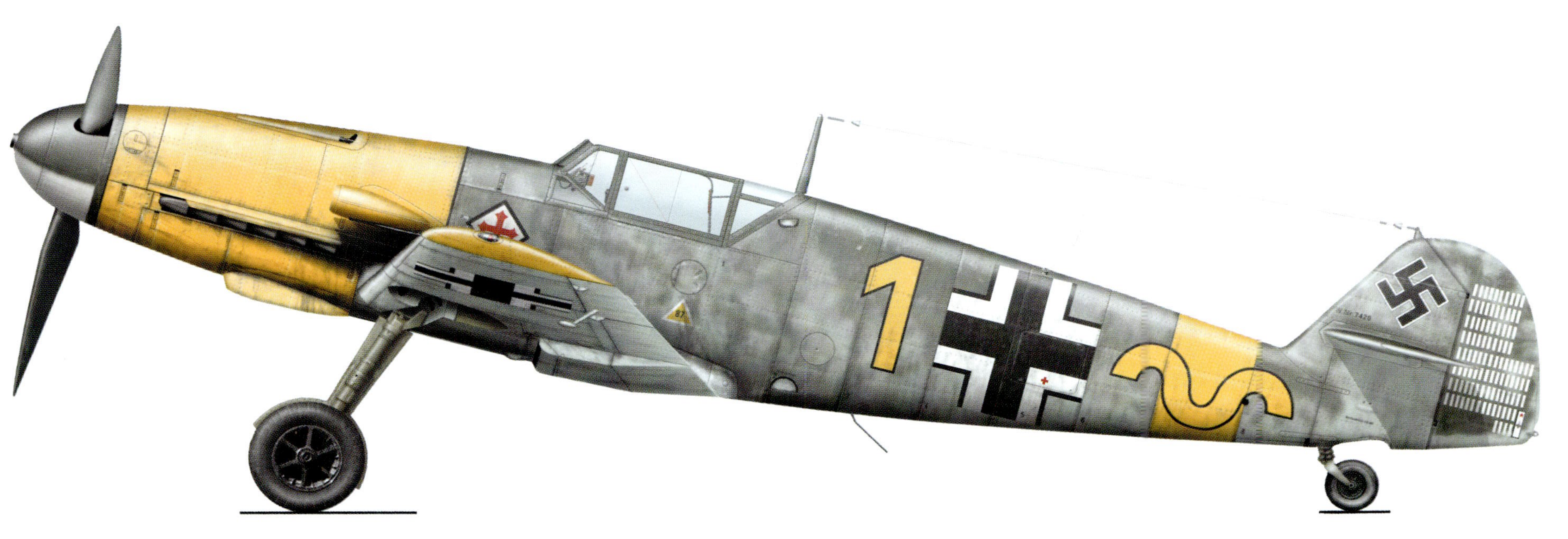

Bf 109 F-4 W.Nr. 7420, Leutnant Hermann Graf, Staffelführer 9./JG 52, Kharkov-Rogan, Soviet Union, May 14, 1942

Japanese at Khalkhin-Gol in 1939 or the Finns during the Winter War of 1939 – 40.

Arguably the most formidable Soviet fighter ace in early 1942, Mayor Boris Safonov, had fought the Luftwaffe in this sector since the opening of the German invasion in 1941. By the turn of the year, Safanov's score stood at sixteen personal and six shared victories, all but two achieved while flying an I-16. That three of the first aviation units adopted as Guards units operated in the Murmansk sector speaks for itself. 72 SAP/VVS-SF was recommissioned 2 GSAP of VVS-VMF in January 1942, and 145 IAP and 147 IAP of VVS-Fourteenth Army were recommissioned 19 GIAP and 20 GIAP, respectively, on April 4, 1942.

A 2 GSAP/VVS-SF Pe-2 is prepared for a combat sortie at Vayenga-1. During the first two months of 1942, VVS SF mustered only three Pe-2s, all in 72 SAP. But, in spite of this minimal presence, these aircraft were quite active. In March 1942, VVS-SF was reinforced with 95 IAP, equipped with eighteen Pe-3s – the heavy fighter version of the Pe-2. (Photo: Rybin.)

A rather used 2 GSAP/VVS-SF MiG-3 at Vayenga Airdrome. 72 SAP/VVS-SF (later 2 GSAP/VVS-SF) was reinforced by a MiG-3-Eskadrilya in July 1941, and four of its MiG-3s survived until 1942. Throughout 1942 only one of these MiG-3s was lost; it was set on fire in an aerial combat on July 19 and burned out just after landing. The three remaining MiGs were transferred to 255 IAP/VVS-SF in the fall of 1942. There they remained (mostly in unserviceable condition) until mid-1943, when they were shifted to VVS-TOF, the Soviet Pacific fleet. Thus the MiG-3's combat history in VVS-sSF was over.

As seen in this photo, Soviet Lapps with their reindeer were used to help with ground service on the Soviet Far North airdromes. These reindeer are transporting bombs on sleighs. (Photo: Soviet Northern Fleet's Museum via Gyllenhaal.)

An increasingly large proportion of the Soviet fighter aircraft in the Far North were Lend-Lease types, most notably Hurricanes in early 1942. (78 IAP/VVS-SF was the first Soviet unit to be equipped with Hurricanes.) This is quite understandable, since much of the American and British Lend-Lease deliveries arrived over the Barents and Norwegian Seas to the northern ports of Murmansk and Arkhangelsk. The first British convoy, code-named *PQ-0*, had left for the Soviet Union on August 21, 1941, and it was followed by convoys *PQ-1* through *PQ-10* during the next six months. The common route went through the Denmark Strait between Iceland and Greenland, always maintaining a position as far to the north as possible. During the first 150 miles of the convoys' journey, fighters from RAF 269 and 330 (Norwegian) squadrons, stationed in British-occupied Iceland, covered the ships from the air. Since all British aircraft carriers were committed to areas of greater importance to the British themselves, the cargo ships were provided with no air cover until they came within reach of the VVS-SF fighters, approximately a day's journey from Murmansk.

The brief daylight hours of the Polar night – for several weeks, darkness reigned around the clock – and adverse weather conditions resulted in all of the first *PQ* convoys arriving at Murmansk or Arkhangelsk, the port in the southern part of the White Sea, without encountering any German major intervention.

Air operations proceeded at a very low tempo during the first months of 1942. "It was damned cold, but we were in a good mood," recalls 6./JG 5's Oberfeldwebel Hugo Dahmer. "There was only a little flying and we passed the time playing cards."[38]

Only in March did climatic conditions permit a increased amount of air activity, and the Germans were stunned by the aggressiveness with which a number of Soviet air strikes were carried out. It started on March 3, when the commander of the Soviet Northern Fleet, Vitse-Admiral Arseniy Golovko, instructed 78IAP/VVS-SF to organize a raid against Luostari Airdrome south of Petsamo in order to hamper the Luftwaffe's effort against the next Lend-Lease convoy, *PQ-12*.

The Soviet fighter unit dispatched twenty-four Hurricanes against the airdrome on March 4. "We flew so low that our propellers almost touched the snow," recalls Starshiy Leytenant Sergey Kurzenkov. The Soviet fighters flew below the horizon of the German Freya radar, and the attack caught the Germans totally unaware. Before the AAA gunners could react, the Soviet fighters swooped down upon the air base with rattling machine guns. RS-82 rocket projectiles exploded all over the parking area, and three He 111s were put out of commission. All of the participating Hurricanes landed safely at their own base, and the pilots were received by General-Leytenant Semyon Zhavoronkov, the commander of the Soviet Naval Air Forces, and General-Mayor Aleksandr Kuznetsov, the VVS-SF commander.

A VVS-SF Hurricane IIB flown by 78 IAP or 2 GSAP. Note the Soviet-installed 20mm ShVAK cannon on the inside of the wing, and 12.7mm BK or 7.62mm ShKAS on the outside of the wing; these replaced the British Vickers .303 machine-guns. One major problem with aircraft of American and British designation was that the Soviet 70- to 74-octane aviation fuel wore down the engines, which were constructed for higher octane ratings. This rapidly reduced their performance and also led to a number of flight accidents. (Photo: Rybin.)

But Zhavoronkov was not fully satisfied with the result of the raid, and decided to launch another twenty-two Hurricanes three hours later against the same target. This time the Germans were alert. Almost all of II./JG 5 was airborne to protect the precious torpedo bombers based on the field. "They showed no mercy," wrote Starshiy Leytenant Sergey Kurzenkov. The air-base raid was warded off, but the Soviet pilots fought well in spite of numerical and tactical disadvantages. They managed to escape with only two Hurricanes missing and filed three victory claims. (Luftflotte 5 registered no losses in aerial combat that day.) One of the downed Soviet pilots, Kapitan

Aleksey Shvedov, even managed to evade capture and returned to the Soviet lines on foot nine days later.

As results of a storm that raged in the Barents Sea from March 6 to March 10 and effective Soviet and Allied counter-air action, the Luftwaffe operation against *PQ-12* was a failure. On March 11 the Zerstörerstaffel 6.(Z)/JG 5 was dealt a hard blow when it lost three Bf 110s to two Tomahawks and a Hurricane from 147 IAP.[39] In return, 147 IAP's Starshiy Leytenant A.V. Yellisev's P-40C was shot down. Two days later, the only bombs that hit any of the *PQ-12* ships – the freighter *Sevzaples* – failed to explode.

With the approach of *PQ-13* at the end of March, the Soviet air offensive against the ground installations of Luftflotte 5 was intensified. By that time, the Soviet aviation command in the Far North held a reassuring numerical advantage. On April 1, VVS-SF, based around Murmansk, reported a strength of 204 serviceable aircraft grouped in seven units (27 IAP, 78 IAP, and 95 IAP; 2 GSAP; 49 RAE; 118 MRAP; and 24 Aviazveno Svyazi).

The Red Army's Karelian Front, responsible for the entire front line along the Soviet borders with Norway and Finland, remained the weakest Soviet army group, but it nevertheless received some reinforcements at the end of 1941 and early 1942. In early April, the units of the Karelian Front opposed to the Germans in northern Norway and Finland and central Finland were: *Fourteenth Army*, with an air force composed of four aviation regiments – 145 IAP, 147 IAP, 197 IAP, and 837 IAP – numbering eighty-four aircraft in the Murmansk area; *Nineteenth Army*, with an air force composed of three aviation regiments – 435 IAP, 609 IAP, and 839 IAP – numbering fifty-nine aircraft in the Kandalaksha area; *Twenty-sixth Army*, with an air force composed of two and a half aviation regiments – 760 IAP, 668 NBBAP, and 17 GShAP – numbering fifty-five aircraft in the Kestenga area near the western coast of the White Sea. *VVS-Thirty-second Army*, mustering fifty-seven aircraft in the Lake Onega area, operated exclusively against the Finns.

Apart from these units, the staff of VVS-Karelian Front oversaw four Polka and one Eskadrilya – 80 BBAP, 137 BBAP, 608 BBAP, 679 TrAP, and 118 ORAE – with a total of eighty-seven aircraft. In addition, 122 IAD was the first aviation unit assigned to the Murmansk Air Defense District (Murmansk PVO).

Bf 110s of 10.(Z)/JG 5 during an escort mission for KG 30 Ju 88s against Murmansk. Tasked to provide KG 30 with escort during long-range missions, the JG 5 Zerstörerstaffel suffered a succession of losses in combat with Soviet fighters in March and April 1942. 147 IAP/20 GIAP, in particular, took a heavy toll of the Bf 110s. (Photo: Roba/Mombeek.)

Even though the southernmost units of these Soviet forces also faced small increments of the Finnish Air Force, the Soviets held a numerical advantage of around four to one against the Luftwaffe in the Far North.

On March 24, I./StG 5 carried out two attacks against the Murmansk port area with limited forces – and managed to score a direct bomb hit on the British freighter *Lancaster Castle*. In return, VVS-SF dispatched six 95 IAP Pe-2s escorted by fourteen 2 GSAP Hurricanes against Luostari Airdrome, where four German planes were reported destroyed and three Hurricanes were lost to German fighter interception.[40]

Compared with other combat zones on the Eastern Front, the scale and tempo of aerial combat in the Far North remained limited. Nevertheless, the loss statistics of both sides reveal a situation quite different from those of other sectors of the Eastern Front. Through March 1942, JG 5 claimed twenty victories against five combat losses. In total, Luftflotte 5 lost eleven aircraft due to hostile activity or unknown causes during that month, and four others were severely damaged.[41] Soviet archival material reveals that in return during the same period, VVS-SF and VVS-Karelian Front lost nineteen aircraft destroyed and eight others with severe or medium damage in aerial combat or to unknown causes.[42]

During the first days of April, I./KG 26 and KG 30's two Gruppen made repeated attempts to locate the ships of *PQ-13*, which had been scattered over a wide area by a heavy storm. Since March 25, Fliegerführer Nord-Ost was entirely focused on the Anglo-American supply shipping. All other activities, such as the interdiction of the Kirov rail line and air-base raids, almost ceased in order to conserve forces for operations against the seaborne Lend-Lease transports. But the rough weather prevented any successful intervention against *PQ-13*. Only two air raids were made against this convoy; Hauptmann Hajo Herrmann's III./KG 30 managed to sink two freighters and U-boats sank three others.

Meanwhile, the Luftwaffe's own airfields were subjected to almost daily air raids. On April 4, 95 IAP's Pe-3s hit Luostari Airdrome twice. Although the Soviets filed optimistic claims of sixteen German aircraft destroyed on the ground, only one

I./KG 26 He 111 was really put out of commission. Nevertheless, the increasing frequency of these air-base raids had the effect of reducing the availability of German fighters for offensive missions, since it compelled the Germans to keep part of their fighter forces on alert status on each airfield. For this reason, Soviet pilots fared well in ensuing air combats.

Three Bf 109s made an unsuccessful interception against the first raid, and during the second mission against Luostari, Northern Fleet's 2 GSAP and 78 IAP claimed six Bf 109s shot down for one Hurricane lost. According to JG 5 files, II./JG 5's Oberfeldwebel Gerhard Hornig and Unteroffizier Arthur Mendl were both wounded, while Leutnant Friedrich Dahn shot down a Hurricane.

An equally stiff combat was fought on April 8 between a Bf 110 Schwarm of 10.(Z)/JG 5 and 20 GIAP/VVS-Fourteenth Army (formerly 147 IAP). Four Hurricanes and two Tomahawks of the latter unit were directed to pursue fifteen Ju 87s of I./StG 5 that were returning after an unsuccessful mission against Murmansk. The Soviets caught up with the Germans near Restikent, southwest of the port city. "Things got pretty rough," Leutnant Gerhard Friedrich, the radio operator in one of the escorting Bf 110s later said.[43] The combat could have resulted in another disaster for the Zerstörerstaffel had it not been for the timely intervention of eight Bf 109s, and the courage and skill of one of the Bf 110 pilots in particular – Oberfeldwebel Theodor Weissenberger. Only one Bf 110 was lost, and Oberfeldwebel Weissenberger countered the attackers by destroying one of the Soviet fighters. His only possible victim was Kapitan Aleksey Pozdnyakov; according to Soviet records, his Tomahawk was destroyed in a taran that killed the pilot. The Stukas managed to slip away without loss. 20 GIAP filed five victory claims, including an amazing record – three tarans in a single engagement, two of them by the same pilot, Starshiy Leytenant Aleksey Khlobystov. Quite sensationally, Khlobystov managed to bring his Tomahawk back to base despite damage suffered in the two midair rammings.[44]

Twenty-four-year old Leytenant Aleksey Khlobystov of 20 GIAP earned fame after the air battle in the Far North on April 8, 1942. 20 GIAP reported five enemy aircraft shot down during this engagement – one Bf 110 shared by Kapitan Aleksey Pozdnyakov and Leytenant I. D. Fateyev; one Ju 87 shared by Kapitan Pozdnyakov, Leytenant Aleksey Khlobystov, and Leytenant Fateyev; one Bf 110 attacked by Serzhant M. Ye. Bychkov and Leytenant V. R. Semen'kov but finally rammed by Khlobystov; one Bf 109 rammed by Kapitan Pozdnyakov; and one Bf 109 rammed by Khlobystov. The only Soviet loss was Kapitan Pozdnyakov, who was killed in his taran. Khlobystov survived a third taran slightly more than a month later but was killed in action on December 13, 1943. (Photo: Seidl.)

20 GIAP reported another success on April 9, when the Tomahawks and Hurricanes of 769 IAP/PVO intercepted a 1.(H)/32 Hs 126 with six Bf 109 escorts from 5./JG 5. The German fighter pilots managed to save the reconnaissance plane but in doing so lost two of their own number. Both pilots bailed out over Soviet-held territory and were captured. One of them, Leutnant Alfred Jakobi, was an ace with ten victories. All of the 20 GIAP airplanes returned safely to base.

The mounting Soviet opposition in the air required that JG 5 be reinforced. Also, the old Bf 109 Es in service with II./JG 5 were gradually phased out and replaced by the faster Bf 109 F (although some Bf 109 Es remained in service with JG 5 well into the summer of 1942). Moreover, the new III./JG 5 was shifted to Petsamo from the Norwegian west coast. II./KG 30 also returned to the Far North from the central combat zone – where it had been dispatched to help stem the tide of the Soviet winter offensive there – and it took part in the series of raids against the Soviet fighter bases. These measures proved sufficient to tip the balance in favor of the Germans.

With bolstered fighter escorts, the bombers and dive-bombers of Luftflotte 5 targeted the port of Murmansk on six occasions during the latter half of April. Two raids were carried out on April 15. During the first, the previously damaged freighter *Lancaster Castle* sustained additional bomb damage. Participating with the escort for this mission, 10.(Z)/JG 5's Oberfeldwebel Theodor Weissenberger bagged a 78 IAP I-16, his eighth victory.

As the Germans returned in force against the same target shortly before nightfall, this time in three waves, three Soviet fighter aviation regiments were scrambled. 20 GIAP was directed against the first wave; the Soviet Northern Fleet's 78 IAP and 2 GSAP followed. They all became locked in combat with a larger number of Messerschmitts than these Soviet pilots had ever seen. "Theo" Weissenberger knocked down two fighters for three kills in one day. Starshiy Leytenant Sergey Kurzenkov describes the combat: "A completely mad air encounter

death. Next, the victorious Bf 109 pilot singled out a second victim, Serzhant N. F. Yepanov. As Yepanov hung in his parachute harness, he saw his victor climb away. Then the victorious German pilot – twenty-one-year-old Unteroffizier Rudolf "Rudi" Müller – triumphantly joined his comrades for the return flight. The Ju 87 airmen, who had escaped any casualties, were no less enthusiastic.

While this fight took place, VVS-Fourteenth Army dispatched a mission against Luostari Airdrome. But before the Soviets reached the target, the German fliers returning from the Vayenga mission spotted them. The Bf 109s immediately attacked, with terrible impact: 20 GIAP's Starshiy Leytenant I. Ya. But and Serzhant A. I. Chibisov, and the SB piloted by 137 SBAP's Mladshiy Leytenant Golovanov were all shot down by "Rudi" Müller, who thus increased his total to fifteen victories.

That evening, the pilots of 6./JG 5 launched a wild party to celebrate the five Soviet planes "Rudi" Müller had claimed during the single sortie.

In total, air combat in the Far North on April 23 resulted in eight Soviet[47] and only one German aircraft lost. Starshiy Leytenant Sergey Kurzenkov of 2 GSAP/VVS-SF later devoted the following lines in his memoir to the formidable "Rudi" Müller:

> During these days [late April 1942], a specially camouflaged Me 109 appeared on the Fascist side. This fighter, painted in stripes, always flew above the main formation of their patrolling fighters. This German pilot and his wingman never took part in group combats. They only jumped pilots that were "dreaming" and had strayed from the others.
>
> We started hunting him, but the Fascist ace wasn't easy to catch.[48]

An attempt by VVS-SF to strike back at the Germans by attacking Kirkenes-Hoybukten Airdrome on April 26 led to further heavy Soviet losses. 6./JG 5 aces Oberleutnant Horst Carganico, Oberfeldwebel Willi Pfränger, and "Rudi" Müller shot down five of the seven participating 95 IAP/VVS-SF Pe-3s, and not a single German aircraft was even damaged on the ground.

Uffz. Rudolf Müller achieved his first victory – against an I-16 – on his first combat mission, on September 12, 1941 (a claim that cannot be located in any Soviet loss registers). During the following twelve months, he increased his score to seventy. By the time "Rudi" Müller was shot down and captured by the Soviets on April 19, 1943, his score had risen to ninety-four. (Photo: Gloeckner.)

Fliegerführer Nord-Ost was well prepared when several months of calm on the ground ended abruptly at the close of April. The Soviet Fourteenth Army made a strong effort to break through the German lines at the Litsa River, forty miles west of Murmansk, and marines of the Northern Fleet made an amphibious landing in the German rear at Motovskiy Bay south of Rybachiy Peninsula. The operation was launched during the night of April 27 – 28, and next day the sky above Motovskiy Bay was filled with aircraft from both sides, supporting their respective ground troops.

At 1348 hours on April 28, 2 GSAP/VVS-SF had another unfortunate encounter with 6./JG 5, resulting in five Hurricanes and four pilots lost. Four of the kills were chalked up by "Rudi" Müller - for his 19-22nd victories. In total, operations on April 28 cost 2 GSAP/VVS-SF seven Hurricanes.

The British-manufactured Hawker Hurricane posed no large threat to the veteran pilots of JG 5, but the Soviet pilots were forced to fly anything available. The men of 27 IAP/VVS-SF were in an even more difficult position as they were still manning old I-153 Chayka biplanes engaged in low-level attacks against the German troops at Motovskiy Bay.

On April 29, 6./JG 5 managed to catch six of these obsolescent planes over the Litsa River, and three had been downed – one by "Rudi" Müller – by the time a flight of Hurricanes arrived on the scene. Under fire from German ground troops, one of the downed and injured Chayka pilots, Leytenant Nikifor Ignatyev, crawled from his I-153 in no-man's-land, back to the Soviet lines. There he reported that he had engaged in a taran over a Bf 109, and he was awarded with the Order of the Red Banner.[49]

The loss figures for both sides reflect the intensified air war in the Far North during April 1942 – with forty-two Soviet aircraft lost and eleven damaged in aerial combat,[50] while Luftflotte 5 recorded twenty-four aircraft lost and eight severely damaged during operations against

Ju 88 A-4 WNr 140171, Hauptmann Siegmund-Ulrich Freiherr von Gravenreuth, Gruppenkommandeur II./KG 30 Adler, Petsamo, Finland, April 1942

VVS-SF Hurricanes cover the Soviet amphibious landing at Motovskiy Bay. Soviet Hurricane pilot Starshiy Leytenant Sergey Kurzenkov recalls: "We carried out several missions each day to cover our troops from the air. Bitter aerial combats led to various results." (Photo: Authors' collection.)

the Soviets. The Soviet losses also include aircraft shot down by the Finns.

The Soviet Fourteenth Army was beaten back with bloody losses, but the 6,000-man 12th Independent Marine Brigade, which had landed at Motovskiy Bay, held out. By May 1 the Red marines had established a ten-by-eight-mile bridgehead. Two days later the German 2d Mountain Division launched a counterattack supported by intense air raids.

Adverse weather prevented most air activity during the first days of May, but both sides launched strong forces into the air to the Motovskiy Bay area when the weather cleared on May 9. In the ensuing combats, a Bf 109, an Hs 126, and three Hurricanes were shot down.

Things got much worse for the Soviets beginning at noon on May 10, when 5./JG 5 engaged the naval 2 GSAP and 78 IAP. The German pilots reportedly shot down six Hurricanes before the twin-engine Bf 110s of 10.(Z)/JG 5 intervened, bagging three more against no losses. Although the Soviets claimed four German fighters, only one was in fact lost. They also recorded five Hurricanes shot down, including four from the 1st Eskadrilya, 78 IAP, alone. Three Soviet pilots were killed and one was injured.

Over the next few hours, 2 GSAP conducted four more missions without spotting any German planes. Then at around 1630 hours on May 10, nine of its Hurricanes were dispatched together with five SBs. Fifteen minutes later as the Soviet formation was approaching the blackened battlefield at the Litsa River, it came across eight I./KG 30 Ju 88s escorted by six Bf 110s. Sergey Kurzenkov recalls: "Suddenly our commander called out: 'Watch out! Above, to the left and to the right, groups of enemy aircraft! Attention, don't lag behind!'"[51]

The Zerstörer pilots pounced on the fatigued Soviet airmen without hesitation – and with terrible impact. Oberfeldwebel Theodor Weissenberger led his Kette of three Zerstörer against the Hurricanes. At 1645, Weissenberger claimed a Soviet fighter shot down. In the next minute a second Hurricane went down under Weissenberger's gun. And at 1648 his voice was heard once again over the radio: "*Abschuss!*" – "Victory!". Weissenberger immediately charged a fourth Hurricane, and at 1650 he scored his fourth victory in this battle. Sergey Kurzenkov continues:

> Two of our aircraft emitted smoke. They were [Kapitan Leonid] Mozerov's and [Starshiy Leytenant V. V.] Kravchenko's planes. They lagged behind and made desperate efforts to defend themselves. Kravchenko managed to shoot down an Me 110 with a well-aimed burst of fire from close distance. Two Fascists concentrated their attacks on him. Suddenly his aircraft broke apart right in front of our eyes. The Kuban Cossak Mozerov barely was able to evade the enemy's attacks. [Kapitan Pavel] Orlov raced to assist him, but it was too late. Several Fascists surrounded Mozerov. The engine in his aircraft was hit and the plane turned into a blazing, red torch. Why didn't Mozerov bail out? Had he been killed? No, he still was alive. He pulled up his aircraft for the last time and rammed a Messerschmitt from below.[52]

By now, the Soviet fighter formation had broken apart, each pilot individually seeking to escape. Weissenberger picked one of the Hurricanes that attempted to get away at low level toward the east. The pursuit lasted two or three minutes, during which Weissenberger fired repeated bursts, each time scoring hits on the desperately zig-zagging Hurricane. Finally, large flames erupted from the Soviet plane and it crashed into the mountaineous terrain below. Weissenberger's wingman noted the time: 1657 hours. Weissenberger had scored five victories in twelve minutes.

The Zerstörer pilots filed hollow claims totalling thirteen Soviet aircraft shot down during this vastly uneven combat. And five Bf 109 pilots claimed three more kills. Starshiy Leytenant Kurzenkov, who made a futile attempt to escape in a Hurricane that had suffered engine malfunction, recounts:

> They approached me from behind and opened fire at short range. My right wing was riddled with bullet holes and caught fire. I turned my aircraft around steeply and managed to disappear into a ravine. The two enemy fighters passed above me at high speed.
>
> The air current extinguished the flames, and I decided to try to make a landing. But my speed was too high and the ravine was too short. A steep mountain wall appeared in front of me. Desperately, I looked for another ravine. There, ahead to the left, was another. I landed my airplane on its belly, and in the next moment everything seemed to crash. I can't remember anything else.[53]

The 2 GSAP ground staff was shocked to find that only four of nine Hurricanes returned to base from this mission. The only consolation was that the five SBs had managed to complete their bombing mission without loss. On the German side, the men of 10.(Z)/JG 5 were in a euphoric mood. Even before the engines of Weissenberger's Bf 110 had been switched off, enthusiastic fliers and ground crewmen surrounded their "Theo", cheering.

In all, JG 5 claimed twenty-seven Soviet aircraft brought down (twenty-two of them Hurricanes) on May 10,[54] against which Fliegerführer Nord-Ost lost no more than two aircraft. Although the German reports were considerably inflated, the May 10 operations cost VVS-SF dearly – ten Hurricanes destroyed and three moderately or seriously damaged.[55]

The Soviet situation on the ground was even worse. With Fourteenth Army halted, it became senseless to maintain the Motovskiy Bay bridgehead, so on May 11 the decision was made to evacuate the landing force. The flotilla of small naval vessels that arrived to evacuate the marines on May 12 was provided with extensive fighter

Kirkenes/Höybuktmoen Airdrome. Surrounded by enthusiastic NCOs of the Zerstörerstaffel, "Theo" Weissenberger shows how he shot down five Soviet fighters on May 10, 1942. Although three were claimed as MiG-3s, all his adversaries were in fact Hurricanes. From the right are Oberfeldwebel Krause, Unteroffizier Pfeiffer, Oberfeldwebel Kurpiers, Oberfeldwebel Munding, Weissenberger, and three unidentified NCOs. This combat was the starting point of Weissenberger's fame. He would end the war with a total of 208 victories, achieved over approximately 400 combat sorties. Weissenberger was killed during a car race on the Nürburgring on June 10, 1950. (Photo: Rautio.)

An American-built Bell P-39 Airacobra in VVS service. When Lend-Lease shipments of Airacobras to the USSR commenced, RAF fighter pilots dismissed the heavy fighter as a "widowmaker" and simply refused to fly it against the Luftwaffe fighters. "Suited for wide, low, and slow circles," was a comment bestowed upon the P-39 by USAAF pilots. The Airacobra had its baptism of fire on the Eastern Front with 19 GIAP, which received sixteen of the type – together with ten P-40 Kittyhawks – in late April 1942. Although the only available instructions and manuals were in English, the assembly of aircraft and training of pilots were carried out rapidly. The first combat involving Airacobras in VVS service took place on May 15, 1942, without loss to either side. Next day, the first loss was suffered when the Airacobra with serial number AH660 was shot down in combat with JG 5 Bf 109s. The pilot – Starshiy Leytenant Ivan Gaydayenko – survived unhurt. (Photo: Viktor Kulikov collection.)

cover. Leytenant Petr Sgibnev of 78 IAP/VVS-SF claimed two of the attacking German aircraft shot down. The evacuation was successfully concluded the next day, but its successful outcome should not obscure the fact that the Soviet attempt to take the initiative in the Far North came to a deplorable end. Not only had the Fourteenth Army been badly crippled, the Northern Fleet had sustained bloody losses. It was evident that the contest between the opposing forces in the Far North was too even to permit either side to break through and achieve its goals.

From a Soviet point of view, the only positive result of the fierce ground battle was that it contributed to saving the next convoy, *PQ-15*, from large-scale Luftwaffe attacks. The need to concentrate Luftflotte 5 to tactical support at the front – in combination with generally bad weather in the Norwegian Sea – allowed only one air raid to be made against *PQ-15* – on May 2, when I./KG 26 He 111 torpedo bombers managed to sink three freighters. In the holds of some of the twenty *PQ-15* freighters that safely entered Murmansk harbor were disassembled, crated American Curtiss P-40E Kittyhawks, an improved version of the P-40 Tomahawk. Also around this time, the first American Bell P-39 Airacobras were delivered to 19 GIAP/VVS-Fourteenth Army in the Murmansk area.

The combat spirits of the VVS airmen in the Far North appear to have remained unbroken despite the steep rise in losses during the spring of 1942. The considerably inflated Soviet victory claims may be viewed in two ways: the strong determintion of these Soviet fliers made them want to shoot down German planes; their determination also led them to exaggerate – or fabricate – the number of their kills, so as not to tarnish their reputations or disappoint their comrades. 20 GIAP's Starshiy Leytenant Aleksey Khlobystov's performance is a typical example of this phenomenon. He earned a widespread reputation for the two tarans he had claimed during the same combat on April 8. And on May 14 he reportedly carried out a third taran shortly after a Bf 109's 20mm shells had set his P-40 on fire. Nevertheless, no German fighter is listed as lost in this area on May 14.

It should be noted that the Soviets had been close to achieving air supremacy in the Murmansk area early in April. Only by doubling the fighter forces of Fliegerführer Nord-Ost were the Germans able to regain the advantage. And still, the Messerschmitt pilots were forced to fight hard to maintain their position.

Bell P-39 Airacobra I, Mladshiy Leytenant Vladimir Gabrinets, 3 Eskadrilya/19 GIAP/VVS-Fourteenth Army/VVS-Karelian Front, Shonguy, Soviet Union, summer 1942

Gabrinets was shot down while piloting this airplane on July 19, 1942; he survived by bailing out.

Part V

Annihilation

After initial successes during the battle of Kharkov, Soviet ground-attack units suffered heavily at the hands of an increased presence of German fighter planes. (Photo: Balss.)

Chapter 16

Carnage at Kerch

A formation of Bf 109 fighters heading for the front lines. Soviet airmen were stunned by the large concentrations of Bf 109s they faced in Crimean skies in May 1942. (Photo: Trautloft.)

In early May 1942 both sides were preparing for a final settlement of the battle of the Crimea. The transfer of the staff of Generaloberst Wolfram von Richthofen's Fliegerkorps VIII, probably the Luftwaffe's best close-support command, to the Crimea during the first week of May was like a dash of cold water to the Soviets. General-Mayor Nikolay Skripko wrote: "The command of VVS-Crimean Front did not take into consideration that the numerical strength of Luftflotte 4 was by no means fixed; it could be considerably increased when the enemy prepared a large offensive operation. And that is exactly what happened at Kerch."[1]

The Luftwaffe built up a formidable force in a matter of days: the bombers of KG 51, KG 55, KG 76, and KG 100; the torpedo planes of II./KG 26; the dive-bombers of StG 77; the fighters of I./JG 3, II., III., and 15.(Kroat)/JG 52, and I. and II./JG 77; and the new ground-attack unit, SchG 1.

On May 7, XXX Corps of General Erich von Manstein´s German Eleventh Army was in position, ready to launch Operation Trappenjagd (Bustard Hunt), the final offensive aimed at annihilating the Soviet Crimean Front. Following artillery preparation and attacks by StG 77 and SchG 1 against Soviet fortifications, XXX Corps opened its assault in the early morning hours of May 8. During most of the day, von Richthofen concentrated his close-support units against the Soviet Forty-fourth Army on the southern flank. Here, the new Hs 129 twin-engine, single-seat ground-attack plane experienced its combat debut with II./SchG 1. After only a few hours, the Soviet command had been deprived of most communication lines with the troops at the front.

Meanwhile, the bomber units of Fliegerkorps VIII went out against the airfields of VVS-Crimean Front and achieved an outstanding success. Following the experience of January, when the Soviet ground operations were hampered because most of its aviation was based in the Taman area on the eastern side of the Straits of Kerch, most of the 176 fighters and 225 bombers assigned to VVS-Crimean Front had been deployed to a few hurriedly constructed airfields on the Kerch Peninsula. With striking similarities to the first day of the war with the USSR, Fliegerkorps VIII easily wrecked most of these overcrowded airfields during the early morning hours of May 8. "After dealing heavy strikes against our airfields, the enemy's aviation started blocking them – preventing our fighters from taking off and intercepting his bombers," wrote General-Mayor Skripko.[2]

Over and over again, Soviet fighter pilots attempted to take off from the forward airfields – only to be pounced on by diving Bf 109s that shot them down before they got more than a few feet off the ground. Apart from scattered aircraft that managed to take to the air during brief intervals in the German air assault, VVS-Crimean Front could launch only one large mission on May 8. Eight 36 IAP I-16s picked up the 214 ShAP I-153 Chayka ground-attack planes over Marfovka Airdrome, twenty-five miles southwest of Kerch, and headed for the front line.

36 IAP's Leytenant Anatoliy Ivanov describes this mission:

> As we were approaching Marfovka Airdrome we met a large number of Fascist bombers, flying considerably higher. They were heading eastward, in several groups of eighteen to twenty planes each. We hadn't seen such quantities since February. The Messerschmitts, divided into separate pairs or in groups of four, flashed past us. They didn't seem to care about us. Apparently their task was to provide the bombers with escort. But a second group of Messerschmitts attacked us immediately above the airfield at Marfovka. By that time the Chaykas were taking off and we took them under our wings. We attempted to fly in the direction of Vladislavovka, but there we were also confronted by a large group of Fascist fighters."[3]

Carrying out close-support attacks in obsolescent I-153s was tantamount to suicide when the Soviets were confronted by Bf 109s. These operations cost VVS-Crimean Front most of its I-153s during the first two days of the German offensive against the Kerch Peninsula. (Photo: Balss.)

Leutnant Hermann Graf, the Staffelkapitän of 9./JG 52 who took part in the interception of the Polikarpov fighter bombers, wrote: "Units from three Geschwader were airborne in the hazy sky over the front line. We forced the bombers to jettison their bombs. My Staffel was positioned low, and we drew a whole lot of ground fire upon us while the fighter combat took place above our heads. Two Me 109s collided and fell in flames to the ground. The pilots bailed out and landed in enemy territory. Then I could see a Russian plane going down."[4]

Hastening to assist the hard-pressed Polikarpov pilots, Leytenant Dmitriy Glinka of 45 IAP hurled his Yak-1 against the Bf 109s and opened fire against one of them, claiming it as shot down. In the next moment, the German wingman had set Glinka's fighter ablaze, and he had to bail out.

Hermann Graf continues: "As we stuck to the bombers a Russian fighter suddenly latched onto my tail, but [Feldwebel Leopold] Steinbatz shot it down at the last moment. Shortly afterward I managed to bag a MiG-1. By this time we were flying at only 1,500 feet altitude, pretty far into the Russian rear area. I knocked down my second enemy at 1058 hours; number three went down at 1102, and number four at 1107."[5]

Of this mission, General-Mayor Skripko concluded laconically: "Heavily outnumbered, the I-153 unit suffered severe losses."[6]

That evening, the staff of III./JG 52 made an astonishing summary of this Gruppe's achievment on the first day of the offensive: It lost only one Bf 109 – Feldwebel Alfred Grislawski made a forced landing[7] – but contributed forty-seven kills to Fliegerkorps VIII's total of fifty-seven aerial victories on May 8. Hermann Graf alone chalked up seven of these victories. The "neighbor Gruppe," Hauptmann Johannes Steinhoff's II./JG 52, was less fortunate: Against only three victories, it lost five

An Hs 129 B-1 of II./SchG 1 on the Eastern Front. This new German ground-attack aircraft saw its first combat with II./SchG 1 during the Kerch offensive in May 1942. Although the dust on the rather primitive front-line airstrips caused severe problems because Hs 129s' Gnôme-Rhône engines lacked adequate dust filters, the unit's aircraft were in relentless action against the Soviet airfields and troop columns on the Kerch Peninsula. On the first day of the German offensive, a Schwarm led by Hauptmann Bruno Meyer claimed the destruction of about forty Soviet aircraft during a single attack against a Kerch airfield.

Hs 129 B-1, 5./SchG 1, Eastern Front, 1942

"Well, but somehow we managed to break out. We were able to start the engine and take off."

Reflecting the desperation on the Soviet side, 119 MRAP/VVS-ChF dispatched three MBR-2 flying boats to raid the German troops on May 10. But when they reached the target area, the rain had stopped and the naval fliers were met by four Bf 109s. Only one MBR-2, piloted by the commander Kapitan Ilya Ilyin (later appointed Hero of the Soviet Union), returned to base.

From noon on May 10, when the downfall had stopped, von Richthofen eagerly launched low-level attacks against the congested Soviet retreat columns stuck in the deep mud on the roads leading to the east. Since the airfields in the Crimea had not dried up, Oberstleutnant Benno Kosch was instructed to dispatch the He 111s of his KG 55 from Dnepropetrovsk Airdrome to carry out this task. And so they did – with a terrible result to both sides. "The horrendous low-level attacks turned the awsome confusion into regular panic," a Soviet report read. Trapped, virtually with their backs against the wall, the Soviet troops opened a fire with all they had against the formations of He 111s that came thundering a few feet above their heads. The bombers flew into a veritable wall of bullets. General Erich von Manstein, the commander of the Eleventh Army, noted that von Richthofen indeed "made terrific demands on the units under his command." KG 55 lost eight He 111s to ground fire on May 10.[14]

Alfred Grislawski took this photo of Hermann Graf in May 1942, when Graf was still a Leutnant. Hermann Graf is one of the most controversial Luftwaffe fighter pilots of World War II. He had an astonishing combat career, scoring two hundred victories in thirteen months in 1941 and 1942. After the war, Graf sided with the Soviets. "He was a really swell guy, respected by everyone," says his old friend Alfred Grislawski. "It is a pity that some people today hold his personal convictions against him." (Photo: Grislawski.)

On May 11 Fliegerkorps VIII was concentrated on the northern flank, causing the Soviet front to crumble in this sector as well. Here, the Soviet Fifty-first Army surrendered while the Forty-seventh Army fell back in disorder.

Flying in his Fi 156 Storch over the territory recently captured on May 11, Generaloberst von Richthofen was stunned by the level of destruction. "Terrible." he noted in his diary: "Corpse-strewn fields . . . I have never seen anything of the kind in this war." The last few pilots of VVS-Crimean Front fought bitterly to the end. "Early in the morning we were already in the air," Leytenant Ivanov wrote about the action on May 11. "Just as we were taking off we were involved in combat with ten or twenty enemy aircraft. That day we fought particularly fiercely to defend the retreating ground troops." 4./JG 52 lost three pilots in combat on May 11, while II./JG 77 had three Bf 109Fs shot down or force-landed.

On May 12 Leutnant Hermann Graf scored his ninetieth victory on his last mission over the Crimea. Later that day his 9./JG 52 was shifted to the Kharkov area to help counter the powerful Soviet tank offensive that had been initiated in this area. In two weeks of action in the Crimean skies, this Staffel had scored ninety-three victories without loss.

The 9./JG 52 would develop into the most successful fighter Staffel of the war, numbering pilots such as the top-scorer of World War II, Erich Hartmann and – in 1941 and 1942 – Hermann Graf in its ranks. It was in the Crimea in May 1942 that this Staffel earned its famous nickname, the Karaya Staffel, which can be credited to Oberfeldwebel Ernst Süss, who had brought a record player from his home leave. All the records Süss had brought with him were broken. The only thing that he could play was a Soviet recording from the Crimean Tartar culture that Süss found in the Crimea. The theme of this song – interpreted by Süss as something like "Karaya, Karaya" – was heard day and night from Süss's living quarters. Süss soon turned Karaya into the signature tune of 9./JG 52, unabashedly singing it loudly on the R/T even during combat missions. Soon, "*Achtung alle Karaya-Männer*" ("Attention all Karaya men") became the general radio call sign of 9./JG 52.

On May 13 the remnants of Crimean Front were heading west, toward the so-called Turkish Rampart located twenty miles to the west of Kerch – the high dirt wall that remained after a deep ditch had been dug across the Kerch Peninsula in the eighteenth century to prevent invasions from Asia. Here the Soviets hoped to halt the Germans. But this attempt was thwarted by intense Luftwaffe attacks.

One of these sorties on May 13 cost the life of 9./StG 77's Oberleutnant Johann Waldhauser, a veteran who had carried out more than three hundred dive-bombing attacks. As it was diving, Waldhauser's Ju 87 sustained a direct hit from AAA fire and exploded in mid-air, killing the pilot and the radio operator, Unteroffizier Martin Kleinert, instantly.

By May 14 German and Romanian troops had crashed across the Turkish Rampart and pushed the Soviets troops toward Kerch, where they were squeezed together in an increasingly narrow area. Leytenant Ivanov witnessed the scenes at Kerch:

> In Kerch harbor there were such large congestions of troops that there was hardly any space to move. Along a ten-mile stretch, the coast was littered with men and equipment. There were very few regular ships available, so tugs, barges, motor boats, and small craft arrived and lay waiting 100 to 200 yards from the docks. The soldiers jumped into the water and started swimming.
>
> Several men made primitive rafts or used tire tubes in an attempt to cross the straits, but the current carried them to Kamysh-Burun, where the Germans were. Wave after wave of Fascist aircraft bombed and strafed the crossings without interruption.

On May 15 Stalin personally called General-Mayor Skripko and instructed him to assume command of the aviation units that had managed to escape to the eastern side of the Straits of Kerch. Skripko immediately dispatched all available aviation units across the straits – the remainder of VVS-Crimean Front that had escaped the carnage at Kerch, three ADD Divizii for nocturnal missions, and 113 AD, equipped with Il-4s (the new designation of the DB-3F), for daylight bombings. What the Soviets feared next was an immediate German invasion of the Caucasus coast. Although this fear eventually proved to be unfounded, it led to a new upsurge in air combat.

As large parts of Fliegerkorps VIII were hastily shifted north to meet the Soviet offensive at Kharkov, much of the German fighter force came to rely upon a few skilled men in JG 77. Two new names appeared here, Hauptmann Gordon Gollob and Hauptmann Heinz Bär.

Gollob assumed command of JG 77 on May 16, 1942, although he only held the rank of Hauptmann. Bär had been sent from IV./JG 51 on the Moscow front to take charge of I./JG 77 five days earlier. Both were highly decorated – Bär with the Swords to the Knight's Cross with Oak Leaves, and Gollob with the Knight's Cross with Oak Leaves. When Bär arrived at I./JG 77, his victory tally stood at ninety-one, and he was eager to reach his one hundredth.

While thousands of Soviet soldiers succumbed at Kerch, Gollob and Bär fought the classic "private war" of German fighter pilots in the "Red Baron style." This is quite indicative to the outlook that many Luftwaffe fighter pilots had on the war by that time. General-Mayor Skripko's Soviet airmen did their utmost to support their doomed troops around Kerch, but they stood little chance of surviving such deadly opponents as these two German aces. On May 16 Gollob and Bär displayed their abilities by respectively shooting down three and two LaGG-3s – thus Gollob ran his victory total to eighty-nine and Bär to ninety-three.

On May 17 Gollob claimed three R-5 biplanes. Soon afterward, he and his wingman found a formation of Soviet fighters.

In contrast to the common fighter tactic of attacking from above, Gollob preferred low-side attacks – to be sure that no one tried to attack him from the blind spot beneath his airplane. A pilot of JG 77 wrote the following account of an event he witnessed when Gollob and his

The Austrian Hauptmann Gordon Gollob served as Zerstörer pilot during the war against Poland in 1939. He eventually was transferred to a single-engine fighter unit, and as the II./JG 3 Gruppenkommandeur earned his reputation as a most skillful fighter pilot during Operation Barbarossa. In early 1942, the new Inspector of the Fighter Aviation Arm, Oberst Adolf Galland, personally recommended Gollob to take command of JG 77. Gollob was sent to Stab/JG 54, where Major Hannes Trautloft tutored him in the duties of a Geschwaderkommodore. Later in the war, when Gollob served in staff positions under Galland's supervision, a deep animosity would develop between him and Galland – with each accusing the other of misuse. Galland was sacked and Gollob took over as the last General der Jagdflieger. Gordon Gollob, who was credited with 150 victories in World War II, passed away on September 7, 1987. (Photo: Trautloft.)

wingman applied this tactic: "They positioned themselves at a low altitude beneath a Russian formation. Then they started climbing in spirals, carefully maintaining their position beneath the enemy formation. Before the tranquilly flying Russians even suspected any mischief, the two planes at the bottom of their formation had been shot down and the two Germans were gone."[15]

Gollob hit the Soviet fighter – a LaGG, he thought – in the belly, saw it go down, and returned home to report his ninety-third victory. When he returned to base, he learned that Bär meanwhile had bagged three MiG-3s, and two other MiG-3s had been claimed by II./JG 77's Hauptmann Heinrich Setz, increasing his tally to seventy-two.

One of the victims of these deadly aces on this day was the Yak-1 pilot Serzhant N. K. Chayka. After suffering severe wounds from the machine guns and automatic cannon in a Bf 109, Chayka struggled at the controls of his damaged Yak-1. He managed to bring it back to his airfield but lost control of it during landing and crashed into another Yak-1. Both planes were destroyed and Chayka was killed.

As a measure of the demoralization caused by the disastrous defeat at Kerch, this Soviet flier flew his U-2 across the straits on June 1, 1942, and landed at Kerch. Hauptmann Heinz Bär allocated two Bf 109s to escort the U-2 to I./JG 77's airfield at Bagerovo, but the Soviet pilot was allowed to fly his own aircraft. This photo shows the Soviet pilot and men of I./JG 77 shortly after the landing at Bagerovo. (Photo: Roba/Mombeek.)

By May 18 the ferocious battle on the ground had been concentrated in the northeastern tip of the Kerch Peninsula and around the city of Kerch. All available Soviet aircraft, including many R-5 and R-Z biplanes intended for night operations, crossed the straits to intervene against the victorious Germans. Gollob was in constant action over the Straits, bringing down six of those biplanes on May 18 and May 19. Unlike most of the Luftwaffe's top aces, who were marked by a strong sense of competition, Gollob allowed Bär to surpass him and enter into the annals of Luftwaffe history as the ninth fighter pilot to reach the 100-victory mark. Gollob wrote in his diary: "I have refrained from reporting four of my last victories. I don't want to reach number 100 so fast, because I fear that my superiors will have me grounded after that."[16]

Heinz "Pritzl" Bär was among the ablest fighter pilots of the Luftwaffe and was famous for his personal charm. In the spring of 1942, he was a favorite of Oberst Adolf Galland, the young Inspector of the Fighter Aviation Arm. Hardly by accident, Galland arrived to inspect Bär's I./JG 77 the same day Bär achieved his one hundredth victory. But Bär also was known for his sensitive and rather undisciplined nature. One year later, when three and a half years of relentless combat activity had worn him to a state at which he refused to carry out any more combat missions, Galland had him relieved of command under humiliating circumstances. After rehabilitating himself during difficult air battles with formations of American heavy bombers over Germany in 1944, Bär was finally posted to Galland's Me 262 unit, JV 44, where he became the top-scoring jet ace and assumed command after Galland was injured in air combat. Heinz Bär was credited with 220 victories in World War II. (Photo: Roba/Mombeek.)

On May 19 a triumphant Bär returned with five victory claims – his kill numbers 99 through 103. Gollob was pleased to note that his JG 77 surpassed its two thousandth victory mark the same day.

Following bitter house-to-house fighting with heavy losses on both sides, Kerch finally fell into German hands on May 20. "It seems to be over at Kerch," Gollob wrote in his diary on May 21. "The Eleventh Army is regrouping for the attack on Sevastopol." Next day, Gollob was summoned to Saki to discuss the air-support operation for the coming offensive against Sevastopol with Oberst Wolfgang von Wild, the Fliegerführer Süd.

A total of 116,405 Soviets would be evacuated across the Straits of Kerch, but another 162,282 were left behind – dead or captured.[17] The Germans also confined 170,000 Soviets, including large numbers of civilians. Soviet aircraft losses during the Battle of the Kerch Peninsula amounted to 417 – including 315 from VVS-Crimean Front.[18]

Stalin's stubborn decision to concentrate all efforts on offensive operations while ignoring the need to fortify defensive positions resulted in the bloody obliteration of all the gains that had been made in the Crimea since late 1941. And this was not the end of the disaster: While the Crimean Front was being slaughtered on the shores at Kerch, another ill-conceived Soviet offensive ended in tragedy three hundred miles to the north, at Kharkov.

When they entered the conquered area at Kerch, Wehrmacht soldiers witnessed the destructive power of the Luftwaffe aerial assault. The peninsula was littered throughout with destroyed vehicles of all kinds, blown up artillery pieces, supply stores in ruins, dead horses, and drifts of Soviet soldiers and civilians killed or maimed in the savage aerial attacks. A field priest in the German 28th Infantry Division wrote in his diary that he had counted one thousand corpses in an area of only one square kilometer. But the attackers also had paid a high price; German and Romanian casualties during the fourteen-day battle were about seven thousand. (Photo: Trautloft.)

 # Chapter 17 

The Battle of Kharkov

While the Soviet Crimean Front fought for its survival, Marshal Sovetskogo Soyuza Semyon Timoshenko, the commander in chief of the Red Army's Southwestern Direction (Southern and Southwestern fronts) opened a powerful offensive in the Ukraine. This strike had been planned long ago. At the end of March, Stalin held a conference with his highest military commanders which in principle was a repetition of the meeting in early January. Stalin complained about the reluctance of the western Allies to open a "second front" and told his commanders that a major new German offensive could be expected after the spring thaws. He then asked his commanders for their opinions as to the possibilities to counter this.

Marshal Sovetskogo Soyuza Boris Shaposhnikov, the Stavka chief of staff, proposed that the defense needed to be flexible and that the bulk of the reserves should be grouped around Voronezh. General Armii Georgiy Zhukov repeated what he had proposed in January: Concentrate the core of the Red Army for an offensive to the west of Moscow while the rest of the front line maintained a defensive posture. Stalin interrupted Zhukov rudely and declared, "We can't remain on the defensive and only wait for the enemy to strike; we have to launch a preventive offensive on a broad front!"

Supported by Peoples' Commissar Marshal Sovetskogo Soyuza Kliment Voroshilov, Timoshenko proposed an offensive in the Southwestern Direction as well, and several days later Stalin instructed him to develop a plan for such an offensive.

On April 10 Timoshenko sent a proposal for the operation to the Stavka, which adopted a revised version on April 28. This plan called for a pincer movement against the German positions around Kharkov.

During winter, the Soviets had managed to establish a bridgehead across the Donets northeast of Kharkov, at Staryy Saltov. To the south of Kharkov, an eighty-mile deep westward bulge had been created at the end of January. By launching a joint operation from these two strongholds, Timoshenko hoped to surround General Friedrich von Paulus's German Sixth Army at Kharkov.

For this purpose, the Southern and Southwestern fronts received a considerable striking force, including 1,200 tanks grouped in several powerful concentrations. For the air support, 926 aircraft of VVS-Southwestern Front, VVS-Southern Front, and the ADD were made ready, including thirty-one fighter aviation regiments.

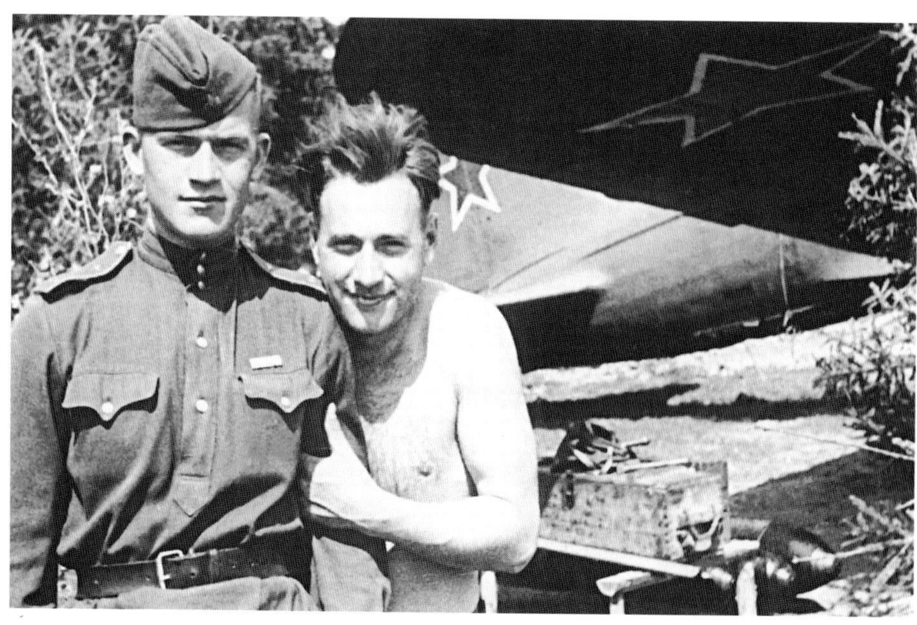

Two Il-4 flyers pose for the photographer at a well-camouflaged ADD airbase. (Photo: Kurayev via Antipov.)

But Timoshenko's troops were beset by the rasputitsa which hampered not only the movements of units but the construction of supply roads and forward airfields as well.[19] On top of this came endless delays due to the Luftwaffe's interdiction of river crossings and other chokepoints in the Soviet rear area. As the attack was about to be initiated, only one third of the ammunition planned for the artillery preparation was on hand.

The Soviet offensive was preceded by intense attacks against the airfields of Fliegerkorps IV in the immediate vicinity of the front line. On May 11, III./JG 77's base at Kharkov was repeatedly bombed by Pe-2s, Il-2s, Su-2s,and fighters of 99 BBAP, 135 BBAP, 431 ShAP, 43 IAP, 148 IAP, 164 IAP, 273 IAP, and 282 IAP. But the Soviets only succeeded in damaging a single Bf 109 on the ground. Five I-16s, all from 282 IAP, were lost during the operation against III./JG 77's Kharkov base on May 11.

Spearheaded by strong tank concentrations, Timoshenko launched his attack to the north and south of Kharkov on May 12. Initially, General Kurt Pflugbeil's Fliegerkorps IV could dispatch nothing but the He 111s of KG 27 and II./KG 55 against the Soviet ground troops. Since the Germans possessed only one Jagdgruppe in this area – III./JG 77, which had just returned from two months of rest and refit in Germany – the Soviets were able to seize control of the skies above the battle area.

The frequency of low-level attacks against the German front lines during the first days of the Soviet offensive had a negative impact on the morale of the German ground troops,[20] but the Soviet dominance in the air relied almost entirely on superior numbers; most Soviet air units were handicapped by the low training standards of the many novice pilots. According to a VVS report, the Pe-2 crews of 99 BBAP felt that when they were intercepted by German fighters they could rely more on seeking refuge in the clouds than on the protection from the MiG-3s of 148 IAP that were tasked to escort them.[21]

Some final words between members of a Soviet bombercrew before they enter their Pe-2 for another combat mission. (Photo: Viktor Kulikov photo collection.)

From May 13, strong Luftwaffe reinforcements started arriving from the Crimea. Among the first was III./JG 52, which included Leutnant Hermann Graf's elite Karaya Staffel, 9./JG 52. Within forty-eight hours, the pilots of III./JG 52 were able to completely alter the situation in the air. The Gruppe received a hot reception when its new operational base was subjected to a sudden low-level attack by a formation of Ishaks on May 12, but III./JG 52 nevertheless retaliated and blasted seven of the attackers out of the sky. One of these kills was the unit's 900th victory,[22] and its losses were limited to one Bf 109.[23] Moreover, this was only the beginning.

An Il-2 armed with RS-82 rocket projectiles. The USSR pioneered the use of aerial rocket projectiles. Taken into service in December 1937, the RS-82 was used in combat for the first time at Khalkhin-Gol in August 1939. Only in 1942 did the USAAF and the RAF make use of similar arms, and the first operational use of rocket projectiles by the Luftwaffe did not take place until 1943. The RS-82 was outfitted with a 5.55-pound warhead containing a .99-pound explosive charge. Its combat range was 5,500 to 6,500 yards. (Photo: Roba/Mombeek.)

On May 13 Leutnant Graf brought down six Soviet aircraft. While engaging about thirty VVS fighters with his Schwarm to the east of Kharkov at 1130 hours, Graf claimed four victories. Included among his victims may have been one of the seven Heroes of the Soviet Union in Kapitan Farit Fatkullin's 929 IAP – Leytenant Arseniy Stepanov, who was killed in aerial combat in this region. An I-16 pilot almost paid back the German ace a few hours later when he managed to riddle Graf's *Yellow 1* with bullets. Graf nevertheless managed to return to the airfield at Rogan with a heavily smoking engine. That afternoon, the LaGG-3s piloted by 512 IAP's Starshiy Leytenants Gennadiy Dubenok, Ivan Motornyy, and Valentin Makarov were shot down during an encounter with III./JG 52.

A formation of Ju 87 Ds over the Eastern Front. Based as close to the front line as possible, the Stukas often arrived at the scene of action within twenty minutes of a request from a ground unit. In his study on the impact of the Luftwaffe's operations during the Battle of Kharkov in May 1942, Oberst Hermann Plocher noted: "Ultimately, the attacks of Fliegerkorps IV became one of the most important factors in preventing the envelopment of Kharkov by the Red Army." The most vital close-support missions carried out by German aircraft in this area undoubtedly were those flown by the Stukas. (Photo: Roba/Mombeek.)

On the same day the Soviet tank forces managed to penetrate the German lines at Staryy Saltov, northeast of Kharkov, and the attack forces inside the bulge south of Kharkov broke through the German lines at Bereka, halfway between Krasnograd and Balakleya. In savage air combat, the Soviet airmen claimed forty Luftwaffe planes, a huge exaggeration. The Germans reported sixty-five Soviet planes shot down – forty-two of them by III./JG 52 Bf 109s.

In spite of their heavy losses, the Soviet air units were fully in action throughout May 14, claiming the destruction of one hundred tanks, three hundred lorries, twenty-five ammunition carts, and one train in the Kharkov battle zone. These figures have little in common with reality, and the VVS continued to pay a high price at the hands of German fighters. In 512 IAP, Starshiy Leytenant Gennadiy Dubenok was shot down by a III./JG 52 Bf 109 for the second consecutive day. III./JG 52 alone claimed 47 more victories – including its 1,000th victory – for the loss of only a single Bf 109. The two most successful pilots were Leutnant Graf, who chalked up 6 kills, numbers 98 through 104, thus becoming the seventh fighter pilot to exceed the 100-victory-mark; and Leutnant Adolf Dickfeld. On May 14 Dickfeld claimed 9 Soviet planes, victories 82 through 90.

The dominant factor in the offensive was Timoshenko's numerical superiority on the ground, not least his large tank concentrations. But as Southwestern Front approached Krasnograd, the full brunt of Fliegerkorps IV fell upon it. By that time, bombers from StG 77, KG 51, KG 55, I./KG 76, and I./KG 77 and ground-attack planes from SchG 1 were operating over this combat zone. In only two days, the Stukas alone claimed the destruction of fifty-four Soviet tanks. On May 15 the Chief of the General Staff of the German Army, Generaloberst Franz Halder, wrote in his diary that "the force of the attack appears to have been broken by the efforts of our Luftwaffe."[24]

On May 15 Kapitan Farit Fatkullin's 929 IAP was instructed to raid the Kharkov-Voychen Airdrome, where large numbers of Bf 109s had been seen arriving. These were the fighters of II./JG 52, which had just been transferred from the Crimea. Hauptmann Johannes Steinhoff led his newly arrived Jagdgruppe in a scramble to meet the attackers.

Three of the Bf 109s singled out Hero of the Soviet Union Leytenant Aleksandr Perepelitsa. The Soviet ace managed to bring down one of the German fighters, possibly the Bf 109 F-4 piloted by Feldwebel Friedrich Schmidt of 6./JG 52. But in the next moment

Ju 87 D-1, StG 2 Immelmann, Eastern Front 1942

A KG 51 Ju 88 returns from a combat mission over the Kharkov battlefield in May 1942. Operating from Zaporozhye Airdrome, the KG 51 Edelweiss crews were in uninterrupted action during the battle of Kharkov. On May 20 and May 21, this Kampfgeschwader carried out 294 individual sorties without loss. Around one-third of these sorties were carried out by III. Gruppe in order to bail out a German troop detachment surrounded between Ternovaya and Varvarovka. "Your untiring energy amazed us, and your actions gave us courage to hold out," a grateful soldier of the enveloped force later wrote to III./KG 51. (Photo: Bernád.)

Perepelitsa's Yak-1 was hit and, fully ablaze, it plunged into one of the airfield hangars. Hauptmann Johannes Steinhoff scored his fifty-fourth victory, which was recorded as a "MiG-3."

Provided with overwhelming air cover, the Germans launched their counterattack on May 17. The provisional Army Group Kleist – First Panzer and Seventeenth armies – advanced northward against the southern shoulder of the Soviet bulge at Slavyansk. The German Sixth Army attacked from the opposite side of the bulge in a classic envelopment maneuver. Strong tank concentrations from both sides clashed in the Volchansk area, northeast of Kharkov. Inside the Bulge, Krasnograd became the focus for ground combat. Thus, four major battles were being fought simultaneously. In each sector, German counterattacks with the strong backing of Stukas and ground-attack planes forced the Red Army to fall back to defend itself. Meanwhile, the bomber crews of Fliegerkorps IV each carried out an average of seven sorties per day against supply lines from the Kupyansk area. These operations blocked all Soviet lines of communication across the Donets River between Izyum and Balakleya and thus laid the foundation for a successful envelopment of Timoshenko's forces.

Soviet fighter pilots made resolute efforts to relieve their ground troops. "The Russian fighter defense was stronger than ever in this area. Frequently, a German Kette came under attack from twenty-five fighters," stated historian Wolfgang Dierich.[25] But the number of Luftwaffe fighters in the air increased daily. I./JG 3 commenced operations in the Kharkov area on May 16, and the Geschwaderstab and the two other Gruppen followed over the next few days.

On May 18, III./JG 52's Leutnant Adolf Dickfeld surpassed all previous records by claiming eleven enemy aircraft shot down, including his one hundredth victory, for which he was awarded the Oak Leaves to his Knight´s Cross.

That the level of opposition in the air had grown considerably was painfully proven to 429 IAP, which lost four of twelve Yak-1s during an escort mission for 13 GBAP near Brigadirovka early on May 19. The 429 IAP pilots were unfortunate to run into Oberleutnant Viktor Bauer's 9./JG 3 on the first combat mission this unit carried out following a month's refit in Germany. Oberleutnant Bauer, Oberfeldwebel Georg Schentke, and Oberfeldwebel Eberhard von Boremski – all Knight's Cross holders, each with more than forty victories to his credit – scored in this engagement. In return, two 9./JG 3 Bf 109s were severely damaged, though 429 IAP claimed six kills.

A Soviet T-34 tank destroyed during a Stuka attack. On May 17, 1942, alone, German airmen claimed to have put fifty-four Soviet tanks out of commission during the battle of Kharkov. (Photo: Creek.)

Meanwhile, Fliegerkorps IV exerted increasing pressure on the Soviet air bases in the region. VVS-Sixth Army reported two raids against Malaya Kamyshevakha Airdrome on May 15 and May 17, one against Brigadirovka Airdrome on May 18, and a series of daily Ju 88 dive-bombings of Levkovka Airdrome from May 16 to May 19.[26]

Marshal Timoshenko realized that his offensive had turned into a bitter fight for survival. It was obvious that the Germans intended to envelop the Soviet forces inside the bulge south of Kharkov. In vain General-Polkovnik Aleksandr Vasilyevskiy, who had been appointed acting Stavka chief of staff after Marshal Shaposhnikov's retirement due to health problems, pleaded with Stalin for permission to evacuate the Bulge. At first Stalin turned this request down, but on May 19 he changed his mind. By then, however, it was too late.

On May 20, von Kleist's attack force had reduced the mouth of the Bulge to less than fifteen miles. From that day on, the Luftwaffe raids against the Donets River crossings in the area were intensified in order to block the evacuation of the Soviet troops from the Bulge. On this day, StG 77 Ju 87s blew up five of the main Donets bridges in this area, and damaged four others. KG 3 Ju 88s in the central combat zone also participated in raids that left scores of burned-out vehicles on the roads in the area. Soviet attempts to break up the advancing German troop columns with air attacks brought diminished success in the face of the Bf 109 fighters.

Timoshenko made a desperate attempt to halt the German advance from the south by launching a strike against von Kleist's flank at Izyum on May 21. All available Soviet fighters were concentrated in this sector to help break the Luftwaffe's dominance in the air.

While escorting an Hs 126 reconnaissance plane in the area northwest of Izyum on May 21, the Rotte composed of Feldwebel Josef Zwernemann and Unteroffizier Heinz Berg of 7./JG 52 was bounced by a formation of MiG-3s. At that moment, Hermann Graf's Rotte appeared on the scene. But before Graf could intervene, Unteroffizier Berg found himself in deep trouble. As he attacked one of the Soviets, a MiG-3 sneaked up beneath him and fired a salvo of RS-82 rocket projectiles. One of the missiles hit the engine or fuel tank of Berg's Bf 109 F-4, which immediately burst into flames. Berg bailed out, but while hanging in his parachute he was shot at by the Soviet fighter.

"By pure coincidence I happened to witness an air combat," Hermann Graf wrote: "Two Me 109s went after a Russian aircraft, but they just couldn't make it. I guess they were beginners. Soon they were in trouble, so I decided to intervene. Thus I achieved my 107th kill. The Kommandeur awarded me with a large cigar."

Unteroffizier Berg was lucky to be provided with the best fighter cover one could wish for – the top ace of the Luftwaffe. "Fortunately, Leutnant Graf and his wingman were circling around my parachute," Berg later wrote.[27]

Further Luftwaffe reinforcements included I./JG 52, which returned with forty pilots and forty-three Bf 109s from more than three months of rest and recuperation in Germany.[28] Reentering combat on May 20, this unit's pilots claimed thirteen Soviet aircraft without any losses of their own in the skies around Kharkov between May 20 and May 22.

Despite intense activity and many large-scale aerial melees, Fliegerkorps IV's combat losses were limited to six planes on May 21 and six more on May 22. Air combat was intensified on May 23, as the Germans managed to close the sack around the Soviet Sixth and Fifty-seventh armies, along with the army-size "Operation Group Bobkin," in the bulge to the south of Kharkov. Operations that day cost Fliegerkorps IV eleven aircraft. The only real setback dealt

A II./SchG 1 Henschel Hs 129 B-1 at Kharkov Airdrome in May 1942. During the first years of World War II, Germany and the Soviet Union each designed a modern ground-attack aircraft type – the Hs 129 and the Il-2. While the latter was a huge success, the Hs 129 proved to be a disappointment. Pilots complained about bad handling characteristics, and the 740-horsepower Gnôme-Rhône 14M engines showed great sensitivity to dust and sand. (Photo: Bernád.)

> I had never felt like that before, not even in air combat.
>
> Eventually we started pulling the corpse of our commander out of the cockpit. We carried him to the shore of a small lake, cleaned his head of blood and mud, and started weeping together.[36]

Clearly marked with the exertion of battle, Starshiy Leytenant Ivan Raube is seen on the wing of his Su-2 immediately after a combat mission in May 1942. By this time, Ivan Raube was deputy commander of 3 AE/210 BBAP and carried out several bombing missions each day. This was a period of hardship for the 210 BBAP Su-2 crews. The heavy losses in Soviet fighter units led to a situation where four Su-2 missions out of five had to be carried out without fighter escort. Ivan Raube was killed on May 28, 1942, when he was shot down by a Bf 109, probably from JG 52. (Photo: Pavlichenko.)

Kazakov's Eskadrilya lost six Pe-2s during this action. It was a terrifying blow to the entire 223 BAD. "Gorbko was very popular with all the airmen. His death and the tragic carnage on 223 BAD brought the entire personnel staff down," wrote General-Mayor Fyodor Polynin, the commander of 2 VA.[37]

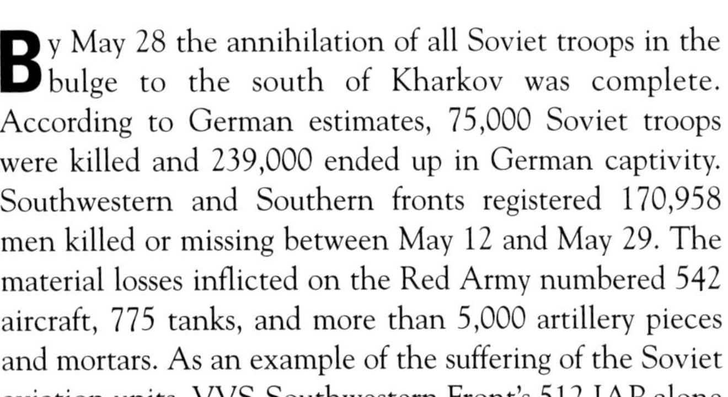

By May 28 the annihilation of all Soviet troops in the bulge to the south of Kharkov was complete. According to German estimates, 75,000 Soviet troops were killed and 239,000 ended up in German captivity. Southwestern and Southern fronts registered 170,958 men killed or missing between May 12 and May 29. The material losses inflicted on the Red Army numbered 542 aircraft, 775 tanks, and more than 5,000 artillery pieces and mortars. As an example of the suffering of the Soviet aviation units, VVS-Southwestern Front's 512 IAP alone filed fifteen LaGG-3s lost in combat between May 12 and May 29, 1942. One of its pilots, Starshiy Leytenant Valentin Makarov, was shot down three times during this period.

Kharkov was a classic battle of encirclement and one of tremendous strategic importance. The Luftwaffe's contribution had been decisive to the outcome. Oberst Hermann Plocher noted: "The Soviet capability to resist in the pocket west of Izyum was greatly influenced by the concentrated and devastating aerial attacks of the [reinforced] IV Fliegerkorps. Extremely heavy losses in men and matériel were inflicted upon these Russian units by the almost around-the-clock assaults from the air."[38]

Fliegerkorps IV claimed the destruction of 596 Soviet aircraft in the air and 19 on the ground, plus 227 tanks, 3,038 motor vehicles, 24 artillery batteries, 2 AAA batteries, 49 separate artillery pieces, 22 railway engines, and 6 complete trains. The cost for all of this was 49 aircraft.

Despite their best and strongest efforts, the VVS airmen had failed to provide their battered ground troops with adequate support. Within a matter of days, the reinforced German fighter establishment had been able to break the backbone of the initially well-organized Soviet low-level attacks.

This defeat underscores the dominant reason for the shortcomings of the VVS during the Battle of Kharkov – inadequate pilot training. Even if the Soviet fliers believed the figure of 200 destroyed German aircraft that the Stavka issued, it was evident that they had nonetheless suffered a huge defeat.

The powerful tank concentrations launched by Marshal Timoshenko during the Kharkov operation were almost totally obliterated in a matter of two weeks. This KV-2 heavy tank was abandoned by its crew after a close hit by a Luftwaffe bomb destroyed its tracks. The Germans claimed the destruction of 1,237 Soviet tanks during the battle of Kharkov in May 1942. Actual Soviet losses of 775 tanks were severe enough. (Photo: Trautloft.)

 Chapter 18 ★

Fire Over Murmansk

On the extreme north flank of the Eastern Front, Generaloberst Hans-Jürgen Stumpff's Luftflotte 5 was preparing a final blow against the northern lifeline of Allied Lend-Lease deliveries to the Soviet Union at Murmansk. Soviet ground forces managed to hold the Germans and Finns at bay, but in the air, the reinforced units of Luftflotte 5's Fliegerführer Nord-Ost gained a marked advantage during the spring. However, on May 17 the German airmen of Luftflotte 5 were once again reminded not to underestimate the Soviet veteran pilots who operated in the Far North. Early that morning an attempt by thirteen KG 30 Ju 88s – escorted by nine II./JG 5 Bf 109s – to attack the ships of the *PQ-15* convoy at Murmansk was beaten back through the combined efforts of Soviet fighters and antiaircraft artillery. The Ju 88 crews jettisoned their bombs far from the target, and turned homeward in two groups. On their return flight seven of these Ju 88s were attacked by eight Hurricanes led by a single P-40 – the latter conspicuously painted in U.S. Navy blue.

This P-40 was one of the two Kittyhawks handed over to the commander in chief of VVS-SF, General-Mayor Aleksandr Kuznetsov, and to the top ace – the commander of 2 GSAP/VVS-SF, Podpolkovnik Boris Safonov – by the American delegation that arrived with *PQ-15* on May 6. Piloting his new fighter, Safonov opened fire on a Ju 88 from three hundred yards and saw it go down in flames. The entire crew was killed.

Soon the fighters were locked into a stiff combat, from which II./JG 5's Oberfeldwebel Willi Pfränger and 2 GSAP's Mladshiy Leytenant I. S. Krivoruchenko did not return. Strangely, more than a year after the melee, in the Fall of 1943, Pfränger suddenly reported himself to a German patrol in the rear area of the Eastern Front's central combat zone! His story was startling.

He was captured after bailing out, then interrogated by Boris Safonov personally. The Soviet report describes Pfränger as "highly self-assured," and mentions that he denied he had been shot down by any Hurricane; he claimed his Bf 109 had been hit by friendly fire. Then Pfränger had the fortune of being subjected to a Soviet attempt to "convert" him. He managed to convince his captors that he would cooperate and was later parachuted into German-held territory. Once on the ground he turned himself in to the first German ground troops he could find.

A group of 78 IAP/VVS-SF pilots – apparently immediately after a combat mission – in front of one of the unit's Hurricane fighters at Vayenga air base near Murmansk. (Photo: Soviet Northern Fleet's Museum via Gyllenhaal.)

A VVS-SF Curtiss P-40E Kittyhawk. The Kittyhawk was developed when the earlier P-40 Tomahawk was reequipped with a new engine and a redesigned fuselage. The 1,150-horsepower Allison V-1710-39 engine and the improved aerodynamics increased the maximum speed of the P-40E to 362 miles per hour at 15,000 feet – compared to the P-40C's 345 miles per hour top speed at 15,000 feet. The main visual difference was the larger radiator, which was shifted farther forward. Another external difference was the increased rear-vision side panels in the rear of the cockpit. Also, armament was increased to six .50-caliber (12.7mm) wing-mounted machine guns. For all this, the Kittyhawk's climbing rate was inferior to that of the Tomahawk – and vastly inferior to that of the Bf 109 F. (Photo: Viktor Kulikov collection.)

During a mission in the Kandalska area on May 17, 1942 – this time escorting I./StG 5 Stukas – an engagement with Hurricanes of 760 IAP cost II./JG 5 two more Bf 109s. While Unteroffizier Karl Heinz Wellner was shot down, Oberleutnant Heinrich Ehrler of 6./JG 5 claimed a "MiG-3" – in fact the Hurricane flown by Serzhant A.I. Bazarov. As the doomed Hurricane went down, it tore straight into a Bf 109 piloted by Unteroffizier Helmut Schattschneider. The unfortunate German managed to nurse his badly crippled plane down to the ground and made a forced landing far behind Soviet lines. Fifteen days later, a totally exhausted Schattschneider reached the German lines by foot.

The air combat on May 18 also testified to the determination of the Soviet fighter pilots in the Murmansk region – despite their numerous losses in recent times. In this action, thirty-two KG 30 Ju 88s managed to attack Soviet and Allied ships in Murmansk and along the coastal waters, but on their return flight a combined force of thirty-seven fighters from VVS-SF and VVS-Fourteenth Army fell upon them. A prolonged fight ensued and the Soviet airmen claimed eight Ju 88s and three Bf 110s shot down. The Murmansk antiaircraft artillery claimed three other German aircraft. Luftwaffe sources confirm the loss of three planes, while Soviet archive material show that three Tomahawks and two Hurricanes – all from VVS-Fourteenth Army – failed to return from this encounter.

Three more Luftwaffe aircraft went missing during anti-shipping operations and attacks against command posts in Murmansk on May 25. One of the pilots lost was Leutnant Friedrich Dahn, a twenty-six victory ace in 5./JG 5. Nevertheless the Germans were able to pay back next day, when three 122 IAD/PVO Hurricanes were shot down for no Luftwaffe losses.

Now a new Allied convoy had been detected by the Germans. *PQ-16* was escorted by RAF Sunderlands and U.S. Navy flying boats, but these aircraft could not prevent 101 Ju 88s from striking at a point southeast of Barents Island on May 27. The Luftwaffe claimed six ships sunk against three planes lost. Five merchantmen and the AAA ship *Empire Lawrence* were in fact sunk.[39] The convoy was heavily attacked again on May 28 and during the night. As it approached Kola Bay (the entrance to Murmansk) on May 30, the somewhat dispersed ships came under renewed Luftwaffe bombing attacks. This time the ships were provided with air cover from VVS-SF, preventing the German airmen from dealing any additional losses to the convoy. But the price paid by the Soviet airmen for this

Mayor Leonid Galchenko achieved seven individual kills while serving with 145 IAP in the Far North during the first three months of the war, and his Eskadrilya developed into the most successful unit of VVS-Fourteenth Army during the first stage of the war. In October 1941, Galchenko was appointed commander of the new 609 IAP, and on June 6, 1942, he was appointed Hero of the Soviet Union. He survived the war with a total of twenty-four individual and twelve shared victories. Galchenko passed away on September 26, 1986. (Photo: Viktor Kulikov collection.)

LaGG-3 (first production series), Kapitan Leonid Galchenko, commander 609 IAP/VVS-Nineteenth Army/VVS-Karelian Front, Afrikanda, Soviet Union, spring 1942

defensive success was very high. In his chronicle of JG 5, German historian Werner Girbig states: "While escorting Ju 87s that were attacking the Allied convoy once again off the Kola Peninsula, and during free hunting missions, the 'Arctic Sea fighters' [on May 30, 1942] managed to shoot down a total of forty-three bombers and seven fighters. [Oberfeldwebel Franz] Dörr, [Oberleutnant Heinrich] Ehrler, and [Feldwebel Walter] Schuck were among the most successful pilots on that day."[40] These figures undoubtedly represent a considerable exaggeration.

Total Soviet aircraft losses in the Far North on May 30, 1942, are not known, but VVS-SF chalked up eight victory claims against only three aircraft lost in combat over the convoy – all from Podpolkovnik Safonov's 2 GSAP/VVS-SF.[41] VVS-Fourteenth Army registered sixteen aircraft lost during the period May 21 through June 1, but the statistics for 122 IAD/PVO for May 30, 1942, are not available.

Displaying an invincible calm, Podpolkovnik Boris Safonov poses in the cockpit of his Curtiss P-40E Kittyhawk in May 1942. On May 15, 1942, Safonov carried out his first flight with his brand-new Kittyhawk after recovering from an appendectomy. Two days later, he scored his first victory (seventeenth total) with this Kittyhawk. Safonov was the undisputed master of Soviet fighter pilots in the Far North in 1941 and early 1942. His personal successes and the great care he took in educating other pilots in fighter tactics contributed a great deal to the achievements of Soviet fighter pilots in the Far North during the first months of the war. His death in late May 1942 was a serious blow for the Soviet fighter units in the Murmansk area. (Photo: Rybin.)

Nevertheless, one of the Soviet losses that day was absolutely irrepairable. Podpolkovnik Safonov took off in his Kittyhawk at 0920 hours this May 30 and flew in the direction of Kildin Island together with three other 2 GSAP aces – Mayor Aleksey Kukharenko, Kapitan Pavel Orlov, and Starshiy Leytenant Vladimir Pokrovskiy. Due to technical trouble, Kukharenko had to abandon the mission and return home.

As the Soviets approached the convoy at the lowest possible altitude, skimming the waves, they spotted a formation of six Ju 88s starting a dive against one of the ships. The Soviet fighter pilots gave full throttle to their engines as they watched the German planes drop their bombs – all of which fell into the sea.

Safonov overtook the first bomber, passed it at high speed, and attacked the second. Pokrovskiy and Orlov attacked the third and fourth bombers. After the first bursts from the Soviet machine guns, the Ju 88s attacked by Pokrovskiy and Orlov broke to the left. The two Soviet fighter pilots decided to follow them, thus losing sight of Safonov.

At an altitude under 600 feet over the gray waves, Pokrovskiy kept chasing one of the Junkers. He emptied all of his ammunition into the fuselage and wings of the enemy plane, which caught fire and dove into the water. Meanwhile, the Ju 88 singled out by Pavel Orlov was down to 90 feet. Orlov blasted away with five or six bursts from his machine guns and hit one of the Ju 88's engines, which began smoking. Then the Ju 88 decreased speed, forcing the Kittyhawk to fly past it. By the time Kapitan Orlov turned after the Ju 88 again, it was gone. Nor was there any trace of Safonov, who could not be reached via R/T, because he operated on another frequency.

At approximately the same time, Soviet ground controllers heard Boris Safonov crying in triumph over the radio: "*Dvukh trakhnul!*" – "I smashed two!" Shortly afterward, his voice was heard again, announcing that he had shot down a third. In fact, nothing beyond these radio calls serves as a foundation for the three final victories that were officially credited to Boris Safonov. It is not known if he actually managed to shoot down *any* enemy aircraft during this combat, but a comparison between Luftwaffe loss files and the claims made by 2 GSAP/VVS-SF shows that 1.(F)/124 and II./KG 30 each lost one Ju 88 to the P-40s that day.

Then followed Boris Safonov's last words over the radio: "My engine is damaged, I have to ditch…"

Curtiss P-40E Warhawk, Podpolkovnik Boris Safonov, 2 GSAP/VVS-SF, Vayenga-1 Airdrome, Soviet Union, May 30, 1942

This airplane was delivered by the Americans in its original US Navy blue scheme.
Note that it has been modified with a non-standard radio antenna.

Thus died one of the most brilliant fighter pilots of World War II. In the course of 234 sorties, resulting in thirty-four air combats, Boris Safonov was officially credited with twenty personal and six collective kills. Numerous Soviet sources give even higher figures. On June 14 Safonov posthumously became the first Soviet citizen to be twice appointed Hero of the Soviet Union during the war against Germany.

Safonov's first fourteen individual kills were achieved while flying an I-16 Ishak. It is quite easy to imagine the rate of success that a pilot like Safonov could have enjoyed had he been outfitted with aircraft of the same quality as his German counterparts.

A comparison between Boris Safonov's personal victories and the first twenty-one victories achieved by Theodor Weissenberger, one of the most outstanding Luftwaffe aces in the Far North, is telling:

VICTORY LIST
Boris Safonov,
individual victories Nos 1-20, plus six shared victories[42]

No.	Date	Aircraft flown	Downed
1	6/24/41	I-16	He 111
*	6/27/41	I-16	Hs 126
2	7/16/41	I-16	Hs 126
3	7/17/41	I-16	Ju 87
4	7/18/41	I-16	Ju 88
5	7/25/41	I-16	Ju 88
6	8/5/41	I-16	Bf 109
7	8/6/41	I-16	Ju 88
8	8/9/41	I-16	Ju 88
*	8/9/41	I-16	Ju 88
*	8/9/41	I-16	Ju 88
*	8/9/41	I-16	Ju 88
9	8/23/41	I-16	Ju 88
10	8/27/41	I-16	Hs 126
*	8/27/41	I-16	Bf 109
11	9/9/41	I-16	Ju 87
12	9/15/41	I-16	Bf 110
13	9/15/41	I-16	Ju 87
14	9/15/41	I-16	Hs 126
*	9/15/41	I-16	Bf 109
15	12/17/41	Hurricane	Bf 109
16	12/31/41	Hurricane	He 111
17	5/17/42	Kittyhawk	Ju 88
18	5/30/42	Kittyhawk	Ju 88
19	5/30/42	Kittyhawk	Ju 88
20	5/30/42	Kittyhawk	Ju 88

(* = shared victory.)

VICTORY LIST
Theodor Weissenberger
Nos. 1 – 21[43]

No.	Date	Aircraft flown	Downed
1	10/24/41	Bf 110	I-153
2	1/24/42	Bf 110	I-18
3	1/24/42	Bf 110	Hurricane
4	2/25/42	Bf 110	Hurricane
5	2/25/42	Bf 110	Hurricane
6	4/8/42	Bf 110	MiG fighter
7	4/12/42	Bf 110	LaGG fighter
8	4/15/42	Bf 110	I-180
9	4/15/42	Bf 110	MiG fighter
10	4/15/42	Bf 110	Hurricane
11	4/23/42	Bf 110	Hurricane
12	4/25/42	Bf 110	Pe-2
13	4/25/42	Bf 110	Pe-2
14	5/10/42	Bf 110	MiG-3
15	5/10/42	Bf 110	MiG-3
16	5/10/42	Bf 110	Hurricane
17	5/10/42	Bf 110	Hurricane
18	5/10/42	Bf 110	MiG-3
19	5/12/42	Bf 110	MiG-3
20	5/15/42	Bf 110	Hurricane
21	6/1/42	Bf 110	Curtiss

In recent years, Russian historian Yuriy Rybin has compared Boris Safonov's victory list with German loss reports and was able to verify between three and twelve of Safonov's first seventeen claims.

For almost a year, the Soviet airmen in the Far North were able to cope with a most difficult combat situation, albeit in the face of significant losses. But in late May 1942 the accumulation of combat strain and the inadequate training of the novice pilots started to show negative effects. Although VVS-Fourteenth Army was reinforced by 80 BAP and 608 BAP, the air-base raids it conducted from May 21 through June 1 achieved poor results: Two hundred and seventy sorties against the German airfields[44] failed to destroy more than a single plane on the ground.

The death of the famous Boris Safonov apparently struck the final blow against the confidence of the fatigued Soviet airmen in the Murmansk sector. On top of this, Mayor Aleksandr Zaytsev, the top-scorer of VVS-Fourteenth Army, was killed while test flying a P-39 Airacobra the same day as Safonov went missing.

Zaytsev remains one of the "forgotten aces" of the VVS. Although he apparently achieved fourteen individual and twenty-one shared victories, his blunt demeanor led him into trouble with his superiors – to the point that a recommendation for his appointment as a Hero of the Soviet Union was withdrawn. Nevertheless, Zaytsev greatly inspired his fellow VVS-Fourteenth Army pilots, and his loss, along with Safonov's, was a heavy blow to the combat spirits of all the Soviet airmen in the Far North.

The first two days of June 1942 were filled with aerial combat activity as Luftflotte 5 was launched in full strength against the *PQ 16* ships that were unloading in Murmansk. Early on June 1 three air raids against the German airfields at Luostari and Höybukten cost the Soviets eight aircraft for the destruction of *no* Luftwaffe planes.[45] Later that day, I/StG 5 and KG 30 carried out four minor raids against Murmansk in which they sank the freighters *Subbotnik* and *Empire Starlight* for the loss of a Ju 87.[46] During Soviet fighter interceptions on June 1, VVS-Fourteenth Army's 20 GIAP lost a brand-new P-40E Kittyhawks flown by Mladshiy Leytenant A. V. Pshenyov, on June 1. Hit in fighter combat – probably by 5./JG 5's Unteroffizier Dietrich Weinitschke – the Kittyhawk went down to the west of Murmansk.

On June 2 the submarine *Shch-404* was damaged during another Stuka air raid against Murmansk. This time the Soviet interceptors managed to shoot down two I./StG 5 Ju 87s,[47] but at the cost five of their own number. Two Hurricanes fell prey to 6./JG 5's Feldwebel Rudolf Müller – quite easily, as the corresponding VVS-SF report indicates: "Instead of carrying out sharp maneuvers and taking advantage of suitable positions for fighter attacks, our pilots confined themselves to sluggish horizontal turns. As a result, a single Me 109 managed to shoot down two Hurricanes in steep high-side attacks."[48]

The weakened Soviet fighter opposition enabled the Luftflotte 5 dive-bombers to sink or damage individual ships. This was a dramatic change compared to the hardships encountered by all Luftwaffe airmen who had hitherto attempted to raid the port of Murmansk, but in order to produce lasting results, the Soviet ability to receive Western military aid from the north had to be destroyed. Hence, Generaloberst Stumpff concentratd his air units against the port installations. After ten days of adverse weather that curtailed most flight activity, he launched his forces against Murmansk with this purpose on June 12. Next day, three raids were undertaken against the same target.

In the ensuing combat with the Soviet fighters that rose to defend the port, Feldwebel "Rudi" Müller once again triumphed by claiming three Hurricanes – including II./JG 5's 500th victory. 78 IAP/VVS-SF filed one Hurricane destroyed in aerial combat – with Starshiy Leytenant Shalayev bailing out – and two other Hurricanes force-landed with battle damage at Murmashi Airdrome. Six days later "Rudi" Müller was awarded the Knight's Cross for his forty-six victories.

German superiority in air combat should not obscure the fact that the German effort was a failure. Air reconnaissance photos showed only limited destruction of the port installations. This captures the situation in a nutshell – while the Bf 109s of JG 5 were the masters of the sky, the strong AAA defending the port of Murmansk prevented any concentrated large-scale bombing attack. "The antiaircraft artillery at Murmansk was the worst I have ever seen," recalls 6./JG 5's Oberfeldwebel Hugo Dahmer. "The port area literally *boiled* with muzzle flashes from the guns below. It was absolutely incredible to see how even a single German airplane managed to survive that antiaircraft barrage."[49]

The repeated attempts by KG 30 to halt the flow of military equipment from *PQ-16* that was brought down along the Kirov rail line likewise achieved only limited success. Here the German airmen noted that Soviet fighter units had been strengthened considerably.[50]

III./KG 30 could testify to the renewed strength of the Soviet fighters following a June 15 mission against the railroad bridge near Kem', 300 miles south of Murmansk. Just as the eighteen Ju 88s wheeled into their dives against the bridge, Kapitan P. V. Vorobyov led four 760 IAP

Two III./KG 30 Ju 88s fly against Convoy PQ-16 in late May 1942. (Photo: Rautio.)

Hurricanes in a frontal attack that forced the Ju 88s to break off. Then four 195 IAP fighters that came up from behind pursued the bombers. Seven German planes were claimed in the ensuing melee, including three by Kapitan Vorobyov. On the other hand, three of the eight Soviet fighters were shot down by the five escorting Bf 110s of 10.(Z)/JG 5 (which carried out its 1,500th sortie on the Eastern Front that day). The returning German bomber crews filed a report describing a terrible air fight, but actual losses were one missing and two severely damaged Ju 88s.

These failures converged to form Stumpff's order to wipe out Murmansk's housing with the intention of depriving the port of its work force. Leaflets urging the inhabitants to leave Murmansk, lest they be subjected to an annihilating fire raid, rained down over the town. On June 18 over one hundred individual German sorties were made during four separate raids against the center of Murmansk. Once again the Germans encountered nothing but weak fighter opposition. Since Soviet records show that VVS-SF airmen carried out a total of 162 sorties to intercept these Germans,[51] it appears that these fighter pilots approached the Luftwaffe formations most cautiously – to put it mildly. "It was hard for us to try and fend off the continuously incoming bombers," Sergey Kurzenkov wrote laconically.[52] VVS-SF filed five victory claims while the actual loss sustained by the raiders was a single Bf 110.[53]

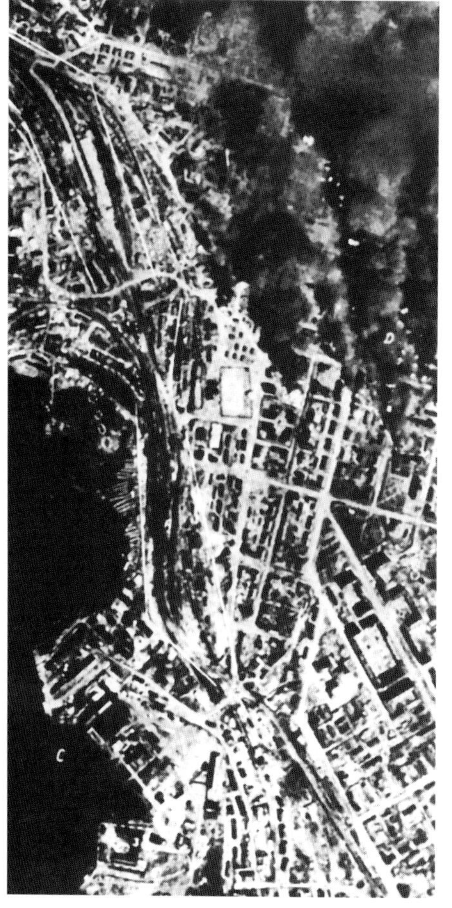

Published in the Luftwaffe magazine *Der Adler,* this aerial photo shows fire spreading through in the residential quarters of Murmansk. Although this was not the intention of *Der Adler,* the photo also reveals that the port area is only lightly damaged. *(Der Adler.)*

Twelve thousand incendiary bombs were dropped, setting almost the entire town of Murmansk on fire. Approximately eight hundred houses, almost half the town's dwellings, were reduced to ashes.

Sergey Kurzenkov recalls this horrifying event:

> Strong winds blew constantly. In the mountains, the dry Arctic birks and the turf were on fire. Smoke clouds covered the Kola Peninsula.
>
> The Fascists made great use of the drying heat and the strong gale... The strong wind made the work of the fire brigade more difficult. In the center of the town, almost all the wooden houses burned to the ground. But the Fascists never succeeded in destroying the harbor.[54]

During the remainder of June, more than twenty follow-up raids were conducted against Murmansk, which was almost totally destroyed. Due to the crippled state of their fighter establishment in the Murmansk area, the Soviets had to rely mainly on their antiaircraft artillery for protective measures.

By this time, the two fighter aviation regiments of VVS-Fourteenth Army that were stationed at Murmashi Airdrome were down at a total of nine serviceable aircraft –

Curtiss P-40Es of 2 GSAP/VVS-SF at Vayenga-2 Airdrome during the summer of 1942. (Photo: Rybin.)

six Kittyhawks and three MiG-3s in 20 GIAP, and no serviceable aircraft at all in 197 IAP![55] The 122 IAD, the PVO Diviziya that had been brought in to provide Murmansk with air cover, was left with only four pilots and nine fighter aircraft by July 1, 1942. It is hardly surprising that the strong determination that had characterized Soviet fighter operations in the Far North to this point changed to the opposite.

Between June 19 and June 30, VVS-SF fighter pilots reported 10 German aircraft shot down – added to the 12 claimed shot down by the fleet's AAA – while the units of Luftflotte 5 noted only 3 combat losses. For the entire period between June 22, 1941, and June 22, 1942, VVS-SF accumulated approximately 300 victory claims – of which 2 GSAP/VVS-SF chalked up 197 (57 since January 1, 1942).[56] VVS-Karelian Front claimed 270 German, 47 Finnish, and 7 unidentified aircraft shot down between June 22, 1941, and June 30, 1942.[57] Of this total, VVS-Karelian Front reported 34 single-engine fighters shot down in June 1942 alone.[58] It is obvious that this represented a large exaggeration, for German and Finnish records list only 2 JG 5 Bf 109s and 3 Finnish fighters lost in operations through June 1942.[59]. Shortly afterwards, the Peoples' Commissar of VVS-SF, Admiral Nikolay Kuznetsov,[60] and the commander of Murmansk PVO, Polkovnik Ivanov,[61] issued orders in which they made it clear that a claim for downing an enemy aircraft would be recorded only when the crash could be confirmed by witnesses.

It should be noted that the JG 5 pilots also showed a propensity to overclaim. Whereas 127 victories were chalked up by JG 5 during June 1942, the Soviet air forces in the Murmansk-Karelian sectors recorded 56 aircraft destroyed in air combat during the same period – including seventeen by VVS-Karelian Front, which also operated against the Finnish Air Force.[62] Eight others sustained "serious" damage, and 15 others sustained "medium" battle damage in aerial combat.[63] Nine additional Soviet aircraft were recorded lost to ground fire, and 13 were reported missing due to unknown causes. Since the Soviet figures include losses all along the Soviet-Finnish front line, they indicate that more than half of the claims made by JG 5 pilots in June 1942 were erroneous. Nevertheless, approximately 10 Soviet aircraft shot down for the loss of only 2 Bf 109s and a Bf 110 was a remarkable achievement by JG 5.

In the summer of 1942 the Bf 109 pilots of JG 5 managed to beat back the strongest Soviet opposition in the air in any single combat zone on the Eastern Front. At the same time, the bombers and Stukas of KG 30 and I./StG 5 displayed that they were capable of intervening with great success against undertakings by Soviet ground forces. Although strong Soviet antiaircraft coverage at Murmansk prevented the German bombers from carrying out a concentrated bombing of port installations, the Germans had wiped out vast areas of the town through horrendous carpet bombing.

The coming of twenty-four hour midsummer sunshine set the stage for an air operation against the next Allied *PQ* convoy in the extreme northern waters.

VVS interdiction effort against the intense Fliegerkorps I operations over the Lyuban Pocket during this period.

How desperate the Soviet situation at Lyuban may have been, the defense of Leningrad was of far greater importance. VVS-Leningrad Front, whose defensive nature is displayed by the fact that it was almost exclusively composed of fighters, also sustained bitter losses and saved its forces for the air defense of Leningrad and the city's supply lifeline across Lake Ladoga. General-Mayor Mikhail Samokhin's air force of the Red Banner Baltic Fleet, VVS-KBF, was primarily occupied covering the Gulf of Finland, which included raids against shipping and ports on Finland's southern coast. Samokhin's airmen were up against the main part of the Finnish Air Force as well as Luftflotte 1. VVS-Leningrad Front and VVS-KBF could muster approximately 150 to 200 serviceable aircraft apiece in the summer of 1942.

Petr Likholetov was among the most skilled fighter pilots of VVS-Leningrad Front during the early stage of the war against Germany. He drew his first blood during the Winter War and served with 159 IAP against Luftflotte 1 from June 1941. He scored his first victory on July 12, 1941, when he downed a Ju 88 while piloting a MiG-3. Likholetov was credited with a total of twenty-five personal and five shared victories during 382 combat sorties. (Photo: Seidl.)

The ice melt on Lake Ladoga naturally destroyed the so-called Ice Road, which had been the lifeline to Leningrad throughout the winter, but as soon as circumstances allowed navigation on the lake, a seafaring supply operation was initiated. The first freight vessel of the Ladoga Flotilya, the tug *Gidrotekhnik*, set to sea from the small port of Kobona on the eastern shore of Lake Ladoga on May 22 and arrived in Leningrad with forty tons of flour. On May 23 the ships brought in another thirty-seven tons of provisions and eighty-five tons of ammunition, and thereafter the shipments increased day by day.

The supply effort alarmed the Germans – who misinterpreted Soviet intentions – and it would be the cause of a major outburst of air combat in the northern combat zone. Hitler was aware that the mass evacuation of Leningrad during the past winter had thrown a spanner into his works for starving the city to surrender, and he assumed that the intention of the intensified shipping effort was to evacuate all civilians. The main intention was not to evacuate civilians, but to bring in supplies. But the returning ships brought civilians back. On May 26 he instructed the commander of Army Group North to concentrate all available forces, "particularly the Luftwaffe," to prevent the evacuation of Leningrad.[64]

Generaloberst Keller immediately went into action, dispatching most of Fliegerkorps I against the Ladoga ports. Here the German airmen would face formidable opposition. The Ladoga ports were defended by powerful AAA forces and some of the best fighter units of VVS-Leningrad Front and VVS-KBF, all assisted by RUS-2 radar stations.

Early on Thursday, May 28, eighty Fliegerkorps I bombers and dive-bombers took off for two major raids against the ports of Kobona and Lednyovo on the eastern shore of Lake Ladoga. Alerted by radar, the Soviet fighters were scrambled and attacked the Germans with fierce determination. The leading group of nine III./KG 1 Ju 88s were met head-on by five 159 IAP MiG-3s commanded by the ace Starshiy Leytenant Petr Likholetov. Six 286 IAP I-16s hurled themselves nose-to-nose against another bomber formation. The German airmen were unprepared to meet such resistance, and the combat formations became scattered as individual bomber pilots attempted to avoid collisions.

Likholetov's fighters attacked one bomber formation after another in the same manner, causing the Germans to spread out, and claiming three Ju 88s and two He 111s in the process.[65] 286 IAP was credited with three victories. One of its pilots, Serzhant Sergey Kotelnikov reportedly brought down a German bomber despite having sustained three bullet wounds and returned to base, making a successful landing. Forty-six holes were counted in his I-16.

Positioned above the veering bombers, intermingled with diving and turning Soviet fighters, the German fighter commander, Major Hannes Trautloft, tried to control the situation. As twenty-two I-16s of 4 GIAP/VVS-KBF, commanded by the famous Starshiy Leytenant Vasiliy Golubev, appeared and attempted to intercept the bombers, Trautloft led his twenty-four Bf 109s into a high-side attack. Two I-16s were badly shot up. Both pilots, one of them the ace Starshiy Leytenant Gennadiy Tsokolayev, were injured and had to disengage.

Bf 109 F-4, Major Hannes Trautloft, Geschwaderkommodore JG 54 Grünherz, Siverskaya, Soviet Union, June 1942
This airplane is the same as that shown in the color profile on page 179. Here it has been resprayed in the typical JG 54 camouflage, consisting of RLM 70 and RLM 71.

Meanwhile, Golubev approached the rear bomber group. "Forward, Vasya!" he radioed to his wingman, Serzhant Vasiliy Zakharov. Next moment they were bounced by a Bf 109 Rotte. "I charged three Ratas that were pursuing a Ju 88," wrote Trautloft. "I got one of the 'Rats' in my gunsight, but it managed to evade my fire through a sharp turn that I wasn't able to follow due to my high speed. Suddenly, I saw bullet tracers passing my cockpit." When he spotted a Bf 109 on his commander's tail, "Vasya" Zakharov increased speed and opened fire on the pursuer. He immediately became targeted by the German's wingman and caught the full burst of the Bf 109's 20mm cannon. A huge ball of fire in the air told Golubev that he had lost Zakharov.[66]

4 GIAP/VVS-KBF returned from combat in disarray. Six German aircraft were reported as shot down, but one of the unit's pilots had been killed, and three were injured. Material losses amounted to eight damaged I-16s. Actual German losses were limited to a KG 1 Ju 88 and a III./StG 1 Ju 87 – against which three victories were claimed.

The stiff-necked nose-to-nose fighter attacks in combination with intense antiaircraft fire had prevented several bomber crews from carrying out their bombing accurately. The gunboat *Bira* was sunk, some loaded trains and a large warehouse were destroyed, and the port installations and the railway station were hit by bombs, but the port remained operational.[67]

The final serial version of the I-16 – Mark 29 – was launched into production in 1940. All 650 were manufactured at Aircraft Production Plant No. 21 in Gorkiy, and the last eighty were completed in 1941. This mark was equipped with a 900-horsepower M-63 engine and could achieve a maximum speed of 290 miles per hour at a flight altitude of 15,000 feet. Armament included one 12.7mm BS, two 7.62mm ShKAS, and six RS-82s rocket-projectiles. (Photo: Authors' collection.)

That evening, around ninety bombers and Stukas were launched against the Ladoga ports. This time they were escorted by sixty-one JG 54 Bf 109s.[68]

Once again alerted by their radar, 158 IAP, 159 IAP, and 4 GIAP/VVS-KBF scrambled twenty-six fighters to cover the eastern ports. But this time, Osinovets on the western shore was the German target, and since the airborne Soviet fighters were not allowed to leave the area they had been assigned to protect, only seven 123 IAP I-16s intercepted the large Luftwaffe formation. Led by Starshiy Leytenant Vasiliy Kharitonov, these Ishaks made a few ineffective gunnery runs, after which they all returned to base.

Nevertheless, the Germans were met by a strong and well-aimed antiaircraft fire that took the wind out of the bombing. The Osinovets provision warehouse and storehouse were set ablaze, and eight railway wagons were destroyed.[69]

"Enormous flames reaching for the dark, cloudy sky offer a terrifying picture," Hannes Trautloft noted in his diary – but the port installations could be made serviceable within a

4 GIAP/VVS-KBF's Starshiy Leytenant Mikhail Vasiliyev returns from a combat mission over Lake Ladoga in his I-16 Mark 17, armed with 20mm ShVAK cannon. Vasiliyev was one of the aces in 4 GIAP/VVS-KBF, where he commanded the 1st Eskadrilya. By April 1942, he had amassed a total of two individual and sixteen shared kills. Vasilyev took part in the fierce air fighting over the Ladoga ports of Kobona and Lednyovo early on May 28, 1942. By that time his score stood at two individual and sixteen shared victories. Vasiliyev was appointed a Hero of the Soviet Union on June 14, 1942. On May 5, 1943, he was killed in action. (Photo: Petrov.)

Polikarpov I-16 Mark 17, Starshiy Leytenant Mikhail Vasiliyev (22 victories), 4 GIAP/VVS-KBF, Lake Ladoga area, Soviet Union, spring 1942

The fighter pilots of 4 GIAP/VVS-KBF made a good account of themselves during the defense of the supply lines across Lake Ladoga during 1942. Through the end of May 1942, this unit was credited with 218 aerial victories – including ninety-two from early February – for the loss of forty-nine pilots and eighty-seven aircraft. Lined up in front of the camera in late May 1942 are (standing, l. to r.) D. Dmitriyev, L. Petelinskiy, Yevgeniy Tsyganov, Valerian Bakirov, S. Suvorkin, G. Lagutkin, D. Sotsenko, Yemelyan Strel'nikov, Filatov, and Potapov; and (seated, l. to r.) are Petr Kozhanov, Mikhail Vasilyev, Boris Mikhailov (the regimental commander), Beznosov, and G. A. Bagirov. (Photo: 4 GIAP/VVS-VMF Museum.)

short time. The Leningrad-bound tonnage brought into Osinovets dropped temporarily, but only from 1,743 tons on May 27 to 1,309 tons on May 28.

Next day, May 29, Fliegerkorps I dispatched four major raids against the supply lines to Leningrad. First, the railroad stations at Volkhovstroy – south of Kobona – and Volkhov were targeted during the morning hours. Since the ports were the prime objects of the Soviet fighter defense in this region, only sixteen P-40s from 158 IAP and 159 IAP were sent into action. A brief skirmish resulted in no German losses[70] and two damaged 159 IAP fighters.[71] One of them was claimed shot down by Leutnant Friedrich Rupp of 7./JG 54.[72]

That evening, Soviet radar stations reported signs of new Luftwaffe raids assembling. These eventually advanced over a wide front south of Leningrad and split into two groups.

The Soviet fighters were scrambled as all available Bf 109-escorted Ju 87s from Stab and III./StG 1 were directed against Kobona, and 150 Ju 88s and Bf 109s went for Osinovets. Nineteen I-16s of 4 GIAP/VVS-KBF managed to break up the Stuka raid with a head-on pass, and Starshiy Leytenant Golubev claimed that he and his I-16 pilots shot down seven Ju 87s for no losses. According to the German loss report, only one Ju 87 was lost. The 11 GIAP LaGG-3s intercepted the Osinovets raid and filed four apparently unsubstantiated claims.[73] Major Trautloft wrote in his diary that he saw four Soviet fighters go down into Lake Ladoga "like blazing torches."

In sum, the Soviets failed to inflict any meaningful material damage on the Luftwaffe during the air battles over Lake Ladoga on May 28 and May 29. But they also gave proof of an increased skill to evade German fighter attacks, and – above all – managed to save the small Ladoga ports from being totally destroyed. On May 30, 4,079 tons of supplies were brought across the lake, and next day the tonnage surpassed 5,000 tons.

The effective fighter and antiaircraft protection of the Ladoga ports, and the need to concentrate Fliegerkorps I against the final battle of the Lyuban Pocket, compelled Generaloberst Keller to discontinue major operations against these targets without the objective being achieved. That the two I./JG 54 Staffeln commanded by Hauptmann Hans Philipp were allotted to carry out fighter-bomber missions against the supply ships may be regarded as a symbolic gesture. Operating from Petäjärvi, a small and well-camouflaged airfield near the Finnish city of Vyborg on the Karelian Isthmus, this detachment carried out 104 sorties without hitting a single ship.[74] From late May 1942 through the end of the year, the Ladoga Flotiliya transported 790,000 tons of goods and 250,000 soldiers to Leningrad, and evacuated 540,000 people, including 490,000 civilians. As a result of the summer shipping effort alone, at least three months of reserve provisions could be accumulated in the besieged city.

South of Lake Ilmen, I./JG 51 was dealt a severe blow on May 29 when its top ace, Leutnant Erwin Fleig, was shot down and bailed out over Soviet territory shortly after downing a MiG-3 for his sixty-sixth victory. When they captured this ace, who once had served as wingman to the legendary Oberst Werner Mölders, the Soviets acquired and confined an important "trophy."

On May 31 four 485 IAP Hurricanes intercepted ten KGrzbV 500 Ju 52s, escorted by four I./JG 51 Bf 109s, and claimed a Ju 52 and two Bf 109s shot down. KGrzbV 500 and I./JG 51 actually recorded one combat loss apiece, while the Gruppenkommandeur of I./JG 51 – twenty-seven-victory ace Hauptmann Josef Fözö – was seriously injured in a landing accident. But these incidents remained isolated exceptions. Although VVS-Northwestern Front – which mustered more than three hundred aircraft in May 1942 – held a substantial numerical superiority, the Bf 109s of I./JG 51 and II./JG 54 were generally masters of the skies in this sector. The Ju 52 that was lost on May 31 was the only combat loss dealt to KGrzbV 500, which continued to fly supplies to the semi-encircled German Demyansk garrison through the month of May.

Ju 52s at Demyansk Airdrome in the summer of 1942. Although a land connection had been opened to the besieged German garrison at Demyansk during the spring of 1942, the corridor was so narrow in some places that it was under constant Soviet fire. Thus, elements of the transport fleet had to continue to airlift supplies to Demyansk. Demyansk Airdrome was a former Soviet airbase, so its runway – 50 yards wide and 900 yards long – was highly suitable for the air bridge. (Photo: Trautloft.)

The scores of inadequately trained airmen that arrived as replacements for the badly mauled units of VVS-Northwestern Front enabled the fighter pilots of I./JG 51 and II./JG 54 to achieve a number of "easy victories" again. Through May 1942, VVS-Northwestern Front registered fifty aircraft missing or shot down in air combat and eighteen lost to ground fire,[75] while I./JG 51 and II./JG 54 lost only four fighters. A comparison of German and Soviet archival data shows that an average of approximately two VVS-Northwestern Front fighters were lost for every German aircraft they shot down in May 1942.

During the last days of May 1942, Fliegerkorps I shifted its focus back to the Lyuban Pocket, where a renewed German offensive managed to conclusively close the sack on May 29. In order to isolate the Soviet battlefield, Stab and III./StG 1 were launched against the railroad station at Malaya Vishera on May 30. Two 2 GIAP MiG-3s made a fruitless interception attempt, and one was shot down by Major Trautloft. The downed pilot, regimental commander Podpolkovnik Petr Metyolkin, was killed.

The dominant task of the German fighters in this area was to interfere with the Soviet supply flights to the Lyuban Pocket. By this time, the He 111s of II./KG 53 organized a Nachtjagdschwarm led by Oberfeldwebel Waldemar Teige that started operating against the Soviet transports during the hours of darkness. The decision to allocate a part of a bomber unit to this task was taken because these crews were experienced in "blind flight" and their He 111s were steady enough to deal with the very slow R-5 and U-2 biplanes. After claiming nine night victories, Oberfeldwebel Teige was awarded the Knight's Cross on June 7 – the first for the airmen in II./KG 53. On the following night he bagged two 662 NBAP U-2s.

The Soviet situation deteriorated considerably on June 10, when the landing strip in the surrounded area, at Finev Lug, fell into German hands. This made the use of the twin-engine PS-84s, which could parachute their cargo from 150 feet flight altitude, even more imperative. The PS-84s allocated to the Lyuban supply operation – a detachment from 1 TAD/ADD, which had arrived at Khvoynaya Airdrome in late May and early June – were commanded by Polkovnik Valentina Grizodubova, one of the most famous female Soviet pilots. But these license-built American-designed DC-3s also suffered dearly at the hands of German night-fighters.

Several JG 54 Bf 109 pilots took advantage of the bright summer nights to join the He 111s in nocturnal hunts over Lyuban. They were guided by nothing but eyesight, but given the bright summer nights and the limited geographical area, all they had to do was to lie in wait above the surrounded area. On the night of June 10, Oberleutnant Günther Fink and Leutnant Hans-Joachim Heyer of III./JG

Bf 109s of 2./JG 51 Mölders and Ju 52s at Demyansk Airdrome. (Photo: Trautloft.)

54 claimed four PS-84s and one "R-2" (an R-5 or R-Z) – one after another – as they arrived during a thirty-minute patrol over the Lyuban pocket.[76]

Generaloberst Keller concluded that the fate of the Lyuban Pocket was settled, so he diverted III./StG 1 to hunt Ladoga shipping the same day. Soviet records confirm that three barges were sunk by the Stuka fliers, but this would remain the only significant Luftwaffe success against the Ladoga shipping throughout 1942.

At the same time, the Volkhov Front – which had been reinstated on June 8 – launched a combined offensive eastward from within the Lyuban Pocket and westward from positions east of the Volkhov River. III./StG 1 was hastily called back to operations against Lyuban, and the Soviet hope of reopening the corridor to the Second Assault Army was scattered in devastating Stuka attacks at Myasnoy Bor. 1 UAG RGK, assigned the task of providing air support for the Soviet offensive, was mercilessly butchered by JG 54 Bf 109s. Meanwhile, the bombers of KG 1 and KG 53 were turning the entire area inside the Lyuban Pocket into a veritable moonscape. A Second Assault Army Starshiy Leytenant wrote in his diary:

While a light drizzle falls on Siverskaya Airdrome, Oberleutnant Günther Fink climbs out of the cockpit of his Bf 109 after his successful sortie over Finev Lug on the night of June 10, 1942, when he teamed with Leutnant Hans-Joachim Heyer to knock down five Soviet transport planes. Fink amassed a total of fifty-six victories, nine of them at night over the Lyuban pocket, before he failed to return from an intercept mission against American heavy bombers on May 15, 1943. (Photo: Trautloft.)

> The damned Germans have gone really seriously into bombing us. They arrive in formations or separately and drop their deadly cargo without pause. And where are our airmen? I have endured for so long, but now I can feel that my nerves can't take this any longer. For how long are we going to starve and remain without tobacco, and allow the cursed Prussians to drop their bombs on us? . . . How much has been destroyed through this aerial bombardment – artillery pieces, tractors, and human lives? It is countless. We are told that a terrible number of people has been killed at Myasnoy Bor. We are like trapped hares. We are really starving. We eat horse flesh…[77]

This 1 TAD PS-84 was shot down by German night fighters near the Lyuban Pocket. Mayor Valentina Grizodubova, who commanded the PS-84-equipped detachment of 1 TAD responsible for the Lyuban supply flights, was the daughter of Russian aviation pioneer Stepan Grizodubov. She had been appointed Hero of the Soviet Union with the two other female pilots – Marina Raskova and Polina Osipenko – after setting the womens' international record for non-stop long-range flying in 1938. (Photo: Roba/Mombeek.)

Between June 5 and June 18, JG 54 claimed twenty-five Soviet transport planes shot down over the Lyuban Pocket. After June 18 troop rations in the Second Assault Army were reduced to forty to fifty grams of dry bread.

Kapitan Nikolay Bogdanov, commanding the "Lyuban detachment" of the new 103 AP/1 TAD, recalls a terrifying encounter with German night-fighters on the night of June 22: "I was alerted by the fact that there was no antiaircraft fire. This could only mean that we had to expect a fighter attack. I instructed my crew to be alert and keep their eyes open, and it was in the nick of time. Suddenly our huge but slow [transports], which were flying singly in a long row, conspicuous in the bright, cloudless sky, came under fighter attack from all directions. Within a few seconds we were stunned to see three of our aircraft falling out of control, blazing like torches."[78]

After this event, the Soviet transport formations were provided with fighter escort, but this did not prevent additional severe losses. On the night of June 22-23, 8./JG 54's Leutnant Erwin Leykauf blasted six Soviet transport planes out of the sky during a fifty-minute mission – his victories eighteen through twenty-three. Leykauf wrote vividly of this event:

> I was feeling slightly annoyed. Hauptmann Reinhard Seiler, with whom I flew as wingman, had shot down two Soviet [PS-84s] right in front of me, and I encountered some trouble with the engine of my Messerschmitt. I was thinking of returning to base when suddenly bullet flares – green, red, and yellow – passed me. A dark shadow flew past. I saw the dark silhouette of a very slowly flying aircraft and throttled back my tired engine. Yes! It was a single-engine biplane, an R-5 transport! It was positioned right in front of the muzzles of my guns. *Ratatatatat* – shrapnel came whirling toward me, and then a bright flame shot out and the Soviet plane plummeted downward in a nice turn.
>
> My engine ran smoothly again, so there was no need to disengage, particularly not since I shortly afterward spotted another shadow. This time it was a really large transport plane. I gave it a couple of bursts, and it disintegrated completely in mid-air, with a large section of one wing, the tailfin, and half the fuselage tumbling down separately toward the ground.
>
> Number three met his fate under most dramatic circumstances. I was a hair's-breadth from colliding with the Soviet plane. As I set him burning, I expected that he would go down, but instead he pulled up. For a brief moment, I could see the blazing plane almost at reaching distance in front of me. As I pulled the stick into my stomach in order to evade a collision, I caught a glimpse of the observer bending forward, shaking the pilot's shoulders. Then the Soviet aircraft turned over and slowly started floating down like a giant torch – a horrendous sight! It crashed into the dark woods below. The burning impact point was only one out of thousands of light points on the ground: exploding artillery shells, antiaircraft bullet flares, and colorful signal flares could be seen everywhere in the night.
>
> Slightly outside the area of encirclement I saw two gray shadows circling around in the sky – Soviet night-fighters. But they could not prevent me from dispatching my fourth victim within minutes. I noticed a row of bomb explosions on the ground. The guys who had dropped those bombs couldn't be far away, I thought – and quite so. Once again I had a "fat" shadow just ahead of me, slow and mighty. I approached him without any

Two JG 54 pilots and their Luftflotten commander: (l. to r.) Leutnant Erwin Leykauf, Hauptmann Reinhard Seiler, and Generaloberst Alfred Keller. Leykauf received his pilot training in 1938 and was posted to JG 26 in May 1940. During the Battle of Britain he was transferred to JG 54, where he achieved the bulk of his success. With seven victories amassed prior to Operation Barbarossa, Leykauf brought down his first Soviet aircraft – an SB – on July 6, 1941, but was himself shot down in the process. Between October 1941 and April 1943, Leykauf served as the adjutant with Hauptmann Reinhard Seiler's III./JG 54, and he ended the war with Me 262-equipped JG 7 (although he never had the opportunity to fly the Me 262 in combat). Reinhard Seiler, a veteran of the Spanish Civil War, attained a total of one hundred victories in World War II before he was shot down on the Eastern Front on July 6, 1943, and so severely injured that he was rendered unfit for combat operations for the remainder of the war. Generaloberst Alfred Keller headed Luftflotte 1 in the northern combat zone of the Eastern Front from June 22, 1941, through July 28, 1943. (Photo: Salomonson.)

difficulty, blasted away my last remaining cannon shells, and for the fifth time this night a flying torch appeared in the sky.

That's all for tonight, I thought. But how was I to let number six get away when he appeared just in front of me? I made an attempt with nothing but my small-caliber machine-guns, but this proved to be sufficient. He caught fire and descended, trailing thick smoke, and exploded on impact.

No angel's song could have sounded sweeter to me than the gruff male voice that sounded in my headphones during my return flight. It was a radio operator from the ground troops who reached me on the air: "Congratulations. I confirm your six victories. Congratulations!"[79]

On the night of June 26, 662 NBAP lost two more U-2s to night-fighters west of the Volkhov River. "The German bandits don't give our airmen the slightest chance to provide us with provisions," the Second Assault Army Starshiy Leytenant wrote in some of the last lines in his diary before he was killed.

In total, JG 54 Grünherz claimed fifty-six night victories over the Lyuban Pocket.

Subjected to almost complete starvation, continuously bombed and shelled, and faced with a numerically and technically superior enemy, the Soviet troops surrounded in the jungle-like marshlands rapidly lost their capacity to resist. The Second Assault Army finally disintegrated completely. On June 28 the entire Lyuban Pocket was overrun by German troops, and all organized resistance ceased. What had been an operation originally intended to break the siege of Leningrad ended with an entire army starving to annihilation. Approximately thirty-seven thousand soldiers disappeared from the Soviet order of battle.

Two weeks later, a German patrol captured General-Leytenant Vlasov, who was hiding alone in a small wooden hut. The disillusioned Soviet General-Leytenant later sided with the Germans and took up arms against his own country.

The German victory at Lyuban was largely a result of efforts by Luftflotte 1 and Fliegerkorps I, which indeed played a major role in Army Group North's containment of all Soviet ground offensives during the period from December 1941 through June 1942. This is remarkable since the dominant structural weakness of Luftflotte 1 was its lack of ground-attack planes. From time to time, a few Stukagruppen of StG 1 and StG 2 served under Keller's command, but the bulk of the offensive missions carried out by Luftflotte 1 were flown by medium bombers. Since Army Group North remained weak in artillery due to both equipment losses during the winter and the higher emphasis placed on other sectors by the High Command, the German ground troops in the northern combat zone were totally dependant on air support.

Word of Erwin Leykauf's successful night combat on June 23, 1942, soon spread among the German ground troops at Lyuban Pocket. This cartoon was sent to Leykauf by one of these soldiers. The text reads: "The night fighter at Somoshkoye Swamp: 'Which one shall I pick next?'" Written on the back side of the drawing is: "The enthusiastic witnesses of the nocturnal victories," signed by seven infantry soldiers. This combat was the pinnacle of Leykauf's career as a fighter pilot. He remained in action throughout the war and achieved a total of thirty-three victories on more than five hundred combat sorties. (Leykauf.)

One of the most decisive factors behind the achievements of Luftflotte 1 was the fighting spirit of JG 54 Grünherz. Commanded by Major Hannes Trautloft, Jagdgeschwader Grünherz was a well-organized and highly efficient fighter unit. Its pilots managed to take and hold control of the air wherever they appeared. Major Fritz Pockrandt, the Gruppenkommandeur of I./KG 53, stated: "Owing to the exemplary protection offered by Trautloft's Jagdgeschwader were we able to evade losses through Soviet fighters for weeks."[80]

The German airlift operation to Demyansk was also brought to a successful conclusion mainly due to the efforts of Major Trautloft's command. There was even a widespread belief among the Soviet airmen that JG 54 Grünherz was made up entirely of the Luftwaffe's best aces. Approximately one thousand Soviet aircraft were reportedly shot down by JG 54 between January and June 1942 – for the loss of only fifty-nine Bf 109s due to hostile action on operations.

After the battle. A view of the terrible destruction in the death trap that became known as the Lyuban Pocket: Fallen Soviet soldiers and destroyed equipment in the totally devastated landscape at Myasnoy Bor, where there had been a narrow corridor between the Soviet main line and the surrounded Soviet Second Assault Army. (Photo: Trautloft.)

The Soviet fighters in the northern combat zone had contributed much to the defensive successes during the German air raids against Leningrad and the Ladoga ports, but they were defeated in the general battle for air superiority. The largest single success in numerical terms was achieved by the VVS-Northwestern Front fighters against the Demyansk airlift operation in late February and March 1942. The operations by the Soviet bombers and ground-attack aircraft opposed to Army Group North rarely managed to achieve more than nuisance results. This also was mainly due to JG 54 Grünherz. In this operational area, the activity of VVS-Northwestern Front against the landing grounds at Demyansk constitutes an exception. In most other cases both sides failed to inflict any significant losses on their enemy through air-base raids – high overclaims notwithstanding.

The generally poor performance by the Soviet air forces in the northern combat zone from January through August 1942 was due both to the efficiency of the German fighter units in the area and qualitative deficiencies on the Soviet side. The most numerous Soviet fighters in this area – LaGG-3s, P-40s, Hurricanes, and I-16s – were inferior or vastly inferior to the Bf 109 F. Furthermore, the problems related to pilot training standards were accentuated in aviation units with a high loss ratio. The fact that obsolete U-2, R-5, and R-Z biplanes were the mainstays of the VVS bomber units in this area indicates that the air war in the northern combat zone did not receive any particularly high priority from the Stavka – contradictory to the fact that the defence of Leningrad remained one of the Stavka's main preoccupations throughout 1942.

In this context, the Soviet stamina deserves to be mentioned. True, battle fatigue spread among the Soviet fliers in the northern combat zone after the exhausting fight in 1941. But under influence of the fortuitous offensives at Moscow and Demyansk, combat spirits resurged during the spring. Although they still could not constitute any serious challenge to Luftflotte 1 – the air forces of KBF, and the Northwestern, Volkhov, and Leningrad fronts were able to remain coherent fighting forces, despite tremendous bloodletting.

Hitler now resumed the idea of launching a major offensive to capture Leningrad, but however dreadful the defeat at Lyuban may have been to the Soviets, it had failed to bring about any major strategic alteration of the situation. While the scattered remnants of what once was the Second Assault Army were rounded up by German troops or succumbed in the marshlands west of the Volkhov, Soviet troops to the east of the river and inside the besieged Leningrad were already preparing for their most powerful offensive so far. The coming summer months would hold many unpleasant surprises for the Germans.

able to stand the enormous physical and mental strain. The most reasonable – and most human – thing to do is to release those pilots who have lost their perseverance from first-line service before they contaminate other pilots or get killed."

Soviet and German accounts indicate that the Soviet naval airmen based inside Sevastopol were generally tougher than their German counterparts. Several statements by Luftwaffe airmen who flew against Sevastopol reveal how impressed the Germans were by the stamina displayed by these Soviet airmen.

Even before the battle, the Luftwaffe pilots knew that, notwithstanding their numerical superiority, it would be a tough fight. This was proven to the fighter pilots of JG 77 on May 27, when a Schwarm from II Gruppe bounced two 116 MRAP/VVS-ChF MBR-2 hydroplanes. The slow seaplanes should have been no match for the Bf 109 F-4s, but the MBRs, piloted by Kapitan Nikolay Tarasenko and Leytenant Yevgeniy Akimov, fought off the fighter attack by turning head-on against the Germans. Unteroffizier Ernst Thoma's Bf 109 was shot down and the remaining three chose to disengage, thus enabling the seaplanes to land safely at Sevastopol.

Unteroffizier Thoma landed in his parachute in the sea near Cape Khersones and was rescued by the Soviets. He was brought to Sevastopol, where he reportedly revealed the number of planes, the location of the parking grounds of the airfields, and other details regarding II./JG 77. The following night, a group of MBR-2s from 116 MRAP/VVS-ChF raided the German airfield in accordance with the information given by the unhappy Ernst Thoma. German sources reveal that Thoma was executed, and his body was found after the German seizure of Sevastopol.

The Soviet Beriyev MBR-2 was the most common flying boat in VVS-VMF throughout the war. It was used in multiple roles – reconnaissance, antisubmarine patrols, bomber (including night-bomber), air-sea rescue, transport, etc. Although a significant number of MBR-2s was lost during the initial stage of the war – 15 MRAP/VVS KBF alone lost seventy-five MBR-2s, three MDR-6s, and forty crews in 1941 – it remained in active service until the last days of the war. The airplane viewed here is a late variant equipped with an 830-horsepower AM-34B engine, which provided the aircraft with a maximum speed of 151 miles per hour at 16,400 feet. The crew consisted of pilot, navigator, and gunner. The armament was made up of two ShKAS machine-guns, one in the nose turret and one in the dorsal turret. (Photo: Rybin.)

Of all the airmen in 3 OAG, the fighter pilots of 6 GIAP/VVS-ChF – later awarded the honorary title Sevastopolskiy – constituted the greatest threat to the Germans in the air over the fortress city. The most famous pilot of this unit was Kapitan Mikhail Avdeyev, an excellent marksman who commanded 1 AE (formerly 5 AE of 32 IAP/VVS-ChF).

On June 1 Avdeyev and his wingman, Starshiy Leytenant Danilko, came close to killing Generaloberst Erich von Manstein. As the two Soviet pilots returned from a reconnaissance mission over the road to Yalta, they spotted a lone motor torpedo boat. Disregarding orders to avoid combat, they immediately put down the noses of their Yak-1s and dived with guns blazing.

Von Manstein had boarded the Italian motor torpedo boat in order to check if the strategically important road from Sevastopol to Yalta could be controlled from the sea. Suddenly machine-gun bullets crashed into the deck. The two Yak-1s dived out of the sun, undetected by the enemy. To the left and right of von Manstein, the port commander of Yalta, Kapitän Joachim von Wedel; the Italian commander of the torpedo boat; and the Generaloberst's faithful driver, Oberfeldwebel Fritz Nagal, fell dead. Von Manstein escaped without injury.[81]

The artillery preparation for the Sevastopol offensive commenced on June 2, the heaviest German artillery barrage ever laid down on the East Front. Besides 1,300 artillery pieces of all calibers – concentrated along a twenty-mile front line – the 600mm *Thor* and *Odin/Karl* guns and the 800mm *Dora* pounded Sevastopol day and night. Meanwhile, the air was filled with bomb-laden German aircraft.

The large scale air operation was launched at 0600 hours on June 2. First to attack were StG 77, KG 76, and I./KG 100 Wiking, then all units of Fliegerkorps VIII mounted "rolling attacks." The Stukas and most of the bombers pounded the Soviet defense positions and airfields around Sevastopol while III./LG 1 concentrated against antiaircraft positions. These aircraft dropped a total of 570 tons of bombs on June 2, and German fighters unloaded five hundred SC 50 splinter bombs.

3 OAG made every effort to support its ground troops. Shturmoviks were in constant action against German positions while the fighters attempted to intercept large formations of German aircraft. But all odds were against the Soviets. On June 2 Fliegerkorps

MBR-2bis, VVS-SF, Soviet Union, 1942

Two Ju 87 Ds prepare for a pin-point dive-bombing attack. The Ju 87 Stuka was the special pride of the commander of Fliegerkorps VIII, Generaloberst Wolfram Freiherr von Richthofen, who had developed the dive-bombing tactic during the Spanish Civil War. German artillery Hauptmann Pickart wrote: "Richthofen indeed was a remarkable man. When the ground troops failed to capture a fortress, he took to the air in his Fieseler Storch and flew to the area in question. From our forward command post we could often see him in the midst of the diving Ju 87s, and my radio operators reported how he explicitly instructed even individual pilots about how they should carry out their attacks. During briefings we noticed how determined he was to help the infantry forward, without any regard to the safety of his own men." (Photo: Roba/Mombeek.)

VIII launched 723 sorties, while 3 OAG could mount only 70. Hauptmann Gollob's fighters, operating from a forward airfield from which the Soviet aircraft taking off in Sevastopol could be observed, recorded two Soviet aircraft shot down on June 2.

While most of Fliegerkorps VIII was occupied against Sevastopol, the He 111 torpedo planes of II./KG 26 were directed against the seaborne supply route from the Caucasus ports to Sevastopol. In the evening of June 2 they sank the tanker *Mikhail Gromov* en route to Sevastopol. But the flotilla leader *Tashkent*, the destroyer *Bezuprechnyy*, and the transport ship *Abkhaziya* escaped destruction and brought military equipment and 2,785 soldiers into the besieged fortress.

The intense air and artillery bombardment continued on June 3, with another 643 sorties carried out against Sevastopol. VVS-ChF dispatched 99 sorties over Sevastopol, including 48 from bases in the northwestern Caucasus, and the German airmen were involved in stiff air combats. Eight German aircraft were claimed shot down (only two were actually lost) against four Soviet naval fighters lost.[82]

Due to the limited geographical area, the same fighter aces on both sides met in combat each day: Hauptmann Gordon Gollob, Oberleutnants Anton Hackl and Heinrich Setz, and Feldwebel Ernst-Wilhelm Reinert were among the most prominent protagonists in JG 77; and Kapitans Mikhail Avdeyev, Konstantin Alekseyev, and Boris Babayev were the leading scorers in 6 GIAP/VVS-ChF. Both sides learned to pay great respect to its adversary. Heinrich Setz, the Staffelkapitän of 4./JG 77, described the initial air combat with "most experienced" Soviet fighter pilots over Sevastopol as "extremely hard."[83] On June 3 Hauptmann Gollob instructed his fighter pilots to avoid "turning combats at low flight altitude."

Kapitan Mikhail Avdeyev, commanding 1 AE of 6 GIAP/VVS-ChF, dedicated a whole chapter in his memoirs to honor a most feared German ace over Sevastopol, whom the Soviet pilots called "Z" – their interpretation of the call sign on the fuselage of this Bf 109 F as a black Latin character "Z". Avdeyev wrote:

> "Z" appeared every day, always with his back protected by other fighters. Usually, he picked his victims carefully, and only rarely were his attacks without success. More than once, I tried to pursue this Fascist, but this proved to be a most difficult undertaking…
>
> It was clear that "Z" was an outstanding pilot, definitely somebody from von Richthofen's inner circle, or maybe even von Richthofen himself…
>
> That damned "Z" deprived us of our sleep and never left us in peace. It was as if he jeered at us. A hundred times I examined my mind to find out different ways to attack him – from above, from below, from the clouds, or from the sun. But these fine theories always were shattered by the realities. "Z" wasn't someone whom you could lure into a trap, or who could be made to lose his nerve through a frontal attack. He was a worthy opponent, and he definitely gave us a lot of headaches.[84]

"Z" was likely Oberleutnant Anton Hackl, the Staffelkapitän of 5./JG 77. Roaming the skies above Sevastopol in his Bf 109 F-4, *Black 5*, in June 1942,

"Toni" Hackl would bring down eleven Soviet aircraft during this battle, making himself the most successful German fighter pilot during the operation. On June 3 a LaGG-3 fell before his guns, bringing his total score to fifty-two. Mikhail Avdeyev was a stunned witness to how swiftly "Z" shot down an Il-2 of 18 ShAP/VVS-ChF in early June:

> The fighters of the 1st Eskadrilya took off first. Three or four minutes later, a dozen Messerschmitts appeared. In that moment, Mayor Gubriy's Shturmoviks were taking off.
>
> Eight Yaks met the Messerschmitts over the sea. Our fast, sudden attack and precisely gauged maneuvers drew the Messerschmitts into combat and prevented them from engaging the Shturmoviks. Then, from somewhere high above, beyond the dogfight, a lone Messerschmitt, which no one had detected, came rushing downward like a vulture. It set one of the Shturmoviks on fire and disappeared at tree-top level. Together with Danilko, I tried to pursue him as he leveled out from the dive, but we were intercepted by four Messerschmitts. We caught a quick glimpse of a black "Z" on the hunter's fuselage side.

Fliegerkorps VIII carried out 585 sorties on June 4 and 555 the next day. But the Soviets did not give in. On June 5 the 3 OAG fighters managed to safeguard the entrance of flotilla leader *Kharkov*, carrying 270 troops, into Sevastopol.

Soviet artillery spotters had located Hauptmann Gollob's forward air base and forced the German fighters to abandon this place through a well-aimed bombardment. At night biplane light bombers of 23 AP/VVS-ChF kept raiding von Manstein's headquarters at Yukhariy Karales.

"Toni" Hackl, who would remain in front-line service during the entire war, rose from the rank of Unteroffizier to Major. He was among the few who survived more than a thousand combat sorties, in which he scored a total of 192 confirmed and 24 unconfirmed aerial victories. Anton Hackl passed away in 1984. (Photo: Sundin.)

Kapitan Mikhail Avdeyev was one of the ablest fighter pilots of 6 GIAP/VVS-ChF, not least during the Battle of Sevastopol. By the time the war with Germany broke out in 1941, Avdeyev had been an active naval fighter pilot for seven years. (Photo: Seidl.)

During the "softening up phase" – from June 2 through June 6 – 3,069 Luftwaffe sorties were made against Sevastopol, and a total of 2,264 tons of explosives and 23,800 incendiary bombs were dropped. Individual German bomber crews made up to *eighteen* sorties daily. Historian Joel Hayward noted that "this hellish blitz was far more ferocious than those inflicted thus far in the war on Warsaw, Rotterdam, London, or Malta."[85] Polkovnik Ivan Laskin, who commanded the Soviet 172d Rifle Division in the northern defense sector of Sevastopol, recalls: "Bombers in groups of twenty to thirty attacked us without caring for their targets. They came in, wave after wave, and literally plowed up the earth throughout our defense area."[86]

On June 7, von Manstein hurled his ground troops against the Soviet lines. While LIV Corps attacked from the north, XXX Corps attempted to advance from the east. Despite the intense "softening-up" bombardment, General-Mayor Petrov's Coastal Army was able to hold its positions. "Earth, water, rock fragments, steel, and cement were intermingled with bleeding corpses," recalls Hauptmann Werner Baumbach, a bomber expert who had been brought in from KG 30 in the Far North due to his particular bombing skills. "And yet, the Russians continued to cling to their ground, their native soil, with unparalleled tenacity."

The same determination was displayed by the airmen of 3 OAG. "Defying our air superiority, the enemy's air force intervened in the ground combat with ground-attack aircraft and fighters," noted a report from LIV Corps. In the evening on June 7, Hauptmann Gordon Gollob wrote in his diary: "My fighters achieved nine victories, while one officer and an Unteroffizier went missing. The Russians are putting up a desperate – and quite skillful – fight. I shot down a LaGG-3, which fell straight into the ground at Sevastopol IV Airdrome and burst into flames. But I also was close to getting shot down myself. I barely managed to reach our own lines with a shot-up radiator." One of the missing pilots, Leutnant Wolfgang Werhagen, an eleven-victory ace in 4./JG 77, was captured after being shot down.

Mikhail Avdeyev describes how the Yak-1s of 6 GIAP/VVS-ChF tied up the Bf 109s that attempted to escort a formation of 18 ShAP/VVS-ChF Il-2s: "Suddenly one of the Messerschmitts broke away from the fighter tussle and headed for the Il-2s, but [Kapitan Konstantin] Alekseyev saw it in time and shot down the German. A second Me 109 was shot down by me, and one more Me 109 fell burning toward the mountains."

Meanwhile, terrible losses were meted out to the German and Romanian ground troops. Already, after only the first day of the offensive, XXX Corps had to discontinue its attacks. On June 8 Generaloberst von Manstein received worrying reports that his 132d Division was approaching "the end of its strength."

The Germans' trump card undoubtedly was their superiority in the air, without which any attempt to seize Sevastopol would have been impossible. The overwhelming German air superiority was too much even for the determined and experienced veterans of 6 GIAP. "For several hours the whole scene was buzzing, howling, and thundering; there was no way for us to repulse the masses of enemy aircraft that kept arriving in wave after wave," recalls Avdeyev. "There were not enough fighters or antiaircraft artillery." Even though 6 GIAP/VVS-ChF claimed nine victories on June 8 – against three Yak-1s lost – it could not prevent German bombers from sinking the destroyer *Sovershennyy* and the survey vessel *Gyuys* in the port of Sevastopol.

Twelve Soviet aircraft were claimed by the pilots of JG 77 – three by Anton Hackl – on June 8. One of the Soviet pilots shot down this day was 6 GIAP's Kapitan Konstantin Alekseyev, who bailed out with severe wounds. "Kostya" Alekseyev had a total score of eleven personal and six group victories, which made him the top ace of the Soviet Black Sea Fleet Air Force at the time. Mikhail Avdeyev recalls the fateful mistake made by Kapitan Alekseyev's wingman: "Together with his wingman, Katrov, he carried out a prolonged dogfight with six Messerschmitts, who attempted to break through to our Shturmoviks. Here the primary task was holding the enemy at bay, not shooting them down. But Katrov couldn't stand it and went after a Messerschmitt that appeared in front of him. This was exactly what the Germans had been waiting for. A pair of Messerschmitts came racing to attack Katrov. Alekseyev tried to overtake them but was himself squeezed between two other fighters, one from each side, which set his aircraft on fire."[87]

Oberleutnant Heinrich Setz described the combat in his diary: "I managed to position myself behind one of these guys several times. My cannon wouldn't fire, and left with only the machine guns I didn't have the sufficient fire power. The Russians proved to be very skilful fliers, and I found myself attacked over and over again. After a prolonged dogfight, I suddenly saw a Yak climbing after a Messerschmitt. I went after him. While turning, I came so close that I almost rammed him. The burst from my machine guns hit his engine and cockpit. He went down and crashed right next to his own airfield."[88]

Oberleutnant Anton Hackl and his Bf 109 F-4, "Black 5", at Oktoberfeld, Crimea, in June 1942. (Photo: Roba/Mombeek.)

On June 9 it was Boris Babayev's turn. That morning the three Yak-1 sections that remained in Mikhail Avdeyev's 1 AE of 6 GIAP/VVS-ChF took off to pave the way through the Bf 109s for Mayor Gubriy's 18 ShAP/VVS-ChF IL-2s. Since the German forward command kept the Soviet airfields inside the fortress under constant surveillance, Generaloberst von Richthofen, from an observation tower located at the front, could personally direct the JG 77 fighters against the Yak-1s when

Bf 109 F-4 WNr 13046, Oberleutnant Anton Hackl, Staffelkapitän 5./JG 77, Oktoberfeld Airdrome, Crimea, Soviet Union, June 1942

Note the beer or wine bottle included in the victory markings on the rudder. This airplane probably had its underside engine cowling exchanged for one that still carries the light blue (RLM 76) color.

Kapitan Mikhail Avdeyev of 6 GIAP/VVS-ChF waves confidently at his ground crew before taking off from his Sevastopol airdrome. (Photo: Author's collection.)

he spotted the dust that was blown up as the Soviet pilots started their engines. Mikhail Avdeyev and his wingman, Katrov, were first to race across the runway, and as soon as the undercarriage of his fighter left the ground he was attacked from above by two Bf 109 pilots. Both Soviet pilots engaged the enemy while Boris Babayev and three other Yak pilots took to the air. Shortly, German reinforcements were called in. The Yak-1 pilots were locked into a severe combat with a large number of German fighter pilots that included Anton Hackl, Heinrich Setz, and Feldwebel Ernst-Wilhelm Reinert.

The Il-2s and three I-16s of 6 GIAP/VVS-ChF took off just as a formation of Ju 88s was approaching with the obvious intention of bombing the airfield. The Bf 109s were occupied with the Yak-1s, so the Shturmoviks and Ishaks managed to slip away to carry out a swift low-level attack against German troops a few miles away.

Boris Babayev bailed out of his blazing Yakovlev, got entangled with the rigging lines of his parachute, and fell with his face downward. He broke his front teeth and fractured his face when he hit the ground. By comparing Soviet and German sources, it is obvious that Babayev's Yak-1 fell prey to "Toni" Hackl – the German ace's fifty-ninth kill.

Ernst-Wilhelm Reinert joined 4./JG 77 on the Eastern Front in June 1941 as an Unteroffizier, and he regularly flew wing on Oberleutnant Heinrich Setz. Reinert soon proved to be a highly talented fighter pilot and developed into JG 77's most successful NCO. When he was awarded the Knight's Cross for fifty-three victories on July 1, 1942, he was still an Unteroffizier. On October 6, 1942 – when he had surpassed his 100-victory-mark – he became the second Feldwebel of the Luftwaffe to be awarded the Oak Leaves. Later Reinert repeated the same rate of success against the USAAF and RAF as he had against the VVS, when he attained fifty-one victories over Tunisia between January and April 1943. Reinert survived the war with a total of 174 victories. (Photo: Reinert.)

The combat was still raging when one of the German pilots caught sight of the Il-2s and I-16s as they returned from their strafing attack. Several Bf 109s turned to intercept them, and the Yak-1s followed to protect their comrades – but in vain. "I dived against a 'bird' which had large areas painted red," Heinrich Setz recalled. "I gave him a burst from my cannon and he exploded in a huge cascade of fire immediately in front of me."[89] Avdeyev's wingman, Katrov, fell to a certain death – Setz's seventy-fourth victory. From his observation tower, Generaloberst von Richthofen saw the Soviet aircraft go down in flames. "It's great fun!" he chuckled. Next, two I-16s were knocked down by Setz and Reinert (the latter's forty-ninth victory). The stiffness of the combat is indicated by that day's entry in Gordon Gollob's diary: "We fought at altitudes between 1,500 feet and the deck. I shot down an I-153, but I was also hit myself and landed close behind our own lines with a burning tire of the landing gear."

In total, 3 OAG/VVS-ChF carried out 144 sorties on June 9 at the cost of eleven aircraft[90] and 6 GIAP/VVS-ChF was left with only four Yak-1s. Thus the bombers and Stukas of Fliegerkorps VIII could attack the supply ships in the port of Sevastopol almost without aerial opposition.

On June 10 the crew of I./KG 100's Leutnant Herbert Klein scored a direct bomb hit on the large transport ship *Abkhaziya* (4,727 tons), which immediately exploded and sank. Other He 111s managed to sink the destroyer *Svobodnyy*.

It was obvious that the few remaining aircraft of 3 OAG were hopelessly inadequate. On June 10 twenty Yak-1s of 45 IAP/5 VA arrived in Sevastopol from the northwestern Caucasus. Next day a group of eight VVS-ChF Yak-1s followed to reinforce 3 OAG. Oberleutnant Heinrich Setz spotted the latter formation just as it approached Sevastopol. Climbing with the sun at his back, Setz put a well-aimed burst into one of the Yaks, which fell to the ground as the German ace's seventy-sixth kill.

These Soviet fighter pilots arrived just as the next German offensive was launched. Provided with close support by StG 77, the German XXX Corps reopened its assault on the southern flank early on June 11. The Stukas were in action over the Soviet positions throughout the day. A report from II./StG 77 on June 11 reads: "Enemy infantry positions on the Zinnober Height was bombed between three and five times by each Staffel from 1430 hours through 1445 hours. In addition, two Ketten strafed enemy positions immediately ahead of our attacking infantry."

The largely inexperienced Soviet replacement airmen could not outweigh the loss of Babayev and Alekseyev, and the air combat situation grew steadily more difficult. On June 12 the four "old" Yak-1s and seven of the "new" were subjected to an attack by at least thirty JG 77 Bf 109s. Mikhail Avdeyev barely managed to escape by means of a daring low-level flight between the houses on

Twenty-year-old Starshiy Leytenant Mikhail Grib poses in front of his Yak-1. On October 17, 1941, 32 IAP/VVS-ChF's 5 AE – commanded by Starshiy Leytenant Mikhail Avdeyev – was reinforced with four pilots and four Yak-1s transferred from 9 IAP. Two of these pilots, Starshiy Leytenant Konstantin Alekseyev and Leytenant Mikhail Grib, soon rose to become among the best pilots of the Eskadrilya, which shortly afterward was redesignated 1 AE of 6 GIAP/VVS-ChF. Mikhail Grib, who was promoted to Starshiy Leytenant in early 1942, amassed a total score of ten victories by August 1942 and was appointed Hero of the Soviet Union that October. By the end of the war, he had carried out more than four hundred combat sorties and his score had risen to seventeen individual victories. (Photo: Seidl.)

The Bf 109 F-4 "Black 4" flown by 8./JG 77's Leutnant Heinz Lüdemann in the air over the Crimea in the summer of 1942. Between June 2 and June 12, the Jagdgruppen based in the Crimea conducted 1,150 sorties in which they claimed eighty-two victories for the loss of eight Bf 109s. (Photo: Lüdemann/Langer via Roba/Mombeek.)

both sides of a Sevastopol street. When he returned to base, he learned that only three of the "new" navy Yakovlev pilots – the unit's political commissar and two inexperienced Serzhants – had survived that day's air fighting, and a 45 IAP pilot had managed to bail out when he was shot down. In his memoirs, Avdeyev wrote laconically: "And next day, the Commissar and his wingmen were no more..." That evening Hauptmann Gollob noted in his diary: "An average of 700 sorties are carried out each day, with approximately 600 tons of bombs dropped. The losses in our aviation units have declined and are now very limited."

Soviet reinforcements kept arriving. On June 12 the cruiser *Molotov* and the destroyer *Bditel'nyy* broke through the German air blockade to deliver 3,341 soldiers, 28 artillery pieces, and 190 tons of ammunition and medical supplies. On June 13 the Luftwaffe concentrated much of their effort against the supply shipping to Sevastopol and sank the transport *Gruziya*, minesweeper *TShch-27*, patrol boat *SKA-092*, motorboat *SP-40*, five barges, and a floating crane in the port of Sevastopol. Aerial combat that day resulted in fifteen victory claims by JG 77. VVS-ChF registered seven aircraft lost over Sevastopol against two victory claims on June 13.[91] Three 45 IAP pilots were also shot down. In a matter of days, 45 IAP lost nine Yak-1s, and most of its novice pilots had been killed.

The Soviet fighter pilots adopted a new tactic in response to German fighter attacks from above. After taking off as fast as they could, they raced out over the sea at low level. Once out of sight of Sevastopol, they climbed high and turned back, diving against the enemy bombers. "Three attacks were made by strong Il-2 formations," an astounded Gordon Gollob wrote on June 14. "These guys have some nerves," Heinrich Setz entered in his diary: "Each day they see their friends go down in flames, and yet they're back in the air with the same enthusiasm next day."[92]

During an air combat on June 15, Mikhail Avdeyev finally managed to get the feared "Z" in his gunsight:

> The sun was already sinking below the horizon. Suddenly I spotted the hated "carrot-colored" plane over the airfield. I called upon all gods to ensure that my engine and guns would not fail, and that my speed wouldn't decrease, so that nothing would go wrong. The matter had become personal: "Z" had become my nightmare, my fixation, the symbol of everything that I hated ferociously... I still don't know the reason for this – either "Z" made a blunder, or my swift attack caught him by surprise – but finally, and not without sensing a fiendish pleasure, I saw "my" *ryzhyy* ["carrot"] cross the threads of my gunsight. I fired one burst. A second. A third. The plane passed by. I turned my head and looked back: Trailing smoke, "Z" raced toward [German] territory. I turned to follow him, but too late; a pack of Messerschmitts intercepted me...
>
> Until today, I don't know if I managed to shoot him down or not, nor do I know if it was General von Richthofen himself, or one of his favorites. But we never saw "Z" again. In vain we looked for his dirty reddish-brown machine in the sky.[93]

Although Avdeyev may have come out with a "moral victory" from his last engagement with the infamous "Z," it is clear that neither "Toni" Hackl nor any other German fighter pilot was shot down over Sevastopol on June 15. Nevertheless, Avdeyev's observation that Hackl disappeared from the skies in this area is correct. On June 14 he received the Knight's Cross during a ceremony led by Gordon Gollob. After that he left for a well-deserved home leave. (Coincidentally Mikhail Avdeyev and Konstantin Alekseyev were appointed Heroes of the Soviet Union on the very same day.)

The 305mm guns of Soviet Coastal Battery 30, also known as Maksim Gorkiy I, played a key role in the Soviet defense of the northern flank at Sevastopol. This photo shows Maksim Gorkiy I after it was blown up by its own crew following the firing of its last shell at the Germans. (Photo: Tieke.)

Thousands of bombs rained upon the city and its fortifications day after day. The combat record of I./KG 100's Hauptmann Hansgeorg Bätcher reads: "Against Sevastopol: June 11, five missions; June 12, three; June 14, four apiece; June 15, three." It seemed incredible to the Germans that the Soviets simply refused to give in.

On June 15 *Molotov* and *Bditel'nyy*, and three submarines broke through to deliver another 3,400 soldiers, 442 tons of ammunitions, 30 tons of fuel, and 12 tons of provisions to Sevastopol. Despite five concentrated Stuka attacks on June 16, the German XXX Corps was unable to advance further and had to turn to the defensive. General-Mayor Petrov reported enthusiastically: "The German soldiers suffer from combat fatigue and are heavily demoralized."

With XXX Corps forced to halt again, the focus of the combat was shifted to LIV Corps in the north. "Fliegerkorps VIII will support LIV Corps with all forces available," the troops of LIV Corps were told before they were thrown against the Soviet Coastal Battery 30, known to the Germans as Fortress Maksim Gorkiy I – the key to the Soviet defense in the north. Between 1515 hours and 1530 hours on June 17, twenty-seven Ju 87s of Hauptmann Alfons Orthofer's II./StG 77 attacked this fortress. A German infantry Leutnant later wrote: "Our Stukas come howling. They dive away over their wings and descend toward 'M.G.' with screaming engines. Over and over again! Their machine guns are spitting small flames. The air trembles from the bomb detonations. Dark smoke and gigantic dust clouds rise..." Stuka pilot Oberleutnant Maué scored a direct bomb hit on one of the gun towers of the fortress, whereafter it was noted that Coastal Battery 30 ceased firing. The Germans assumed that Maué had destroyed the battery, but Soviet records show that the fortress was able to withstand all bomb hits – even by 1,000-kilogram bombs – without suffering internal damage. The battery simply had run out of ammunition. In any case, this proved to be the turning point of the entire battle. When Coastal Battery 30 became inactive, LIV Corps was able to open a breach into the Soviet lines north of the Severnaya Bay, opposite to the city of Sevastopol.

It became increasingly difficult for the Soviets to counteract against the Germans, who had the attacker's advantage of choosing where to locate the main effort.

On June 18 the flotilla leader *Kharkov* was severely damaged by a close hit near Khersones. And eight 18 ShAP Il-2s and a number of escort fighters were bounced by some twenty Bf 109s during takeoff from Sevastopol's Khersonesskiy Mayak Airdrome. Within a few minutes Gordon Gollob sent one Il-2 and one LaGG-3 back to the ground. Other pilots of JG 77 were credited with four kills. Since Gollob earlier had refrained from reporting four of his victories, his two kills on June 18 were officially recognized as his hundredth and hundred-and-first victories – which earned him a mention in the OKW Bulletin the following day.

On June 19 German ground troops reached the northern shore of Severnaya Bay and were able to subject the Soviet airfields to intense artillery fire, which destroyed four 3 OAG aircraft on the ground and almost completely paralyzed Soviet air activity. The German LIV Corps reported: "No enemy air activity." On June 19 Oberleutnant Heinrich Setz and his Schwarm patrolled above Sevastopol from 0300 hours, searching for an opportunity to achieve his eightieth victory. Only after twelve hours did the Bf 109 pilots spot the first Soviet aircraft. Setz dived on a group of Soviet fighters that were taking off and shot at a LaGG-3 that crashed straight onto Khersonesskiy Mayak Airdrome. Setz then made a quick escape.

To the Luftwaffe's considerable relief the large antiaircraft raft PZB-3 (Floating Antiaircraft Battery No. 3) – known to the Soviets as *Ne tron' menya* ("Don't touch me") – in Severnaya Bay was destroyed by 2./KG 51's Oberleutnant Ernst Hinrich that evening.[94] Generaloberst von Richthofen, who personally witnessed the conspicuous explosion of the antiaircraft raft from the cockpit of his Fieseler Storch, was so enthusiastic that he immediately called Hinrich's commander and told him that the successful pilot would be awarded the Knight's Cross.

On June 20 the lack of antiaircraft cover made it impossible for the minelayer *Komintern* to enter the port of Sevastopol with its load of supplies. This failure brought on the rapid deterioration of the SOR's already desperate shortage in ammunition and fuel. Thus, on that day the decision was made to fly out all Soviet amphibian planes and bombers. And on the same day a GST (a license-built American Catalina) from 80 AE/VVS-ChF, based in the northwestern Caucasus, was intercepted by I./JG 77 Bf 109s near the Kerch Peninsula and ended up as Feldwebel Ottokar Pohl's fifth victory, which resulted in the death of Kapitan Chebanik, the 80 AE/VVS-ChF commander.

But the Germans were also at the end of their strength. The stiff Soviet resistance had completely worn down the German ground troops; several Eleventh Army regiments had been brought down to a few hundred men each. Indeed, von Manstein recalled that one regiment reported a strength of one officer and eight men![95] The aviation units had been saved from heavy losses, but the long period of intense combat activity was exhausting the airmen, which was further complicated by a mounting supply shortage when the bulk of deliveries were shifted to units in the Ukraine that were preparing for the commencement of the major German summer offensive a few days hence. The KG 51 historian, Wolfgang Dierich, wrote: "Because of the ammunition shortage, every bomb had to be dropped singly. This meant that each crew had to carry out a daily 25 – 30 dive-bombings from 11,000 feet down to 2,500 feet. In the hot summer temperatures this led to an extreme physical strain."[96]

The OKH also was growing impatient, demanding that Fliegerkorps VIII – described by von Manstein as "a condition for victory"[97] – should be shifted north to participate in the new summer offensive. A compromise was achieved: The staff of Fliegerkorps VIII and several aviation units were shifted to the Ukraine on June 23, while some units were left in the Crimea under the new Fliegerführer Krim, commanded by Fliegerführer Süd, Oberst Wolfgang von Wild.

Von Manstein opted for a decision through an amphibian landing on the southern shore of Severnaya Bay at the outskirts of Sevastopol. In preparation, von Wild dispatched his units in a concentrated bombardment against Sevastopol's inner fortification belt. While the German troops lay waiting in their trenches, the Luftwaffe bombers and Stukas kept coming throughout June 23, unloading their deadly cargo over a small area. "The thick smoke that rose from Sevastopol completely covered the horizon," Gordon Gollob wrote in his diary. And still, the airmen of 3 OAG kept fighting, as Gollob noted on June 23: "We drop bombs against ships and quays in the western part of the bay, and strafe vehicles and other targets of opportunity. But although the Sevastopol IV airfield is subjected to continuous shelling from our antiaircraft artillery, Russian aircraft continue to take off and land at this place." That day, Oberleutnant Setz was amazed to see a lone I-153 carrying out what he thought of as "aerobatics" above Khersonesskiy Mayak Airdrome. "One minute later, I destroyed the biplane," Setz wrote – his eighty-first victory, which can be confirmed in Soviet loss records.[98]

Added to von Manstein's problems, shortages in fuel deliveries to the Crimean airfields started to affect Luftwaffe operations over Sevastopol; the number of sorties carried out each day was cut in half compared to the opening phase of the offensive. But 3 OAG was in an

was among the 95,000 Soviet troops captured during the battle of Sevastopol; he was eventually executed by the SS at the Flossenburg concentration camp.

Soviet resistance at Sevastopol had been crushed following an eight-month siege. It is clear that this immense German victory could not have been achieved without the contribution made by Fliegerkorps VIII and its successor, Fliegerführer Krim, which launched 23,751 sorties between June 2 and July 3, 1942, during which time the German bombers dropped 20,529 tons of bombs. According to German sources, 123 Soviet airplanes were destroyed in the air (including 118 by German fighters) and another 18 were destroyed on the ground. StG 77 carried out 7,708 combat sorties and dropped 3,537 tons of bombs. In I./KG 100, Hauptmann Hansgeorg Bätcher alone flew 116 bombing missions during the Battle of Sevastopol. Total Luftwaffe combat losses over and around Sevastopol were limited to 23 aircraft destroyed and 7 damaged.[106]

As usual, the most outstanding fighter pilots received the highest awards: Hauptmann Gollob was awarded the Swords to his Knight's Cross with Oak Leaves and Oberleutnant Heinrich Setz and Oberleutnant Friedrich Geisshardt – both from JG 77 – received the Oak Leaves to their Knight's Crosses. The Eleventh Army commander, Erich von Manstein, was not even awarded the Oak Leaves to his Knight's Cross following the victory at Sevastopol, but he was promoted to Generalfeldmarschall.

On July 5 a victory banquet was held in the old Czarist castle Livadia at Yalta. All Eleventh Army unit commanders, from battalion commanders up, and several Luftwaffe unit commanders, took part. But to remind the participants of the stiff fight that had been offered by the defenders of Sevastopol, Soviet aviators crashed the gate. Based on information from partisans, SB bombers of 5 VA's 6 BAP carried out a surprise raid in the middle of the night, which sent the festively dressed officers tumbling toward the basement and caused severe bloodshed among their drivers waiting outside.

This unserviceable Il-2 was captured on the ground by victorious German ground troops. (Photo: Roba/Mombeek.)

The Sevastopol defenders – including the 3 OAG airmen – had stunned the world by their long and tenacious resistance. This cost the German Eleventh Army more than 24,000 casualties, and participating Romanian units lost approximately 4,000 men. Between May 25 and July 1, 3 OAG carried out 3,144 sorties, including 1,621 ground-attack sorties. According to Soviet accounts, they destroyed fifty-seven tanks, sixty enemy aircraft in the air, and forty-three enemy aircraft on the ground. They lost sixty-nine airplanes and fifty airmen doing so.

The eight-month defensive fight for Sevastopol became an example for the upcoming battle of Stalingrad. By the time the exhausted troops of the German Eleventh Army raised their flag over Sevastopol, the Wehrmacht had already embarked upon meeting its destiny at Stalin's city.

Part VI

Conclusions

While a group of civilians constructs a dugout, these 840 BAP/ADD airmen are waiting for their next bombing sortie in their Il-4. Displaying determination and composure, these fliers were absolutely certain of victory, as were most servicemen in the Red Army by this time. The inscription on the photo reads: "Dyagilevo, 1942, summer." Dyagilevo was the airfield at which 840 BAP was formed by combining 820 BAP, 821 BAP, and 840 BAP in April 1942. This bomber aviation regiment would operate with success from Dyaglievo throughout the summer of 1942 and during the Battle of Stalingrad. (Photo: Kurayev.)

Chapter 21

Twice Resurgent

January through June 1942 was a period of dramatic change in the war between Germany and the Soviet Union. Within only a few months, a situation that had seemed to promise an imminent Soviet victory turned into the diametric opposite. The air war over the Eastern Front during the same period was characterized by a resurgence of both the Luftwaffe and the VVS. This development is particularly astonishing regarding the latter. Following a sharp decrease in the summer of 1941, Soviet opposition in the air mounted steadily until overextension once again brought it into decline. As for the Germans, only through a combination of economizing on resources, creating local points of concentration, and – to a certain extent – scrapping its resources in other theaters was the Luftwaffe able to recover from its disastrous downfall in January 1942, and only then could it achieve large successes in late spring and early summer.

Ready for another encounter with Luftwaffe Bf 109s. Starshiy Serzhant G. A. Pozhidayev served as gunner and radio operator in a 128 BBAP Pe-2 in the central combat zone in 1942. (Photo: Viktor Kulikov photo collection.)

The Luftwaffe had played a vital role during the Blitzkrieg in Poland, France, and the Balkans; it had been roughly handled during the Battle of Britain; and it had saved the entire Axis situation in the Mediterranean area. But the Eastern campaign proved to be its greatest test.

By concentrating aviation units at the major territorial points of conflict, the Luftwaffe commanders proved their skill in making maximum use of their force's relatively limited aerial resources. The intimate cooperation between air and ground units was an important factor that contributed to the German military's achievements. Attacks by Luftwaffe bombers, Stukas, and ground-attack planes played a significant role during every single major ground battle between January and June 1942. Operating against enemy shipping, only a handful of Kampfgruppen had managed to contain large naval forces in the Black Sea. Aerial reconnaissance had provided the army commanders with invaluable information about Soviet troop movements, most notably during the Red Army's offensive at Kharkov in May 1942. Transport planes – of which the bulk were old but still effective three-engine Ju 52s – had saved the army's supply situation on numerous occasions, and had even succeeded in providing engulfed ground troops with the means necessary to continue fighting – most notably at Sukhinichi, Demyansk, and Kholm.

During the battles at Kerch and Kharkov in May 1942, and at Sevastopol in June 1942, the Luftwaffe once again demonstrated its capacity to isolate a battlefield from the air, with considerable success to the German ground troops as a result. But these events could only take place due to a concentration of the bulk of available German aircraft to a limited territory, and inevitably at the expense of other sectors. The Luftwaffe in 1942 never was able to achieve the same kind of total isolation of an entire combat zone that had settled the fate of large Soviet ground contingents at Minsk, Uman, and Kiev in 1941.

Krasnogvaredysk Airdrome, March 12, 1942. The tailfin of Hauptmann Hans Philipp's I./JG 54 Bf 109 F – displaying eighty-nine victory markings – is attired with victory laurels to celebrate the pilot's receipt of the Swords to the Knight's Cross with Oak Leaves. The extreme focus on individual aerial victories in the Luftwaffe led to very high personal scores among the best fighter pilots. At the same time, other duties in which fighter pilots of other air forces were involved – most notably the direct intervention in ground battles through strafing – were largely neglected by the Jagdflieger. (Photo: Wagner/Stein via Rosipal.)

The air combat tactics predominantly used by the German fighter pilots also gave them a considerable advantage over their adversaries, who were instructed to stick to World War I-style air-combat tactics during most of the first twelve months of the war against Germany.

A report issued by the Soviet 485 IAP in June 1942 described the dominant German fighter tactic as follows:

> Encountered by our fighters, the Germans as a rule evade turning combat. Instead they carry out surprise attacks against aircraft in the rear of our formations, diving from above or attacking from below. During the engagements between Me 109s and our Hurricanes, the following method was noted: One pair is flying in the opposite direction from the sun, obviously with the intention to reveal themselves, while another pair is flying higher, covered by the sun. If our Hurricanes

But local tactical achievements should not obscure the fact that the Luftwaffe in 1942 was substantially less powerful than it had been in 1941. The Luftwaffe in 1942 was unable to bring about a repetition of the mass destruction of Soviet aircraft on the ground that had been a vital precondition to the victories in the summer of 1941. Soviet countermeasures and the heavy demands of close-support operations in the immediate vicinity of the front kept the Luftwaffe from doing so. In reality, only a couple of hundred Soviet aircraft were destroyed during German air-base raids during all of 1942.

In certain areas, however, the Luftwaffe was able to maintain its dominating edge. With the exception of the Soviet Western Front, the Soviet air forces mainly were outfitted with relatively obsolescent equipment throughout most of the first half of 1942. The situation perhaps was worst in the northern combat zone – between Lakes Ladoga and Ilmen – where the bulk of the Soviet aircraft were old light biplane bombers – R-5s, R-Zs, and U-2s. Reliable radio transmitters – a standard in all Luftwaffe combat aircraft – remained a scarcity in Soviet single-engine combat planes. Whereas the quality of the German pilots still was at the highest level, abbreviated pilot training schemes provided VVS front-line units with novice pilots barely able to handle their combat planes.

Siverskaya, May 9, 1942. II./JG 54's Leutnant Horst Hannig and Leutnant Hans Beisswenger are awarded the Knight's Cross for forty-eight and forty-seven victories, respectively. Under the influence of the C-in-C of the Luftwaffe, Hermann Göring, the fighter pilots undoubtedly were the "darlings of the Third Reich." No achievements in the war led to high promotions and awards as rapidly as scoring aerial victories. Twelve of the fourteen servicemen of the Wehrmacht who were awarded the Swords to the Knight's Cross with Oak Leaves to June 1942 were fighter pilots, and the first five to receive the highest military award – the Diamonds to the Knight's Cross with Oak Leaves and Swords – all were fighter pilots. (Photo: Höfer.)

> attempt to charge the pair that reveal themselves, they are attacked from the rear by the upper pair. In this way, Serzhant Gorb and Mladshiy Leytenant Lunev were killed.[1]

Thus, the reasons for the continued high level of German claims of downed Soviet aircraft is perfectly clear.

Seven German fighter pilots surpassed their personal 100-victory marks on the Eastern Front during the first half of 1942. 9./JG 52's Oberleutnant Hermann Graf amassed a record tally of 111 victories by late June 1942, all of which had been achieved on the Eastern Front. Graf's score of sixty-nine kills during the first six months of 1942 set the pace for the performances by aces such as JG 54's Oberleutnant Max-Hellmuth Ostermann with forty-nine; JG 77's Hauptmann Herbert Ihlefeld, with forty-six victories achieved between January and June 1942; and JG 51's Leutnant Hans Strelow, who increased his victory total from twenty-seven to sixty-eight between January and May 1942.

According to German figures, the following combat losses were sustained by the VVS and the Luftwaffe on the Eastern Front during the first six months of 1942:

	SOVIET AIRCRAFT DESTROYED				**GERMAN AIRCRAFT LOSSES**		
	In air combat	By AAA	On the ground	**Total**	In the air	On the ground	**Total**
Jan	207	43	77	**327**	138	20	**158**
Feb	554	106	232	**892**	176	10	**186**
Mar	1,040	100	251	**1,391**	192	30	**222**
Apr	443	98	111	**652**	111	14	**125**
May	1,394	308	108	**1,810**	230	22	**252**
June	1,561	267	76	**1,904**	199	28	**227**
TOTALS	**5,199**	**922**	**855**	**6,976**	**1,046**	**124**	**1,170**

The average of five Soviet aircraft claimed shot down in air combat for every German plane lost on combat missions is increased to a staggering twenty victories for every loss in the Jagdgeschwader.

While the German claims of Soviet aircraft destroyed on the ground approaches a tenfold exaggeration, the overclaim rate regarding the number of Soviet aircraft shot down was less than 2:1. It should be noted that Germany's allies in the war against the USSR made comparatively limited claims against the Soviet Air Force. The Finns reportedly shot down 458 Soviet aircraft during all of 1942 (355 in air combat and 103 by AAA) – against 34 losses of their own; and the small air force of the Italian expeditionary force on the Eastern Front claimed 47 air kills from January through September 1942, for the loss of ten aircraft.

The Soviets claimed 3,012 German aircraft shot down in aerial combat and 1,197 by ground fire, plus 1,059 reportedly destroyed on the ground, during the period January 1 through June 22, 1942.

The monthly losses by each individual Luftwaffe Geschwader on the Eastern Front are shown in Appendix I. In the VVS, the disparity in loss rates between various aviation regiments is notable. A large part of the total losses sustained by a VVS aviation regiment frequently occurred during a small number of incidents, when its airmen were caught in a position of disadvantage by a tactically or numerically superior Bf 109 formation. As an example, the following combat losses were registered by these VVS aviation regiments for the period January through June 1942: 7 GShAP lost eighteen Il-2s; 74 ShAP lost nineteen Il-2s; 8 GBAP lost five bombers; 88 IAP lost three I-16s. 485 IAP lost fifteen Hurricanes between April and June 1942, and 427 IAP lost seventeen Yak-1s against ten victory claims in June 1942 alone.[2] There were several cases when individual VVS aviation regiments were literally wiped out after only a few weeks of fighting over an area covered by a strong concentration of Luftwaffe forces, in some cases even in a single engagement.

Luftwaffe bombs throw up huge fountains of earth and dust during an air raid against a Soviet air base in early summer 1942. Not least due to improved Soviet tactics of dispersing and concealing their aircraft on the ground, the Luftwaffe was unable to repeat its enormous successes during air-base raids on the Eastern Front after the summer of 1941. For example, VVS-Northwestern Front – which lost 522 aircraft in German air-base raids between June 22 and July 31, 1941, alone – registered no more than thirty-four aircraft destroyed in air-base raids during the entire period January through June 1942. The 855 Soviet aircraft claimed destroyed on the ground by the Luftwaffe during the first six months of 1942 represent a considerable exaggeration. (Photo: Kriegstagebuch I./SKG 10 via Bobek.)

In comparison, the Luftwaffe's KG 1 filed forty-one Ju 88s lost on operations during the first half of 1942, and StG 2 lost thirty-eight Ju 87s on operations. The Luftwaffe Geschwader – roughly equivalent to three VVS aviation regiments – that suffered the heaviest losses during the first half of 1942 was JG 54 Grünherz, which registered fifty-nine combat losses but nevertheless brought home approximately one thousand victories during the same period.

During the first days of the war between Germany and the Soviet Union in June 1941, there were a number of cases when Luftwaffe units on the Eastern Front were dealt relatively heavy losses in a single day. But with the loss of the cream of experienced VVS pilots and unit commanders, heavy single-day losses did not happen again on the Eastern Front (except for the Ju 52 transport units at Demyansk) until later in the summer of 1942. Instead, there was a steady rate of attrition of generally two or three combat losses in each Luftwaffe Geschwader on the Eastern Front each week during the first half of 1942. Thus many German airmen apprehended the air war over the Eastern Front during this period as less hazardous compared to the air war over Western Europe – with the Murmansk sector as the only exception. But statistics show that the accumulated effect of relentless combat sorties carried out in the East brought the chances of survival down to the same level as in the West at this stage. Thirty-seven pilots of JG 26's three Gruppen, operating against the RAF over the English Channel, were killed or reported as missing during the first half of 1942. JG 54, operating three Gruppen on the Eastern Front, lost exactly the same number of pilots – thirty-six – pilots during the same period. I./JG 27 lost seven pilots in the North African skies, and II./JG 5 lost thirteen pilots in the Murmansk sector of the Eastern Front.

The increasing experience accumulated by the Luftwaffe veterans further increased the gap in quality between the core of Luftwaffe aces and the majority of the fliers on the Soviet side. Nevertheless, the VVS, also predominantly hobbled by an outmoded tactical doctrine, gave a relatively good account of itself in many types of combat despite its shortcomings. Soviet bombers and – most significant – ground-attack planes dealt heavy blows against Army Group Center early in 1942 and at Kharkov in May 1942. German accounts particularly underline the efficiency of the Il-2-equipped Shturmovik units. Summarizing the appraisal of several Wehrmacht commanders in 1942, Luftwaffe Generalleutnant Walter Schwabedissen wrote: "As early as the beginning of 1942 Russian ground-attack aviation had, for the most part, recovered from the defeat of 1941. During the course of the 1941 – 1942 winter operations, it proved to be even superior to the Luftwaffe on several occasions. From then on the Germans observed the gradual strengthening of Russian ground-attack aviation despite the personnel and materiel losses suffered."[3] Schwabedissen also noted that during the initial phase of the Kharkov battle in May 1942, Soviet ground-attack aircraft "operated in conjunction with attacking infantry and armor. These offensive operations were properly coordinated with regard to time and space, and the targets were well selected, plans were effectively executed and correlated so that the operations produced a considerable effect on the Germans, especially on their morale."[4]

Although it was designed as a long-range bomber fleet, the ADD contributed to the VVS's tactical achievements; it did carry out some limited strategic raids, but in general, the uninterrupted crisis at the front forced its deployment mainly in the tactical role.

The Soviet airmen continued to challenge the Luftwaffe for superiority in the air throughout the difficult period of January through June 1942. Just as in 1941, the VVS was able to secure local air supremacy on a number of occasions during the first half of 1942: in the central combat zone in January, over the Crimea in February, and at Kharkov during the opening of Marshal Timoshenko's ill-fated May offensive.

The VVS fighters maintained a predominantly defensive footing throughout the period, and they also gained their most significant achievements during the first half of 1942 in the task of local air cover. VVS and PVO fighters, in cooperation with powerful antiaircraft concentrations, managed to prevent any successful German air raids against Moscow and Leningrad, and against the supply line to Leningrad across Lake Ladoga. But the Soviet fighters largely failed to provide VVS bombers, ground-attack planes, and ground troops with enough air cover against Luftwaffe attacks in sectors where the Germans had concentrated their air forces. The most successful offensive operation by VVS fighters in the period January through June 1942 was achieved against the German airlift operation to Demyansk. Nevertheless, the air force involved – VVS-Northwestern Front – almost bled itself white in the process.

The widening qualitative gap between the Luftwaffe aces and the mass of the Soviet airmen also had its equivalent within the VVS. Veterans such as Podpolkovnik Boris Safonov, Mayor Aleksandr Zaytsev, Mayor Vasiliy Zaytsev, Mayor Ivan Kleshchyov, and Kapitan Mikhail Avdeyev rose high above the average aviators of both the VVS and the Luftwaffe. The twenty

Mayor Georgiy Gromov, commanding 20 GIAP's 2d Komsomolets Zapolyar'ya Eskadrilya in the Far North, poses in front of his Kittyhawk fighter, which displays fifteen victory stars, in mid-1942. Four of these stars are red with a white outline – indicating individual victories – while eleven stars only have a white outline, indicating Gromov's shared kills. This was a common way of marking individual and shared victories on Soviet fighters. During the first twelve months of the war, a core of experienced Soviet pilots rose high above the average skills of most VVS airmen. It was not uncommon that they adorned their personal aircraft in an individualistic manner, even though doing so contradictory to the official collective attitude of Soviet society. (Photo: Viktor Kulikov photo collection.)

individual and six shared victories Boris Safonov attained by the time of his death in late May 1942 placed him in the lead of the Soviet fighter aces.

In all air forces at war, a relatively small number of aces have been responsible for a large proportion of all aerial victories, but this tendency was particularly accentuated in the VVS during the early stages of the war. For instance, 402 IAP claimed 26 aerial victories during the first half of 1942. Of this total, Leytenant Ivan Likhobabin scored 12 individual and shared victories. On the German side, II./JG 77 provides a good example. The most successful pilot in this Jagdgruppe, Hauptmann Heinrich Setz, contributed 36 victories to the total of 262 amassed by this Gruppe on the Eastern Front during the first half of 1942. In III./JG 52, Oberleutnant Hermann Graf was responsible for about 1 in 4 of this Gruppe's victories from January through June 1942.

Although the size of the Luftwaffe on the Eastern Front grew from about fifteen hundred aircraft in January 1942 to approximately twenty-five hundred a half year later, 1942 was the year in which the Luftwaffe's state as a mere supplement to the army became permanent. While the Luftwaffe went into a long-term decline, the Soviet air forces experienced a gradual but steady growth in both numbers and quality.

That the Red Army was able to recover from heavy losses had been painfully demonstrated to the Germans, and it was clear that new powerful Soviet offensives would again be staged unless the Germans could strike a devastating blow against the USSR. Western Lend-Lease deliveries of military equipment increased each month, and – even more important – the industries that had been evacuated east from the western parts of the USSR in the fall of 1941 were coming on line at a surprisingly fast pace. By mid-1942 the crisis emanating from the hasty redeployment of entire factory complexes in the eastern areas of the Soviet Union had been largely overcome. Although German intelligence reported an output of 600 to 700 Soviet tanks each month, the actual figure was three times higher; an average of 1,863 Soviet tanks were produced monthly during the first half of 1942. The output of Soviet combat aircraft increased from 3,301 in the period January through March 1942 to 4,967 in the period April through June 1942.

Time was running against Hitler, and the crisis deriving from the disastrous winter battles had been far from overcome when on April 5, 1942, he issued his instruction for the next major offensive. The new offensive plan, Operation Blau, intended to deal a decisive strike against the most vulnerable point of the Soviet economy: the oil fields in the Caucasus.

By the time German troops were marching up into position to launch their summer offensive, the Red Army was entering an amazing resurgence. New and better war equipment – not least new and better aircraft – were arriving at the front at an increasing pace. The restructuring of the VVS was in full swing, and Soviet aerial tactics were being reappraised.

The German fighter pilots of I./JG 53 Pik As, who returned to the Eastern Front from Sicily at the end of May 1942, immediately noted that Soviet opposition in the air had grown far more dangerous than it had been the previous year. One month later the Wehrmacht embarked on the fateful road that would lead it to the city that carried Josef Stalin's name – Stalingrad. To the airmen of the Luftwaffe, the summer of 1942 on the Eastern Front would be completely different than anything they had previously experienced, much less expected.

Appendices

Appendix I 

Luftwaffe Combat Losses on the Eastern Front January-June 1942

The following table is a compilation of available Luftwaffe unit loss records, mainly the unit daily loss reports to Generalquartiermeister der Luftwaffe. It should be noted that most of these files are not one hundred percent complete. The actual Luftwaffe losses on the Eastern Front in 1942 undoubtedly were higher than the figures below indicate. But it is clear that the majority of the aircraft combat losses of the Luftwaffe units below are included here.

The figures relate to aircraft totally lost or written off–damage degrees of 60 percent or higher, according to Luftwaffe terminology – due to either enemy activity or "unknown reasons."

The authors would like to express their particular gratitude to historian Mr. Matti Salonen for his extensive assistance regarding the material below.

Unit	January		February		March		April		May		June		Total		Grand Total
	air	*grnd*	*air*	*grnd*	*air*	*grnd*	*air*	*grnd*	*air*	*grnd*	*air*	*grnd*	*air*	*grnd*	
JG 3	–	–	1	0	5	0	2	0	14	0	6	0	28	0	**28**
JG 5	1	0	5	0	5	0	10	1	9	0	3	2	33	3	**36**
JG 51	4	0	11	0	2	1	1	0	3	2	9	0	30	3	**33**
JG 52	6	0	2	0	4	0	0	2	19	2	15	0	46	4	**50**
JG 53	–	–	–	–	–	–			0	1	7	0	7	1	**8**
JG 54	8	5	14	1	10	0	8	0	11	1	8	3	59	10	**69**
JG 77	2	3	1	0	9	4	2	1	14	0	6	0	34	8	**42**
KG 1	10	0	5	1	6	0	8	0	7	0	5	1	41	2	**43**
KG 3	8	0	1	0	4	0	9	0	8	4	8	0	38	4	**42**
KG 4	11	0	11	0	4	0	1	0	5	0	7	1	39	1	**40**
KG 26	2	0	2	0	1	0	0	1	5	2	5	0	15	3	**18**
KG 27	3	1	7	0	10	0	6	0	6	0	6	2	38	3	**41**
KG 30	3	0	1	0	3	0	9	0	13	0	2	5	31	5	**36**
KG 40	0	0	0	0	0	0	0	0	0	0	0	0	0	0	**0**
KG 51	5	0	2	0	2	0	4	0	6	0	5	3	24	3	**27**
KG 53	5	0	3	0	7	0	3	0	4	1	7	0	29	1	**30**
KG 54	2	0	9	0	5	0	0	0	3	1	2	0	21	1	**22**
KG 55	3	0	2	0	3	0	1	0	19	1	8	0	36	1	**37**
KG 76	13	0	6	0	1	1	1	0	5	0	6	0	32	1	**33**
KG 77	1	0	6	2	3	0	1	0	3	0	2	0	16	2	**18**
KG 100	3	0	2	1	2	0	1	0	1	0	0	0	9	1	**10**
KLG 1/KG 6	–	–	–	–	–	–	0	1	4	1	1	1	5	3	**8**
(H)Aufkl	3	4	4	1	2	2	1	0	7	0	8	1	25	8	**33**
(F)Aufkl	19	0	12	1	16	6	6	4	9	0	8	1	70	12	**82**
K406,906	2	0	0	0	0	0	0	0	1	0	0	0	3	0	**3**
StG 1	0	0	5	0	6	0	7	0	14	2	4	0	36	2	**38**
StG 2	5	0	9	1	9	5	9	0	3	0	3	0	38	6	**44**
StG 5	0	0	1	0	1	0	2	0	4	0	9	0	17	0	**17**
StG 77	3	0	1	0	5	5	2	1	4	0	3	0	18	6	**24**
SchG 1	3	0	6	0	4	1	1	0	15	0	14	0	43	1	**44**
ZG 1	2	0	6	0	2	0	–	–	0	0	9	0	19	0	**19**
ZG 2	–	–	–	–	–	–	–	–	0	0	20	0	20	0	**20**
ZG 26	4	0	6	0	2	3	–	–	–	–	–	–	12	3	**15**
Transport and miscellaneous	7	7	35	2	59	2	16	3	14	4	3	8	134	26	**160**
Totals	138	20	176	10	192	30	111	14	230	22	199	28	1046	124	**1170**
Grand Totals	**158**		**186**		**222**		**125**		**252**		**227**		**1170**		

NOTES:
Transport and miscellaneous aircraft include all transport aircraft combat losses on the Eastern Front, and all other Ju 52 combat losses on the Eastern Front. Liaison aircraft are not included.

K 406 and K 906 = Küstenfliegergruppe 406 and Küstenfliegergruppe 906.
Heeresaufklärungs units – (H) Aufkl – included: 1., 2., 4. (H)/10; 1., 5. (H)/11; 1., 2., 3., 4., 5., 6., 7. (H)/12; 1., 2., 3., 4., 5., 6., 7., 11. (H)/13; 1., 3., 4. (H)/14; 1., 2., 3., 4., 5., 6. (H)/21; 1., 2., 3., 4. (H)/23; 1., 2., 3., 4., 5., 6. (H)/31; 1., 2., 3., 4., 5., 6., 7. (H)/32; 2., 3.(H)/33; 1., 2., 3., 4., 5., 6.(H)/41; 7.(H)/LG 2.
Fernaufklärungs units – (F) Aufkl – included: 3.(F)/10; 2., 3., 4. (F)/11; 1., 2., 3. (F)/22; 3. (F)/31; 3.(F)/33; 3., 4.(F)/121; 4., 5.(F)/122; 1.(F)/124; 7.(F)/LG 2; Aufkl.Ob.d.L.; SAGr. 125.

THE THIRTEEN AIR ARMIES ON THE SOVIET-GERMAN FRONT IN 1942

Air Army	Date of formation order	Operational sector in 1942
1 VA	May 5, 1942	Western Front
2 VA	May 5, 1942	Bryansk Front (May through July 7, 1942)
		Voronezh Front (from July 7, 1942)
		Operationally subordinated to Southwestern Front November 19 through December 19, 1942
3 VA	May 5, 1942	Kalinin Front
4 VA	May 7, 1942	Southern Front (May through July 28, 1942)
		Don Operative Group of Northcaucasian Front (July 28 through mid-August, 1942)
		Northern Group of Transcaucasian Front (from mid-August 1942)
5 VA	June 3, 1942	Northcaucasian Front (June through July 28, 1942)
		Coastal Operative Group of Northcaucasian Front (July 28 through August 17, 1942)
		Northcaucasian Front (August 17 through September 1, 1942)
		Black Sea Group of Transcaucasian Front (from September 1, 1942)
6 VA	June 6, 1942	Northwestern Front
7 VA	November 10, 1942	Karelian Front
8 VA	June 9, 1942	Southwestern Front (June through July 12, 1942)
		Stalingrad Front (July 12 through August 7, 1942)
		Southeastern Front (August 7 through September 28, 1942)
		Stalingrad Front (September 28 through December 31, 1942)
13 VA	November 20, 1942	Leningrad Front
14 VA	July 27, 1942	Volkhov Front
15 VA	July 22, 1942	Bryansk Front
16 VA	August 8, 1942	Stalingrad Front (September 4 through September 28, 1942)
		Don Front (from September 28, 1942)
17 VA	November 15, 1942	Southwestern Front

the commander in chief of the Troops of the Home Air Defense (Voyska PVO Strany). With this, the formation of IA PVO as a branch of the Troops of the Home Air Defense was completed. Prior to this, the fighter units allocated to the Home Air Defense had been part of the VVS and were subordinated to the Troops of the Home Air Defense only in an operational sense.

In 1942 the Troops of the Home Air Defense was composed of antiaircraft artillery, fighter aviation, searchlight units, and the Troops of the VNOS (Aerial Observation, Information, and Communication). These formations were responsible for air cover over the major administrative and economical centers, objects behind the front, communication centers, and points of strategic reserve concentration. Prior to the war, the territory of the Soviet Union was divided into PVO zones, which in turn were divided into brigade districts of the PVO. In November 1941 the PVO zones in the European part of the Soviet Union were reorganized into two corps districts of the PVO (the Moscow Corps District and the Leningrad Corps District) and thirteen divisional districts of the PVO. In the other areas of the Soviet Union (Transcaucasus, Middle Asia, Siberia, and the Far East), the PVO zones were not reorganized.

The district of the PVO was a territorial formation, to which all PVO assets (antiaircraft artillery, fighter aviation, searchlight units, and VNOS troops) within a certain territory were subordinated. At the end of 1941 and in early 1942, three new divisional districts of the PVO were formed. In April 1942 the Moscow Corps District of the PVO was reorganized into the Moscow Front PVO, while the Leningrad Corps District of the PVO was reorganized into the Leningrad Army of the PVO. In May 1942 the Baku Army of the PVO was formed from the Transcaucasian PVO Zone. During the same period, the Gorkiy, Stalingrad, and Krasnodar divisional districts of the PVO were reorganized into corps districts of the PVO.

In May 1942 the Troops of the Home Air Defense in the European part of the Soviet Union was composed of three operational formations (the Moscow Front of the PVO, the Leningrad Army of the PVO, and the Baku Army of the PVO), sixteen corps and division districts of the PVO, and fourteen brigade districts of the PVO. On May 1, 1942, these formations mustered a total of 1,168 fighter aircraft, 4,576 antiaircraft cannon, 2,068 antiaircraft machine guns, and 2,267 searchlights.

The fighter aviation of the Home Air Defense was organizationally divided into three fighter aviation corps (6 IAK of the Moscow Front PVO, 7 IAK of the Leningrad Army PVO, and 8 IAK of the Baku Army PVO), thirteen fighter aviation divisions, and nine independent fighter aviation regiments.

VVS-VMF (Naval Air Forces)

C-in-C General-Leytenant Semyon Zhavoronkov

The Soviet Navy also had its independent air arm, and the four Soviet fleets and a number of flotillas were assigned their own air forces. The fleets based in the European part of the Soviet Union fielded the following air forces.

★ VVS-SF – the air force of the Northern Fleet
★ VVS-KBF – the air force of the Red Banner Baltic Fleet
★ VVS-ChF – the air force of the Black Sea Fleet.

Throughout 1942 the strengths of the air forces of those three fleets were constantly shifting, depending on the war situation, the relative importance of the regions of operations, and so on.

A special feature of the Soviet Naval Aviation in 1942 was the creation of provisional ("temporary") aviation groups from all aviation units of the naval aviation in the various operational regions. Thus, on January 2, 1942, VVS-KBF formed an aviation group intended for operations in the Novaya Ladoga sector. By the time it was formed, this aviation group mustered sixty-four aircraft from 57 ShAP, 5 IAP, 13 IAP, 71 IAP, 13 OIAE, and 42 ORAE of VVS-KBF.

In VVS-ChF all aircraft operating from within Sevastopol were organized into 3 OAG (Special Aviation Group) during the last months of the defense of this city.

GVF (Civil Aviation)

Chiefs of the Main Directorate of GVF:
General-Mayor Vasiliy Molokov (until May 15, 1942)
General-Leytenant Fyodor Astakhov (from May 15, 1942)

At the outbreak of the war, the Soviet Civil Aviation was operationally subordinated to the Peoples' Commissariat of the Defense. While a part of the GVF carried out civil transport flights in the rear areas, another part was mobilized for combat service. By July 1941, six special aviation groups of the GVF were formed on the basis of the territorial detachments of the GVF, and the personnel of these aviation groups were conscripted into the Red Army. These special aviation groups of the GVF were subordinated to the military councils of the fronts and armies.

The main job of these groups was transportation of military supplies and personnel, evacuation of injured soldiers, supplying partisan detachments in the enemy's rear area, and liaison flights.

On April 26, 1942, the Main Directorate of the GVF was subordinated to the commander in chief of VVS-KA, while the chief of the Main Directorate of the GVF was appointed deputy commander in chief of VVS-KA.

The structure of Soviet aviation was significantly altered in 1942. High losses and the ensuing sharp decline in the numerical strength of the Soviet aviation led to a simultaneous decline in the number of aircraft and airmen available to the individual aviation units. The basic tactical formation remained the Zveno (flight) of three aircraft. Throughout 1942, the Eskadrilya (squadron) usually comprised three Zveno. The fighter aviation four-plane Zveno, divided into two Para (pair), was adopted on large scale only in mid-1942.

In early 1942 the most common structure of the Polk (regiment) was two nine-plane squadrons and a staff flight – altogether an assigned strength of twenty aircraft. Only a small number of VVS regiments (mainly Guards units) were provided with an assigned strength of thirty-two aircraft (three squadrons of ten aircraft each plus a staff flight). In time, the twenty-plane regiment was found to be too small and unsuitable for the task provided to a Polk. As increasing numbers of aircraft arrived from production lines, thirty-two-plane regiments became more and more common from mid-1942.

In the Long-range Aviation, attempts were even made to form ten-plane regiments, but combat practice demonstrated the ineffectiveness of this structure, so by the spring of 1942, the ten-plane regiments were reformed into three ten-plane squadrons.

The standard strength of an aviation division was two or three regiments, but some aviation divisions consisted of four to six regiments.

There were purely fighter, purely bomber (and high-speed bomber and heavy bomber), and purely ground-attack Divizii and Polka, and composite Divizii and Polka. Apart from this, there were some independent Eskadril'i, OAE.

Appendix IV

Rank Equivalency

VVS	Luftwaffe	USAAF
Enlisted		
Krasnoarmeyets	Flieger	Private
Yefreytor	Gefreiter	Private First Class
	Obergefreiter	Corporal
	Hauptgefreiter	
NCOs		
Mladshiy Serzhant	Unteroffizier	Staff Sergeant
Serzhant	Unterfeldwebel	Sergeant
Starshiy Serzhant	Feldwebel	Technical Sergeant
Starshina	Oberfeldwebel	Master Sergeant
Warrant Officers		
	Oberfähnrich	(Officer Candidate)
	Stabsfeldwebel	Sergeant Major
Commissioned Officers		
Mladshiy Leytenant		Flight Officer
Leytenant	Leutnant	Second Lieutenant
Starshiy Leytenant	Oberleutnant	Lieutenant
Kapitan	Hauptmann	Captain
Mayor	Major	Major
Podpolkovnik	Oberstleutnant	Lieutenant Colonel
Polkovnik	Oberst	Colonel
General Officers		
General-Mayor	Generalmajor	Brigadier General
General-Leytenant	Generalleutnant	Major General
General-Polkovnik	General	Lieutenant General
General Armii	Generaloberst	General (4-star)
Marshal Sovetskogo Soyuza	Generalfeld-marschall	General of the Army
	Reichsmarschall	

Soviet political ranks and their equivalents

Rank of Political Instructor	*Equivalent Regular Army Rank*
Mladshiy Politruk	Leytenant
Politruk	Starshiy Leytenant
Starshiy Politruk	Kapitan
Batal'yonniy Komissar	Mayor
Starshiy Batal'yonny Komissar	Podpolkovnik
Polkovoy Komissar	Polkovnik
Divizionny Komissar	General-Mayor
Korpusnoy Komissar	General-Leytenant
Armeyskiy Komissar Vtorogo Ranga	General-Polkovnik
Armeyskiy Komissar Pervogo Ranga	General Armii

Appendix V

The Highest Military Awards

THE IRON CROSS AWARDS OF THE WEHRMACHT IN 1942

Das Eiserne Kreuz 2. Klasse.
The Iron Cross Second Class.

Das Eiserne Kreuz 1. Klasse.
The Iron Cross First Class.

Das Ritterkreuz des Eisernen Kreuzes.
The Knight's Cross of the Iron Cross. About 7,500 were awarded during World War II, including about 1,730 to servicemen of the Luftwaffe.

Das Ritterkreuz des Eisernen Kreuzes mit Eichenlaub.
The Knight's Cross with Oak Leaves. A total of 860 were awarded during World War II, including 192 to servicemen of the Luftwaffe.

Das Ritterkreuz des Eisernen Kreuzes mit dem Eichenlaub mit Schwertern.
The Knight's Cross with Oak Leaves and Swords. A total of 154 were awarded during World War II, including 41 to servicemen of the Luftwaffe.

Das Ritterkreuz des Eisernen Kreuzes mit dem Eichenlaub mit Schwertern und Brillanten.
The Knight's Cross with Oak Leaves, Swords, and Diamonds. A total of 27 were awarded during World War II, including 12 to servicemen of the Luftwaffe.

Das Grosskreuz des Eisernen Kreuzes.
Only awarded once, to Reichsmarschall Hermann Göring, the commander in chief of the Luftwaffe.

Note:
Each of the above orders could be awarded to an individual only once.

MILITARY AWARDS OF THE SOVIET UNION IN 1942

Orden Krasnoy Zvezdy.
The Red Star Order. More than 2,860,000 were awarded during the wars against Germany and Japan from 1941 to 1945.

Orden Krasnogo Znameni.
The Red Banner Order. More than 580,000 were awarded during the war.

Orden Lenina.
The Lenin Order. More than 41,000 were awarded during the war.

Geroy Sovetskogo Soyuza.
Hero of the Soviet Union. More than 11,000 men and women – including 2,420 members of the VVS – were appointed Heroes of the Soviet Union during the war. Of these, 104 – including 65 members of the VVS – were appointed twice, and three – including two members of the VVS – were appointed Heroes of the Soviet Union three times. The appointment as a Hero of the Soviet Union was the highest recognition for courage or remarkable feats. It was not a military "award"; it was an honorary title. The men and women who were appointed Heroes of the Soviet Union were simultaneously awarded the Lenin Order and the Golden Star Medal. The Golden Star Medal was the token of a special distinction, not an award in itself. In the few cases when individuals were appointed Heroes of the Soviet Union a second or a third time, they also were awarded with a second and a third Golden Star Medal, respectively.

Orden Otechestvennoy Voyny 1-y (Pervoy) and 2-y (Vtoroy) stepeni.
The Order of the Patriotic War of the First and Second Grades, established on May 20, 1942. More than 350,000 awards of the First Grade and more than 1,000,000 awards of the Second Grade were made during the war.

ORDERS ESTABLISHED FOR COMMANDERS OF THE RED ARMY ***for "remarkable achievements in the organization and guidance of combat operations and for the successes achieved during these operations":***

Orden Suvorova 1-y (Pervoy), 2-y (Vtoroy) and 3-y (Tretyey) stepeni.

The Suvorov Order of the First, Second, and Third Grades was established on July 29, 1942. More than 390 awards of the First Grade, more than 2,800 awards of the Second Grade, and more than 4,000 awards of the Third Grade were made during the war.

Orden Kutuzova 1-y(Pervoy), and 2-y (Vtoroy) stepeni.

The Kutuzov Order of the First and Second Grades. More than 660 awards of the First Grade, and more than 3,300 awards of the Second Grade were made during the war.

Orden Aleksandra Nevskogo.

The Aleksandr Nevskiy Order. More than 42,000 were awarded during the war.

Note:

Each of the above orders could be awarded to the same individual several times.

Chapter Notes

Part I: The Legacy of Barbarossa

1. Glantz and House, *When Titans Clashed: How the Red Army Stopped Hitler*, p.87.
2. Haupt, *Army Group Center: The Wehrmacht in Russia 1941 – 1945*, p. 103.
3. TsVMA. Via Carl-Fredrik Geust.
4. Via Carl-Fredrik Geust.
5. *JG 54 "Grünherz" Archiv*, courtesy of Günther Rosipal.
6. TsAMO, f. 11, op. 2, d. 129, 1. 66 – 77; *Russkiy arkhiv: Velikaya Otechestvenaya; T. 17 – 6*, p. 427.
7. Haupt, *Army Group North: The Wehrmacht in Russia 1941 – 1945*, p. 109.
8. TsAMO, f. 228, op. 724, d. 32.
9. Interview with Aleksandr Pavlichenko.
10. Pokryschkin, *Himmel des Krieges*, p. *141*.
11. *Kriegstagebuch des Oberkommandos der Wehrmacht*, vol. II, p. 808.
12. Prien, *Geschichte des Jagdgeschwaders 77*, pp. 877 – 888.
13. VVS-Southern Front Documents. TsAMO.
14. Rolf Dieter Müller, *Das "Unternehmen Barbarossa" als wirtschaftlicher Raubkrieg*, in *Der deutsche Überfall auf die Sowjetunion*, pp. 138 – 141.
15. Ibid., p. 144.
16. Yefimov, *Nad polem boya*, p. 86.
17. Interview with Hansgeorg Bätcher.
18. 230 ShAD Documents. TsAMO.
19. Pokryschkin, 140 – 141.
20. Ibid., p. 136.
21. Ibid., p. 137.
22. Schmidt, *Sowjetische Flugzeuge*, p. 22.
23. *Kriegstagebuch des Oberkommandos der Wehrmacht*, vol. III, p. 166.

Part II: Soviet Resurgence

1. Interview with Arkadiy Kovachevich.
2. Kiehl, *Kampfgeschwader "Legion Condor" 53*, p. 185.
3. *Traditionsgeschichte der I./Jagdgeschwader 52*, pp. 40 – 41.
4. TsAMO, f. 208, op. 2511, d. 1185, 1. 89 – 96; *Russkiy arkhiv. Velikaya Otechestvenaya; T. 15 (4 – 1) Bitva pod Moskvoy*, p. 284.
5. Kovachevich interview.
6. Plocher, *The German Air Force Versus Russia, 1942*, p. 104.
7. TsAMO, f. 351, op. 1053, d. 699, 11. 5 – 8; TsAMO, f. 351, op. 10756, d. 7, 11. 43 – 71.
8. Murray, *Luftwaffe: Strategy for Defeat 1933 – 45*, p. 168.
9. *Zvezdy nemerknyschev slavy*, pp. 289 – 291.
10. *Kriegstagebuch des Oberkommandos der Wehrmacht*, vol. III, p. 199.
11. *Meldungen über Flugzeugunfälle und Verluste bei den fl. Verbände (täglich) Gen. Qu. 6. Abt.* Bundesarchiv/Militärarchiv. Hereafter cited as *Generalquartiermeister der Luftwaffe*.
12. *Führerbefehl vom 8. Januar 1942 betr. Verteidigung aller Stellungen;* OKW/WFSt/Op.(1) Nr. 420013/42 g – Kdos. Chefs.; *Kriegstagebuch des Oberkommandos der Wehrmacht*, vol. IV, p. 1264.
13. TsAMO, f. 212, op. 2002, d. 251, 11. 41, 50.
14. Plocher, p. 111.
15. Stahl, *Kampfflieger zwischen Eismeer und Sahara*, p. 207.
16. VVS-Western Front Documents. TsAMO.
17. Steinhoff, *In letzter Stunde: Verschwörung der Jagdflieger*, p. 91.
18. *Generalquartiermeister der Luftwaffe*. Via Matti Salonen.
19. Ibid.
20. Ibid.
21. TsAMO, f. 208, op. 2589, d. 150, 1. 7 – 14.
22. TsAMO, f. 208, op. 2511, d. 1185, 1. 89 – 96.
23. TsAMO, f. 208, op. 2589, d. 150, 1. 7 – 14; *Russkiy arkhiv. Velikaya Otechestvenaya; T. 15 (4 – 1) Bitva pod Moskvoy*, p. 290.
24. TsAMO, f. 218, op. 161877, d. 4, 1. 32; Fyodorov, *Aviatsiya v bitve pod Moskvoy*, p. 250.
25. Figures based on the daily loss reports to *Generalquartiermeister der Luftwaffe*.
26. *Traditionsgeschichte der I./Jagdgeschwader 52*, p. 39.
27. Aders and Held, *Jagdgeschwader 51 "Mölders,"* p. 105.
28. TsAMO, f. 208, op. 2589, d. 150, 1. 7 – 14; *Russkiy arkhiv. Velikaya Otechestvenaya; T. 15 (4 – 1) Bitva pod Moskvoy*, p. 291.
29. Radtke, *Kampfgeschwader 54*, p. 134.
30. Antipov, *Patriots or Red Kamikaze?*
31. TsAMO, f. 213, op. 2070, d. 15, 11. 9, 10; Fyodorov, p. 237.
32. TsAMO, f. 35, op. 11290, d. 147, 11. 116, 118; Fyodorov, p. 237.
33. TsAMO, f. 213, op. 2070, d. 15, 11. 9, 10; Fyodorov, p. 237.
34. Fast, *Das Jagdgeschwader 52*, vol. II, p. 56.
35. TsAMO, f. 221, op. 1374, d. 8.
36. Via Hans-Ekkehard Bob.
37. *Staffel-Chronik der III. Jagdgeschwader 54, 7. Staffel*.
38. Via Hans-Ekkehard Bob.
39. *Khronika Velikoy Otechestvennoy voyny Sovetskogo Soyuza na Baltiyskom more i Ladozhskom ozere*, vol. II., January 1, 1942.
40. *Staffel-Chronik 9./JG 54*.
41. *Khronika Velikoy Otechestvennoy voyny Sovetskogo Soyuza na Baltiyskom more i Ladozhskom ozere*, vol. II., January 4, 1942.
42. *Staffel-Chronik der III. Jagdgeschwader 54, 7. Staffel*.
43. *JG 54 "Grünherz" Archiv*, courtesy of Günther Rosipal.
44. Via Hannes Trautloft.
45. Haupt, *Army Group North: The Wehrmacht in Russia 1941 – 1945*, p. 119.
46. Brütting, *Das waren die deutschen Stuka-Asse 1939 – 1945*, p. 27.
47. *Chronik der I./JG 54*, p. 34.
48. *Khronika Velikoy Otechestvennoy voyny Sovetskogo Soyuza na Baltiyskom more i Ladozhskom ozere*, vol. II., January 25, 1942.
49. *Chronik der I./JG 54*, p. 34.

50. 6 VA/VVS-Northwestern Front Documents. TsAMO.
51. *Khronika Velikoy Otechestvennoy voyny Sovetskogo Soyuza na Baltiyskom more i Ladozhskom ozere*, vol. II., February 14, 1942.
52. *Chronik der I./JG 54*, p. 35.
53. *JG 54 "Grünherz" Archiv*, courtesy of Günther Rosipal.
54. Via Ferdinando D'Amico.
55. VVS-Southwestern Front Documents. TsAMO.
56. Figures based on the daily loss reports to *Generalquartiermeister der Luftwaffe*.
57. VVS-Southern Front Documents. TsAMO.
58. Quoted in Prien, *Geschichte des Jagdgeschwaders 77*, p. 899.
59. Prien, *Geschichte des Jagdgeschwaders 77*, p. 900.
60. TsAMO, f. 319, op. 4799, d. 25.
61. TsAMO, f. 319, op. 4798, d. 22.
62. VVS-Southern Front Documents. TsAMO.
63. Dickfeld, *Footsteps of the Hunter*, p. 81.
64. Ibid., p. 82.
65. *Pravda*, February 17, 1942.
66. War Diary 88 IAP. TsAMO.
67. Dickfeld, p. 84.
68. Deutsche Dienststelle (WASt).
69. Interview with Aleksandr Pavlichenko.
70. 230 ShAD Files. TsAMO.
71. VVS-Southern Front Documents. TsAMO.
72. *Generalquartiermeister der Luftwaffe*. Via Matti Salonen.
73. *Kriegstagebuch des Oberkommandos der Wehrmacht*, vol. III, p. 217.
74. *Pobratimyy Nikolaya Gastello*, p. 269.
75. Plocher, p. 162.
76. Red Army general staff report, quoted in Hayward, *Stopped at Stalingrad: The Luftwaffe and Hitler's Defeat in the East*, p. 35.
77. Wolf-Dietrich Huy in Prien, *Geschichte des Jagdgeschwaders 77*, p. 904.
78. Balke, *Kampfgeschwader 100 "Wiking,"* p. 102; Brütting, *Das waren die deutschen Kampffliegerasse 1939 – 1945*, p. 150.
79. Interview with Hansgeorg Bätcher.
80. *Tageseinsatz-Meldung Fliegerführer Süd, 20. 2. 42.*
81. Ibid.
82. *Tageseinsatz-Meldung Fliegerführer Süd, 21. 2. 42.*
83. Prien, *Geschichte des Jagdgeschwaders 77*, p. 915.
84. *Tageseinsatz-Meldung Fliegerführer Süd, 24. 2. 42.*
85. Major Hansgeorg Bätcher, Flight Book.

Part III: Stalemate

1. Plocher, *The German Air Force Versus Russia, 1942*, p. 71.
2. Major Hans-Ekkehard Bob, Flight Book.
3. Prien and Stemmer, *Messerschmitt Bf 109 im Einsatz bei der III./Jagdgeschwader 3*, p. 154.
4. VVS-Northwestern Front Documents. TsAMO.
5. *Generalquartiermeister der Luftwaffe*. Via Matti Salonen.
6. Plocher, p. 73.
7. Via Hans-Ekkehard Bob.
8 *Staffel-Chronik 9./JG 54*.
9. 154 IAP Documents. TsAMO.
10. *M.I vozvrashalis s pobedoy*, pp. 49 – 58.
11. Major Wolfgang Späte, Flight Book.
12. *Staffel-Chronik 9./JG 54*.
13. *Staffel-Chronik 9./JG 54*.
14. Salisbury, *De 900 dagarna*, p. 100.
15. *Generalquartiermeister der Luftwaffe*. Via Matti Salonen.
16. Hardesty, *Red Phoenix: The Rise of the Soviet Air Power 1941 – 1945*, p. 83.
17. *Generalquartiermeister der Luftwaffe*. Via Matti Salonen.
18. Gundelach, *Kampfgeschwader General Wever 4*, p. 170.
19. War Diary 108 *"Rava Russkiy"* GvShAP. Via Aleksandr Pavlichenko.
20. Plocher, p. 73.
21. Figures based on the daily loss reports to *Generalquartiermeister der Luftwaffe*.
22. Ibid.
23. 6 VA/VVS-Northwestern Front Documents. TsAMO.
24. Haupt, *Army Group North*, p. 138.
25. Figures based on the daily loss reports to *Generalquartiermeister der Luftwaffe*.
26. Prien and Stemmer, *Messerschmitt Bf 109 im Einsatz bei der III./Jagdgeschwader 3*, p. 484.
27. 108 *"Rava-Russkiy,"* GvShAP Arkhiv.
28. TsAMO, f. 148a, op. 3763, d. 126, l. 74.; *Russkiy arkhiv: Velikaya Otechestvenaya: Stavka VGK: Dokumenty i materialy: 1942 god. T. 16 (5 – 2)*, p. 145.
29. Major Wolfgang Späte, Flight Book.
30. Haupt, p. 139.
31. Rosipal, *Jagdgeschwader 54 Grünherz: Verluste 1940 – 1945*, ed. Günther Rosipal; *Generalquartiermeister der Luftwaffe*.
32. 6 VA/VVS-Northwestern Front Documents. TsAMO.
33. 402 IAP Documents. TsAMO.
34. *JG 54 "Grünherz" Archiv*, courtesy of Günther Rosipal.
35. 485 IAP Documents. TsAMO.
36. Ibid
37. Ibid.
38. Röhricht, *Probleme der Kesselschlacht, dargestellt an Einkreisungs-Operationen im Zweiten Weltkrieg*, p. 140 – 141, op. *Kriegstagebuch des Oberkommandos der Wehrmacht*, vol. III, p. 43.
39. VVS-Northwestern Front Documents. TsAMO.
40. Glantz and House, *When Titans Clashed*, p. 340.
41. Murray, *Luftwaffe: Strategy for Defeat*, pp. 169 – 170.
42. *Generalquartiermeister der Luftwaffe*. Via Matti Salonen.
43. *Khronika Velikoy Otechestvennoy voyny Sovetskogo Soyuza na Baltiyskom more i Ladozhskom ozere*, vol. II., April 4, 1942.
44. Gundelach, p. 171.
45. *Khronika Velikoy Otechestvennoy voyny Sovetskogo Soyuza na Baltiyskom more i Ladozhskom ozere*, vol. II., April 18, 1942.
46. Via Hans-Ekkehard Bob.
47. *Khronika Velikoy Otechestvennoy voyny Sovetskogo Soyuza na Baltiyskom more i Ladozhskom ozere*, vol. II., April 19, 1942.
48. *Pobratimyy Nikolaya Gastello*, pp. 300 and 315.
49. Via Hannes Trautloft.
50. *Khronika Velikoy Otechestvennoy voyny Sovetskogo Soyuza na Baltiyskom more i Ladozhskom ozere*, vol. II., April 24, 1942.
51. Ivanov, *Krylia nad morem*.
52. *Velikaya Otechestvenaya den' za dnyom*, in *Morskoy Sbornik*, 3/1992.
53. Starck, *Allmän sjökrigshistoria, del 2 1942 – 1945*, p. 132.
54. Boëthius, M-P, *Heder och samvete: Sverige och andra världskriget*, p. 54.
55. *Generalquartiermeister der Luftwaffe*. Via Matti Salonen.
56. Radtke, *Kampfgeschwader 54*, p. 139.
57. Antipov, *Patriots or Red Kamikaze?*
58. Obermaier, *Die Ritterkreuzträger der Luftwaffe; Band I, Jagdflieger 1939 – 1945*, p. 55.
59. Dyachenko, *Nasledniki Nesterova*, p. 102.
60. *Fernschreiben VIII. Fliegerkorps, 4. 4. 1942*, VIII. Fliegerkorps, Ia geh; Radtke, p. 141.
61. TsAMO, f. 213, op. 2070, d. 19, l. 9.; Fyodorov, *Aviatsiya v bitve pod Moskvoy*, p. 245.
62. TsAMO, f. 213, op. 2070, d. 15, ll. 14, 15.; Fyodorov, p. 247.
63. Figures based on the daily loss reports to *Generalquartiermeister der Luftwaffe*.
64. Murray, p. 168.
65. *Kriegstagebuch des Oberkommandos der Wehrmacht*, vol. III, p. 166.
66. TsAMO, f. 346, op. 52133, d. 3, ll. 147 – 148; Fyodorov, p. 243.
67. TsAMO, f. 213, op. 2070, d. 19, l.5 – 6; Anishchenkov and Shurinov, *Tret'ya Vozdushnaya*, p. 31.
68. *Geroi ognennykh let*, pp. 46 – 48.
69. 630 IAP/PVO Log Book. TsAMO.
70. 630 IAP/PVO Documents. TsAMO.
71. Görlitz, *Model: Der Feldmarschall un sein Endkampf an der Ruhr*, 6th ed., p. 121.

Part IV: German Resurgence

1. *Krasnaya Zvezda*, March 12, 1942.
2. Combat Diary, 88 IAP. TsAMO.
3. Via Ferdinando D'Amico.
4. VVS-Southern Front Documents. TsAMO.
5. Statement by Kurt Schade.
6. Ibid.
7. 88 IAP Documents. TsAMO.
8. VVS-Southern Front Documents. TsAMO.
9. Figures based on the daily loss reports to *Generalquartiermeister der Luftwaffe*.
10. VVS-Southern Front Documents. TsAMO.
11. 15./JG 52 Log Book. Via Tomislav Haramincic.
12. Ibid.

Bernád, D. *Rumanian Air Force: The Prime Decade, 1938 – 1947*. Carrollton: Squadron/Signal Publications, 1999.
Beskorovayniy, A. I. *Geroi ryadom*. Moscow: DOSAAF, 1979.
Bessmertyen podvig ikh vysokiy. Tula: Priokskoe knizhnoe izdatel'stvo, 1983.
Bock, R. *Sowieckie Lotnictwo Morskie 1941 – 45*. Warsaw: AJ Press, 1996.
Bodrikhin, N. *Stalinskiye Sokoly*. Moscow: NPP Delta, 1997.
——· *Sovyetskiye Asi*. Moscow: ZAO KFK "TAMP," 1998.
Boëthius, M-P. *Heder och samvete: Sverige och andra världskriget*. Stockholm: Norstedts, 1991.
Bogdanov, N. G. *V nebe Gvardeyskiy Gatchinskiy*. Leningrad: Lenizdat, 1980.
Boyd, A. *The Soviet Air Force Since 1918*. London: Macdonald and Janes, 1977.
Boyevoy put' Sovyetskogo Voyenno-Morskogo Flota. 4th ed. Moscow: Voyenizdat, 1988.
Boykov, P. M. *Na glavnykh napravlyeniyakh*. Moscow: Voyenizdat, 1984.
Bracke, G. *Gegen vielfache Übermacht*. Stuttgart: Motorbuch Verlag, 1977.
Brown, J. *Ryssland kämpar*. Stockholm: Steinsviks bokförlag, 1943.
Brütting, G. *Das waren die deutschen Kampffliegerasse 1939 – 1945*. Stuttgart: Motorbuch Verlag, 1975.
——· *Das waren die deutschen Stuka-Asse 1939 – 1945*. 3rd ed. Stuttgart: Motorbuch Verlag, 1979.
Buchner, H. *Stormbird: Flying Through Fire as a Luftwaffe Ground Attack Pilot and Me 262 Ace*. Aldershot: Hikoki Publications, 2000.
Bucurescu, I., et al: *Aviatia Romana-Pe frontul de est si in apararea teritotiului*. Romania: Tehnoprod, 1993.
Burov, A. V. *Tvoi Geroi Leningrad*. Leningrad: Lenizdat, 1970.
——· *Ognennoye Nebo*. Leningrad: Lenizdat, 1974.
——· *Blokada Den'za Dnyem*. Leningrad: Lenizdat, 1979.
Carell, P. *Unternehmen Barbarossa: der Marsch nach Russland*. Frankfurt-am-Main: Verlag Ullstein, 1963.
——· *Verbannte Erde: Schlacht zwischen Wolga und Weichsel*.
Frankfurt am Main: Verlag Ullstein, 1966.
Chazanov (Khazanov), D. *Bitwa nad Moskwa*. Series *Nawieksze Bitwy Wieku*. Warsaw: ALTAIR, 1977.
——· *Nad Stalingradem*. Warsaw: Wydawnictwo Altair, 1995.
Davtyan, S. M. *Pyataya Vizdushnaya*. Moscow: Voyenizdat, 1990.
Denisov, K. D. *Pod nami—chernoye more*. Moscow: Voyennoye izdatel'stvo, 1989.
Der deutsche Überfall auf die Sowjetunion: "Unternehmen Barbarossa" 1941. Edited by Ueberschär, G. R. and W. Wette, Frankfurt am Main: Fischer Taschenbuch Verlag, 1999.
Dickfeld, A. *Footsteps of the Hunter*. Winnipeg: J. J. Fedorowicz Publishing, 1993.
Dierich, W. *Kampfgeschwader 51 "Edelweiss."* Stuttgart: Motorbuch Verlag, 1975.
——· *Kampfgeschwader 55 "Greif."* Stuttgart: Motorbuch Verlag, 1975.
Dolgov, I.A.: *Zolotye Zvezdy Kalinintsev*. 2nd ed. Moskovskiy rabochiy, Moscow 1983.
Dolnikov, G. U. *Letit stal'naya eskadrilya*. Moscow: Voyenizdat, 1993.
Dorokhov, A. P. *Geroi chyernomorskogo neba*. Moscow: Voyenizdat, 1972.
Dyachenko, G. Kh. *Nasledniki Nesterova*. Moscow: Voyenizdat, 1963.
Dzhurayev, T. D. *Vyernye syny Rodiny*. Tashkent: Uzbekistan, 1964.
Einsiedel, H. *I Joined the Russians*. New Haven: Yale, 1958.
Encyclopedia of the Holocaust. *New York: Macmillan Publishing Company, 1990*.
Erickson, J. *The Road to Stalingrad: Stalin's War with Germany*. Vol. I. New York: Harper & Row, 1979.
Fast, N. *Das Jagdgeschwader 52*. Bergisch Gladbach: Bensberger Buch-Verlag, 1988 – 1992.
Fiest, U., N. E. Harms, and M. Dario. *The Fighting 109*. Devon: David & Charles Ltd., 1978.
Fuglewicz, W. *Skrzydla niosa odwet*. Warsaw: Wydawnictwo MON, 1975.
——· *Minuta nad twierdza*. Warsaw: Wydawnictwo MON, 1977.
——· *Rakietowym w czolgi*. Warsaw: Ministerstwo Obrony Narodowej, 1979.
——· *Stalinowskie sokoly*. Gdynia: AJ Press, 1995.
Fyodorov, A. G. *Aviatsiya v bitve pod Moskvoy*. Moscow: Nauka, 1975.
——· *V nebe Petlaykovy*. Moscow: DOSAAF, 1976.
——· *Zvezdy nemerknyschev slavy*. 3rd ed. Simferopol: Tavriya, 1984.
Gaczowski, B. *Atakuje taranem*. Rzeszow: Krajowa Agencja Wydawnicza, 1985.
Galland, A. *Die Ersten und die Letzten; Jagdflieger im zweiten Weltkrieg*. Munich: Franz Schneekluth Verlag, 1953.
Geroi ognennykh let. 3rd ed. Yaroslavl: Verkhnye-Volzhskoye knizhnoye izdatel'stvo, 1985.
Geroi Sovyetskogo Soyuza. Moscow: Voyenizdat, *1987*.
Geroi Sovyetskogo Soyuza Mogilyevchane. Minsk: Polyma, 1965.
Geroi—Volgogradtsy. Volgograd: Nizhne-Volzhskoe knizhnoe izdatel'stvo, 1967.
Geroyam Rodiny—slava! Petrozavodsk: Kareliya, 1985.
Geust, C.-F., K. Keskinen, and K. Stenman. *Soviet Air Force in World War Two: Red Stars*. Kangsala: Ar-Kustannus Oy, 1993.
Girbig, W. *Jagdgeschwader 5 "Eismeerjäger."* Stuttgart: Motorbuch Verlag, 1975.
——· *Im Anflug auf die Reichshauptstadt*. Stuttgart: Motorbuch Verlag, 1977.
——· *. . . mit Kurs auf Leuna: Die Luftoffensive gegen die Treibstoffindustrie und der deutsche Abwehreinsatz 1944 – 1945*. Stuttgart: Motorbuch Verlag, 1980.
Glantz, D. M., and J. House. *When Titans Clashed: How the Red Army Stopped Hitler*. Lawrence: University Press of Kansas, 1995.
Golubev, V. F. *Krylia krepnyt v boyu*. 2nd ed. Leningrad: Lenizdat, 1984.
——· *Vtoroye dykhanie*. 2nd ed. Leningrad: Lenizdat, 1988.
Görlitz, W. *Model: Der Feldmarschall und sein Endkampf an der Ruhr*. 6th ed. Munich: Universitas Verlag, 1993.
Grechko, S. N. *Reshyeniya prinimalis'na zyemlye*. Moscow: Voyenizdat, 1984.
Green, W. *Warplanes of the Third Reich*. London: Macdonald, 1970.
Grichenko, I. T., and N. M. Golovin. *Podvig*. 3rd ed. Kharkov: Prapor, 1983.
Groehler, O. *Geschichte des Luftkriegs*. Berlin (GDR): Militärverlag, 1981.
Grif sekretnosti sniat. Poteri vooruzhennykh sil SSR v voynakh, boyevykh deystviyakh, i voyennykh konfliktakh. Moscow: Voyenizdat, 1993.
Gubin, B. A., and V. A. Kiselyov. *Vos'maya vozdushnaya*. Moscow: Voyenizdat 1986.
Gundelach, K. *Kamfgeschwader "General Wever" 4*. Stuttgart: Motorbuch Verlag, 1978.
Haase, O. *Stirb und werde: Aus zwei Jahren Russlandkrieg des Jagdgeschwaders Trautloft*. Berlin: 1943.
Hafner, and Meiller. *Flieger Fiende Kameraden*. Rastatt: Erich Pabel Verlag, 1962.
Halder, F. *Kriegstagebuch*. Edited by Hans-Arnold Jacobsen. Stuttgart: W. Kohlhammer Verlag, 1964.
Hardesty, V.: *Red Phoenix: The Rise of the Soviet Air Power 1941 – 1945*. Washington, D.C.: Smithsonian Institution Press, 1982.
Haupt, W. *Army Group Center: The Wehrmacht in Russia 1941 – 1945*. Atglen: Schiffer, 1997.
——· *Army Group North: The Wehrmacht in Russia 1941 – 1945*. Atglen: Schiffer, 1997.
——· *Army Group South: The Wehrmacht in Russia 1941 – 1945*. Atglen: Schiffer, 1998.
Hayward, J. *Stopped at Stalingrad: The Luftwaffe and Hitler's Defeat in the East*. Lawrence: University Press of Kansas, 1998.
Held, W., H. Trautloft, and H.-E. Bob. *Die Grünherzjäger*. Friedberg: Podzun-Pallas Verlag, 1985.
Herrmann, H. *Bewegtes Leben: Kampf-und Jagdflieger 1935 – 1945*. 2nd ed. Stuttgart: Motorbuch Verlag, 1986.
Inozemtsev, I. G. *Krylatye zaschitniki Severa*. Moscow: Voyenizdat, 1975.
——· *Pod krylom—Leningrad*. Moscow: Voyenizdat, 1978.
——·*Tarany v Severnom nebe*. Moscow: Voyenizdat, 1981.
——· *V nebe Zapolyar'ya i Karelii*. Moscow: Voyenizdat, 1987.
Istoriya Vyelikoy Otyechyestvyennoy Voyny Sovyetskogo Soyuza 1941 – 1945. Moscow: Voyenizdat, 1960.
Ivanov, A. L. *Skorost', manyovr, ogon'*. Moscow: DOSAAF, 1974.
Ivanov, P. N. *Krylia nad morem*, Moscow: VIMO, 1973.
I vozvrashchalis' s pobedoy. Leningrad: Lenizdat, 1986.
Jackson, R. *The Red Falcons: The Soviet Air Force in Action, 1919 – 1969*. New York: International Publications Services, 1970.
Jacobsen, H.-A., and J. Rohwer. *Entscheidungsschlachten des zweiten Weltkrieges*. Munich: Bernard & Graefe Verlag, 1960.
Jagdgeschwader 54 Grünherz: Verluste 1940 – 1945. Edited by Günther Rosipal. Salzwedel/Hannover: Forschungsgruppe 45, 1998.
Jakovlev, A. *Livets mål*. Stockholm: Rabén & Sjögren, 1969.
Jatkosota-Kronikka. Jyväskylä: Gummerus Kustannus Oy, 1991.
Jochim, B. K. *Oberst Hermann Graf: 200 Luftsiege in 13 Monaten*. Rastatt: Erich Pabel Verlag, 1970.
Jukes, G. *Stalingrad—vändpunkten*. Stockholm: Aldus, 1972.
Kabanov, S. I. *Na dalnikh podstupakh*. Moscow: Voyenizdat, 1971.
Kaberov, I. A. *V Pritsele—Svastika*. Leningrad: Lenizdat, 1983.
Kalinin, V. V., and D. G. Makarenko. *Geroi podvigov na Kharkovschine*. Kharkov: Prapor, 1970.

Karpov, V. *The Commander*. London: Brassey's, 1987.

Kaufov, Kh. Kh. *Orel umirayet v polyete*. Nalchik: Elbrus, 1970.

Kavalery Zolotoy Zvezdy. Donetsk: Donbas, 1976.

Keskinen, K., K. Stenman, K., and K. Niska: *Suomen ilmavoimien historia*. Vol.VII, *Venäläiset hävittäjät, Tietoteos*. Forssa: Forssan Kirjapaino Oy, 1977.

Khametov. M. I. *V nebe Zapolyarya*. Moscow: Politizdat, 1987.

Khanin, L. *Geroi Sovyetskogo Soyuza—syny Tatarii*. Kazan: Tatknigozdat, 1963.

Khronika Velikoy Otechestvennoy voyny Sovetskogo Soyuza na Baltiyskom more i Ladozhskom ozere. Vol. II. Compiled by Makarskiy, Podpolkovnik N. V., Kapitan 2-go ranga M. A. Krekshin and Polkovnik N. N. Alikhov, supervised by Lebedev, Kapitan 1-go ranga A. N. Edited by Dolin, Kontr-Admiral M. M. Moscow, Leningrad: Voyenmorizdat, 1945.

Khronika Velikoy Otechestvennoy voyny Sovetskogo Soyuza na Severnom teatre c. 1.01.42 – 30.6.42 gg. Vol. II. St Petersburg: Galeya-Print, 1999.

Kiehl, H. *Kampfgeschwader "Legion Condor" 53*. Stuttgart: Motorbuch Verlag, 1996.

Kilmarx, R. A. *A History of Soviet Air Power*. New York: Frederick A. Praeger, 1962.

Kislitsyn, A. S. *Oveyannye slavoy*. Chelyabinsk: Yuzhno-Ural'skoe knizhnoe izdatel'stvo, 1965.

Kozhevnikov, M. N. *Komandovaniye i shtab VVS Sovyetskoy Armii v Velikoy Otyechestvyennoy Voyny 1941 – 1945*. Moscow: Nauka, 1977.

Kozlov, N. A. *V ognye srazhyeniy*. Grozny: Chechyeno-Ingushskoye knizhnoye izdatelstvo, 1968.

Kriegschronik Band XIV. Franz F. Winter, ed. *Die deutschen Jagdflieger*. Munich: Universitas Verlag, 1993.

Kriegstagebuch des Oberkommandos der Wehrmacht 1939 – 1945.

Krzeminski, C. *Walczyli i polegi za Polske*. Warsaw: KAW RSW Prasa—Ksiazka-Ruch, 1977.

Kurowski, F. *Balkenkreuz und Roter Stern*. Friedberg: Podzun-Pallas Verlag, 1984.

Kursenkow, S. G. *Jagdflieger*. Berlin (GDR): Deutscher Militärverlag, 1964.

Kusnezow, N. G. *Gefechtsalarm in den Flotten*. 3rd ed. Berlin (GDR): Militärverlag, 1984.

Kuzovkin, A. I., and A. T. Belyayev. *Orlinoye plemya Kolomentsev*. Moscow: DOSAAF, 1985.

Lavrinenkov, V. *Vozvrascheniye v nyebo*. Moscow: Voyenizdat, 1974.

Lee, A. *The Soviet Air Force*. New York: John Day Company, 1962.

Liddell-Hart, B. H. *The Other Side of the Hill*. Vol. III, *Through German Eyes*. 1st ed. London: Cassell and Company Ltd., London, 1948.

Lorents, Y., and E. Zeeh. *Andra världskriget*. Stockholm: Natur & Kultur, 1940 – 1945.

Luganskiy, S. *Nyebo ostayetsya chistym: Zapiski voyennogo letchika*. Alma-Ata: Izdatelstvo *Zhazushi*, 1970.

Lyudi geroicheskoy profesii. Moscow: DOSAAF, 1976.

Mahlke, H. *Stuka: Angriff: Sturzflug*. Berlin: Verlag E. S. Mittler & Sohn, 1993.

von Manstein, E. *Verlorene Siege*. Bonn: Athenäum Verlag, 1955.

Maslennikov, Yu. I. *Taktika v boyevykh primerakh*. Moscow: Voyenizdat, 1985.

Maslow, M. *Istrebiteli I-16*. Moscow: Armada, 1997.

Meroño, F. *Aviadores Españoles en la Gran Guerra Patria*. Moscow: Editorial Progreso, 1986.

Michulec, R. *Stalinowskie sokoly*. Gdynia: AJ Press, 1995.

Minakov, V. *Gnevnoye nebo Tavridy*. Moscow: DOSAAF, 1985

——- *Baltiyskiye sokoly*, St Petersburg: Politekhnika, 1995

Morgan, H. *Soviet Aces of World War 2*. London: Osprey/Reed International Books, 1997.

Morozov, M. E. *Morskaya aviatsiya Germanii 1939 – 1945. Chast' 1. Torpedonostysy*, Moscow: Armada, 1996.

Murray, W. *Luftwaffe: Strategy for Defeat 1933 – 45*. London: Grafton Books, 1985.

Na pole ratnom. Moscow: Moskovskiy rabochiy, 1977.

Nashi Zemlyaki—Geroi Sovyetskogo Soyuza. 3rd ed. Cheboksary: Chuvashskoe knizhnoe izdatel'stvo, 1980.

Nauroth, H. *Stukageschwader 2 Immelmann*. Preussisch Oldendorf: Verlag K. W. Schütz, 1988.

Neulen, H. W. *Am Himmel Europas: Luftstreitkräfte an deutscher Seite 1939 – 1945*. Munich: Universitas Verlag, 1998.

Noggle, A. *A Dance with Death: Soviet Airwomen of World War II*. College Station: Texas A & M University Press, 1994.

Novikov, A. A. *V Nebe Leningrada*. Moscow: Voyenizdat, 1970.

Nowarra, H. J. *Über Europas Fronten: Das technisch-historische Porträt der Ju 52*. Rastatt: Erich Pabel Verlag, 1978.

Nowotny, R. *Walter Nowotny: Berichte aus dem Leben meines Bruder*. Leoni: Druffel-Verlag, 1957.

Obermaier, E. *Die Ritterkreuzträger der Luftwaffe: Band I—Jagdflieger 1939 – 1945*. Mainz: Verlag Dieter Hoffmann, 1966.

——- *Die Ritterkreuzträger der Luftwaffe 1939 – 1945: Band II—Stuka-und Schlachtflieger*. Mainz: Verlag Dieter Hoffmann, 1976.

Pavlov, G. R. *Odnopolchane*. Moscow: DOSAAF, 1985.

——- *Krylya muzhestva*. Kazan: Tatarskoye knizhnoe izdatel'stvo, 1988.

Plocher, H. *The German Air Force Versus Russia, 1942*. USAF Historical Division, Air University. New York: Arno Press, 1966.

Pobratimy Nikolaya Gastello. Moscow: MOF "Pobyeda-1945 GOD," 1995.

Podvigi vo imya Otchizny. 2nd ed. Kharkov: Prapor, 1985.

Podvigom slavny tvoi zemlyaki. Zaporozhye: Zaporozhskoe knigo-gazetnoe izdatel'stvo, 1962.

Pokryschkin [Pokryshkin], A. I. *Himmel des Krieges*. Berlin (GDR): Deutscher Militärverlag, 1970.

——-*Na istrebitele*. Novosibirsk: Novosibgiz, 1948.

——- *Krylya istrebitelya*. Moscow: Voyenizdat, 1948.

——- *Nebo voyny*. Moscow: Voyenizdat, 1980.

——- *Poznat sebia v boyu*. Moscow: DOSAAF, 1986.

Polak, T., and C. Shores. *Stalin's Falcons: The Aces of the Red Star: A tribute to the Notable Fighter Pilots of the Soviet Air Forces, 1918 – 1953*. London: Grub Street, 1999.

Polyanskiy, V. V. *10 lyet s Vasiliyem Stalinym*. Tver: Vikant, 1995.

Polynin, F. P. *Boyevyye marshruty*. 2nd ed. Moscow: Voyenizdat, 1981.

Prien, J. *"Pik-As:" Geschichte des Jagdgeschwaders 53*. Eutin: Struve-Druck, 1990, 1991.

——- *Geschichte des Jagdgeschwaders 77*. Eutin: Struve-Druck, 1992 – 1994.

Prien, J. / Stemmer, G.: *Messerschmitt Bf 109 im Einsatz bei der III./Jagdgeschwader 3*. Eutin: Struve-Druck, n.d.

——- *Messerschmitt Bf 109 im Einsatz bei der II./Jagdgeschwader 3*. Eutin: Struve-Druck, n.d.

——- *Messerschmitt Bf 109 im Einsatz bei Stab und I./Jagdgeschwader 3*. Eutin: Struve-Druck, 1997.

Prien, J. *Jagdgeschwader 53: A History of the "Pik As" Geschwader Volume 2: May 1942 – January 1944*. Atglen: Schiffer Military History, 1998.

Prussakov, G. K. *16ya vozdushnaya: Voyenno-istorichyeskiy ochyerk o boyevom puti 16-y vozdushnoy armii 1942 – 1945*. Moscow: Voyenizdat, 1973.

Pshenyahik, G. A. *Sovyetskie Voyenno-vozdushnye sily v bor'bye s Nemetsko-fashistskoy aviatsiyey v lyetnyeosyennyey kampanii 1941 g*. Moscow: Voyenizdat, 1961.

——- *Doyetim do Odera*. Moscow: Voyenizdat, 1985.

Pstygo, I. I. *Na boevom kurse*. Moscow: Voenizdat, 1989.

Radtke, S. *Kampfgeschwader 54*. Munich: Schild Verlag, 1990.

Rajlích, J., and J. Sehnal. *Slovensti Letci 1939 – 1945*. Kolín: Vydavatelství Kolinske noviny, 1991.

Rajlich, J., Z. Stojczew, and Z. Lalak. *Sojusznicy Luftwaffe, czesc 1*. Warsaw: Books International, 1997.

Rechkalov, G. A. *V nebe Moldavii: Vospominaniya voyennogo letchika*. Kishinev: Kartya moldovenyaske, 1967.

——- *Dymnoye nebo voyny*. Sverdlovsk: Sredne-Uralskoye knizhnoe izdatel'stvo, 1968.

Relling, A. *Oberleutnant Anton Hafner*. Rastatt: Erich Pabel Verlag, 1972.

Röhricht, E. *Probleme der Kesselschlacht, dargestellt an Einkreisungs-Operationen im Zweiten Weltkrieg*. Karlsruhe: Condor-Verlag, 1958.

Roman, V. *Aerokobra vstupyut v bo*. Kiev: Aerokhobbi, 1993.

Rudel, H.-U. *Trotzdem*. Göttingen: Verlag K. W. Schütz, 1970.

Rudenko, S. I. *Krylya Pobedy*. Moscow: Voyenizdat, 1976.

Rumyantsev, N. M. *Lyudi legendarnogo podviga*. Saratov: Privolzhskoe knizhnoe izdatel'stvo, 1968.

Russkiy Arkhiv: Velikaya Otechestvennaya: Stavka VGK: Dokumenty i materialy: 1942 god. T 16 (5 – 2). Moscow: TERRA, 1996.

Russkiy arkhiv: Velikaya Otechestvenaya: T. 15 (4 – 1) Bitva pod Moskvoy. Moscow: TERRA, 1997.

Salisbury, H. E. *The 900 Days: The Siege of Leningrad*. New York: Harper & Row, 1969.

——- *The Unknown War*. New York: Bantam Books, 1978.

——- *De 900 dagarna*, Stockholm: Bonniers, 1997.

Samsonov, A. M. *Stalingradskaya bitva*. Moscow: Nauka, 1988.

Schmidt, H. A. F. *Sowjetische Flugzeuge*. Berlin (GDR): Transpress Verlag, 1971.

Schreier, H. *JG 52: Das erfolgreichste Jagdgeschwader des II. Weltkrieges*. Berg am See: Kurt Vowinckel Verlag, n.d.
Schwabedissen, W. *The Russian Air Force in the Eyes of German Commanders*. USAF Historical Division, Air University. New York: Arno Press, 1960.
Seaton, A. *The Russo-German War 1941 – 1945*. New York: Praeger Publishers, 1970.
Seidl, H. *Stalin's Eagles: An Illustrated Study of the Soviet Aces of World War II and Korea*. Atglen: Schiffer, 1998.
Semyonov, A. F. *Na vzlyote*. Moscow: Voyenizdat, 1969.
Shevchuk, V. M. *Komandir atakuyet pervym*. Moscow: Voyenizdat, 1980.
Shirer, W. *Det tredje rikets uppgång och fall*. Stockholm: Forum, 1989.
Sims, E. H. *Jagdflieger: Die grossen Gegner von einst*. Stuttgart: Motorbuch Verlag, 1980.
Skripko, N. S. *Po tseliam blizhnim i dal'nim*. Moscow: Voyenizdat, 1981.
Skulski, P., J. Bargiel, and G. Cisek. *Asy frontu wschodniego*. Wroclaw: Ace Publication, 1994.
Sokoly. Leningrad: Lenizdat, 1971.
Sovetskiye VVS v Velikoy Otechestvennoy Voyne 1941 – 1945. Moscow: Voyenizdat, 1986.
Stahl, P. W. *Kampfflieger zwischen Eismeer und Sahara*. Stuttgart: Motorbuch Verlag, 1995.
Starck, M. *Allmän sjökrigshistoria, del 2 1942 – 1945*. Stockholm: Bonnier / Marinlitteraturföreningen, 1972.
Steinhoff, J. *Kampen om Messinasundet*. Malmö: Berghs förlag, 1973.
——. *In letzter Stunde: Verschwörung der Jagdflieger*. Munich: Paul List Verlag, 1974.
Sto Stalinskih sokolov v boyah za rodinu. Moscow: Voyenizdat, 1949.
The Soviet Air Force in World War Two. New York: Doubleday & Co., 1973.
Tieke, W. *Kampf um die Krim 1941 – 1944*. Erbland: Selbstverlag Wilhelm Tieke, 1975.
Toliver, R. F., and T. J. Constable. *Das waren die deutschen Jagdfliegerasse 1939 – 1945*. Stuttgart: Motorbuch Verlag, 1973.
Tolstoy, N. *Stalin's Secret War*. London: Pan Books, 1982.
Uchebnik boytsa i mladshego komandira podrazdeleniy mestnoy PVO. Moscow: Upravleniye protivovozdushnoy oboronyy RKKA, Voyenizdat, 1939.
Valtonen, H. *Luftwaffen Pohjoinen Sivusta*. Jyväskylä: Gummerus Kirjapaino Oy, 1997.
Velikaya Otechestvenaya Voyna. Tsyfry i fakty. Moscow: Prosveshcheniye, 1995.
Vershinin, K. A. *Chetvertaya vozdushnaya*. Moscow: Voyenizdat, 1975.
Vo imya Rodiny. Moscow: Politizdat, 1982.
Voyska Protivovozdushnoy Oborony Strany. Moscow: Voyenizdat, 1968.
V sozvyezdii slavy. 2nd ed. Volgograd: Nizhne-Volzhskoe knizhnoe izdatel'stvo, 1976.
Wennerström, S. *Röda vingar*. Stockholm: Allhems förlag, 1946.
Werth, A. *Russia at War 1941 – 1945*. New York: Dutton, 1964.
Whelan, J. R. *Hunters in the Sky*. Washington, D.C.: Regnery Gateway, 1991.
Woroshejkin, A. W. *Jagdflieger*. Berlin (GDR): Deutscher Militärverlag, 1976.
Yakimenko, A. *V atake—mech*. Moscow: DOSAAF, 1973.
Yakimov, G. *Pike v byessmyertiye*. Alma-Ata: Kazakhstan, 1973.
Yefimov, A. Ye. *Nad polem boya*. Moscow: Voyenizdat, 1976
Yemelyanenko, V. B. *V Voyennom Vozdukhe Surovom*. Moscow: Sovyetskaya Rossiya, 1985.
Yeryomin, P. *Vozdushnye boytsy*. Moscow: Voyenizdat, 1987.
Yevstigneyev, K. A. *Krylataya gvardiya*. Moscow: Voyennoye izdatel'stvo, 1982.
Zakharov, G. N. *Ya istrebitel*. Moscow: Voyenizdat, 1985.
Zankiskiyev, Kh. Kh. *Syn gor—sokol Baltiki*. Nalchik: Elbrus, 1971.
Zholudev, L. V. *Stalnaya eskadrilya*. Moscow: Voyenizdat, 1972.
Zhukov, Yu. *Odin "MiG" iz tysyachi*. Moscow: Molodaya Gvardiya, 1963.
Zimin, G. V. *Taktika v boyevykh primerakh*. Moscow: Istrebitel'naya aviatsionnaya diviziya, Voyenizdat, 1982.
——. *Istrebiteli*. Moscow: Voyenizdat, 1988.
Zolotye zvezdy. Dnepropetrovsk: Promin', 1967.
Zvezdy doblesti ratnoy. 2nd ed. Novosibirsk: Zapadno-Sibirskoe knozhnoe izdatel'stvo, 1986.
Zvezdy Nemerknyschey slavy. 3rd ed. Simferopol: Tavriya, 1984.

Periodicals

Aeroplano.
Der Adler.
Air Combat.
Airfoil.
AviaMaster.
Aviatsiya i Kosmonavtika.
Aviatsia i Vremia.
Classic Wings Downunder.
The Dispatch Magazine.
Fly Past.
Jägerblatt.
Jet und Prop.
Krasnaya Zvezda.
Luftwaffe Verband Journal.
Militaria.
Mir Aviatsii.
Morskoy Sbornik.
Pravda.
Skrzydlata Polska.
Vestnik Vozdushnogo Flota.
Voyenno-Istoricheskiy Zhurnal.
VVS i PVO.

Internet Sites

The Age of Information has supplied Mankind with a new and expanding forum for exchange of information, the Internet. In recent years, several Internet sites have evolved with a supply of high-quality information in the field of aviation history. The authors have received invaluable material for this book directly from and via the following Internet sites, whose owners have undertaken considerable research work. Without depreciating the value of any other Internet site mentioned below, the authors wish to acknowledge particularly the work done by Mr. Ruy Horta to establish a worldwide interface between aviation historians and aviation history enthusiasts.

Air Operations During the Battle of Kursk by Pawel Burchard. http://www.geocities.com/dedeusz/
Biplane Fighter Aces from the Second World War by Håkan Gustavsson. http://www.dalnet.se/~surfcity/
Eagles Over Norway by Andreas Brekken. http://www.stormbirds.com/eagles/
The History Net. http://www.thehistorynet.com/home.htm
Jagdgeschwader 54 Home Page by Bob Wartburg. http://www.jps.net/wartburg/index.htm
Luftwaffe Fighter Aces and their Aircraft by Claes Sundin. http://hem.passagen.se/galland/index.html
The Luftwaffe Homepage by Michael Holm. http://www.ww2.dk/
146th Guards Fighter Regiment PVO. By Vlad Antipov. http://www.geocities.com/giap_146/
SIG Luftwaffe Homepage by Olve Dybvig. http://home.online.no/~odybvig/
Russian Aviation Museum by Alexandre Savine. http://hep2.physics.arizona.edu/~savin/ram/
Russian Military Forum by Valera Potapov. http://www.netale.net/cgi-bin/mb.cgi?warclub1
Soviet Women Pilots in the Great Patriotic War by R. Silva. http://pratt.edu/~rsilva/sovwomen.htm
12 O'Clock High by Ruy Horta. http://www.xs4all.nl/~rhorta/
Traditionsgemeinschaft JG 52 & Luftwaffen - JG 52 - Museum e.V. http://www.jg52.de
War is Over: Soviet and Russian Aviation. By Vladislav Arhipov. http://wio.newmail.ru/
WW II Ace Stories by Dariusz Tyminski. http://www.elknet.pl/acestory/

Acknowledgments

This book could not have been written without the help of Luftwaffe and VVS veterans and a large number of historians, aviation history enthusiasts, and many others. The authors are deeply grateful for the interest, encouragement, and kindness of these people, who have shown that history and historical facts belong to all of us, and that it is in our common interest to cooperate in uncovering every part of Mankind's history.
We wish to express our gratitude to: Radek Adamec, Brigadier Captain Christian Allerman, Alfons Altmeier, Ferdinando D'Amico, Aleksey V. Andreev, Sergey V. Andreev, Vlad Antipov, Vladislav Arhipov, Michael Balss, Vsevolod Bashkuev, Tony Belobrajdic, Holger Benecke, Kjell Bergström, Lars-Eric Bergström, Dénes Bernád, Christian Berring, Jan Bobek, Andreas Brekken, Mike Bryazgin, Pawel Burchard, Craig Busby, Don Caldwell, Sven Carlsen, Brian Cauchi, Michael Case, Yevgeniy Chizikov, Martin J. Cobb, John Crump, Paulo Dario, Larry deZeng, Andrey Dikov, Tadeusz Dobrowecki, Doug Drabik, Chris Dunning, Eugene Dvurechenski, Olve Dybvig, Nigel Eastaway, Santiago A. Flores, Josef Fregosi, Carl-Fredrik Geust, Octavian Ghita, Dr. Rainer Göpfert, Alexey Gretchikine, Franek Grabowski, Jürgen Grislawski, Pascal Guillerm, Håkan Gustavsson, Eric Hammel, David R. Hames, Lutz Hannig, Tomislav Haramincic, Thomas Hasselberg, Jim Haycraft, Joel Hayward, Nick Hector, Carlos Herrera, Michael Holm, Magnus Holmqvist, Ruy Horta, Ivanova Maya Ivanovna, Ossi Juntunen, Polkovnik Vsevolod Kanaev, Dmitriy Karlenko, Peter Kassak, Chuck King, Christian Kirsch, Saso Knez, General-Leytenant Aleksandr Anatolevich Kudriavtsev, Martti Kuvalainen, Vitse-Admiral Yuriy Kvyatkovskiy, Knut Larsson, Sean Leeman, Brigadier General Håkan Linde, Kari Lumppio, Oleg Maddox, Alexander Makienko, Raimo Malkamäki, Francis Marshall, Alexey Matvienko, William Medcalf, George Mellinger, Rolf Mewitz, Yekaterina Mikhailova, Eric Mombeek, Mike Mucha, Egor Nazarenko, David Nieto, Mathias C. Noch, Doug Norrie, Bogdan Pavelyev, Donald Pearson, Jim Perry, Erik Pilawskii, Rodion Podorozhny, Valera Potapov, Robert E. Potter, Dr. Jochen Prien, Rune Rautio, Ondrej Repka, Jean-Luis Roba, Ivan I. Rodionov, Günther Rosipal, Yuriy Rybin, Pär Salomonson, Matti Salonen, Vitaly Samodurov, Greg Sango, Alexandre Savine, Yuri V. Shakov, Alan Scheckenbach, Andreas Schmidt, Anneluise Schreier, Reinhard Schröder, Hans Dieter Seidl, Yuriy V. Shakhov, Mark Sheppard, Grzechu Slizewski, Hans E. Söder, James Sterrett, Harold E. Stockton, Claes Sundin, Lieutenant Commander B. John Szirt, Peter Taghon, Kevin Troha, Dariusz Tyminski, Rustam Usmanov, Hannu Valtonen, Peter Vollmer, Dave Wadman, Manfred Wägenbaur, Bob Wartburg, Pierre Watteeuw, Carl-Johan Westring, Brigadier General Björn Widmark, Dave Williams, Mike Young, Director Lyudmila P. Zapryagayeva, Vyacheslav M. Zaretsky, Jan Zdiarsky, and Admiral Vasilyevich Zelenin.

World War II VVS airmen: Starshina Petr Andreyevich Shvets, General-Leytenant Petr Vasilyevich Bazanov, Starshiy Leytenant Mikhail Petrovich Devyatayev, Polkovnik Nikolay Ivanovich Gapeyonok, Starshiy Leytenant Vasiliy Matveyevich Garanin, General-Mayor Semyon Vasilyevich Grigorenko, Kapitan Viktor Alekseyevich Grubich, Starshiy Serzhant Leonid Yakovlevich Klabukov, General-Leytenant Arkadiy Fyodorovich Kovachevich, General-Mayor Viktor Aleksandrovich Kumskov, Starshina Vasiliy Vasil'evich Kurayev, General-Leytenant Boris Dmitrievich Melyokhin, Polkovnik Vladimir Vladimirovich Onishenko, Polkovnik Aleksandr Aleksandrovich Pavlichenko, General-Mayor Georgiy Vasilyevich Pavlov, General-Leytenant Viktorovich Rybakov, Starshiy Leytenant Aron Shavelevich Shapiro, Petr Andreyevich Shvets, Kapitan Vera Tikhomirova, and General-Mayor Ivan Petrovich Vasenin.

World War II Luftwaffe airmen: Oberst Gerhard Baeker, Major Gerhard Barkhorn, Oberstleutnant Hansgeorg Bätcher, Major Hans-Ekkehard Bob, Leutnant Hugo Broch, Hauptmann Hugo Dahmer, Generalleutnant Adolf Galland, Unteroffizier Arthur Gärtner, Oberleutnant Rudolf Gloeckner, Oberst Gordon M. Gollob, Major Alfred Grislawski, Leutnant Norbert Hannig, Oberst Hajo Herrmann, Oberfeldwebel Karl-Heinz Höfer, Leutnant Udo Hünerfeld, Felix Lademann, Major Friedrich Lang, Major Heinz Lange, Oberleutnant Erwin Leykauf, Leutnant Friedrich Lüdecke, Unteroffizier Friedrich Lühring, Major Günther Rall, Oberleutnant Ernst-Wilhelm Reinert, Oberleutnant Kurt Schade, Unteroffizier Heinrich Scheibe, Leutnant Ernst Scheufele, Oberst Johannes Steinhoff, Oberst Hannes Trautloft, and Oberfeldwebel Dieter Woratz.

To any helpers whose names we may have missed, please accept our apologies and our implied gratitude.

Index